D1575441

The Rorschach: A Comprehensive System, in two volumes
  by John E. Exner, Jr.
Theory and Practice in Behavior Therapy
  by Aubrey J. Yates
Principles of Psychotherapy
  by Irving B. Weiner
Psychoactive Drugs and Social Judgment: Theory and Research
  edited by Kenneth Hammond and C. R. B. Joyce
Clinical Methods in Psychology
  edited by Irving B. Weiner
Human Resources for Troubled Children
  by Werner I. Halpern and Stanley Kissel
Hyperactivity
  by Dorothea M. Ross and Sheila A. Ross
Heroin Addiction: Theory, Research and Treatment
  by Jerome J. Platt and Christina Labate
Children's Rights and the Mental Health Profession
  edited by Gerald P. Koocher
The Role of the Father in Child Development
  edited by Michael E. Lamb
Handbook of Behavioral Assessment
  edited by Anthony R. Ciminero, Karen S. Calhoun, and Henry E. Adams
Counseling and Psychotherapy: A Behavioral Approach
  by E. Lakin Phillips
Dimensions of Personality
  edited by Harvey London and John E. Exner, Jr.
The Mental Health Industry: A Cultural Phenomenon
  by Peter A. Magaro, Robert Gripp, David McDowell, and Ivan W. Miller III
Nonverbal Communication: The State of the Art
  by Robert G. Harper, Arthur N. Wiens, and Joseph D. Matarazzo
Alcoholism and Treatment
  by David J. Armor, J. Michael Polich, and Harriet B. Stambul
A Biodevelopmental Approach to Clinical Child Psychology: Cognitive Controls and
Cognitive Control Theory
  by Sebastiano Santostefano
Handbook of Infant Development
  edited by Joy D. Osofsky
Understanding the Rape Victim: A Synthesis of Research Findings
  by Sedelle Katz and Mary Ann Mazur
Childhood Pathology and Later Adjustment: The Question of Prediction
  by Loretta K. Cass and Carolyn B. Thomas
Intelligent Testing with the WISC-R
  by Alan S. Kaufman
Adaptation in Schizophrenia: The Theory of Segmental Set
  by David Shakow
Psychotherapy: An Eclectic Approach
  by Sol L. Garfield
Handbook of Minimal Brain Dysfunctions
  edited by Herbert E. Rie and Ellen D. Rie
Handbook of Behavioral Interventions: A Clinical Guide
  edited by Alan Goldstein and Edna B. Foa
Art Psychotherapy
  by Harriet Wadeson
Handbook of Adolescent Psychology
  edited by Joseph Adelson
Psychotherapy Supervision: Theory, Research and Practice
  edited by Allen K. Hess

Continued on back

THE UNCONSCIOUS
RECONSIDERED

The Unconscious Reconsidered

Edited by

Kenneth S. Bowers

and

Donald Meichenbaum

University of Waterloo
Waterloo, Ontario, Canada

A WILEY-INTERSCIENCE PUBLICATION

JOHN WILEY & SONS

New York • Chichester • Brisbane • Toronto • Singapore

Copyright © 1984 by John Wiley & Sons, Inc.

All rights reserved. Published simultaneously in Canada.

Reproduction or translation of any part of this work
beyond that permitted by Section 107 or 108 of the
1976 United States Copyright Act without the permission
of the copyright owner is unlawful. Requests for
permission or further information should be addressed to
the Permissions Department, John Wiley & Sons, Inc.

Library of Congress Cataloging in Publication Data:

Main entry under title:

The Unconscious reconsidered.

(Wiley series on personality processes)
"A Wiley-Interscience publication."
Includes indexes.
1. Subconsciousness.   2. Personality.   I. Bowers,
Kenneth S.   II. Meichenbaum, Donald.   III. Series.

BF315.U63   1984   154.2   84-5201
ISBN 0-471-87558-9

Printed in the United States of America

10 9 8 7 6 5 4 3 2 1

To

Ernest R. Hilgard
who, in too many ways to enumerate,
has exemplified for me
what it means to be a psychologist.
This book is small thanks for all
that he has done over the years to encourage me,
and to foster my career.
K.B.

J. Barnard Gilmore
whose friendship and collaboration
have continually enriched me.
D.M.

Contributors

KENNETH S. BOWERS, Department of Psychology, University of Waterloo, Waterloo, Ontario, Canada

KURT W. FISCHER, Department of Psychology, University of Denver, Denver, Colorado

J. BARNARD GILMORE, Department of Psychology, University of Toronto, Toronto, Ontario, Canada

JOHN F. KIHLSTROM, Department of Psychology, University of Wisconsin, Madison, Wisconsin

JEAN-ROCH LAURENCE, Department of Psychology, Concordia University, Montreal, Quebec, Canda

DONALD MEICHENBAUM, Department of Psychology, University of Waterloo, Waterloo, Ontario, Canada

JOHN C. NEMIAH, Department of Psychiatry, Harvard Medical School and Psychiatrist-in-Chief, Beth Israel Hospital, Boston, Massachusetts

CAMPBELL PERRY, Department of Psychology, Concordia University, Montreal, Quebec, Canada

SANDRA L. PIPP, Department of Psychology, University of Colorado Medical School, Denver, Colorado

DANIEL N. ROBINSON, Department of Psychology, Georgetown University, Washington, D.C.

Foreword

To all of us who continue to hope that observations from the laboratory and from the clinic can be mutually enriching, this book will be very welcome. Its contributors include individuals who have distinguished themselves as experimenters and as clinicians (and some, such as the editors, who have distinguished themselves in both realms). Their thoughtful reflections cover a range of topics and perspectives so wide that I cannot imagine a reader so sated with knowledge and wisdom that he or she will not learn something new or be surprised, provoked, and spurred to think further. At the same time, running through these diverse contributions is a set of themes that reverberate, mutually clarify and highlight, and provide a valuable and pleasing coherence.

I will not go into much detail about these themes, for the editors have themselves astutely identified and articulated them in their Introduction. Instead I will highlight one or two points that particularly interest me and suggest a number of additional perspectives and bodies of work that might provide an interesting counterpoint to what is here included.

A very important clarification is introduced by the editors in their discussion of the relation between conscious and unconscious determinants of behavior and experience. As they suggest, we should not be thinking of two radically separate realms or two separate kinds of psychological determination. Rather, we can fruitfully understand unconscious influences very largely in terms of how they shape conscious perception and thought. Thus behavior can indeed be a function of the person's phenomenal field—conscious experience is neither trivial nor epiphenomenal—but the phenomenal field itself is a product of considerably more mental activity, as well as more sensitivity to environmental events, than we are able to notice or report.

In considering this latter aspect—unconscious sensitivity to environmental events—we may note that an interest in unconscious processes need not be restricted to baleful influences of primitive or antisocial drives nor to a conception of a kind of salient control that shows we are not masters in our own houses. As Bowers' interesting chapter indicates, considering unconscious events need not leave us feeling reduced; it can also help us appreciate that we do and see *more* than we were aware of, that the power we bring to bear in furthering our own conscious intentions (of which scientific discovery is but one instance) is also greater than we had recognized.

An interesting perspective on the question of the relation between conscious and unconscious thought is provided in a recent work by David Shapiro (1982) which complements his earlier classic, *Neurotic Styles* (Shapiro, 1965). Shapiro shows us a structure to consciousness itself that is so elaborate that one begins to wonder precisely where consciousness ends and unconscious processes begin. Rather than a picture of the unconscious as a completely separate realm influencing consciousness of another (and largely superficial) entity, Shapiro's account is one of levels of articulation of awareness (in Bowers' terms, we might say levels of noticing). His analysis bears resemblances in some ways to Rogers' (1959) phenomenological emphasis, as it does to Sartre (1956) and other existentialist writers. All these thinkers share a skepticism about the particular way that psychoanalysis presents the unconscious (about the spatial metaphor of the unconscious as a separate place, for example, or the sharply dichotomous conception of conscious and unconscious) yet at the same time an interest in the phenomena that intrigued Freud and a recognition of the limited nature of our everyday awareness. In effect, they suggest much that Bowers and Meichenbaum suggest in their Introduction—that whatever we might mean by the unconscious, it does not simply represent the "true" source of our experiences while consciousness sits as a pretty cover that hides the reality; rather unconscious influences operate *through* consciousness—are even, we might say, the more shadowy patterns *of* consciousness, not a realm apart.

In spite of this, these positions do not ignore the issue that Freud had in mind when he differentiated the "descriptive" unconscious from the "dynamic" unconscious. Some things we are not aware of because we are simply turning to something else or because they are trivial, not worth focal attention. Others are not in awareness precisely because they are *not* trivial, because full awareness of them would be threatening. Here, in what are probably the most significant instances of unconscious processes, we have *motivated* unawareness. Not all the theorists mentioned would use these precise terms—some would oppose them vigorously—but in one way or another all take into account our distaste for noticing some aspects of our experience and our active efforts to see things in a way that is more comfortable or familiar. All note as well that this tendency can cause us serious difficulty.

This seems to me the conceptual ground that has the most united clinical observers over the years and it must be said that even in this book it is the notion that most divides the clinicians and the experimenters. There is certainly nothing intrinsically incompatible between cognitive and information-processing notions on the one hand and clinical ideas about defensive warding off of certain experiences on the other. Indeed in recent years a number of dynamically oriented clinicians have presented analyses in terms of cognitive and information-processing concepts (e.g., Klein, 1970; Peterfreund, 1971; Wachtel, 1981). Nonetheless, despite the editors' generally accurate statement that this book's authors have not rushed to disavow classical psychoanalytic formulations, the chapters that stress cognitive and information-processing models do tend to give short shrift to concepts of impulse and defense, or to motivated mis- or non-perception (non-noticing in Bowers' terms).

Bowers' own discussion of the controversies that surrounded research on subliminal perception is masterful. The difference between definitions that serve within a limited laboratory paradigm and those that are needed to deal seriously with life as most of us live it has never been pointed out more sharply than in Bowers' pithy warning that we should avoid the highways if forced-choice criteria be taken as signifying seeing. But even Bowers' discussion has an interesting omission: the subliminal perception and stimulation work was intimately linked in the "new look" perception research with another controversial concept (or phenomenon, depending on one's conviction)—that of "perceptual defense." In reviewing the evidence in this area in 1973 I concluded that by any clinically useful definition of perception, there was overwhelming evidence that motivational factors influenced perception and that avoidant motives in particular can lead us not to notice what we otherwise might; indeed some of the strongest evidence was provided by those such as Eriksen, who later questioned the concept (Wolitzky & Wachtel, 1973). I am not aware of any later work that would lead me to conclude differently. The concept of defense is still at the heart of the clinical importance of unconscious processes and it would have been interesting to see each of the chapter authors address it explicitly from their perspectives.

In a related vein, I would call the attention of readers of this book to the work of Lloyd Silverman and his associates over the last two decades. Silverman's (1976, 1978) carefully designed experiments have repeatedly found effects of subliminal stimulation that seem to require understanding in terms of the activation of specific psychodynamic conflicts. Silverman chooses the content of the subliminal stimulus to be consistent with hypothesized areas of conflict for particular groups and compares the effects of such stimuli to those of a variety of relevant control stimuli for different groups. In a large number of parametrically varied studies he has found a pattern of effects which seem hard to explain without psychoanalytic concepts of unconscious conflict and fantasy. Significantly, the results are not obtained when the stimuli are presented at a level capable of producing conscious experience and report.

Silverman's consistent findings pose a serious challenge to those who dismiss psychoanalytic notions—a challenge which has largely been met by ignoring the findings rather than by serious methodological critiques. Some of Silverman's findings are nothing short of startling (even to someone like myself who is familiar and comfortable with psychodynamic thinking) and the difficulty of assimilating them into mainstream experimentally oriented psychology is easy to understand. But any effort to assess the evidence for unconscious processes and their nature is incomplete without coming to terms with this remarkable body of work.

As is befitting, given the areas where the two editors have particularly made their mark, there is much in this volume about hypnosis and about cognition. In a sense, this represents a sweep from the area where unconscious processes were first scientifically studied (hypnosis) to the area where its most recent considerations have lain (cognition). Along the way, the volume expands into other areas where fresh perspectives are offered, such as cognitive developmental psychology and psychobiology. Robinson's chapter on psychobiology is a charming and sophisticated account that should be a caution to anyone who is tempted to view physiology as a shortcut or substitute for close scrutiny of psychological data in their own right.

The authors of these chapters share an admirable quality of scholarliness and historical sense. One fruit of these historical forays is a reexamination of the ideas of Pierre Janet. The reader is likely to be struck by the number of references to Janet in these various chapters, even in the psychoanalytic chapter by Nemiah. (Perry and Laurence make it clear that Freud and Janet, though fellow pioneers of the unconscious, were not on the best of terms.) Much of the new interest in Janet is due to Ernest Hilgard's employment of a "neo-dissociation" theory to account for the findings of his own seminal research on hypnosis as well as the findings of many others. Similar notions are discussed in an interesting fashion in Kihlstrom's chapter in this volume. One may speculate whether recent psychoanalytic interest in the concept of "splitting"—which, like dissociation, is differentiated from repression in terms of "horizontal" and "vertical" splits—may also present possibilities of bringing to bear some of Janet's ideas in areas that have been of interest to Freudians.

Also significant for its bringing to bear another major tradition in areas of traditional Freudian concern is Fischer and Pipp's exploration of the development of unconscious thought. Drawing on the tradition of Piaget and of American cognitive-developmental psychology, these authors argue that in fact unconscious thought undergoes development just as conscious thought does. It must be noted that their definition of unconscious processes is not fully consonant with the psychoanalytic idea with which it can easily be confused. But their heuristic assumption that fractionation is a natural state for all psychological processes unless an effort is made to integrate them is an intriguing one which at once introduces order and simplicity to diverse observations and invites an examination of complexity. In recent years, there has been a resurgence of interest in the specificity of behavior and experience depending on the environmental context, as well as an effort to integrate such an emphasis with what we also know about psychological structure and coherence (cf. Bowers, 1973; Mischel, 1968; Sullivan, 1953; Wachtel, 1973, 1977a, 1981). Further inquiry along these lines is likely to prove very fruitful.

Meichenbaum and Gilmore note the increasing influence of efforts to bridge the gaps between behavioral and psychodynamic approaches and appropriately include their own chapter among such efforts. There are many points of convergence between their cognitive-behavioral route to such a bridge and those which have begun on the psychodynamic side of the abyss. They describe, for example, how confirmatory bias can lead to behavior which evokes responses in others that provide "pseudoconfirmation." Such vicious circles have been described from a psychodynamic point of view as well (e.g., Wachtel, 1973, 1977b, 1981, 1982). Their call for active behavioral efforts to complement and activate the therapeutic value of "raising consciousness" reflects a concern similar to that which led some psychodynamic therapists to seek to integrate behavioral methods into their work (e.g., Wachtel, 1977a). Their emphasis on schemas that have both an ideational and an affective component is consonant with efforts to use the notion of schema to clarify the implications of central psychodynamic concepts. A recent paper, for example, has shown how the Piagetian notion of schema in particular, with its emphasis on assimilation and accommodation, can clarify and modify the psychoanalytic concept of transference (Wachtel, 1981). [Goldfried (1983) has suggested that the schema concept may be ideal for bridging the gap among various orientations.] Finally, Meichenbaum and Gilmore's concern that the role of environmental influences be given due weight along with the role of unconscious processes in the individual is evident as well in integrative efforts starting from the psychodynamic side (e.g., Wachtel, 1973, 1977b, 1981).

This is by no means to suggest that their cognitive-behavioral model is but a carbon copy or mirror image of integrative psychodynamic efforts. There are differences in style, investigative strategy, and primary observational base that seem to go along with differences in one's original intellectual background, and these differences are essential to explore further. Meichenbaum and Gilmore, for example, seem to have a greater faith than I do in systematic straightforward rationality. In contrast, notwithstanding the departures we have each made from our points of origin, my own psychodynamic roots are reflected in a greater concern with conflict, motivation, and the gradually accumulating consequences of fears learned in the state of helplessness in which we all began our lives. I suspect we will each converge still further, but it is best at present to take the differences as well as the convergences seriously; I have consistently been forced to learn more by the challenge of cognitive and behavioral formulations that shared some of my assumptions but questioned others, and I would hope it is a two-way street.

I have at times in my career been pessimistic about my chosen field. Reading some of our journals can leave the impression that psychologists have a kind of tunnel vision that excludes both historical perspective and the truly important questions one would expect psychology to address. This book is a wonderful antidote to such pessimism. It is a model of how psychological science can address the truly significant with imagination, discipline, and—a delightful bonus on many of these pages—wit. The reader is invited both to enjoy and to learn.

PAUL L. WACHTEL

City University of New York

REFERENCES

Bowers, K.S. Situationism in psychology: An analysis and critique. *Psychological Review*, 1973, *80*, 307–336.

Breger, L. *Clinical-cognitive psychology: Models and integrations*. Englewood Cliffs, N.J.: Prentice-Hall, 1969.

Goldfried, M.M., & Robins, C. On the facilitation of self-efficacy. *Cognitive Therapy and Research*, 1983, *6*, 34–41.

Klein, G.S. *Perception, motives, and personality*. New York: Knopf, 1970.

Mischel, W. *Personality and assessment*. New York: Wiley, 1968.

Peterfreund, E. Information, systems, and psychoanalysis. *Psychological Issues*, Monograph No. 25/26. New York: International Universities Press, 1971.

Rogers, C.R. A theory of therapy, personality, and interpersonal relationships, as developed in the client-centered framework. In S. Koch (Ed.), *Psychology: A study of a science* (Vol. 3). New York: McGraw-Hill, 1959, pp. 184–256.

Rosenblatt, A.D., & Thickstun, J.T. Modern psychoanalytic concepts in a general psychology. *Psychological Issues*, Monograph No. 42/43. New York: International Universities Press, 1977.

Sartre, J.P. *Being and nothingness*. New York: Philosophical Library, 1956.

Shapiro, D. *Neurotic style*. New York: Basic Books, 1965.

Shapiro, D. *Autonomy and rigid character*. New York: Basic Books, 1982.

Silverman, L.H. Psychoanalytic theory: The reports of my death are greatly exaggerated. *American Psychologist*, 1976, *31*, 621–637.

Silverman, L.H. The subliminal psychodynamic activation method: Overview and comprehensive list of studies. In J. Masling (Ed.), *Empirical studies in psychoanalysis* (Vol. 1). New York: Erlbaum, 1978.

Sullivan, H.S. *The interpersonal theory of psychiatry*. New York: Norton, 1953.

Wachtel, P.L. Psychodynamics, behavior therapy, and the implacable experimenter: An inquiry into the consistency of personality. *Journal of Abnormal Psychology*, 1973, *82*, 324–334.

Wachtel, P.L. *Psychoanalysis and behavior therapy: Toward an integration*. New York: Basic Books, 1977. (a)

Wachtel, P.L. Interaction cycles, unconscious processes, and the person-situation issue. In D. Magnusson and N. Endler (Eds.), *Personality at the crossroads: Issues in interactional psychology*. Hillsdale, N.J.: Erlbaum, 1977, pp. 317–331. (b)

Wachtel, P.L. Transference, schema, and assimilation: The relevance of Piaget to the psychoanalytic theory of transference. *Annual of Psychoanalysis*, Vol. 8. New York: International Universities Press, 1981, pp. 59–76.

Wachtel, P.L. Vicious circles: The self and the rhetoric of emerging and unfolding. *Contemporary Psychoanalysis*, 1982, *18*, 273–295.

Wolitzky, D.L., & Wachtel, P.L. Perception and personality. In B. Wolman (Ed.), *Handbook of general psychology*. Englewood Cliffs, N.J.: Prentice-Hall, 1973, pp. 826-857.

Series Preface

This series of books is addressed to behavioral scientists interested in the nature of human personality. Its scope should prove pertinent to personality theorists and researchers as well as to clinicians concerned with applying an understanding of personality processes to the amelioration of emotional difficulties in living. To this end, the series provides a scholarly integration of theoretical formulations, empirical data, and practical recommendations.

Six major aspects of studying and learning about human personality can be designated: personality theory, personality structure and dynamics, personality development, personality assessment, personality change, and personality adjustment. In exploring these aspects of personality, the books in the series discuss a number of distinct but related subject areas: the nature and implications of various theories of personality; personality, characteristics that account for consistencies and variations in human behavior; the emergence of personality processes in children and adolescents; the use of interviewing and testing procedures to evaluate individual differences in personality; efforts to modify personality styles through psychotherapy, counseling, behavior therapy, and other methods of influence; and patterns of abnormal personality functioning that impair individual competence.

IRVING B. WEINER

University of Denver
Denver, Colorado

Contents

Introduction   1

1. Mental Processing Outside of Awareness: The Contributions
    of Freud and Janet   9
        Campbell Perry and Jean-Roch Laurence

2. The Unconscious and Psychopathology   49
        John C. Nemiah

3. Development of the Structures of Unconscious Thought   88
        Kurt W. Fischer and Sandra L. Pipp

4. Conscious, Subconscious, Unconscious: A Cognitive Perspective   149
        John F. Kihlstrom

5. Psychobiology and the Unconscious   212
        Daniel N. Robinson

6. On Being Unconsciously Influenced and Informed   227
        Kenneth S. Bowers

7. The Nature of Unconscious Processes: A Cognitive-Behavioral
    Perspective   273
        Donald Meichenbaum and J. Barnard Gilmore

Author Index   299

Subject Index   307

THE UNCONSCIOUS
RECONSIDERED

Introduction

This book emerged as a possibility several years ago as the editors, en route for a day of sailing, found themselves in friendly disagreement over the need for invoking unconscious determinants to account for human thought and action. The argument turned to the question of what Freud's concept of the unconscious might be today, given the recent advances in biology, psychiatry, and psychology. This fueled an interest in getting other people to reconsider the notion of the "unconscious." After a period of reflection about how to proceed, we approached potential contributors with the charge to write a detailed analysis of unconscious processes from a particular perspective. Hence this book contains chapters that consider the unconscious from a historical perspective and from the points of view of psychopathology, developmental psychology, information processing, biopsychology, social cognition, and psychotherapy. We think each contributor discharges this assignment with admirable scholarship, insight, and elan.

It may nevertheless seem vaguely perverse to publish a book on unconscious determinants of thought and action just as more and more books, chapters, and articles appear in the psychological literature extolling the need for consciousness in human thought and action. As just one illustration, Richard Jessor (1981), based on his large-scale study with thousands of high school students, recently argued that "it is the perceived environment that is most likely to yield '...the thing that psychology has always been really after throughout its history' (Brunswick, 1943, p. 266)—invariant relations between environment and action" (p. 317). Since, according to Jessor, the perceived environment is phenomenally represented, the implication is strong that the environment guides and directs behavior by virtue of being *consciously* perceived.

That behavior is for the most part consciously controlled is an assumption shared by many psychologists who have rebelled against a mindless behaviorism; it is a position that both the present editors would have endorsed at one time. But each of us, for somewhat different reasons, has begun to worry about the implicit assumption that human behavior is by and large controlled by phenomenologically accessible perceptions (i.e., is consciously controlled). Surely there are times when a person's conscious experience seems somehow insufficient to account for one's behavior. Consider the following episode.

A young, attractive, and already powerful Quebec politician with an extraordinary career in front of him and the devotion of thousands of constituents behind him—recently walked into one of Canada's largest department stores and shoplifted a $120 sport coat. He was caught, fined $300, and the story was widely publicized in the Canadian press. As a consequence, the man resigned his cabinet seat in disgrace. According to newspaper accounts of the incident, the shoplifter was very puzzled by his action. He called the theft "probably an attempted political suicide...I didn't need that coat. I could have paid for it many times over." (The 35-year-old cabinet minister's salary was $65,095 a year, and he was a bachelor.) In another account, he stated that taking the jacket "was neither premeditated nor calculated....Now it's done. My unconscious made me do an act that I never would have thought of doing myself." While we have to be cautious about accepting such protestations at face value, this politician's comments are reminiscent of the biblical Paul's lamentation: "I do not understand my own action. For I do not do what I want, but I do the very thing I hate."

Such a lapse in the ability of conscious experience to provide a sensible account of one's own behavior may be relatively infrequent, but its occurrence is revealing. It is one of the very few times that a person is confronted with reasonably compelling evidence, however indirect, that more is moving behavior than meets the eye. While such a gap in an individual's mental life is uninformative about the truly important determining conditions of the behavior in question, at least it implies the existence of *some* sort of influence operating on human behavior that is not well represented in consciousness, and which therefore needs to be inferred or otherwise identified.

It is our impression, however, that most of the time people manage some account of their behavior that preserves at least the illusion of conscious control over their action. Often these post hoc accounts are referred to as rationalizations, and typically they are more persuasive to the person trying to account for his behavior than they are to an impartial judge. Consider, for example, the following illustration.

In a recent court case, a middle-aged man of considerable prominence and regard in the community pleaded guilty to nine counts of sexual assault on preadolescent girls, and to one count of engaging in intercourse with a girl younger than 14. There was some indication that he had in fact had some sort of sexual contact with more than 50 young girls over a period of several years. Several of these girls were his legal wards; others were local neighborhood girls. The defendant claimed that at the time he thought sexual relationships with young girls were a means of fostering feelings of love and closeness while helping them at the same time to achieve maturity. "At the time, I literally had no conscious sense of the horrible things I was doing and only in retrospect [do] I understand what I was doing."

In general, then, it is our impression that people's perceptions and actions are typically coordinated, as Jessor suggests, so that the former are experienced as generating, predicting, and explaining the latter. To assume otherwise, that is, to assume that action derives from some source other than conscious perception and experience, is to admit immediately that behavior is unconsciously determined—a very threatening admission indeed. For once we give up the anchoring influence of conscious perception and experience as the primary indicator of why we behave the way we do, *anything* seems possible: Simply buying a cigar can be swollen with libidinous implications. More seriously, the absence of *conscious* control is often regarded as the absence of any control at all, thereby raising the prospect of behavior run riot.

But let us review "the evidence." A young cabinet minister throws his political career away by stealing a $120 sports coat; a prominent middle-aged man engages in sexual misconduct over an extended period of time with prepubescent girls; torture takes place on a daily basis in many so-called civilized countries; 6 million Jews were killed in the World War II holocaust; and according to many experts, we are very likely to blow ourselves up in a nuclear Armageddon. Evidently, as far as human behavior is concerned, anything *is* possible, and has been taking place for millennia—despite various religious and moral injunctions for us to conduct ourselves in a humane and civilized manner.

If the mere prospect of taking unconscious determinants seriously means that anything would be possible, does the fact that almost anything and everything has *already* occurred help to document the existence of unconscious influences on thought and action? Perhaps not as a strictly logical conclusion. But certainly there is an implication that the acts of perversity, inhumanity, and self-destructiveness mentioned above and reported daily in the newspapers do not derive exclusively from rational and conscious considerations—however much people may wish or believe their behavior to be rational and consciously controlled.

What has become more and more compelling to us, however, is that unconscious influence is not merely a psychological deus ex machina—to be invoked when (and only when) conscious accounts of behavior are found wanting. Rather it seems to us that conscious perception and experience are *themselves* subject to the vagaries of unconscious influence. To illustrate, a full-blown paranoid no doubt harbors conscious thoughts of being the target of various plots against his safety and security. Precipitate action may well proceed from this rather bizarre but compelling perception of the world. And a person newly fallen in love may have conscious experiences that "naturally" lead to uncharacteristic and even irrational actions that would never be considered under normal circumstances. What is more, the paranoid or lover may inadvertently behave in ways that engender events which further confirm his or her view of the world. This entire interpersonal process may occur in an entirely automatic, unwitting, and unconscious manner. The question then is not simply how to account for the outward behavior of a paranoid or lover. We must ask as well: What has led the person to experience the world in a way that leads naturally to such behavior?

Our answer to this question, in rough outline, is that many factors laid down in one's personal history and development, together with current informational input (at least some of which is itself not represented in consciousness) interactively conspire to influence our conscious experience and behavior. There is no compelling reason to assume that these influences must be represented in consciousness in order to guide human thought, feeling, and action, and the various contributions to this book detail how such influences are in fact frequently unconscious. At this point, it is perhaps sufficient to elaborate briefly on the notion that conscious experience is at least in part unconsciously determined.

First of all, conscious experience need not resemble the unconscious influences that helped form it. This is particularly striking in the psychodynamic notion of reaction formation in which anger, for example, is completely cut off from consciousness, but nevertheless helps to determine an overweening "niceness" in what the person says and does. In general, then, the contents of consciousness do not necessarily reveal in any obvious or direct way the kind or quality of the unconscious influences that originally helped generate the conscious experience. Indeed if this were not the case—for example, if an overdetermined "niceness" were immediately and automatically recognized by the perpetrator for what it was—then there would be little or no reason for having transformed the anger into its opposite.

More generally the contents of consciousness often serve as a heavy curtain separating people from the unconscious determinants of both their actions and their experience of it. For clearly whatever is present in consciousness is by definition vividly, directly, and focally represented in immediate experience, whereas this is obviously *not* the case for whatever is unconscious. Consequently, when trying to appraise or understand one's own thoughts and actions, it is natural to do so in terms that are vividly and focally represented in immediate experience. In other words, precisely because conscious experience can be so compelling, the contents of consciousness are frequently and unquestioningly accepted as providing a valid account of one's actions, however misleading or mistaken they may be. Thus those newly in love or the paranoid may experience their behavior as reasonable and well-informed, rather than as deriving from unconscious influences that affect both the behavior and how it is experienced. More generally, history has repeatedly taught us that the most perverse, evil, and unconscionable actions against humanity are seldom deemed by their perpetrators as perverse, evil, or unconscionable; on the contrary they are experienced as necessary (under the circumstances), patriotic, or even (heaven help us) as God's will. Thus as Polanyi (1964) argued, humanity's moral passions can infect the most obscene policies and practices, thereby permitting them to be experienced as justified, and at the same time obscuring their unconscionable and unconscious sources.

Finally, the impact of unconscious influences on conscious perception and experience is especially evident when it leads to gross psychopathology (see Nemiah, this book). Indeed early proponents of unconscious influences on human thinking and behavior argued rather emphatically that unconscious influences needed to be acknowledged *only* in people who were psychologically disturbed. This was clearly Pierre Janet's position, as Perry and Laurence imply in their contribution to this book. It was a distinctly Freudian view that unconscious influences are visited upon those who are psychologically intact as well as those who are not. However, it was one thing to concede that a person who is psychologically disturbed might be haunted by unconscious ghosts, and quite another to propose that even those who were firmly embedded in reality and committed to rationality could nevertheless be responding to forces that were not part of their conscious agenda. *That* was an assault on the basic assumptions of what it meant to be fully human, as passed down from generation to generation at least since the teaching of Aristotle.

The Freudian assumption that unconscious influences are at work even in those most committed to reality and rationality still has the power to incense those who think Freud may be saying something about *them*—which of course he was. Yet as Bowers asserts in his chapter, scientific progress depends vitally on the fact that scientists—the very archetypes of rationality—remain open and responsive to tacit, unconscious features of their experience. The unconscious can inform thought in a way that explicit evidence alone often fails to do (Polanyi, 1964). Evidently those who are most intuitively in touch with reality are no less responsive to unconscious influences on thought and action than those people who are seriously burdened with psychological problems they do not understand. Obviously, however, the nature and quality of the unconscious influences at work in the intuitive scientist differ considerably from those that produce the human suffering of the mentally disturbed. In other words, some people are more fortunate, by dint of their particular developmental and learning histories, in the kinds of unconscious factors that exert contemporary influence on their thought, feeling, and behavior. Fischer and Pipp's chapter in this book is an extended developmental analysis of how unconscious processes can be expressed in both normal and pathological behavior.

Whether or not a particular unconscious influence generates mental mayhem or intuitive musings, the process at work is indisputably psychological. Robinson's chapter on the unconscious and biopsychology is emphatic on this point. For example: "Neuronal activity...as with all purely physical events is utterly neutral with respect to psychological formulations [of repression]. Such activity *derives* its psychological significance from these formulations, not vice versa." In other words, the language of neuroanatomy and neurophysiology simply does not embody or refer to psychologically significant realities such as cognitive structure, repression, or the experience of the color red—though, of course, without a brain nothing psychological could occur. We can be assured, therefore, that advances in brain structure and function will not render the present book obsolete; only conceptual and empirical advances in the psychology of unconscious processes could do that. While the editors obviously are not in a position to predict which of the proposals in the current anthology will be rendered quaint and antiquated with time, we can identify several themes that have emerged as salient and substantial reconsiderations vis-à-vis the unconscious as classically conceived.

First of all, there has been no rush to disavow the classical formulations of psychoanalysis. Indeed Nemiah's chapter on the role of unconscious processes in psychopathology could not have been written if the author had not been deeply and broadly informed by psychoanalysis. It is a chapter based on clinical observation, and exploits to full advantage the case history method for generating insights into the human condition. While there are limitations to the case history approach, they are by and large different from the limitations of controlled laboratory investigations, some of which are addressed in Bowers's chapter. The difficulties in coming to some adequate understanding of unconscious influences on human thought, feeling, and behavior are sufficiently pervasive and profound that we can ill afford to ignore insights from the consulting room any more than we can afford to overestimate the value of laboratory findings simply because they are based on experimental methodology.

It is in this spirit that Kihlstrom's contribution to this book, perhaps the most experimentally oriented in emphasis, nevertheless challenges contemporary models of cognition with a variety of clinical evidence, including multiple personality, somnambulism, and findings from hypnosis. At the same time, the chapter by Meichenbaum and Gilmore and the one by Fischer and Pipp, though having a distinctly clinical flavor, nevertheless display a keen appreciation of what laboratory findings can add to the insights of clinical and naturalistic observation. It is this willingness on the part of the contributors to utilize evidence from both experimental and clinical contexts that is a thematic departure from the classical position enunciated by psychoanalysis. Freud was on record as having little time for experimental inquiry into the nature of unconscious influence on human thought and conduct. We think he was wrong in this pronouncement.

A third striking theme that emerges in this anthology is the recrudescence of dissociation as an important mechanism by which psychological influences can be rendered unconscious. The historical chapter by Perry and Laurence is an elegant addition to the literature on how dissociative processes initially constituted a robust alternative to the psychoanalytic preference for a repressed unconscious. The Freudian view ultimately gained ascendance over that of Pierre Janet's dissociative account, partly by dint of Freud's prepossessing personality and capacity for engendering discipleship. The reemergence of dissociation owes something to Henri Ellenberger's (1970) remarkable book *The Discovery of the Unconscious* and something to Hilgard's (1977) neodissociative theory of hypnosis. Moreover, as Robinson states in his chapter, dissociation as a mechanism for rendering certain influences unconscious is far more congenial to contemporary models of information processing than is repression. For these as well as additional reasons, dissociation is once again a popular concept, and we think it is here to stay. Kihlstrom's contribution goes a long way toward justifying this assertion.

Kihlstrom highlights a fourth theme that also figures prominently in the contributions of Robinson and Bowers—the heuristic value of information-processing models of perception and memory as they contribute to an understanding of unconscious processes. This domain of inquiry is diverse and not always open to claims for perception without awareness—whether in the guise of subliminal perception or some other form of unconscious perception. Yet as several contributors indicate, the evidence in favor of "perception without noticing" (Bowers's phrase) now seems compelling.

The emphasis on information processing leads naturally toward a consideration of externally presented information as a source of unconscious influence. This development represents another thematic shift away from the classical psychoanalytic view, which emphasized the largely intrapsychic nature of unconscious influences. However, the emergence of external information as a source of unconscious influence should not be overstated. Bear in mind that research in information processing is naturally disposed to employ experimental methods. This strong methodological preference is simply not well tuned to the operation of transference, resistance, and the unwitting expression of impulse, conflict, and defense so sensitively addressed in Nemiah's chapter. As we implied earlier, the all-too-human tendency to identify "legitimate" psychological investigation with certain favored methodology must be firmly resisted, since it almost inevitably generates truncated conceptualization. Thus the emphasis on information processing evident in several contributions to this book should be seen as supplementing rather than replacing the classical, psychoanalytic view of "unconscious," and as correcting some of its intrapsychic excesses by offering a tempered consideration of how external constraints can be influential without being conscious.

In the final analysis, the mind and the environment "need" each other, as far as a balanced understanding of the human condition is concerned. The contributions of Fischer and Pipp and of Meichenbaum and Gilmore are especially clear on this point. Each of these chapters emphasizes the operation of Piagetian-like cognitive structures or schemas that develop and differentiate with the organism's experience. Without a relatively complex environment that forces accommodative efforts on the part of the person, the mind would never develop internal representations of the external complexities to which it must adapt. According to this view, "normal" failures to adapt simply indicate that the difficulties and complexities presented by the environment exceed the available "secondary processing" capacities of the person attempting to deal with them. Alternatively, failures of adaptation can index the reduced ability of a person to deal with an environment. Such pathological failures of adaptation are often due to disrupting invasion of affect and impulse that actively interferes with the person's ability to cope, even though the environment in question would not ordinarily present excessive demands on the person's unimpaired skills and abilities. It is precisely these pathological failures of adaptation that led both Freud and Janet to an appreciation of intrapsychic and largely unconscious influences in thought and behavior (see Perry and Laurence, this book), and this tradition is sensitively portrayed in Nemiah's chapter on unconscious processes in psychopathology.

What is worth underlining here is that it is precisely the role of affect and impulse that is not yet well integrated into the literature on information processing. By and large, investigators of this tradition are interested in the "generalized human mind"—that is, the Wundtian mind that minimizes the importance of individual differences, let alone the pronounced deficits that characterize severe psychopathology. Within treatment variance is a source of nuisance and annoyance to many such investigators. Yet these differences are basic to a clinician probing the subtleties of a particular person's (mal)adaptations. What is more, such individual differences are not simply a result of peremptory impulses and affects; as Meichenbaum and Gilmore indicate, these differences are also a result of a person's core beliefs, assumptions, and dispositions developed over a lifetime. As the authors make clear these basic individuating schema are often as invisible and unconscious in their functioning as they are pervasive in their impact. Since these cognitive schemas or structures are internalized representations of the person's history of adaptation, they represent a potent *intrapsychic* source of unconscious influence.

The diversity and pluralism represented by an individual's repertoire of cognitive schemas is one of the conceptual distinctions that most separates the thrust of the present book from classical psychoanalysis. Freud's inveterate identification of sex and aggression as *the* crucial sources of unconscious influence is simply not reflected in most of the contributions to this book. One does not have to deny the importance of these twin pillars of psychoanalytic theory in order to resist claims for their exclusive provenance over matters unconscious. Indeed one could argue that Freud *underestimated* the extent to which thought, feeling, and behavior are subject to unconscious influences by his championing of sex and aggression as matters of the unconscious. Perhaps if he had not tied the possibilities for unconscious influence so closely to the notions of sex and aggression, Freud may have gained easier and earlier acceptance of his revolutionary insights into the human condition.

We hope that these introductory remarks are sufficient to put our readers in touch with the important themes that emerge in this book; in any event, it is time for the contributors to speak for themselves. We wish our readers well, and hope that they will find as much satisfaction in perusing the book as we had in guiding it through completion.

REFERENCES

Brunswick, E. Organismic achievement and environmental probability. *Psychological Review,* 1943, *50,* 255–272.

Ellenberger, H. *The discovery of the unconscious.* New York: Basic Books, 1970.

Hilgard, E.R. *Divided consciousness: Multiple controls in human thought and action.* New York: Wiley, 1977.

Jessor, R. The perceived environment in psychological theory. In D. Magnusson (Ed.), *Toward a psychology of situations: An interactional perspective.* Hillsdale, N.J.: Erlbaum, 1981.

Polanyi, M. *Personal knowledge: Toward a post-critical philosophy.* New York: Harper and Row, 1964.

CHAPTER 1

Mental Processing Outside of Awareness: The Contributions of Freud and Janet

CAMPBELL PERRY AND JEAN-ROCH LAURENCE

The notion that cognitive processing can occur outside of awareness is not a new one; several scholars have noted that such a belief can be found in the writings of such diverse thinkers as Leibnitz, Kant, Herbart, and Hartmann (Ellenberger, 1970; Klein, 1977; Prince, 1929/1970). More recently, such an emphasis has appeared in the work of Hilgard (1973, 1974, 1977, 1979). The most major and all-encompassing attempt to account for cognition without awareness is, of course, by Sigmund Freud (1856–1939). Freud's theorizing about the unconscious has sufficiently pervaded psychological and psychiatric thought (not to mention popular beliefs about mental functioning) that Morton Prince in 1928 complained that "Freudian psychology has flooded the field like a full rising tide, and the rest of us were left submerged like clams buried in the sands at low water" (Nemiah, 1979, p. 318).

There is much justification for Prince's lament, since he himself followed an alternative line of thinking which was contemporaneous with that of Freud. This alternative account of mental processing, and particularly of cognition out of awareness, was initiated by Pierre Janet (1959–1947). In his book *L'Automatisme psychologique* (1889), which predated Freud's first major exposition of unconscious mental processes in *The Interpretation of Dreams* (1900) by a decade (and

This chapter was prepared while the first author was in receipt of Natural Sciences and Engineering Research Council (NSERC) of Canada Grant No. A6361 and the second author held an NSERC Postdoctoral Fellowship. We acknowledge NSERC's support with gratitude. Special thanks to Dorothy Redhead, Elizabeth Chau, and Trenny Cook for the careful typing of the manuscript during its preparation, and to the editors of this volume for their critical comments and encouragement of earlier drafts of this chapter.

an earlier formulation by Freud and Breuer in 1895 by several years), Janet proposed a theory of *désagrégation* (often translated into English incorrectly as *dissociation*). He argued that in various neurotic conditions, ideas and cognitive processes could become detached from the mainstream of consciousness, whereupon they had the power to form neurotic symptoms, and in some cases, secondary personalities. They could, however, be tapped by hypnosis, and by this method could be reintegrated with the ego and with consciousness. More crucially, Janet believed that in the normally functioning individual, no unconscious (or subconscious, as he preferred to call it) existed; it was only when certain events intervened in a person's life to create *désagrégation* that a plurality of psychic processes occurred. This, as is well known, is in complete contradiction to the Freudian view that the Unconscious is at work in such diverse normal activities as dreaming, humor, slips of the tongue, errors, creativity, as well as neurotic symptoms and psychosis.

Janet's beliefs were incorporated into the theorizing of such contemporary and subsequent investigators as Alfred Binet in France, Edmund Gurney and F.W.H. Myers in England (though the efforts of the British investigators were directed to establishing scientific evidence for the paranormal), and Boris Sidis and Morton Prince in the United States. Until recently, however, these alternatives to Freud remained at the periphery of psychological and psychiatric thinking. This is, in part, the result of the recent rediscovery of hypnosis by psychology in general. More important, Hilgard's (1973, 1974, 1977, 1979) major efforts to reformulate late nineteenth century and early twentieth century dissociation theory in terms of contemporary cognitive psychology, developing what he has described as "neodissociation" theory, has refocused interest upon the position of Janet and certain other thinkers of a *désagrégation* ilk.

By Freud's own admission, Janet's observations constituted a significant point of departure for his own investigation of mind and mental processes. The emphasis of this essay therefore is upon Janet and Freud, and the issues and problems that their particular approaches to cognitive processes outside of awareness continue to raise. The more recent theoretical and empirical work of Hilgard is briefly surveyed in order to evaluate the current status of thinking on this issue.

FREUD AND JANET

In his fascinating biography of Freud, Ernest Jones (1964) states:

> Pierre Janet, who has erroneously been regarded as a predecessor of Freud's, adopted in the eighties the alternative method of approach. He devised some beautiful and very ingenious experiments which led to some vivid descriptive conclusions, but they brought him not one step nearer to the forces at work. (pp. 70–71)

It is very clear from their writings that Freud and Janet had a barely concealed mutual animosity, though each, at times, paid respect to the work of the other. An examination of what each said about the other indicates, among other things, that Jones was in error in denying Janet's claim to be a predecessor of Freud; as indicated already. Freud acknowledged Janet's contribution to his own thinking, despite his personal dislike of him. He believed, however, that Janet had taken the wrong path in his theorizing about unconscious mental processes while he had not. Janet's feelings about Freud were mutual.

They were contemporaries. Freud, born in 1856, was Janet's elder by three years; Janet, who died in 1947, outlived Freud by almost eight years. Amazingly, they never met; nor did they correspond. Jones (1964) quotes a letter from Freud to Marie Bonaparte in 1937, two years before his death, part of which concerns a request made by Janet's son-in-law, Edouard Pichon, who had written to Freud, asking him to permit Janet to visit him. The reply was:

> No, I will not see Janet. I could not refrain from reproaching him with having behaved unfairly to psychoanalysis and also to me personally and never having corrected it. He was stupid enough to say that the idea of a sexual aetiology for the neuroses could only arise in the atmosphere of a town like Vienna. Then when the libel was spread by French writers that I had listened to his lectures and stolen his ideas he could with a word have put an end to such talk, since actually I never saw him or heard his name in the Charcot time: he has never spoken this word. You can get an idea of his scientific level from his utterance that the unconscious is *une façon de parler.* No, I will not see him. I thought at first of sparing him the impoliteness by the excuse that I am not well or that I can no longer talk French and he certainly can't understand a word of German. But I have decided against that. There is no reason for making any sacrifice for him. Honesty the only possible thing; rudeness quite in order. (pp. 633–634)

Things were more complex between Freud and Janet than these quotations from Jones would suggest. While it may be true that Freud and Janet never met, they were aware of each other's work from a very early stage. The earliest reference to Janet made by Freud, that we can find, is in a letter to Fliess dated July 10, 1893 (Freud, 1977). In it, he stated that "our work on hysteria has at last received proper recognition from Janet in Paris." Although Janet was quite fulsome in his praise of Breuer and Freud's work, it is possible that his expression of it may have been perceived as condescending. For example, he wrote:

> We are glad to find that several authors, particularly MM. Breuer and Freud, have recently verified our interpretation *already somewhat old,* of subconscious fixed ideas with hystericals. (Janet, 1894/1901, p. 290, italics added)

Elsewhere, in the same book, Breuer and Freud are represented as having expressed "very well the idea we have long maintained" (p. 408). Certainly, when

Freud came to write an encyclopedia article on psychoanalysis he made a curious distinction between who observed first, and who published first. He stated:

> The theoretical ideas put forward at the time by Breuer and Freud were influenced by Charcot's theories upon traumatic hysteria and could find support in the findings of his pupil, Pierre Janet, which, though they were published earlier than the *Studien,* were in fact subsequent to Breuer's first case. (Freud, 1922, p. 108).

This account, however, was written after many years of disparaging references to each other in both the writings of Freud and Janet, although initially Freud wrote glowingly of Janet. For example, Freud (1893a) spoke of the "highly remarkable discoveries in reference to anaesthetic patients" (p. 35) of Binet and the two Janets.[1] In the same year (Freud, 1893b) he stated that "I must agree completely with the views expressed by Janet in the latest numbers of *Archives de Neurologie*; hysterical paralyses demonstrate their truth just as well as anaesthesias and psychic symptoms do" (p. 55). Again, in a subsequent paper (Freud, 1894), there is reference to "the fine work carried out by P. Janet, J. Breuer, and others" (p. 60), and Janet's "ingenious paper" is referred to elsewhere in the same essay. It is around this time, however, that Freud began to express polite and open disagreement with Janet. For instance, he wrote:

> With this new turn in the theory, Breuer and I ... recede from Janet who assigns too great importance to the splitting of consciousness as a characteristic of hysteria. (Freud, 1894, p. 65)

From here on, their relationship deteriorated, as the following quotations from Freud indicate:

> We hold this opinion with the French school (Janet) which, by the way, owing to too crude a schematization, refers the cause of hysterical symptoms to an unconscious *idée fixe.* (Freud, 1904, p. 261)

And

> The emphasis held by Janet on the *idée fixe* which becomes transformed into a symptom amounts to no more than an extremely meagre attempt to schematization. (Freud, 1905, p. 137)

Even so major a thinker as Freud, however, could fall into self-serving argumentation, as when he wrote that the idea

> that the memory of a premature sexual experience is always found as the specific cause of hysteria does not agree with Janet's psychological theory of the neurosis, nor with any other; but it does harmonize perfectly well with my own hypotheses, described elsewhere, on the "defense neuroses." (Freud, 1896, pp. 151–152)

The history of animal magnetism, for instance, reminds us that two observations, though logically consistent with each other, can still both be empirically false.

Others in the psychoanalytic movement held Janet in similar low esteem. In a letter to Freud of June 28, 1907, Jung wrote:

> My experience on the trip was *pauvre*. I had a talk with Janet and was very disappointed. He has only the most primitive knowledge of Dem. pr.[2] Of the latest happenings, including you, he understands nothing at all. He is stuck in this groove and is, be it said in passing, merely an intellect and not a personality, a hollow *causeur* and a typical mediocre bourgeois. (McGuire, 1974, p. 33)

Elsewhere, in another letter to Freud of September 11, 1907, Jung added to this portrait of Janet. "Janet," he wrote, "is a vain old buffer, though a good observer. But everything he says and does now is sterile" (McGuire, 1974, p. 86).

Freud's most trenchant criticisms of Janet are to be found in "On the History of the Psychoanalytic Movement" (Freud, 1914a). The Seventeenth International Congress of Medicine had been held in London the previous summer, and Janet had presented a far from favorable critique of psychoanalysis. In this historical report dated February 1914, Freud described Janet's paper in the following terms:

> In Paris itself, a conviction still seems to reign (to which Janet himself gave eloquent expression at the Congress in London in 1913) that everything good in psychoanalysis is a repetition of Janet's views with insignificant modifications, and that everything else is bad. At this congress, indeed, Janet had to submit to a number of corrections by Ernest Jones, who was able to point out to him his insufficient knowledge of the subject. Even though we deny his claims, however, we cannot forget the value of his work on the psychology of the neuroses. (pp. 316–317)

Janet's London Congress paper was reprinted verbatim[3] in two parts in *The Journal of Abnormal Psychology* (Janet, 1915a,b) and drew a reply from Ernst Jones in a later issue of that journal for that year (Jones, 1915). He expanded it subsequently; it formed the basis of Chapter 11 of *Psychological Healing* (Janet, 1919/1925, pp. 589–698), and his main criticisms of psychoanalysis, which are primarily methodological, are summarized in *Principles of Psychotherapy* (Janet, 1923/25, pp. 41–46). The allegation that Janet regarded everything good in psychoanalysis as a repetition of Janet is expressed in all of these sources in a much more specific manner than is suggested by Freud (1914).

Thus having characterized Freud as a "foreign physician," Janet (1923/1925) proceeded to accuse Freud of, in effect, plagiarizing his ideas. He wrote:

> ... he changed, first of all the terms that I was using: what I had called psychological analysis he called psychoanalysis, what I had called psychological system, ... he called complex; he considered a repression what I considered a restriction of consciousness, what I referred to as a psychological dissociation, or as a moral fumigation, he baptized with the name of catharsis. (p. 41)

Further, he considered the difference between psychoanalysis and psychological analysis "to be true and profound" but, he added, "it must be sought, not in the observations and doctrines which are almost identical, but in the method of study and the general conception that one gathers from these doctrines" (Janet, 1915a, p. 32).

It is also true that Janet dismissed certain Freudian innovations, in particular Freud's replacement of hypnosis with free association and Freud's method of dream analysis, both of which Janet considered to convey strong demand characteristics to report material that conformed with psychoanalytic hypotheses. He characterized it thus for free association:

> Freud's disciples advise having the patient seated in an easy chair while the physician places himself behind him and directs him to relax and speak aloud all the thoughts which enter his mind. This seems to me to be a very mediocre and somewhat naive proceeding, for in spite of every precaution the patient is conscious of the surveillance and, more than one would think, arranges his words to produce a certain effect...The patient should be observed unknown to himself, when he believes himself alone, as I have often done.... (Janet, 1915a, p. 12)

A similar critique was presented for Freud's method of dream collection. He did not doubt that dreams were valuable in understanding the patient's symptoms. As with free association, however, the criticism was of a methodological nature. He wrote:

> Freud does not seem to concern himself, as do so many writers, with disturbances of memory which transforms many dreams, or with the systematization that the dream undergoes at the moment of waking. He limits himself to noting and to accepting the related dream, as it stands, that the patient gives him some hours or days after its occurrence. He does not attempt to criticize this recital. (Janet, 1915a, p. 15)

In his reply to Janet, Jones (1915) misunderstood the methodological nature of Janet's criticisms. On the issue of free association, Jones dismissed Janet's critique with a rhetorical question. He wrote, "Does Professor Janet seriously believe that Professor Freud, who deliberately withholds from his patients all knowledge of psychoanalysis except what they discover for themselves, conveys, consciously or unconsciously to them such impressions?" (p. 407).[4]

He gave similar short shrift to Janet's criticisms of the Freudian dream collection method. His response was directed only to Janet's criticism that Freud appeared unconcerned by the observation that dreams become systematized at the moment of waking, and it ignored the more telling methodological point concerning the interval between the occurrence of the dream and its recounting during an analytic session. He wrote.

> So little is this the case that Freud, who in his detailed study of this interesting process has offered for the first time a precise explanation of it, coined a special

term to denote it, 'secondary elaboration," this being one of the four great mechanisms under the headings of which he describes the process of dream-formation. (Jones, 1915, p. 406)

One aspect of Janet's London Congress report on psychoanalysis appears to have particularly enraged Freud. He accused Janet of stating that the sexual atmosphere of Vienna was responsible for Freud's overemphasis of sexuality. In evaluating the sexual etiology of traumatic neuroses proposed by Freud, Janet wrote:

> It is difficult to accurately determine the proportion of neuropaths in whom (sexual) troubles of this kind are found, first, because observations have not always been precisely conducted to this end, and, next, this number must be extremely variable according to the environment in which observations are made....If Freud simply said that his estimate was very high, that in the district where his observations were made genital preoccupations and sexual disturbances are more frequent than elsewhere, I should not presume to contradict him. I have always thought that Paris was pre-eminent in this respect. (Janet, 1915b, p. 164).

It is not known what reading or representation of Janet's remarks at the 1913 London Congress led Freud to denounce his views in vehement terms. He wrote:

> We have all heard of the interesting attempt to explain psycho-analysis as a product of the peculiar character of Vienna as a city; as recently as 1913 Janet did not disdain to employ this argument, although he himself is undoubtedly proud of being a Parisian.... Now honestly, I am no local patriot; but this theory about psychoanalysis always seems to be quite exceptionally stupid, so stupid, in fact, that I have sometimes been inclined to suppose that the reproach of being a citizen of Vienna is only a euphemistic substitute for another reproach which no one would care to put forward openly. (Freud, 1914a, p. 325)

In actuality, Janet was defending Freud from what he considered to be the more extreme and ill-founded criticism of psychoanalysis. Thus one writer accused Freud of suggesting "sexual matters to them in some way and causes them to reply accordingly to his wish." The same author also believed that Freud would take the most commonplace sexual remark seriously, "that he stops when he obtains such a clue and puts it into a mental constellation, which he fabricates" (Janet, 1915b, p. 175). Janet noted that he found this a curious observation, and added:

> Friedländer and Ladame proposed a still more curious explanation, namely, that Vienna had a special sexual atmosphere, that it had a sort of *genius loci,* a local demon who epidemically reigns over the population, and that in this environment an observer is inevitably led to accord an exceptional importance to questions relative to sexuality. (Janet, 1915b, p. 175)

Janet stated that while he believed that there was some truth to both allegations, the real problem, in his opinion, lay in Freud's tendency to overgeneralize. This point is presented most succinctly elsewere, where Janet argued:

> Instead of agreeing with all of the preceding observers that one finds memories of this sort in *some* neuropaths psychoanalysis asserts, and therein lies its originality, that one finds such memories in *all* neuropaths....If they are not readily established in all patients, it is because one has not known how to make the patient acknowledge them, or has not known how to discover them behind his reticence. (Janet, 1923/25, p. 43)

Perhaps Janet's most interesting rebuke of Freud comes in his evaluation of psychoanalysis. He described it as

> the last incarnation of those practices at once magical and psychological that characterized ("animal") magnetism. It maintains the same characteristics, the use of imagination and the lack of criticism, the vaulting ambition, the contagious fascination, the struggle against orthodox science. It is possible that it will also meet undeserved appreciation and decline; but like magnetism and hypnotism, it will have played a great role and will have given a useful impulse to the study of psychology. (Janet, 1923/25. p. 46)

There is one final irony in this ill-fated interaction between Freud and Janet. As we have seen, one reason for Freud's refusal to meet Janet in 1937 was his belief that Janet had not attempted to dispel rumors that Freud had plagiarized Janet's ideas. Certainly it is true that Janet believed that Freud had done exactly this by a simple switch of terminology.[5] Notwithstanding, in June 1915, four months after Freud had written his history of the psychoanalytic movement, there was a meeting of the Paris Psychotherapy Society, in which Freud, in absentia, was the object of a number of acrid attacks. Interestingly, it was Janet who spoke in Freud's defense. He noted that it was neither "courteous nor just" that a session devoted to Freud's work had generated only criticism. He added:

> Admitting the part of errors and exaggerations, the general theory served as a basis for valuable studies. Psychoanalysis has contributed numerous data to the knowledge of neuroses, of sexual psychology and psychopathology. "Let us acknowledge these merits; our unavoidable criticisms should not detract us to show our regard for the fine work and the important observations of our Viennese colleagues." (Ellenberger, 1970, p. 821)

Subsequently, Janet published his defense of Freud in the *Revue de Psychothé*rapie in 1915, which has been described as "an act that took courage" (Ellenberger, 1970, p. 344), given that World War I was in progress and relations between France and Germany were comparable to those of two scorpions in a bottle.

We have documented the relationship in such detail only because subsequent authors have tended to discuss it fragmentarily or else have not even mentioned

Janet (Fine, 1979). The impression is left that either Janet had no claim at all to having influenced Freud's thinking or that he did (as Freud willingly indicated), but that his contribution to an understanding of unconscious mental processes was minimal and/or trivial. Only Cole (1970) gives a balanced though brief rendition of the enmity that existed between Freud and Janet. He noted:

> Janet began to realize just how greatly Freud was going to diverge from his path as, one after another, Freud's brilliant studies appeared, and his new methods, his total revision in the theory of mental illness, were advocated by a tightly knit coterie that grew dogmatic and aggressive, and which finally succeeded in convincing the bulk of the psychiatric profession....By 1925 the cleft had so deepened that Janet's reviews and criticisms characterized the new Viennese school in caustic terms, as something bizarre and puerile, as a method that twisted facts and treated patients in an unprofessional manner. Freud never forgave Janet these critical shafts. (p. 280)

Neither did Freud's followers; long after the London Congress of 1913, Janet was the object of several attacks from psychoanalysts. Perhaps one of the most original critiques came from a French psychoanalyst, Madeleine Cavé (1945). She accused Janet of *hurried plagiarism* upon the publication of Breuer and Freud's paper of 1893. She wrote that Janet had published in 1889 the case of Marie without understanding how and why the patient had been cured. After the publication of Breuer and Freud's paper Janet finally understood what had happened to his patient and hurriedly published other cases pretending that Freud had imitated him. Although her attack was historically incorrect, as Ellenberger has pointed out (1970), it certainly did not enhance Janet's acceptance by the younger psychoanalytic generation.

Now that the dust has settled on an acrimonious dispute between the two main proponents of the belief in unconscious mental processes, it is possible to reevaluate their respective contributions. That our conceptualizations of the unconscious come primarily from psychoanalysis is historically understandable. Such conceptualizations are, however, far from complete, so that an understanding of the divergences of theory between Freud and Janet may serve to effect a rapprochement of their views, and, in the process, extend our understanding of how cognition may be influenced by processes of which we are not always aware.

PRECURSORS OF FREUD AND JANET

Regardless of whether one is Freudian or Janetian in outlook, it is difficult to attribute one or the other with the discovery or creation of the unconscious. Freud and Janet differed markedly in their social origin and milieu, but they were witnesses of a period of history in which the idea of unconscious processes influencing the human mind was ascendant in literature and philosophy. Such ideas were especially alive in the rising movement of paranormal phenomena emanating from England, the United States, and, to a lesser extent, France. In the scientific world of this period, physiology and neurology were dominating the scene, whereas psychology was struggling to find an exact methodology to explain human behavior. No major theory of the human mind had yet developed, although a few isolated individuals had already planted the seed from which the Freudian and Janetian ideas were to evolve. It is difficult to ascertain the exact influence that these early writers had on the thinking of Freud and Janet, but most of the important concepts that influenced their thinking had been enunciated during the mid-nineteenth century.

In the case of Freud, it is quite clear, for example, that he was following and expanding on the ideas of such writers as Moritz Benedikt (1835–1920), G.T. Fechner (1801–1887), and J.F. Herbart (1776–1841), to mention but a few. Already in 1864, Benedikt had proposed that hysteria was rooted in some functional disorder of the patient's sexuality. By 1868 he had placed major emphasis on the consequences of sexual frustrations, using the term libido in relationship to early dysfunctions of sexual life (Ellenberger, 1978). Benedikt particularly stressed the careful exploration of the patient's sexuality by directed questioning, and discouraged the use of hypnosis in psychotherapy, on the grounds that patients should be able to confront their problems in their normal waking state. Fechner's influence on Freud can be seen in *Beyond the Pleasure Principle* published in 1920. The principle of pleasure-unpleasure was a concept borrowed from Fechner. In fact, Freud connected the pleasure principle to Fechner's more general principle of the tendency to stability. Fechner had already proposed a "topographical concept" of the mind that would be the starting point of Freud's own topology (Ellenberger, 1970). Finally, the concept of repression can be traced back to Herbart, who introduced the notion of dynamism in the relationships between conscious and unconscious perceptions. Herbart viewed the threshold of perceptions as a surface where perceptions were continuously fighting one another, in order to avoid being repressed.

Janet, on the other hand, had a passion for history and cited all the sources from which he drew, emphasizing the analogies between his conceptions of mental life and those of earlier writers. Although several authors had already noticed the relationship between early traumatic experiences and some functional disorders, it is only with the publication of Janet's *L'Automatisme psychologique* in 1889 that the question was taken up by psychology. As early as 1649, Descartes, in his book *Les Passions de L'Ame,* had given two examples of traumatic memories affecting subsequent behaviors that had persisted long after the memories were forgotten. Janet reports that after the publication of his first observations he found a short book where the theory of psychological disaggregation was already laid down. The manuscript was 93 pages long and had been published in 1855, under the title "Seconde lettre de Gros Jean à son évêque au sujet des tables parlantes, des possessions et autres diableries."[6] Unfortunately this manuscript was anonymous.

Many authors who influenced Janet's thinking can be identified. Hippolyte Taine had published a treatise in 1870 called "De l'intelligence," where the problem of hypnosis was thoroughly explored; Janet drew heavily from it in his

1889 book. Maine de Biran, a philosopher, emphasized the ability of the mind to process information out of awareness. Janet (1889) described him as the true precursor of experimental psychology. Even if these two authors were of considerable influence in the writings of Janet, some others are also worth mentioning, because they particularly pointed either to the reality of nonconscious processing of information or to the ability of the mind to be active at different levels.

Richet, for example, was the first to talk about the changes in personality that can be observed both in healthy individuals and in hysterical patients. He was in fact the first experimenter to reinaugurate the study of hypnotism in France in the second half of the nineteenth century, following a period of long decline. Studying unconscious processes, Richet was the first to point out that a sort of permanent semisomnambulism existed within the individual which he characterized as an unconscious ego or an unconscious activity; according to Richet this unconscious ego was constantly on the watch, formed inferences, and performed acts, all unknown to the conscious ego. Janet not only acknowledged the work of Richet, but kept the notion of semisomnambulism in *L'Automatisme psychologique.*

Another extremely proficient psychologist of the nineteenth century was Théodule Ribot, who devoted his life to the study of psychopathology. Again, throughout his works can be found the idea of multiple levels of consciousness. In his work *The Diseases of the Personality* (1885) Ribot wrote:

> The unity of the ego, in the psychological sense of the word, is the cohesion for a given time of a certain number of states of clear consciousness, accompanied by others less clear, and by a multitude of physiological states which, although not themselves conscious like the others, yet operate as much as they. Unity means co-ordination. (p. 46)

In this passage the foundations of Janet's concept of psychological disaggregation can already be seen.

Finally, it would be difficult to ignore the contributions of Alfred Binet and Jean Martin Charcot to Janet's thinking. Binet was a contemporary of Janet, and an extremely refined investigator in the field of hypnosis. Following the publication of *L'Automatisme psychologique,* Janet continuously referred to the works of Binet. It is, however, Janet who exerted the most dramatic change in Binet's thinking about hypnosis. Before the publication of Janet's book, Binet was mainly concerned with the physiology of hypnosis and was trying to relate Charcot's discoveries to physiological dysfunctions of the nervous system. After 1889, however, Binet started looking at the hypnotic phenomena in mostly psychological terms, particularly in his 1889–1890 papers where he concluded that "all those experiments on hypnosis pointed to the fact that the limits of introspection are not those of consciousness, and that where we have not consciousness, there is not necessarily unconsciousness" (1905, p. 43).

Finally, there is the work of Charcot, although the identification of Janet as a former pupil of Charcot was probably detrimental to the success of Janet's ideas. In fact, Janet was not a pupil of Charcot. When he arrived at the Salpêtrière he was already a well-known researcher with ideas of his own. Although he respected Charcot's work he always, when possible, avoided working with Charcot's patients. But it was not until 1919 that Janet recognized in his writings that Charcot's three stages of hypnotism were what he called "cultist hypnotism," thus echoing Bernheim's expression of 1911 (Guillain, 1959). But already in 1889 Janet was especially aware of the influence of the hypnotist upon the hypnotized subject. He used the term plasticity to describe the state that made hypnotized individuals particularly sensitive to the demands of the experimenter.

The work of Charcot, and particularly his enormous influence in subjecting the phenomena of hypnosis and hysteria to the scrutiny of psychological investigation was a major accomplishment. Who better than Freud could summarize its value?

> He [Charcot] had the creative idea to reproduce these symptoms in an experimental way among patients by putting them in a hypnotic or a somnambulistic state. He also found that certain paralyses were the results of symbolizations which dominate the mental processes of patients having a certain predisposition. It was because of Charcot's conceptions that Pierre Janet, Bleuler and others were able to develop a theory of the neuroses which was acceptable to science. (cited in Codet & Laforgue, 1925, p. 801)

With these remarks in mind, we turn to the works and writings of Freud and of Janet.

FREUD'S FORMULATIONS OF THE UNCONSCIOUS[7]

Throughout his working life, Freud espoused two major formulations of the unconscious; as indicated earlier the first was presented in *The Interpretation of Dreams,* and the second in *The Ego and the Id.* Both are presented here not only because they have often been confused by subsequent writers, but also because they illustrate many of the problems of theorizing about unconscious mental processes and processings. An earlier formulation of the unconscious, predating that of *The Interpretation of Dreams,* can be traced through *A Project for a Scientific Psychology* (1895) and *The Origins of Psychoanalysis* (1977), which consists mainly of a selection of Freud's correspondence with Fleiss (see especially Letter 62 of December 6, 1896). In the interests of parsimony, these initial formulations are not discussed.

Freud's First Formulation (1900)

In his first major attempt to explain cognition without awareness, Freud subdivided mental processes into conscious, unconscious, and preconscious. By definition, these notions are simple enough. Freud (1900) stated that "consciousness appears to us as a sensory organ which perceives a content proceeding from another source" (p. 224). Put simply, consciousness is what we are aware of, be it from the external environment or from internal sensations such as hunger, thirst, sexuality, pain, or anger.

The preconscious (Pcs) was defined in more dispositional terms as ideas that are *capable* of becoming conscious; that is, they are ideas that can become a part of consciousness, even though a person may not be thinking of them at any particular time. This division of Cs and Pcs recognizes the simple fact that a person is unable to think about everything at once; that when we are trying to recall the words of a poem, we are not trying to solve a mathematical problem, although if one is not concentrating fully on recalling the poem, other thoughts may intrude. James (1890) put it elegantly when he described consciousness as "like a bird's life, it seems to be made of an alternation of flights and perchings" (p. 243).

More significantly, Freud saw the preconscious at this stage as a sort of buffer zone between the unconscious and the conscious system; as he put it, "The system Pcs is like a screen between system Ucs and consciousness" (p. 544). Elsewhere, he states in italics that "the only course that psychotherapy can pursue is to bring the Ucs under the domination of the Pcs" (p. 518), a notion to which we return later.

The unconscious (Ucs) was at this stage seen as a system of ideas which has no access to consciousness except through the preconscious "in the passage through which the excitation-process must submit to certain changes" (Freud, 1900, p. 491). It consists of ideas and impulses, usually of a sexual and an aggressive character, which, during early childhood, have been repressed—that is, banished to the unconscious. The process of repression is more comprehensively discussed in subsequent works such as *Three Contributions to the Theory of Sex* (1905b).

The most interesting aspect of Freud's earlier formulation of mental processing concerns the mechanisms of censorship. In *The Interpretation of Dreams,* Freud presents two accounts of censorship that are somewhat at variance with each other. Early in this book, he appears to conceive of censorship in dynamic terms; he states that

> we should then assume that in every human being there exists, as the primary cause
> of dream-formation, two psychic forces (tendencies or systems), one of which forms
> the wish expressed by the dream, while the other exercises a censorship over this
> dream-wish, thereby enforcing on it a distortion. The question is, what is the nature
> of the authority of this second agency by virtue of which it is able to exercise its
> censorship? (p. 223)

But connected with this notion of force/tendency/system (and it is not clear whether Freud is using the terms synonymously or as successive approximations of an idea) is a more animistic notion. In elaborating on the censoring process, he states that the "second instance (i.e., censorship) lets nothing pass without exercising its rights, and forcing modifications that are pleasing to itself upon the candidates for admission to consciousness" (p. 224).

This more animistic notion is elaborated subsequently, by referring to the censoring agent as "the guardian of our psychic health" (p. 510). He then proceeds to present his now famous account of dream-formation, based on the premise that the unconscious, as a repository of repressed ideas, requires a safety valve to allow some discharge of accumulated pressure, in much the manner of a pressure cooker. Since the ideas and particularly the impulses stored in the unconscious would create psychic pain, if not trauma, to consciousness if they were recognized explicitly, some form of circumvention is needed. The latent content of the dream (namely the unconscious material from which it is derived) has to be sanitized in some manner so that what is dreamed (the manifest content) is innocuous to consciousness.

Freud's solution to the problem of how this occurred was ingenious, though the language was highly metaphorical. He proposed that the "guardian" needed to sleep at the time the person was sleeping, or at least to reduce vigilance. Accordingly, he proposed that:

> when the critical guardian goes to rest—and we have proof that his slumber is not profound—he takes care to close the gates to motility. No matter what impulses from the usually inhibited Ucs may bustle upon the stage, there is no need to interfere with them; they remain harmless because they are not in a position to set in motion the motor apparatus which can alone operate to produce any change in the outer world. Sleep guarantees the security of the fortress which has to be guarded. (p. 510)

In his preface to the American edition of *A General Introduction to Psychoanalysis* (1920), G. Stanley Hall describes the 28 lectures it consists of as "elementary and almost conversational" (pp. 5–6). Nevertheless, Freud's description of the interplay between conscious, preconscious, unconscious, and censorship shows a remarkable similarity in conceptualization and exposition to one of his earlier formulations of 1900. He wrote 20 years later for the layman in terms that are strikingly similar to those he had previously used to address a more professional audience. He stated:

> The crudest conceptions of these systems is the one we will find most convenient, a spatial one. The unconscious system may therefore be compared to a large ante-room, in which the various mental excitations are crowding upon each other, like individual beings. Adjoining this is a second, smaller apartment, a sort of reception-room, in which consciousness resides. But on the threshold between the two there stands a personage with the office of door-keeper, who examines the various mental excitations, censors them, and denies them admittance to the reception-room when he disapproves of them. You will see at once that it does not make much difference whether the door-keeper turns any one impulse back at the threshold, or drives it out again once it has entered the reception-room; that is merely a degree of his vigilance and promptness in recognition. Now this metaphor may be employed to widen our terminology. The excitations in the unconscious, in the ante-chamber, are not visible to consciousness, which is of course in the other room, so to begin

with they remain unconscious. When they have pressed forward to the threshold and have been turned back by the door-keeper, they are *"incapable of becoming conscious";* we call them *repressed.* But even those excitations which are allowed over the threshold do not necessarily become conscious; they can only become so if they succeed in attracting the eye of consciousness. This second chamber therefore can suitably be called *the preconscious system.* In this way the process of becoming conscious retains its purely descriptive sense. Being repressed, when applied to any single impulse, means being able to pass out of the unconscious system because of the door-keeper's refusal of admittance into the preconscious. The door-keeper is what we have learned to know as resistance in our attempts in analytic treatment to loosen the repression. (Freud, 1920, pp. 305–306)

To further complicate matters, Freud, in his essay "The Unconscious" (1915), began to anticipate a subsequent revision of the conscious/unconscious/preconscious/censor (censorship) model which was stated formally in *The Ego and the Id* (1923). In this particular formulation, he spoke in terms of censorship, rather than in terms of the door-keeper/censor metaphor. He postulated a second system of censorship between preconscious and conscious, but noted that "we shall do well not to regard this complication as a difficulty, but to assume that to every transition from one system to that immediately above it (that is, every advance to a higher stage of mental organization) there corresponds a new censorship" (p. 124). The implications of multiple censorships are discussed in the following section. For the present, the important issue concerns censorship, be it conceived of in system or animistic terms. In examining Freud's writings on the matter, the striking feature, particularly when he discussed guardians and gate-keepers, is that he made certain covert assumptions.

Consider what a system of censorship as conceived by Freud entails. Such a system appears to have knowledge which is inaccessible to consciousness. This system or entity knows what is acceptable to consciousness; something that does not appear to be available to consciousness itself. Censorship (the guardian or gate-keeper) knows also what is contained in the unconscious; something again that is inaccessible to consciousness. It appears to be a knower that knows things about both consciousness and the unconscious, but it remains independent of and unknown to consciousness. The parallel with Richet's conceptualization of the unconscious (described in the previous section) is striking.

Freud's Second Formulation (1923)

The Ego and the Id (1923) marked a major alteration in Freud's conceptualization of mental functioning. While some of this alteration was anticipated earlier, as noted previously (Freud, 1912, 1914b, 1915), the final set of revisions is presented in the 1923 paper. The main innovation presented in this paper is the grafting of the tripartite division of Conscious/Preconscious/Unconscious to a second tripartite division of mind in terms of Ego/Id/Super Ego.

It is not entirely clear why Freud felt compelled to make this major revision of theory. He stated:

> In the further course of psycho-analytic work, however, these distinctions (i.e., conscious, preconscious and unconscious) have proved to be inadequate, and for practical purposes, insufficient. This has been clear in more ways than one; but the decisive instance is as follows. We have formed the idea that in each individual there is a coherent organization of mental processes; and we call this his *ego*. (Freud, 1923, p. 7).

From Freud's (1923) subsequent description of the ego, the nature of the dilemma appears to center around his earlier guardian/door-keeper/censor notion, since its functions are not attributed to the ego. He described it in the following terms:

> It is to this ego that consciousness is attached; the ego controls the approaches to motility—that is, to the discharge of excitations into the external world; it is the mental agency which supervised all its own constituent processes, and which goes to sleep at night, though even it exercises the censorship on dreams. From this ego proceed the repressions, too, by means of which it is sought to exclude certain trends in the mind not merely from consciousness but also from other forms of effectiveness and activity. In analysis these trends which have been shut out stand in opposition to the ego, and the analysis is faced with the task of removing the resistances which the ego displays against concerning itself with the repressed. (p. 7)

It would appear that the main basis for postulating a dualistic ego—one conscious, the other unconscious—was Freud's observation that patients, in analysis, would stop free associating at times when Freud's clinical judgment was that he was coming close to repressed material. He stated that he could even tell the patient that "he is dominated by a resistance" (p. 7), but that the patient would usually continue to be unaware of it. He added that some patients would guess that a resistance was at work from the unpleasurable sensations that such an event generated; but Freud added, "He does not know what it is or how to describe it" (p. 7). From all of this, Freud concluded:

> Since, however, there can be no question but that this resistance emanates from his ego and belongs to it, we find ourselves in an unforeseen situation. We have come upon something in the ego itself which is also unconscious, which behaves exactly like the repressed—that is, which produces powerful effects without itself being conscious and which requires special work before it can be made conscious. From the point of view of analytic practice, the consequence of this discovery is that we land in endless obscurities and difficulties if we keep to our habitual form of expression and try, for instance, to derive neuroses from a conflict between the conscious and the unconscious. We shall have to substitute for this antithesis another, taken from our insight into the structural conditions of the mind—the antithesis between the coherent ego and the repressed one which is split off from it. (p. 7)

Freud attempted to explain how a part of consciousness might be unconscious, but basically the details are immaterial to the present discussion. The important point is that Freud has raised an issue which prevails as a problem today, even though he had discussed, and rejected, this very notion eight years earlier. In discussing the problems of self-analysis, he observed that there appeared to be some "special hindrance" (Freud, 1915, p. 102) to individuals obtaining a true self-knowledge, which led him to conclude:

> Now this method of inference, applied to oneself in spite of inner opposition, does not lead to a discovery of an unconscious, but leads logically to the assumption of another, second consciousness which is united in myself with the consciousness I know. But at this point criticism may fairly make certain comments. In the first place, a consciousness of which its own possessor knows nothing is something very different from that of another person and it is questionable whether such a consciousness, lacking, as it does, its most important characteristic, is worthy of any further discussion at all. Those who have contested the assumption of an unconscious system in the mind will not be content to accept in its place an unconscious consciousness. (Freud, 1915, p. 103)

At this stage, however, Freud was unwilling to come to terms with this apparent impasse. Having discussed other criticisms of an unconscious consciousness, he gave tentative support for such a notion mainly on the grounds that analysis indicates that individuals may possess characteristics and peculiarities that are alien to them, and which run directly counter to consciousness. From this, he concluded in 1915:

> This justifies us in modifying our inference about ourselves and saying that what is proved is not a second consciousness in us, but the existence of certain mental operations lacking in the quality of consciousness. We shall also, moreover, be right in rejecting the notion of "subconsciousness" as incorrect and misleading. The known cases of *"double conscience"* (splitting of consciousness) prove nothing against our view. They may most accurately be described as cases of a splitting of the mental activities into two groups, whereby a single consciousness takes up its position alternately with either the one or the other of these groups. (pp. 103–104)

Basically, the notion of "mental operations lacking in the quality of consciousness" is a semantic evasion of the problem. It is typical of Freud, however, that he continued to be puzzled by this paradox for several more years, before reversing himself in 1923.

It was a problem that he was never able subsequently to resolve. In his last will and testament, *An Outline of Psychoanalysis,* published posthumously in 1940, he admitted what in Freud's terms, considering the enormity of his contribution to the understanding of the mind, was tantamount to defeat. He wrote:

> The preconscious condition, which is characterized on the one hand by having access to consciousness and on the other hand by being linked with the verbal residues, is nevertheless something peculiar, the nature of which is not exhausted by these two characteristics. The proof of this is that large portions of the ego, and in particular of the superego, which cannot be denied the characteristic of being

preconscious, none the less remain for the most part unconscious in the phenomenological sense of the word. We do not know why this must be so. We shall attempt later on to attack the problem of the true nature of the preconscious. (pp. 42–43)

In sum, Freud left us with two tripartite divisions of the mind and a paradox of how they are interrelated. On the one hand, mental processes are divided structurally in terms of whether they are involved with instinctual gratification (id), reality monitoring (ego), or morality (super ego). On the other, the mental processes are available to consciousness, ranging from complete unavailability (unconscious), potential availability (preconscious), and complete availability (conscious).

Conceptually, there is no reason to doubt that some id impulses, particularly involving sexuality and aggression, are completely unavailable, and others are fully conscious. The same can be said for super ego impulses; morality can be blind, or it can equally be almost biblical in the expansiveness of its formulation.

The paradox comes with the Freudian conceptualization of ego. Whatever the mechanisms are that monitor reality, a certain amount of this cognizing, in the Freudian view, takes place out of awareness. Even though much successful decision making, judgment, and problem solving follow orderly, logical, and conscious pathways, a certain amount of such processing, which varies among individuals, takes place out of awareness—it is what is ordinarily called intuition. Although Freud has been dead for more than 40 years, we are probably no closer to understanding this unconscious consciousness than Freud himself was. Nevertheless, there does appear to be a phenomenon that requires understanding, since it appears to be one of the central aspects of mental life.

L'AUTOMATISME PSYCHOLOGIQUE (1882–1888)

Pierre Janet published *L'Automatisme psychologique* in 1889. It was a summary as well as an expansion of his work and reflections of the previous seven years. Janet was a teacher of philosophy at Le Havre during this period. He was interested in both history and psychology. With the help of Dr. J. Gibert and Powilewicz he was able to study a number of patients who were to lead him into the psychological world of hysteria and neurosis. He was interested also in hypnosis and the work that was going on at the Salpêtrière under the supervision of Charcot.

It is not possible here to go into Janet's work or life in detail and, therefore, only the main points of his work as it pertains to the study of consciousness, and particularly his views of unconscious processes, are discussed. To know more about Janet's personal life and to obtain a global idea of his contributions to the field of psychotherapeutics, the reader should consult either the excellent chapter on Janet in Ellenberger's *The Discovery of the Unconscious* (1970), or Janet's own writings. In line with contemporary French psychology, Janet was much more interested in psychopathology than in the psychology of normality. In all his works and particularly in his 1889 book, he emphasized that his observations were made on patients, and any extension to healthy, normal individuals should be attempted with extreme care. At the time when Janet wrote *L'Automatisme psychologique,* he was not yet a medical doctor; for this reason he tried to avoid invading this field of expertise. Consequently Janet defined himself as a scientist devoted to the methodological investigation of certain abnormal phenomena in humans.

Very early in his work, Janet challenged Charcot's ideas about hysteria and hypnosis. When he began his researches, Janet always insisted upon seeing only new patients, patients who had not been treated or hypnotized by other therapists before him. Janet took that position after he had examined and studied one of his now famous patients, Léonie. When Léonie first began therapy with him, Janet was amazed to find that she was the only one to display all the characteristic stages of Charcot's major hysterical crisis, as well as most of the phenomena that had been historically identified with somnambulism. A thorough inquiry into Léonie's past history revealed that she had been a patient at the Salpêtrière and had been since an early age hypnotized by a number of physicians and lay hypnotists. This led Janet to conclude with a certain wry humor that a clinician could recognize by whom a patient had been treated by the way this patient behaved. But more important, this observation led him to establish his own research methodology and to devote himself not only to the careful observation of new patients but to a complete investigation of the history of hypnosis.

Following the episode with Léonie, Janet adopted a series of methodological guidelines that he was to maintain throughout his working life. Three of these guidelines are worth mentioning since they represent the first elements in the elaboration of Janet's psychotherapeutic approach. Janet always required that (1) each patient be seen alone to avoid contamination by outside observers, especially if these patients were subjected to artificial somnambulism; (2) everything the patient said and did be carefully written down as nearly verbatim as possible; and (3) the complete life history of each patient be taken in order to understand his or her particular background. It is by following these three guidelines that Janet wrote *L'Automatisme psychologique.*

Although *L'Automatisme psychologique* is a curious blend of psychological observations and philosophical reflections that may at first repel the serious reader, three main themes can be extracted fom it; (1) memorial processes, perceptual synthesis, and adaptation; (2) psychological disaggregation; and (3) psychotherapeutic intervention. Memorial processes and perceptual synthesis are at the core of Janet's observations. Memories are studied through all their phases from the simplest sensations (if such things exist) to the multiple processing of complex information that is synthesized into the idea of the personality allowing the individual to adapt to new situations.

From some abnormalities in these processes, Janet derived his concept of psychological disaggregation; that is, the progressive narrowing of the field of consciousness that inevitably leads to psychoneurosis, hysteria, fixed ideas, and the classical manifestations of artificial somnambulism. A treatment orientation is elaborated as well, but only with difficulty, since he never advocated a single treatment. Janet never sought to create a therapeutic system; he should be seen as always experimenting. He abhorred generalizations and loved the particulars. All his life, with great energy, he tried not to generalize, recognizing the complexity and the elusive nature of the mind. As a consequence, he protested energetically against any system that purported to dissect the mind into little black boxes (and especially psychoanalysis) in the same way that he violently attacked in his early years those who saw only simulation and suggestion in hypnotic phenomena.

Before examining the three basic themes presented in *L'Automatisme psychologique,* it may be of interest to note that two historical facts gave Janet the impetus to investigate unconscious processes. The first one that seems to have influenced all of his research was Chevreul's (1825) discovery and explanation of ideomotor action. Chevreul had devised a new experimental approach that demonstrated that the movements of the divining rod and the pendulum resulted from unconscious muscular movements of the subject caused by unconscious thoughts. For Janet this demonstration of the influence of thought upon action was decisive; he became convinced that any thought is first of all translated into movements and that the study of psychopathological conditions where movements are inhibited (e.g., catalepsy) would be the best way to understand how thoughts are formed and organized. Psychological automatism, which he defined as the opposition between the creative activity of the mind and its reproductive capacity, was to become central in his evaluation of consciousness.

The second impetus to Janet's investigation of unconscious processes was his acquaintance with the phenomenon of posthypnotic suggestion. Janet explained the execution of a posthypnotic suggestion by the persistence at a subconscious level of the initial suggestion given by the hypnotist. It is interesting to note that the same type of observation was to convince Freud of the reality of the unconscious (Ellenberger, 1970). In his introduction to *L'Automatisme psychologique,* he wrote: "Consciousness does not reveal all the psychological phenomena that occur in us; this is an undisputable truth that we will try to confirm once again" (1889, p. 23)[8]

Memory, Perceptual Synthesis, and Adaptation

For Janet memory was responsible for ensuring the continuity of mental life; memorial processes were continually active from the onset of the first sensation (birth) to the ending of the last one (death). The different perceptions, however, were not solely responsible for one's own consciousness; a second process was at play in determining the individual's personality. Grafted upon the processing capacity of the memory system was a second system which at all times was organizing and synthesizing the incoming information in the light of previous integrated memories. The harmonious functioning of these two systems resulted in what the individual would perceive as his or her personality, and his or her self-perception. Any malfunctioning in either the perceptual or synthesizing systems would result in some form of psychopathology.

In Janet's view, mental life starts with the simplest expression of any reaction to the environment. Sensations, whether they be visual, auditory, gustatory, or tactile, represent the foundations of what will become a memory. Innumerable simple sensations are processed into the perceptual system from outside as well as inside the organism. The organism responds to these sensations in an automatic way, allowing adaptive movements to occur. Janet believed that these adaptive movements ranged from simple ones like a child's grasping reflex (reflecting the response of the neurophysiological system to the environment) to more complex ones like the development of a psychophysical malfunctioning (reflecting the responses of the psychological system of the individual). Such complex psychophysiological responses had been exemplified by Janet's brother Jules (1889/1890) in his studies of the neurotic disturbances of urination, and more particularly anuria.

In the writings of Janet's predecessors, the overwhelming tendency was to attribute any unconscious manifestation to the physiological systems of the organism. Any disturbance, whether psychological or physiological, was thought of as primarily based in the biological organism. Janet's originality stemmed from his conviction that there existed psychological disturbances that were reflected in the biological or physical systems. He was basically emphasizing the psychological part of what we know today as psychosomatic diseases, so that his thinking was contrary to the mainstream of his period. What Janet called psychological automatisms occurred when a perturbed psychological response would bypass consciousness and manifest itself at the expense of the organism, rather than being integrated by the main perceptual synthesis system.

While a good number of these sensations are actually perceived, not all are; Janet thought that the perfectly healthy, normal individual should be able to process and perceive all sensations, but he knew this ideal individual could not exist. The perceived sensations formed but the basis of the memory system; they had to be organized, aggregated, synthesized into a single major percept before being integrated into the individual's personality. Only then would an individual be able to behave in an adaptive fashion. The main percept, once integrated, became available to the individual self-perception. What is important to realize here is that the main percept will quite often bear little resemblance to its constituent parts. Moreover, percepts are always changing in the light of subsequent incoming information: they contain both memories and new sensations that will form the basis of an ever-evolving self-perception. But this self-perception is not a mere association of ideas; it is an active synthesis that unites new phenomena in a continuously newly formed perception of self-unity (Janet, 1889, p. 295).

It is unfortunate that even today Janet's views are still equated with the notion of the association of ideas as being the main principle of the mind. This misunderstanding was, however, present at the outset. Binet (1889), in an article on the alterations of consciousness in hysterics, refuted the idea that the mechanism underlying the phenomenon of double consciousness resulted from a lack of association of ideas, a lack of communication between the elements of both consciousnesses. He was obviously attacking Janet's conception. However, in the same article (footnote 2, p. 169) following a letter by Janet, Binet rectified his position. He says:

> Mr. Pierre Janet, to whom I allude in the text and to whom I have communicated my observations, tells me that by dissociation he did not intend to designate a phenomenon contrary to the association of ideas. For him a dissociated state is a state that is not reappropriated by the idea of the ego and of the personality thereby escaping this superior synthesis. Mr. Janet does recognize that my mistake was due to the ambiguity of the expression *mental dissociation*. (Binet, 1889, p. 69)[9]

What Janet was proposing, then, was to look at the personality of the individual as an aggregation of memories that had been altered by a synthesis process. The result of the synthesis process and its integration into the main personality allowed the individual to adapt to his or her environment. Thus by the time a person reflects upon his or her self-perception, he or she is acting on the third element of the triad of perception, synthesis, and adaptation. It then becomes extremely difficult to decipher what part an original memory played in the subsequent behavior of the individual; one can only hypothesize that a memory had positive or negative valence in the life of the individual.

This integrative process, however, is not by itself available to consciousness at all times, although it is amenable to consciousness. When Janet started to examine the mental life of his patients, he was amazed by the discrepancy between the symptoms that they exhibited and their lack of introspection into their origins. By the use of hypnosis or artificial somnambulism, he was able to reinstate in these patients some introspective mechanisms that could lead them to bring back to consciousness some part of the integrative process that had assumed an automatic way of functioning outside of the mainstream of consciousness. This observation led him to the formulation of the concept of mental disaggregation, which was to be central in his understanding of some psychoneurotic processes.

La Désagrégation Psychologique

One has to keep in mind that Janet concerned himself primarily with the study of neuroses and particularly of fixed ideas (*idées fixes*), rather than with normal individuals. Although he recognized that the work of Binet and Richet, for example, emphasized that disaggregation could be experimentally elicited in healthy individuals, Janet could never go so far as to say that the phenomenon could be found in everyone. It has already been noted that this phenomenon was different from a simple disassociation of ideas, but rather represented a failure to synthetize information and incorporate it or, as Janet would later put it, a failure to adapt to new information. In a revised introduction (1893) of *L'Automatisme psychologique,* Janet felt a need to specify what he meant by *désagrégation.* He recognized that his previous descriptions were only simple and clear cases that did not represent the complexity of such a phenomenon. He said:

> We have said and repeated many times that this second group of phenomena were extremely suggestible; that the name and even the personal form were determined by exercises and suggestions; that this personality formed in such a way can be educated, take on habits; that in experiments it will constantly collaborate with the normal personality. Often, phenomena determined in one layer of consciousness will act upon, produce a remarkable back-lash on another system. The caprices, the preferences of both the subconscious or normal personality interact at all times to complicate further the experiments. (Janet, 1893/1977, p. 17)[10]

Janet wanted to point to the difficulty of studying these phenomena in isolation and to the complex interaction between the different elements of consciousness. As an example, Janet cites a passage of Erasme Darwin taken from his book *Zoonomia* (1801):

> I remember seeing this young and beautiful artist practicing with her teacher her singing part while playing on the piano-forte with grace and sensibility; I could, by looking at her, see some emotion that I could not understand; at the end, she started to cry. It's only then that I realized that while she was singing and playing, she was contemplating her beloved canary that was suffering and did die during that time. (Vol. I, p. 332)

For Janet the complexity of the behaviors and the emotions displayed by the young artist were a good example of the continuum that formed what he called consciousness. From basic physiological processes (automatisms), which indicate that the organism is in some way aware of what is happening to it, to the highest form of self-consciousness (creativity) as exemplified by the artist in the creation of his or her work, lies the field or the domain of consciousness.

Although most individuals vacillate somewhere between these two extremes, Janet was interested in people at both ends of the continuum: patients who had lost some of their capacity for perceptual synthesis and functioned in a more or less automatic fashion; and creative individuals, able to extract new ideas from previous perceptions and associations. Consciousness can then be seen as a field in the same sense that the organism possesses a visual field. Processes like attention bring into focus particular elements that are in this field and relegate other elements of perception that are not current objects of attention to the background.

There exists, then, in consciousness ideas that pertain to its mainstream as well as collateral and coexisting images and sensations. So although the sensation is still present, as can be demonstrated experimentally, the idea of the sensation is not in the field of consciousness. Depending upon a person's present mental state, the field of consciousness will change, synthesizing different sets of sensations; many examples can be found in everyday life whether it be in dreams, daydreaming, distraction, drunkenness, or love. In the normal individual, however, unattended sensations and perceptions will always reach consciousness at some point; for Janet the unconsciousness is only momentary, related to selective attention or distraction. The field of consciousness scans its entire domain continually. In the unhealthy individual, there is a shrinking of the field of consciousness (*rétrécissement du champ de la conscience*), which reduces the number of simultaneous phenomena that can be scanned. This shrinking of consciousness gives rise to what Janet identified as subconscious processes, that is, ongoing mental processes that were unperceived by consciousness.

Janet was the first author to use the word subconscious, in an attempt to differentiate these psychological processes that seemed to have their origins in some psychological disturbances from unconscious processes that were linked to some physiological malfunctions and were not amenable to consciousness. He believed that the phenomenon of *désagrégation* and its subconscious manifestations were primarily abnormal ones—that is, pathological conditions found only in neurotic patients. Though Janet did not generalize his conclusions to the perfectly healthy individual, he perceived dissociation as a potentiality of the conscious apparatus that could occur in certain individuals, otherwise normal, at particular times in their lives. Janet did not see these dissociative phenomena as being an actual part of the psychic apparatus, and in this sense alone his theorizing differed markedly from that of Freud.

Janet derived his beliefs about subconscious processes from his observations of both hysterical patients and his experiments with induced or artificial somnambulism. He was fascinated by two phenomena seen in somnambulism: amnesia and posthypnotic suggestion. These two phenomena could only be explained by the hypothesis that there was, apart from the waking consciousness, a subconscious that remembered what had happened during the somnambulistic episode and could, for example, allow the subject to carry on a posthypnotic suggestion at the expense of the waking consciousness. Because the patients or subjects could not explain why they were performing such actions, Janet called their behaviors subconscious acts, implying explicitly a consciousness below normal waking consciousness. Further, this consciousness could be tapped in artificial somnambulism. This led Janet to write, for example, about suggested anesthesia in the following terms: "In a suggested systematic anesthesia, the sensation is not eliminated. It is displaced, removed from normal consciousness, but can be found as part of another group of phenomena, like another type of consciousness" (1889, p. 274). As will be seen later, Hilgard's neodissociation theory is extremely close to this Janetian notion.

What Janet then realized is that his patients under a somnambulistic influence displayed alternating sets of memories; one that pertained to their waking state and one that pertained to their hypnotic episodes. Furthermore, both sets of memories had the potential to aggregate and synthetize a new self-perception, giving the impression that the patient actually had two personalities. These patients exhibited what he called psychological disaggregation, allowing the mind to become functionally split off into different, although interrelated, parts.

What Janet observed in his somnambulistic subjects and called alternating memories he also observed in hysterical patients out of hypnosis. In these patients, however, memories were much more intricately related. This is a major point in Janet's theorizing that has often been neglected. Janet never theorized that the disaggregated parts of consciousness were autonomous, that is, completely independent of one another. In fact, the different parts were interrelated and interfered with one another. Each different part drew from the same perceived sensations even if they were not, later on, synthesized in the same, unique percept. This dynamic interaction occurring at a subconscious level was held by him to be responsible for the emergence of dissociated behaviors in either hysterical neurosis or somnambulistic episodes.

What caused the phenomenon of disaggregation to happen was what Janet described as a state of psychological misery. This psychological misery could arise from a number of different causes ranging from heredity to physiological accidents to moral causes. Under such conditions, the organism is deprived of a part of its psychic energy and in order to function must withdraw consciousness from certain sensations, perceptions, and memories. It is this weakening of the synthetic activity of the mind that leads to psychological disaggregation. Thus by trying to adapt to some psychological distress, the individual involuntarily restricts his or her own field of consciousness. Fortunately, this process can be reversed by altering the mental health of the patient. Typical examples of this process could be seen in the different analgesias displayed by hysterical patients.

Once initiated, this dissociative process had a tendency to repeat itself. Janet saw it as a permanent state of distraction or selective attention. In patients suffering such distraction one sensation came to dominate and attract automatically associated memories, images, and sensations. An automatic loop was formed where only the same type of sensations were perceived and synthetized, leaving other sensations outside the purview of consciousness. In this pathological condition, ignored sensations could be brought again into the focus of consciousness by means of hypnosis.

At the beginning of treatment only sensations and images could be reinstated. However, as the therapist continued to work with the patient, these memories could be reassembled, organized, and, to a certain point, synthetized into a new personal perception. The individual would then exhibit alternating sets of memories, or at least some latent sets of disaggregated memories became available to his or her consciousness. In the hysterics or the somnambulists this second set of memories would then slowly build up, manifesting itself in the phenomenon of double consciousness. Janet was always extremely careful in describing cases of multiple personalities. He always pointed out that the phenomenon of psychological disaggregation was an extremely suggestible process and that the mere act of discovering it in a patient was the first step toward its establishment as a second well-organized entity within the psychic apparatus.

Psychological disaggregation can then be seen as a symptom of some psychological maladaptation occurring in the life of an individual. One of the causes of the process was a traumatic memory and the subsequent development of a fixed idea, but not invariably so. Here again Janet was drifting further away from Freud (although Freud had not at that stage begun writing about traumatic memories). The maladaptive process of disaggregation could also be rooted in the environment, in the contextual demands put upon the individual quite apart from personal traumatic events; or, it could be a long-term process rather than a dramatic occurrence related to the onset of a particularly distressing event. It is thus important to understand that this phenomenon of disaggregation does not have any universal qualities; it can only be substantiated in a certain number of patients and, as Janet would later point out, trying to fit everyone into the same model could lead to some tragic cases of mistreatment.

THERAPEUTIC PRINCIPLES

In 1889 Janet had few ideas about the treatments to offer to the different types of patients he encountered. Psychological analysis, as it came to be known, was not a system that evolved out of one man's thinking, but was instead the result of years of psychological practice and innumerable communications between a number of practicing therapists. It was not until the publication of *Psychological Healing* (1919/25) and *Principles of Psychotherapy* (1923/25) that Janet actually put together the results of his experiments and experience. Very early in his career, however, he had elucidated some basic premises for therapy that were to become the foundation of his view of mental functioning. It is to this early period of his development that we will turn our attention in order to understand why Janet opposed and, to a certain extent, resented Freud's psychoanalytic system.

One of Janet's contributions to psychology was to reconcile the physiological tendencies of the medical system to a more psychological view of mental illness. The task was not easy and, in a sense, the fact that he had moved to La Salpêtrière did not help him. As soon as Charcot died in 1893, Janet was the victim of some of his medical colleagues who wanted to return to a more conservative way of treating patients. He was quickly isolated and experienced many difficulties in pursuing his researches (Ellenberger, 1970).

Janet's first treatment innovation concerns the importance that he placed on obtaining a personal history of the patient. Each patient's personal history was taken in the course of a very detailed examination. It was Janet's idea that you cannot treat a patient that you do not know. But he went further than to just record the history; he promoted the idea of checking that history with people around the patient, family and friends, in order to better understand how each patient had adapted to his or her own life history. This way of interacting with the patient led him very early to the uncovering of traumatic memories or at least memories that were recalled as being traumatic by the patient.

The case of Marie (Janet, 1889; see Nemiah, this volume) was probably the most dramatic case reported in these early years and exemplified the effect of a traumatic memory—or as Janet preferred to call it, the effect of a fixed idea. Marie's blindness and hemiplegia were cured by the uncovering of particular events that had taken place in her youth. However, it was not the uncovering of that special memory which was responsible for the cure, but rather the modification of that memory. The individual who maintains a fixed idea of an event does not exactly have a memory of that event, and it is only for clearness of speech that Janet spoke of traumatic memory. This view was again based on the idea that self-perception is not merely reminiscence and association of different memories, but the integration or synthesis of all the live events into a new perception. The patient or subject is often incapable of verbalizing the event that we call a memory, but such a person nonetheless suffers the consequences of a difficult historical event that he or she has been unable to solve.

For Janet, going back to find the memory and determining whether or not it is historically accurate is only the first step in the process of therapy. Once access has been gained to the memory, whether it be through interview, dream recording, or hypnosis, this memory must be either transformed or liquidated. Here Janet had some insight into the workings of memory, seeing it not only in terms of its reconstructive capacity with all the possibilities of confabulation that such a process entails, but also in terms of its creative capacities. He saw memory as an act of creation. The transformation or the liquidation of a particular memory that had some subconscious activity was the essential step toward the reestablishment of mental health. The subconscious was not for Janet a constant in the psychic economy of the mind; in fact, it was not even a constant in psychoneuroses. This point was one of the major criticisms Janet made of psychoanalysis; he believed that it had reified and systematized a potential for subconscious processes in some psychoneurotics into an ever-present Unconscious that pervaded the mental life of everyone.

Over and above the examination of a patient's life history, Janet also advocated the careful examination of the patient's daily activities in the hospital. Each patient was to be carefully examined not only in his or her normal everyday state of mind, but also during sleep or induced somnambulism. Janet went so far as to awaken patients at night in order to have them recall what they were dreaming, looking in this first description of the oneiric content for clues that would help the therapeutic treatment. It was only when these alert and altered states investigations were concluded that the appropriate treatment could be applied.

Thus what was a means of diagnosing psychopathology in Janet's practice was to become a mode of treatment in psychoanalysis. But for Janet the treatment of psychopathological disturbances was to be considered in the light of the patient's psychic economy. The function of such careful examination was to provide the means by which a reequilibrium of the psychic forces could be achieved. Hypnosis represented one particular way through which patients could come to adapt to their new perceptions and reinstate a normal, healthy way of functioning. Keeping these preliminary notions in mind, it becomes easier to understand the criticisms that Janet launched on psychoanalysis as the popularity of this movement increased, and why he viewed psychoanalysis as a rather limited therapeutic technique in the field of psychopathology.

One of the reasons that Janet expanded his position from the initial concept of subconsciousness to a global evaluation of the patient's psychic economy in later years was the observation that reliving and working out a traumatic memory was not always beneficial for the patients. Even when it was, the positive results were usually short-term and the process had to be started all over again. This observation, combined with the fact that it was often impossible to demonstrate either the presence of traumatic memories in certain patients (Janet estimated that in about 25 percent of his patients no traumatic memory could be unveiled) and the role that they played in the ongoing pathological behaviors, led Janet to adopt a holistic therapeutic approach. Treatment was aimed at reestablishing the equilibrium between the psychic energy displayed by a patient and the level of psychological tension he or she was experiencing. As early as the 1900s, Janet incorporated into his therapeutic approach elements of behavioral and ecological interventions based upon his awareness of the importance of automatisms in human functioning and the plasticity of the human mind in response to contextual and environmental demands. One can better understand Janet's reactions toward psychoanalysis when the holistic approach to the human mind that he advocated is contrasted with what he considered to be Freud's simplistic and reductionist view of human potentialities.

JANET'S CRITIQUE OF FREUDIAN PSYCHOANALYSIS

Although it is clear from what we have seen that Janet did not particularly appreciate the amazing popularity of psychoanalytic concepts, he still had a great respect for the contributions of Freud in the field of psychoneuroses. He recognized that the main concept of repression would continue to form "a part of mental pathology under the name of 'Freud's syndrome'" (Janet, 1925, p. 649) and that "psychoanalysis has rendered great service to psychological analysis" (p. 656). But apart from Janet's overt animosities toward Freud, he nonetheless had more professional criticisms of psychoanalysis in terms of both its method and its theoretical constructs. Janet mainly attacked what he saw as the exaggerations surrounding the uncovering of the traumatic memories and their associated sexual content, the concept of repression, and most of all, the interpretation of dreams.

It is interesting to note that for Janet, psychoanalysis was a philosophical and a medical system; he does not refer to it as a psychological system. He saw psychoanalysis as one part of a more global therapeutic modality which he called "mental disinfection by the dissociation of traumatic memories" (p. 601). He attacked psychoanalysis for what he saw as its excessive use of the concept of the unconscious in the same way that he attacked the then popular parapsychological movements. Although he was pleased to see that one of his concepts, namely the activation of subconscious phenomena, was widely accepted, he was at the same time worried by its grossly exaggerated use in the explanation of the human mind.

Janet did not understand the sudden popularity of the psychoanalytic method; he could not find anything new in it. Careful observation of patients and obtaining detailed life histories were already part of his own methodology, and their inclusion into psychoanalysis added nothing new to the field of psychotherapies. Free association was for Janet a simple-minded method, especially in regard to the influence of the therapist on the patient's verbalizations. "I do not think much of the method, and I regard those who advise it as somewhat simple-minded, for the patient still feels himself to be under observation, and will be more inclined than we are apt to suppose to arrange his words so as to produce a definite effect" (p. 603). This criticism also found its place in his critique of the sexual theory of neurosis and the interpretation of dreams.

Indeed, probably because Janet regarded himself more as an experimentalist, he preferred Jung's word association test that measured the patient's reaction time to specifically chosen words as a better method to discover areas of problems in the patient. But even that he regarded as a promising new laboratory method and certainly not as a valid clinical tool. He believed that if the therapist knows in advance what he or she is looking for, then it will be found by the test; but if there is nothing to be found, the delayed associations will be linked to some irrelevant memories that may have nothing to do with the neurosis present at the time. Janet gives the following example:

> It has seemed to me that every word capable of arousing emotion of whatever kind, even mere surprise, will cause a more or less considerable delay and will modify the association. A strange or shocking word introduced into a list of ordinary words will arouse a surprise of this kind. I have secured delays of from six to nine seconds by suddenly pronouncing such improper words as "merde" or "votre cul" in the middle of a list of permissible words. Yet the subject, with whose mental condition I had long been acquainted, had no traumatic memory connected with either of these words. (p. 653)

These remarks on the psychoanalytic methods exemplify what concerned him most, namely, that in Freudian analysis a fact has to fit the theory rather than the other way around. He saw such procrustean hazards, particularly in the overgeneralization given to the concept of repression, to the notion of traumatic memory, and probably most of all to the sexual theory of neurosis.

It is interesting to note that this was not the first time that Janet confronted a sexual explanation of some psychoneuroses. In his early years, before the publication of *L'Automatisme psychologique,* Janet had been struck by the then well accepted fact that hysterical patients had some kind of malfunction of sexuality. This idea was well accepted in Charcot's time, and had led to a doctrine concerning the erogenous zones of hysterial women, zones that could only be triggered by a male investigator. These sexual malfunctions could also be observed in one of the phases of Charcot's "great hystero-epileptic attack," during which women would take provocative positions and utter obscenities. In order to elucidate such deviance, Janet studied a number of his patients' sexual lives and conduct. In none of them did he find any sign of the pseudo-hypereroticism that had for years been accepted as a pathognomic sign of hysterical pathologies. He reported that he did not find more abnormalities in the sexual behaviors of these patients than in the normal individuals, and certainly nothing that justified their reputation as causal agents underlying neurosis.

From the beginning, Janet accepted the idea that a traumatic memory was an important factor in the aetiology of psychoneuroses. He vehemently opposed, however, the idea that it was the only causal factor. He recognized in his own patients this genuine inability both to know what is going on in the mind and to verbalize it. The reliving or uncovering of such memory did not automatically lead to the patient's recovery, indicating to him that other factors were at play in the neurotic process. And even if such traumatic memories were uncovered, it did not indicate that they were still active and related to the ongoing neurosis. Even more troublesome was the Freudian idea that not only can such traumatic memories be found in all neuropaths, but that these memories always show an underlying sexual conflict, the epitome of which was the Oedipus complex. As Janet remarked early in his discussion of psychoanalysis:

> The psychoanalyst contention is that in the absence of such a (sexual) mishap metamorphosed into a traumatic memory, there is no neurosis. If it is not easy to detect the existence of such a traumatic memory of a sexual mishap in every neurotic patient, this is because the doctor has not succeeded in making the patient admit what has happened, has not been able to break down the patient's reticence....I must content myself with having given a few indications of the way in which, notwithstanding the subject's dissimulations, and despite his forgetfulness, it is possible to show that underlying every case of neuropathic disorder there is a traumatic memory with a sexual content. (1919/1925, p. 614)

Janet believed that this a priori belief of the psychoanalytic movement was reflected in its construct of repression and transference and most of all in the analytic technique of dream interpretation—and he was not alone in questioning these ideas. Many critics were asking why Freud saw sexuality wherever he looked; some of them even tried to explain this remarkable illusion. Aschaffenburg (1906), for example, thought that Freud must question his patients regarding their sexual life in a peculiarly impressive manner to obtain from them what he wanted to hear. Forel in France expressed the same concern:

> I consider that Freud, through his gross exaggeration in this matter of the traumatic memory as a cause of nervous disorder, and above all by the way in which he generalizes the theory and applies it to cases in which the patient has no such memories, himself as a rule, suggests to his patients all sorts of notion (sexual for the most part) which are far more likely to be hurtful than helpful. (1905, p. 214)

Other authors like Friedländer and Ladame went as far as to suggest that the explanation lay in a peculiar kind of sexual atmosphere in Vienna. Janet accepted this interpretation as an example of the influence of the context and milieu upon the beliefs and expectations of patients. As we have seen, this view was particularly ridiculed by Freud, who misunderstood it. What Janet was proposing was that one should look at the demands imposed on the patient by the therapist's beliefs, and the context in which they came forth as an explanation of the findings of Freud.

Finally, Janet expressed extreme skepticism toward the undue use of interpretation by psychoanalysts. He regarded interpretation or the symbolical construction used by these therapists as probably the part of the method that was most open to confabulation both from the therapist and the patient. The problem again lay in the observation that this form of thinking could lead a therapist to find whatever he or she wished to find, and could have serious drawbacks for the patient. Further, Janet could not believe that the dream recounted by the patient had not already undergone some transformations by the time it was communicated to the therapist, which would then be further transformed by the therapist's interpretation.

The justification of this interpretative technique had its roots in the concept of repression, which became so central to Freudian thinking. It is only by accepting such a mechanism as repression that the systematic generalization of the subconscious traumatic memory could be advocated. Janet accepted in part the concept of repression, but did not agree with the Freudian interpretation of it. For Janet repression was one of the possible mechanisms leading to the development of subconscious mental disaggregation. It was a transient stage in a series of mental operations that soon transcended it. In a normal, healthy individual, repression did not leave any trace; what was excluded from consciousness was by the same token excluded from memory. Repression was not a normal defense mechanism, but a morbid disturbance, a consequence of mental weakness (shrinking of the field of consciousness) already present in the patient. Janet was especially reluctant to admit that a psychopathological process could be due to the patient's will (motivation). In Janet's terms, the struggle against the emergence of an undesired tendency was more a function of suggestion, emotion, and fatigue already at play in the patient's psychic apparatus. Repression could be the cause of the struggle for psychic equilibrium, but it could also be the consequence of an ongoing disequilibrium. In trying to resolve this dilemma, Janet wrote: "Psychological analysis hesitates between these interpretations and awaits the light which the development of the illness throws upon them" (Janet, 1915a, p. 33). Janet believed repression must not be hypothesized in each patient, but must be observed and documented: before being applied to facts, it should be confirmed by facts.

Overall, however, Janet did not completely reject psychoanalysis. He recognized the value of the studies on neurosis, the various types of sexual sentiment, and the development of thought in childhood that had been emphasized by the psychoanalysts. "In due time," Janet wrote, "the overstrained generalizations and fanciful symbolism which today seem typical of psychoanalysis, and which separate the doctrine from other scientific studies, will be forgotten" (p. 656).

In later years Janet was to propose a dynamic view of mental processes in his book *From Anguish to Ecstasy* (1926), but again he avoided any form of typology. He did not advocate any specific psychotherapy but rather tried to examine the mind as a general system of psychotherapeutic economics. He always acknowledged the complexity of the human mind and would excuse himself to his readers when the tried to simplify the intricacies of consciousness using economic analogies. One of the great advantages of Janet's theorizing is that it leads to scientific investigation and, as will be seen later, such investigations are now starting to be conducted by contemporary researchers.

AN EVALUATION OF THE UNCONSCIOUS

Freud and Janet agreed that cognitive processing could take place out of awareness; they differed in terms of their respective methodologies and theoretical accounts of how this occurred. Put simply, Freud believed in an Unconscious as a sort of repository for repressed and ego threatening ideas and impulses. By contrast, Janet opted for a simpler formulation in which he argued that under conditions of stress, integrative skills deteriorate, which in turn leads to ideas becoming detached from the mainstream of consciousness.

In terms of theory, there is no a priori reason for preferring one formulation to the other: each is equally valid. Virtually any phenomenon that cannot be attributed to conscious control can be equally attributed to a Freudian Unconscious and to a Janetian disaggregation of ideas. The fact that much of what we infer about unconscious mentation comes from clinical observations, rather than from rigorous experimentation, only serves to compound the problem.

It is compounded further by Freud's own insistence that the notion of an unconscious is an assumption which is not only necessary and legitimate, but for which "we possess manifold *proofs*" (Freud, 1915, p. 99). Further on, he stated:

> When, after this, it appears that the assumption of the unconscious helps us to construct a highly successful practical method, by which we are enabled to exert a useful influence upon the course of conscious processes, this success will have won us an incontrovertible proof of the existence of that which we assumed. (p. 99)

This was no mere slip of the pen. In one of his last essays, Freud (1938) spoke of the unconscious as one of two "hazardous hypotheses" (p. 377) which form the cornerstone of psychoanalysis. In defense of the assumption of an unconscious, he cited two examples. One involved a slip of the tongue by the President of the Austrian Parliament, who opened a sitting of the Lower House by stating "'I take notice that a full quorum of members is present and herewith declare this sitting closed'" (p. 379). Freud explained this slip of the tongue as follows:

Many of the previous sittings of the House had been disagreeably stormy and had accomplished nothing, so that it would be only too natural for the President to think at the moment of making his opening statement: "If only the sitting that's just beginning were finished: I would much rather be closing than opening it": When he began to speak he was probably not aware of this wish—not conscious of it—but it was certainly present and it succeeded in making itself effective, against the speaker's will, in his apparent mistake. (p. 380)

Freud then reasoned that if all such slips of the tongue and pen, of misreading and of mishearing, could be similarly shown to involve similar unconscious mentation, "It would really be no longer possible to dispute the fact that mental acts which are unconscious do exist and that they are even sometimes active when they are unconscious and that they sometimes get the better of conscious intentions" (1938, p. 380).

His second example was of a posthypnotic suggestion which he had seen Bernheim administer in 1889. Here it was suggested that a patient would open Bernheim's umbrella, indoors, when a particular signal was given. When asked subsequently by Bernheim why he had done this, the patient explained that because it was raining, Bernheim would want to open his umbrella in the room before venturing outside. Freud took such demonstrations as further evidence for unconscious mental acts.

We would agree. The question is not whether unconscious mentation occurs. It is rather whether a Freudian unconscious had greater explanatory power than a Janetian hypothesis of *désagrégation*. At the level of theory, both have equal claims to being able to accommodate the phenomena under investigation.

From this the most that can be inferred is that mental processing occurs outside of awareness, and that it is, at times, contrary to the person's conscious volition. How it occurs is still to be determined; what Freud and Janet present us with are alternative hypotheses, and we are left in the position of either finding means to choose one or the other, or else developing further hypotheses in order to account for phenomena which cannot be accommodated easily under the rubric of conscious phenomena.

"UNCONSCIOUS CONSCIOUSNESS"

The major paradox that we have inherited from Freud is his late-appearing belief that there are unconscious aspects of consciousness. Such a view may appear to be inherently self-contradictory, but there is some evidence to suggest that Freud may have been very close to the mark.

In recent years, Hilgard (1973, 1974, 1977, 1979) has single-handedly revived interest in Janet's thinking, by formulating what he calls a neodissociation theory. The purpose here is not so much to disally himself from Janet, but rather from critics who have viewed nineteenth-century dissociation theory as "an all-or-nothing interpretation of the separateness or noninterference between dissociated activities. The originators of the concept held no such extreme positions" (Hilgard, 1977, p. 12).

The main tenet of neodissociation theory is that mental functioning may be regulated by multiple and overlapping control systems that are not always available to consciousness. A major strength of the approach is that it seeks to account for psychopathology, while providing, also, a viable theory of hypnosis; in addition, Hilgard seeks to bring this approach to bear upon normal functioning where dual processing takes place, such as when a person drives an automobile while engaging in a spirited conversation.

Despite these broader aims, Hilgard has provided experimental data bearing on his position using studies of hypnotic analgesia as his reference point in highly hypnotizable individuals (see J.F. Kilhstrom's chapter in this book for an overview of the experimental findings). This latter fact is of major importance. One of the major criticisms of psychoanalysis from a positivistic point of view is that its theoretical constructs are not easily subjected to experimental scrutiny. As Janet points out: "But we cannot accept this explanation (the concept of repression) as true, simply because it may be possible" (Janet, 1915a, p. 32). As far as possible, theoretical constructs should be supported by objective data.

As the years go by since Freud's contributions to the exploration of unconscious processes, more than 250 different psychotherapies have emerged out of the disappointment encountered in the practical application of psycho-analysis (Herink, 1980). Among psychoanalysts there is even a tendency to avoid talking about cures anymore; indeed, some argue that psychoanalysis should be valued for what it brings to an individual's life experience, whether or not there is a subsequent cure (see Chertok, 1979, 1982 for a discussion of French psychoanalytic movements).

On the other hand, many of Janet's theoretical constructs can be experi-mentally investigated, as Hilgard has demonstrated repeatedly. By successfully devising an experimental analogue of Janet's mental disaggregation concept, Hilgard has opened up the possibility of a reconciliation between Janet's concepts and the unconscious consciousness which so puzzled Freud during the last 25 years of his life.

Hilgard's findings have elicited various reactions ranging from complete acceptance (Hebb, 1975, 1982) to cautious criticisms (Laurence & Perry, 1981; Neisser, 1979) to total rejection (Spanos & Hewitt, 1980; Spanos, 1983). But already his major findings have been replicated and extended to a considerable degree (Perry & Laurence, 1980; Laurence & Perry, 1981; Nogrady, McConkey, Laurence, & Perry, 1983). these studies may be of ultimate major importance for the understanding of how information is processed outside of awareness. Their special significance may reside in the fact that they demonstrate empirical differences between highly hypnotizable individuals in terms of the manner in which information is processed.

Since high hypnotizability is found in approximately 10–15% of the population (Hilgard, 1965) it remains to be seen what implications these findings hold for hypnotically less responsive individuals. But such studies provide one starting point for an understanding of nonconscious cognition. What this may mean ultimately for an understanding of the various Freudian unconsciousnesses on the one hand and for the Janetian notion of *désagrégation* of ideas is currently beyond the realm of speculation. The important point is that empirical differences in mental processing have been demonstrated consistently and reliably, and they can be shown to be independent of subject compliance and experimenter demand characteristics (Nogrady et al., 1983), two of the major criticisms that Janet launched on Freud's methodology. The major task now is to build upon these initial observations in the hope that they will provide a solid base upon which a psychology of nonconscious mentation can be constructed.

There is one final, and major, lesson to be derived from the careers of Freud and Janet. They were the first major investigators to provide a systematic attempt to understand psychical events outside of awareness. From a very early stage, however, their differences submerged their obvious similarities of orientation, interest, and intent. Few episodes in the history of the social sciences so amply illustrate the deleterious effects of treating science as an athletic contest in which there can only be one winner, as opposed to a collaborative enterprise in which differences become a stimulus for proposing better theories and methods for understanding complex phenomena. So much of the time that Freud and Janet expended in mutual crucifixion could better have been put into extending an understanding of the question which so vitally concerned both of them. Our present understanding of mental processes outside of consciousness might well be less fragmentary than it currently is had they collaborated rather than contested.

NOTES

1. Freud referred to Pierre Janet and his younger brother Jules. Jules Janet (born in 1861) became a physician and a specialist in urology. He was greatly interested in psychology, especially looking at neurotic disturbances of urination. He also shared his brother's interest in hypnosis.

2. Dementia praecox.

3. In Footnote 1 of Janet (1915a, p. 1) he states that the paper was "presented before the Section of Psychiatry, XVII, International Congress of Medicine, London, 1913." This implies that he did not alter it for Journal presentation; if he did, the writing style suggests that changes were minor. It reads more like it was written for the ear than for the eye.

4. Some authors have suggested that Freud's clinical practice was not as neutral as this disclaimer implies. For instance, Malcolm (1982) describes analysis with Freud in the following terms: "He conducted therapy as no classical Freudian analyst would conduct it today—as if it were an ordinary human interaction in which the analyst could shout at the patient, praise him, argue with him, accept flowers from him on his birthday, lend him money, and even gossip with him about other patients" (p. 37). Other analysts of this period went further; Malcolm refers also to a letter from Freud to Ferenczi in 1931 in which he correctly criticizes Ferenczi's practice of

kissing his patients, and points to the broader ramifications of such a practice. Again, within the context of what Freud termed a didactic analysis (as opposed to a therapeutic one) with the then 47-year-old Hilda Doolittle, Freud, then 77 years old, is reported to have pounded the back of the analytic couch on which the patient was reclining, and said: "The trouble is, I am an old man—*you do not think it worth your while to love me*" (p. 166).

5. Roazan (1976) reports a similar observation. He states: "One of the reasons Freud preferred the term 'unconscious' to 'subconscious' was that Janet had used the latter" (p. 74).

6. Second letter from Gros Jean to his cardinal about talking tables, possessions, and other devilry.

7. Although Janet's ideas about the unconscious predated those of Freud by a few years, we have chosen to discuss Freud's formulations first in order that the point of departure between the two can be more readily appreciated.

8. "La conscience ne nous fait pas connaître tous les phénomènes psychologiques qui se passent en nous; c'est une vérité indiscutable que nous espérons confirmer encore."

9. "M. Pierre Janet, que je vise dans le texte, et auquel j'ai communiqué mes observations, m'écrit que par dissociation, il n'a pas entendu désigner un phénomène contraire à l'association des idées; pour lui, un état dissocié est un état qui n'est point ramené à l'idée du moi et de la personalité et qui échappe à cette synthèse supérieure. M. Janet reconnait lui-même que l'ambiguité de l'expression *dissociation mentale* explique mon erreur (Binet, 1889, p. 169).

10. "Nous avons dit et répété bien des fois que ce second groupe de phénomènes était extrêmement suggestible; que le nom et même la forme personnelle étaient déterminées par des exercices et des suggestions; que cette personalité, ainsi formée, s'éduquait, prenait des habitudes; que dans les expériences elle collaborait sans cesse avec la personnalité normale. Bien souvent, des phénomènes déterminés dans l'une des couches de la conscience avaient une action, un contre-coup remarquable sur l'autre système de phénomènes. Les caprices, les préférences de la personnalité subconsciente comme de la personnalité consciente interviennent à chaque instant pour compliquer les expériences."

REFERENCES

Aschaffenburg, G. Die beziehungen des sexuellen I eben zur Entstehung von Nerven-und Geisteskrankheiten. *Munchener Medizinische Wochenschrift, 1906, 53,* 1793–1798.

Benedikt, M. Beobachtungen über hysterie. *Sonderdruck aus Zeitschrift fur praktische Heilkunde,* 1864.

Benedikt, M. *Elektrotherapie.* Vienna: Tendler & Co., 1868.

Binet, A. Recherches sur les altérations de la conscience chez les hystériques. *Revue Philosophique de la France et de l'Etranger, 1889, 27,* 135–170.

Binet, A. *On double consciousness.* Chicago: Open Court, 1905. (Originally published 1889–1890; reprinted as a new edition, 1896.)

Cavé, M. *L'Oeuvre paradoxale de Freud. Essai sur la théorie des névroses.* Paris: Presses Universitaires de France, 1945.

Chertok, L. *Le non-savoir des Psy.* Paris: Payot, 1979.

Chertok, L. Hypnose, hystérie, psychanalyse. *Annales Médico-Psychologiques,* 1982, *1,* 45–65.

Chevreul, M.E. "Lettre à M. Ampère." *Revue Des Deux Mondes,* 1833, 2nd ser., *2,* 258–266.

Chevreul, M.E. *De la baguette divinatoire, du pendule explorateur, des tables tournantes, au point de vue de l'histoire, de la critique et de la méthode expérimentale.* Paris: Mallet-Bachelier, 1854.

Codet, H., & Laforgue, R. L'influence de Charcot sur Freud. *Progrès Médical,* 1926, *30,* 801–802.

Cole, L.E. *Understanding abnormal behavior.* Scranton, Pa.: Chandler, 1970.

Darwin, E. *Zoonomia, or the laws of organic life* (3rd ed.). London: J. Johnson, 1801.

Ellenberger, H.F. *The discovery of the unconscious: The history and evolution of dynamic psychiatry.* New York: Basic Books, 1970.

Ellenberger, H.F. *Les mouvements de libération mythique et autres essais sur l'histoire de la psychiâtrie.* Montréal: Editions Quinze, 1978.

Fine, R. *A history of psychoanalysis.* New York: Columbia University Press, 1979.

Forel, A. *Die sexuelle frage.* Munich: Reinhardt, 1905.

Freud, S. On the psychical mechanism of hysterical phenomena. In Ernest Jones (Ed.), *Sigmund Freud: Collected papers* (Vol. 1). New York: Basic Books, 1959. (Originally published 1893.) (a)

Freud, S. Some points in a comparative study of organic and hysterical paralysis. In Ernest Jones (Ed.), *Sigmund Freud: Collected papers* (Vol. 1). New York: Basic Books, 1959. (Originally published 1893.) (b)

Freud, S. The defence neuro-psychoses. In Ernest Jones (Ed.), *Sigmund Freud: Collected papers* (Vol. 1). New York: Basic Books, 1959. (Originally published 1894.)

Freud, S. Project for a scientific psychology. In S. Freud, *The origins of psychoanalysis. Letters to Wilhelm Fleiss, drafts and notes.* 1887-1902. New York: Basic Books, 1977. (Originally published 1895.)

Freud, S. L'hérédité et l'étiologie des névroses. *Revue Neurologique,* 1896, *4,* 161–168.

Freud, S. The interpretation of dreams. In A.A. Brill (Ed.), *The basic writings of Sigmund Freud.* New York: Modern Library, Random House, 1938. (Originally published 1900.)

Freud, S. Fragment of an analysis of a case of hysteria. In Ernest Jones (Ed.), *Sigmund Freud: Collected papers* (Vol. 3). New York: Basic Books, 1959. (Originally published 1905.) (a)

Freud, S. Three contributions to the theory of sex. In A.A. Brill (Ed.), *The basic writings of Sigmund Freud.* New York: Random House, 1938. (Originally published 1905.) (b)

Freud, S. A note on the unconscious in psychoanalysis. In Ernest Jones (Ed.), *Sigmund Freud: Collected papers* (Vol. 4). New York: Basic Books, 1959. (Originally published 1912.)

Freud, S. On the history of the psycho-analytic movement. In Ernest Jones (Ed.), *Sigmund Freud: Collected papers* (Vol. 1). New York: Basic Books, 1959. (Originally published 1914.) (a)

Freud, S. On narcissism: An introduction. In Ernest Jones (Ed.), *Sigmund Freud: Collected papers* (Vol. 4). New York: Basic Books, 1959. (Originally published 1914.) (b)

Freud, S. The unconscious. In Ernest Jones (Ed.), *Sigmund Freud: Collected papers* (Vol. 4). New York: Basic Books, 1959. (Originally published 1915.)

Freud, S. *A general introduction to psychoanalysis.* New York: Washington Square Press, 1967. (Originally published 1920.)

Freud, S. Two encyclopaedia articles (A) Psychoanalysis. In Ernest Jones (Ed.), *Sigmund Freud: Collected papers* (Vol. 5). (Originally published 1922.)

Freud, S. *The ego and the id.* New York: Norton, 1962. (Originally published 1923.)

Freud, S. Some elementary lessons in psychoanalysis. In Ernest Jones (Ed.), *Sigmund Freud: Collected papers* (Vol. 5). New York: Basic Books, 1959. (Originally published 1938.)

Freud, S. *An outline of psychoanalysis.* New York: Norton, 1949. (Originally published 1940.)

Freud, S. *The origins of psycho-analysis: Letters to Wilhelm Fleiss, drafts and notes: 1887–1902.* New York: Basic Books, 1977.

Freud, S., & Breuer, J. *Studies on hysteria.* New York: Avon, 1966. (Originally published 1895.)

Guillain, G. *J-M. Charcot, his life, his work.* Pierce-Bailey (Ed.). New York: Paul B. Hoeber, 1959.

Hebb, D.O. Science and the world of imagination. *Canadian Psychological Review,* 1975, *16,* 4–11.

Hebb, D.O. Hilgard's discovery brings hypnosis closer to everyday experience. *Psychology Today,* May 1982, pp. 52–54.

Herink, R. *The psychotherapy handbook.* New York: New American Library, 1980.

Hilgard, E.R. *Hypnotic susceptibility.* New York: Harcourt, Brace & World, 1965.

Hilgard, E.R. Dissociation revisited. In M. Henle, J. Jaynes, & J. Sullivan (Eds.), *Historical conceptions of psychology.* New York: Springer, 1973.

Hilgard, E.R. Toward a neo-dissociation theory: Multiple cognitive controls in human functioning. *Perspectives in Biology and Medicine,* 1974, *17,* 301–316.

Hilgard, E.R. *Divided consciousness: Multiple controls in human thought and action.* New York: Wiley, 1977.

Hilgard, E.R. Divided consciousness in hypnosis: The implications of the hidden observer. In E. Fromm & R.E. Shor (Eds.), *Hypnosis: Developments in research and new perspectives.* New York: Aldine, 1979.

Hilgard, E.R., Morgan, A.H., & Macdonald, H. Pain and dissociation in the cold pressor test: A study of hypnotic analgesia with "hidden reports" through automatic key pressing and automatic talking. *Journal of Abnormal Psychology,* 1975, *84,* 280–289.

Hilgard, E.R., Hilgard, J.R., Macdonald, H., Morgan, A.H., & Johnson, L.S. Covert pain in hypnotic analgesia: Its reality as tested by the real-simulator design. *Journal of Abnormal Psychology,* 1978, *87,* 655–663.

James, W. *The principles of psychology.* New York: Holt, 1890.

Janet, J. *Les troubles psychopathiques de la miction. Essai de psycho-physiologie normale et pathologique.* Thèse médicale, 1889–1890, No. 216; Paris: Le francois, 1890.

Janet, P. *L'Automatisme psychologique.* Paris: Alcan, 1889.

Janet, P. Psychoanalysis. *The Journal of Abnormal Psychology,* 1914–1915, *9,* 1–35 (W.G. Bean, trans.) (a)

Janet, P. Psychoanalysis. *The Journal of Abnormal Psychology,* 1914–1915, *9,* 153–187. (W.G. Bean, trans.) (b)

Janet, P. Valeur de la psycho-analyse de Freud. *Revue de Psychothérapie et de Psychologie Appliquée,* 1915, *29,* 82–83.

Janet, P. *Principles of psychotherapy.* London: Allen and Unwin, 1925. (Originally published as *La Médicine psychologique.* Paris: Flammarion, 1923.)

Janet, P. *Psychological healing: Historical and clinical study* (2 vols.) New York: Macmillan, 1925. (Originally published as *Les médications psychologiques.* Paris: Alcan, 1919.)

Janet, P. The mental state of hystericals. In Daniel N. Robinson (Ed.), *Significant contributions to the history of psychology 1750–1920,* Series C, Medical psychology, Vol. 2, P. Janet. Washington, D.C.: University Publications of America, 1977. (Originally published as *Contribution à l'étude des accidents mentaux chez les hystériques.* Thèse de médicine, Paris, 1893.)

Janet, P. *Etat mental des hystériques: Les accidents mentaux.* Paris: Rueff, 1894. (English translation, 1901.)

Janet, P. *De l'angoisse à l'extase.* Paris: Alcan, 1926.

Jones, E. Professor Janet on psychoanalysis: A rejoinder. *The Journal of Abnormal Psychology,* 1914–1915, *9,* 400–410.

Jones, E. *The life and work of Sigmund Freud.* L. Trilling & S. Marcus (Eds.). London: Penguin, 1964.

Klein, D.B. *The unconscious: Invention or discovery? A historico-critical inquiry.* Santa Monica, Ca.: Goodyear, 1977.

Knox, V.J., Morgan, A.H., & Hilgard, E.R. Pain and suffering in ischemia. *Archives of General Psychiatry,* 1974, *30,* 840–847.

Laurence, J.-R., & Perry, C. The "hidden observer" phenomenon in hypnosis: Some additional findings. *Journal of Abnormal Psychology,* 1981, *90,* 334–344.

Malcolm, J. *Psychoanalysis: The impossible profession.* New York: Vintage, 1982.

McGuire, W. (Ed.), The Freud/Jung letters: The correspondence between Sigmund Freud and C.G. Jung. Princeton, N.J.: Princeton University Press, 1974.

Myers, F.W.H. *Human personality and its survival of death.* London: Longmans, Green, 1918. (Originally published 1906.)

Neisser, U. Is psychology ready for consciousness? (Review of *Divided consciousness: Multiple controls in human thought and action* by E.R. Hilgard). *Contemporary Psychology,* 1979, *24,* 99–100.

Nemiah, J.C. Dissociative amnesia: A clinical and theoretical reconsideration. In J.F. Kihlstrom and F.J. Evans (Eds.), *Functional disorders of memory.* Hillsdale, N.J.: LEA, 1979, pp. 303–323.

Nogrady, H., McConkey, K., Laurence, J.-R., & Perry, C. Dissociation, duality, and demand characteristics in hypnosis. *Journal of Abnormal Psychology,* 1983, *92,* 223–235.

Perry, C.W., & Laurence, J.-R. Hilgard's "hidden observer" phenomenon: Some confirming data. In M. Pajntar, E. Roškar, M. Lavric (Eds.), *Hypnosis in psychotherapy and psychosomatic medicine.* Ljubljana, Yugoslavia: University Press, 1980, pp. 75–79. (Proceedings of the 2nd European Congress of Hypnosis in Psychotherapy and Psychosomatic Medicine, Dubrovnik, Yugoslavia, May 1980.)

Prince, M. *Clinical and experimental studies in personality.* Westport, Conn.: Greenwood, 1970. (Originally published 1929.) (a)

Prince, M. *The unconscious: The fundamentals of human personality normal and abnormal.* New York: Macmillan, 1929. (b)

Ribot, T. *Les maladies de la personnalité.* Paris: Alcan, 1885.

Roazan, P. *Freud and his followers.* New York: Meridian, 1976.

Sidis, B. and Goodhard, S.P. *Multiple personality: An experimental investigation into the nature of human individuality.* New York: Greenwood, 1958. (Originally published 1904.)

Spanos, N.P. The hidden observer as an experimental creation. *Journal of Personality and Social Psychology,* 1983, *44,* 170–176.

Spanos, N.P., & Hewitt, E.C. The hidden observer in hypnotic analgesia: Discovery or experimental creation? *Journal of Personality and Social Psychology,* 1980, *39,* 1201–1214.

Taine, H. *De l'Intelligence* (2 vols.). Paris: Hachette, 1870.

CHAPTER 2

The Unconscious and Psychopathology

JOHN C. NEMIAH

When the ultimate history of psychiatry is written, it will perhaps be seen that Charcot's famous clinic at the Salpêtrière was one of those nodal points where seemingly unrelated facts converged in new and seminal ways of observing and thinking. Founded in the latter half of the nineteenth century, it became under Charcot's guidance a meeting place for the study of hysterical and hypnotic phenomena and as the century waned attracted Pierre Janet to its staff. Appointed head of a newly created laboratory of experimental psychology, Janet could continue in a clinical setting his psychological exploration of hysterical patients that had already brought him scientific reknown during his earlier investigations at le Havre.

JANET AND DISSOCIATION

In 1889 Janet published his thesis, *L'automatisme psychologique,* in which he made a systematic presentation of his initial observations and formulations. Among these was a detailed description of the unusual illness of a young woman whom he studied over the course of a number of months. Marie, he writes[1]

> was brought from the country to le Havre since they thought her insane and almost despaired of her ever being cured....After a period of observation it was easy to determine that the illness consisted of recurrent symptoms regularly accompanying her menses....As her menses approached, Marie's character would change; she would become somber and passionate, which was unusual for her, and would suffer from pains and nervous twitchings in all her limbs. Despite this, everything would go fairly smoothly during the first day, but scarcely twenty hours after its appearance her menstrual flow would suddenly cease, and her whole body would be seized by a shaking chill followed by an acute pain starting in her stomach and rising to her throat, after which she would begin to have major hysterical crises. The convulsions, although very violent, did not last long and never manifested

characteristic epileptiform movements, and were followed by an exceedingly long and intense delirium.... The delirium alternated with the convulsions for 48 hours, with only short movements of respite in between. The episode would end with copious vomiting of blood, following which everything returned pretty much to normal. After a day or two of rest Marie would calm down and would remember nothing that had transpired. During the interval between these major symptoms associated with her menses, she maintained...a variety of highly changeable anesthesias, and in particular a total and continuous blindness in her left eye....

This illness, so obviously related to her menstrual periods, seemed entirely physical in nature and of little interest to the psychiatrist. I was thus initially not particularly concerned with this patient. At the most, I made a couple of attempts to hypnotize her,...but I avoided doing anything that might have disturbed her at the time of her periods, when her major symptoms appeared. Thus she remained in the hospital for seven months, during which time a variety of medications and hydrotherapy were employed without producing the slightest effect. Moreover, therapeutic suggestions, especially those directed at her menstrual difficulties, had only a bad effect and increased her delirium.

Toward the end of the eighth month she complained of her sad plight and said despairingly that she felt that everything was about to begin all over again. "See here," I said to her out of curiosity, "tell me what happens when you are going to be sick?" "Why you know perfectly well—everything stops, I have a bad chill, and then remember nothing of what follows." I wished to have precise information concerning the manner in which her periods had begun and how they had been interrupted. She did not reply with any clarity since she appeared to have forgotten a large part of the details about which she was questioned. I thought then of putting her into a deep somnambulistic state, capable, as has been seen, of recovering apparently forgotten memories, and I was thus able to recall the exact memory of a scene that she had never been aware of before except in the most incomplete fashion. At the age of 13 she had had her first period, but, either as the result of some childish idea or of a conversation she had overheard and misunderstood, she got it into her head that there was something shameful about the process and tried to find a way of stopping her menstrual flow as quickly as possible. Approximately 20 hours after her period had started, she went out secretly and plunged herself into a large tub of cold water. Her action was completely successful, her period was suddenly arrested, and despite a severe shaking chill that followed, she was able to return home. She was ill for some time thereafter and for several days was delirious. Everything quieted down, however, and her periods did not recur for five years. When they did reappear, they were accompanied by the difficulties I have already described. Thus if one compares the sudden arrest of her menses, the shivering and the pains that she now recounts in her waking state, with the account she gave in somnambulism (which, moreover, was indirectly confirmed), one arrives at the following conclusion: Each month the scene of the cold bath is repeated, leading to the same arrest of the menses and to delirium.... In her normal state of consciousness, however, she knows nothing about that and is quite unaware that her shivering is brought on by a hallucination of cold. It is possible, therefore, that this scene occurs below consciousness and brings on all the rest of her difficulty in its train.

Finally, I wished to explore the blindness in her left eye, but Marie objected to it when she was awake, stating that she had been that way since birth. It was easy to demonstrate by means of hypnotic somnambulism that she was mistaken. If one changed her into a small child of 5 by the usual procedures, she recovered the sensation she had had at that age, and one could observe that she saw very well with both eyes. It was when she was 6 that the blindness had begun. What were the circumstances? Marie persisted in saying, when she was awake, that she had absolutely no idea. During hypnotic somnambulism, and by means of successive transformations in which I had her relive the principal scenes of her life at that age, I determined that the blindness had begun at a specific moment in connection with a trifling incident. She had been forced, despite her outcries, to sleep with a child of her own age *the left side of whose face was covered with scabs.* Marie herself, some time afterward, developed similar scabs, which appeared almost identical and had exactly the same distribution. These scabs reappeared for several years and then were completely cured, but it was noticed that from that point on *the left side of her face was anesthetic and she was blind in her left eye.* She has since always maintained this anesthesia, or rather, to stick within the realm of observation, to whatever past period in her life I regressed her by suggestion, she always had the same anesthesia.... I made the same attempt as before at curing her symptoms. I brought her back to the period of contact with the child of whom she had such horror. I caused her to believe that the child was very attractive and had no scabs, but she was only half convinced. After having her repeat the scene twice, I was successful, and she fearlessly caressed the imaginary child. The sensation in the left side of her face reappeared without difficulty, and when I woke her up, Marie saw clearly with her left eye.

It is now five months since these experiments were made. Marie no longer manifests the slightest sign of hysteria, she feels well and grows increasingly stronger. Her physical appearance has radically changed. I do not attach any greater importance to this cure than it merits, and I have no idea how long it will last, but I find this history interesting as demonstrating the importance of fixed unconscious ideas and the role they play in certain physical illnesses as well as in emotional disorders. (pp. 436-440)

In this clinical account, written nearly a hundred years ago, one finds observations and a psychological conception of symptom formation of considerable sophistication. Janet skillfully employs hypnotic techniques, especially age regression, that are still effectively used by modern hypnotists. One should note particularly his recognition of the role of unconscious ideas in the production of somatic symptoms. As the ideas emerge in the expanded consciousness of the somnambulistic state, one can see that the patient's symptoms reproduce exactly the ideational form and content.

Janet's Model of the Mind

In other writings, Janet expands on the psychopathological mechanisms that are adumbrated in the case of Marie (Janet & Raymond, 1903). Central to his theoretical scheme is the concept of dissociation—that process (and state) by which ideas escape from conscious awareness and recall, and are rendered unconscious (or "subconscious," to use Janet's terminology). In his model of the human mind, the ego is the keystone of the conceptual arch. In the psychologically healthy individual, the ego (and the related sense of self) is aware of and in control of all psychological functions—thoughts, memories, volitions, actions, and emotions. The ego maintains its psychological dominance by virtue of an innate psychological energy that allows it to bind together all the human psychic functions in a unified, organized whole. In certain individuals, however, the quantum of psychological energy is insufficient for the ego's binding function, and as a consequence specific psychic components fall away from conscious control—that is, they are *dissociated.* Once dissociated, they may then, as we have seen, produce pathological symptoms in the remaining ego. In this formulation the presence of dissociated mental contents is in itself an indication of a pathological psyche.

A further question remained to be answered to complete Janet's psychopathological formulation: What is it that leads in the first place to the lowered psychic energy that compromises the ego's binding power and permits dissociation to occur? For Janet the answer was basically a genetic one. Because of their heredity, he postulated, certain individuals are born with an inherently insufficient amount of that energy. In some it may always be below the threshold required for the proper functioning of the ego; in such persons, dissociative phenomena will occur spontaneously. In others, although the energy is less than normal, it is sufficient for integrated ego functioning in ordinary circumstances. If, however, accidental factors lower the quantum of energy, it will, because of inadequate reserves, drop below the critical level and dissociation will supervene; among these accidental factors are serious physical illnesses or emotionally stressful events, such as major losses or other traumatic events that cause a significant and prolonged expenditure of mental energy.

It should be noted that for Janet, except insofar as they might lead to a diminution of mental energy, emotions were not a primary element in the psychogenesis of symptoms. The essential etiological factor was the dissociated *idea,* which, if it were dissociated, inevitably stamped itself on the ego in its own image in the form of a pathological symptom. *Why* a dissociated idea should return as a symptom, what motivational force led to its intrusion on the ego, were questions neither asked nor answered in Janet's theory. His explanation was focused primarily on the *cognitive* aspect of mental processes (i.e., on the *formal* congruence of dissociated ideas and symptoms). Emotions played only a small role in his theoretical explanation of symptom formation.

FREUD AND PSYCHOLOGICAL CONFLICT

It remained for Freud to introduce this latter element as a major, if not central, factor in psychogenesis. Freud, it will be remembered, traveled to Paris in the

1880s to study neuropathology with Charcot at the Salpêtrière, became fascinated with the intensive study of hysterical patients he found in progress there, and returned to Vienna to pursue his own psychopathological studies, initially in partnership with his older colleague Josef Breuer.

In one of their earliest collaborative papers, Breuer and Freud (1893) focused their attention on the cathartic treatment of hysterical symptoms. Like Janet, Breuer and Freud recognized that such symptoms could be the result of traumatic experiences which were "...completely absent from the patients' memory when they are in a normal psychic state" (p. 9). "Hysterics," they proposed, "suffer mainly from reminiscences" (p. 7). But they went further than Janet in pointing out that it was not only the *cognitive* element of the memory of the traumatic event that was dissociated, but the *affect* associated with it as well. Furthermore, the removal of hysterical symptoms by psychological measures required bringing into consciousness both the unconscious memory and the affect attached to it. They wrote:

> We found, to our great surprise...*that each individual hysterical symptom immediately and permanently disappeared when we had succeeded in bringing clearly to light the memory of the event by which it was provoked and in arousing its accompanying affect, and when the patient had described that event in the greatest possible detail and had put the affect into words.* Recollection without affect almost invariably produces no result. The psychical process which originally took place must be repeated as vividly as possible; it must be brought back to its *status nascendi* and then given verbal utterance. (p. 6)

From these comments it is clear that for Breuer and Freud, affect is the central pathogenic element: Though the cognitive aspect of the memory may determine the *form* of the symptom, it is by itself unable to produce a symptom if the driving force of the affect is absent. It is, then, memories of traumatic events still retaining their affect that are responsible for the appearance of symptoms. But why do some memories of traumatic events "persist...with astonishing freshness and with the whole of their affective colouring" (p. 9)? Most traumatic events, as the authors point out, normally arouse an overt emotional response which brings about a discharge of their affects and allows the memories to become insignificant and to fade into forgetfulness, without any subsequent emergence of hysterical symptoms. It is only those memories that have been separated from consciousness before this normal and customary discharge of the affective element has occurred that can produce hysterical illness. The central problem, therefore, lies in understanding why the memories and their affects are separated from consciousness in the first place. Why, in other words, does dissociation take place?

Janet, as we have seen, invoked genetic factors, or as Freud (1894) put it in a paper published a year after the appearance of what he called his and Breuer's "Preliminary Communication." "According to the theory of Janet...the splitting of consciousness (i.e., dissociation) is a primary feature of the mental change in hysteria. It is based on an innate weakness of the capacity for psychical synthesis.... which ... is evidence of the degeneracy of hysterical individuals" (p. 46). We shall pass over Breuer's suggestion of the causal role of "hypnoid states" (which was similar in its basic conception to Janet's view) and focus directly on Freud's notion of "defense hysteria." Introduced quietly, almost tentatively, in his first analytic writings (1894, 1896a, 1896b), the concept on which it rests is now the foundation stone of the entire psychoanalytic structure. In the passage in which he first uses the term, Freud (1894) writes:

> I may provisionally present my cases of defence hysteria as "acquired" hysteria, since in them there was no question either of a grave hereditary taint or of an individual degenerative atrophy. For these patients whom I analyzed had enjoyed good mental health up to the moment at which *an occurrence of incompatibility took place in their ideational life* —that is to say, until their ego was faced with an experience, an idea or a feeling which aroused such a distressing affect that the subject decided to forget about it because he had no confidence in his power to resolve the contradiction between the incompatible idea and his ego by means by thought-activity. (p. 47)

We should pause to reflect on these sentences, for they introduce a concept that goes far beyond Janet's important formulations and that markedly effected the subsequent course of the study and understanding of psychopathology. Freud's notion is a simple one. Certain ideas, fantasies, memories, impulses, and feelings are so unacceptable to the self, so frightening, saddening, painful, or disgusting that they are *forcefully excluded* from conscious awareness. Though thus rendered unconscious and beyond voluntary recall (i.e., "split-off" from consciousness or "dissociated"), they are nonetheless capable, as we have already seen, of producing derivative, ego-alien symptoms. With this concept of *psychological conflict,* Freud makes possible a dynamic understanding of symptom formation and provides the background for the later development of psychodynamic theory and the treatment techniques based on it.

Psychological Conflict Exemplified—Alice V

Before proceeding to a discussion of the refinements and extensions of analytic concepts that followed on Freud's initial formulation of psychological conflict, let us examine the manifestations of such a conflict in a young woman. Her clinical story will give more tangible meaning to the concepts we have thus far described in a more abstract fashion, and at the same time will point to clinical and theoretical features not evident in these first steps toward creating a psychodynamic explanation of symptom formation.

At 25, Alice V was already the mother of five children. Her illness had started several months before her admission to the hospital. Although she was initially vague about the circumstances surrounding the onset of her symptoms, she described easily enough the sudden irruption into consciousness of "obscene thoughts" that distress her deeply. These consisted of mental images of herself and her father, naked, engaged in sexual activity. When they occurred, she would try desperately to push them out of her mind by shaking her head or thinking of other things. But to no avail, for the mental pictures invariably forced themselves back onto her attention with a power of their own. Asked for the details, she replied with hesitation that they were "just thoughts about sex. Sometimes I would ask him and sometimes he would ask me. I could see pictures of him in my mind—you know, with no clothes on." As the images persisted relentlessly day after day, the patient became increasingly anxious and depressed to a point where she was sufficiently disabled to require hospitalization.

The thoughts were not only deeply distressing, but Alice was surprised at their character for she had never liked her father and could not understand why they should portray such intimacy between them. In fact, she protested, she had always tried to avoid him, and found it difficult to talk to him when she was forced to be with him. He was, she said, "poison" to her. In the context of discussing this relationship, she recollected that her symptoms had started at the end of a period of a week during which her father had gone out of his way to be friendly and helpful to her in connection with a temporary financial difficulty that had overtaken her and her husband.

As Alice continued to talk about her father, a curious tone of ambivalence emerged. Initially she could say only harsh things about him—that he was always mean, sarcastic, and rejecting. Indeed, a quality of vehemence in her insistence on how unpleasant and hateful he was struck the listener as being a case of "protesting too much," and when the patient at length commented, "I sort of feel as though I missed something," she was asked to elaborate. "My mother," she replied, "said he was good to me when I was little, and he used to sing songs to me and take me on his lap, but I don't remember. I only remember when he was mean to me . . . I just am glad when he keeps on talking to me mean the way he always does. . . . I just wouldn't know what to do if he was nice to me." Asked "Was there a time when you wanted him to be nice to you?" the patient answered. "When I was little . . . I wanted just to know that he did love me a little bit. I guess I always wanted him to be nice to me, but when I stop and think about him, I guess I didn't want him to be nice to me." The doctor then commented, "It sounds as though a part of you wants to be close to your father." In response the patient burst into sobs and blurted out, "I don't know how to be close to my father. I am too old to care about my father now."

When the patient had regained her composure, she recalled a memory of an event she had not thought of since it had occurred some 15 years previously. When she was 11, she reported, while in the livingroom with her father, she had suddenly had the mental image of herself in a sexual embrace with him. Terrified, she had run into the kitchen to find her mother. There had been no subsequent recurrence of such imagery (until the onset of her current illness, that is), and the episode had remained forgotten until its recall during the interview. Its emergence into consciousness then, however, amplified the history of her illness and pointed to an earlier transient outbreak of the same symptoms whose severity had caused her hospitalization as an adult.

It had not been easy for the patient to tell the doctor of this recovered memory. She became increasingly agitated and tearful, hung her head to hide her face, and covered her ears with her hands. Between sobs and in an almost whisper, she confessed that she was then and there thinking of her father with his clothes off. Presently, after a pause and still agitated, she revealed a new bit of information—that as a child she had slept in a crib in her parents' bedroom. "I slept in their room till I was five," she said hesitantly and anxiously. "I was in a crib for a long time. I can't remember—I can't remember. I never thought about that before. I don't remember—," she broke off, overcome by convulsive sobs. Encouraged to continue, the patient became quieter and said, "When I was very young, my father used to take me to bed and tell me stories. I didn't even think about that. I was very little . . . I remember once my father being very mad and yelling at me real loud. He just yelled so loud at me when I was in the crib."

Nothing more was forthcoming during that interview, but the following day the patient added a new detail to the account of the onset of her illness that she had not remembered when initially giving her history. At the end of the period during which her father had been making the friendly overtures that had so troubled her, and the night before the sudden outbreak of her symptoms, Alice had had a nightmare. She was, she dreamed, at a zoo. It was nighttime, and she heard strange noises in the darkness. She asked an animal keeper standing next to her what these noises were. "Oh," he replied casually, "that's only the animals mating." She then noticed a large gray elephant lying on its right side in the grass in front of her. As she watched, she saw the creature moving its left hind leg up and down as if it were trying to get up onto its feet. At that point in the dream she awoke with a sense of terror and during the morning experienced the first episode of the frightening imagery of sexual activity with her father.

In direct association to the dream, the patient recovered a long-forgotten childhood memory of an episode that had occurred during her fourth or fifth year. She had awoken one night while in her crib in her parents' bedroom, to observe her parents naked, engaging in sexual intercourse. They suddenly became aware of her watching them and sprang quickly apart. The patient remembered seeing her mother hastily pulling the bedclothes around her to hide her nakedness; her father, meanwhile, rolled over, half on his back, half on his left side. The patient noticed his erection, and then saw him lift up his left leg as he sat up and yelled at her crossly to go to sleep, at which she hid her head under the covers and pretended to doze off.

It was not easy for the patient to communicate these memories. She spoke haltingly, in a low voice, and was visibly ashamed and anxious. Throughout the entire recital she discharged a great quantity of affect, but after doing so appeared considerably relieved and emotionally composed. Following the interview, she became increasingly relaxed, cheerful, and outgoing on the ward. Of particular note was the complete disappearance of her central symptom—the sexual imagery involving her father and herself, which until that point in her hospital stay had continued to plague her regularly. Her improvement was sustained, and the patient was discharged within a week. When she was examined again two months later in a clinic follow-up visit, she reported that there had been no recurrence of her symptoms, that she was feeling well, and that all was going smoothly at home with her family.

If we compare the cases of Marie and Alice V, we find points of striking similarity, but we can also observe certain important differences. With regard to their likeness, both of them had experienced traumatic experiences; in both, the memories of the experiences had been lost to conscious recall (i.e., dissociated) only to return as ego-alien symptoms whose form reproduced, in part at least, the content of the unconscious memories; in both, traumatic pathogenic events could be traced back to early childhood (in Marie this was true only of her ocular symptoms); and in both, stressful life events had occurred in association with derivative symptoms (in Marie this applied only to the symptoms related to her menses).

The differences are equally notable. In Marie's illness, although the traumatic memories and the painful nature of the affects attached to them were readily apparent, one was not provided with clinical evidence of defensive psychological forces actively preventing their conscious recall. Perhaps this was because such evidence did not exist in Marie's clinical behavior, or perhaps because Janet's theoretical views of dissociation led him to overlook it. In Alice's illness one cannot escape a recognition that her pathogenic memories were not only painful but were a source of conflict to her that led to their being actively rendered unconscious by repression. This could be seen not only in the painful struggle, the anxiety, and the intense effort that accompanied the emergence during clinical interviews of long-forgotten memories; it was evident too in the exaggerated hatred for and avoidance of her father with whom the painful memories were closely associated. In Alice's sobbing agitation as she gained insight into the pathogenesis of her symptoms, we are privy to the kinds of observation that led Freud to the concept of dynamic psychological conflict. And in Alice's relief from symptoms once the battle was won and the unconscious had become conscious, accompanied by the discharge of almost overwhelming affects, we see, too, the therapeutic effectiveness of emotional catharsis to which Freud called attention—although more is, of course, involved in the therapeutic process than catharsis alone.

THE UNCONSCIOUS AND SYMPTOM FORMATION

In our brief therapeutic encounter with Alice V we observe still more aspects of the role of the unconscious in bringing about psychopathological states. Although we elaborate on them later, two of these require our initial attention here: (1) the nature of the unconscious pathogenic material against which defenses are erected and (2) the unconscious nature of the psychological defenses themselves.

The Nature of Unconscious Contents

Thus far in our consideration of the unconscious elements underlying the surface symptoms we have been concerned with memories of traumatic events. These were central to Janet's view of psychogenesis, and they similarly formed the basis of Freud's first formulation of the theory of symptom formation—especially in hysterical neuroses. In Freud's early clinical investigation of hysterical patients he invariably found that his patients (all women) gave a history of a childhood sexual encounter by an older man, in most instances their fathers. This led to the publication of an early classic paper (Freud, 1896a) in which he ascribed the specific etiology of adult hysteria to these early seductions, the memories of which had been repressed. It was only when subsequent clinical observation showed him that the actuality of the seductions could not be substantiated by information obtained from relatives and others who had known his patients that he began to doubt the validity of his theoretical formulations. In the letters to Fliess (Bonaparte, 1954) one can trace the often despairing course of his thinking as he abandoned his hard-won initial theory and came gradually to the recognition that the alleged incidents of seduction reported to him by his patients were recollections not of actual events but of early childhood fantasies. This discovery led him to the further recognition that the fantasies were the wish-fulfilling derivatives of childhood sexual drives directed to the parent of the opposite sex. This in turn led to the elaboration of the facts of childhood sexuality, and to an understanding of its development and culmination in the Oedipus complex—a formulation that was confirmed in many of its details through the observation of the stages of growth and development in infants and children themselves (Freud, 1900, 1905).

The abandonment of the traumatic theory of the psychoneuroses did not invalidate Freud's basic concept of psychological conflict; it merely changed the elements that entered into that conflict. In the new theory, it was the sexual drive and its derivative fantasies and affects that became subject to repression, especially when the drive retained a strong incestuous coloring as a result of distortions of its normal evolution in the course of childhood growth and development. In this newer form, the psychogenesis of adult neuroses was viewed as being both dynamic and developmental. Symptoms were evoked in the adult when environmental stimuli touched on current unconscious conflicts that traced their origin back to childhood developmental arrests. By the same token, a full understanding of a neurotic illness (and its adequate treatment) could be the result only of bringing into consciousness all of the present and past elements of the underlying conflict.

In the observations of the phenomena that emerged during the clinical interviews with Alice V we find evidence favoring this newer formulation. At first glance it appears that one has uncovered a memory of a childhood traumatic event. The recollection of seeing her parents in intercourse went back to her fourth or fifth year; judged by the painful affect that accompanied its emergence into consciousness, it was clearly an intensely disturbing memory; and the resistance one encountered in helping the patient bring it forth pointed both to its conflictual nature and to the defenses the patient employed to keep it out of her conscious awareness. Furthermore, one can readily observe from the content of the memory and from its associational connection with the patient's symptoms that it played a central role in determining the nature of the symptoms—sexual imagery involving her father is a central theme of both the memory and the symptomatic image.

There is, however, one major and significant difference between the form of the memory of the event and its symptomatic reproduction. In her memory the patient sees her mother and father making love; in the frightening thought that irrupted unbidden into her adult consciousness, *she* and her father are in a sexual embrace. She has substituted herself for her mother. This altered imagery is her own fantasy, not a reproduction of fact, and represents an incestuous wish for her father's love. Her childhood observation of her parents' lovemaking (and one suspects that the incident she recalled to memory was not an isolated event but that having slept in their bedroom she may have been witness to repeated episodes of a similar nature) coincided with her own childish longings for her father that constituted a part of her normal growth and development. The latter, intensified when her childhood observations of actual sexuality fell on the soil of her natural oedipal drives and fantasies, became fixated in their normal evolution and resolution, and remained in her unconscious as a source of lifelong conflict. The intensity of the conflict is evident not only in the form of her adult symptoms and the overwhelmingly frightening, disorganizing quality of the affects associated with them, but also in her adult relationship with her father, which we must now examine in more detail.

Unconscious Psychological Defenses

We have noted that after uncovering the many elements of Alice's psychological conflict it was evident that she had a highly ambivalent relationship to her father—hating and avoiding him on the one hand, yet longing for his love on the other. The latter aspect of her feelings, however, was not apparent on the surface. She was aware only of the fact that her father made her so uncomfortable that she would do anything she could to avoid seeing him or having any contact with him; similarly she insisted (almost too protestingly, it seemed) that she felt nothing but dislike for him. Both the longing and the traumatic memories associated with it were initially entirely removed from her consciousness; her avoidance, her dislike, and her repression of memories all acted as defenses to keep the anxiety-provoking attraction to her father out of consciousness. If one examines these defenses, one can distinguish subtle differences among them. In her avoidance behavior, and to some extent in her emphasizing her dislike for her father, there is an element of conscious volitional choice. The same cannot be said of her repression of the underlying memories; these are simply gone, absent from consciousness without any awareness that they have been banished. She has not consciously chosen to exclude them from consciousness (that is, she has not merely chosen voluntarily to suppress them); the act of repression itself is an unconscious process that occurs without any participation on the part of her conscious volition. Ego defenses against drives, in other words, like the drives themselves, may have the quality of being unconscious, of operating entirely outside the sphere of conscious awareness. In an examination of the patient that follows we shall elaborate on that proposition and shall at the same time be able to expand our observation of the nature of the defenses themselves.

A Case of Phobia

In his book *The Unconscious,* Morton Prince describes the illness of a woman who was the object of extensive clinical investigation (Prince, 1924). The patient consulted him because of an extreme fearfulness of towers and church steeples that caused her to avoid any sight of them. She could not remember exactly when and how the phobia had begun, but thought it had first appeared around her fifteenth year. The symptom, understandably, markedly limited her activities and movement around the city where she lived. To facilitate associations that might give a clue to the genesis of the phobia, Prince hypnotized the patient and induced automatic writing. Without her conscious knowledge of what she wrote, her hand scrawled the following message: "G.M. church and my father took my mother to Bi—where she died and we went to Br—and they cut my mother. I prayed and cried all the time that she would live and the church bells were always ringing and I hated them" (p. 391).

While writing these words the patient was consumed by anguished crying as if "she were living over again the period described in the script." On being awakened from the hypnotic trance the patient regained her composure, and when questioned about what she had written was able without any emotion at all to describe the events to which the automatic writing referred. When she was 15, she had been living in England with her mother, who had been taken with a serious illness requiring surgery, from which she died. While her mother was hospitalized, the patient was in constant fear that her mother would not survive and twice a day prayed in a church near her hotel for her mother's health. "The chimes in the tower of the church," reported Prince, "... sounded every quarter hour, they got on her nerves; she hated them; she could not bear to hear them, and while she was praying they added to her anguish. Ever since this time the ringing of bells has continued to cause a feeling of anguish... It was the *ringing* of the church bells, or the *anticipated ringing* of bells, that caused the fear... When she saw a tower she feared lest bells should ring.... She could not explain why she had never before connected her phobia with the episode she described" (pp. 392–393).

In this fragment of a clinical history we are able to observe a complex process of symptom formation. As the patient's story evolved, it became evident that the fear of towers and church steeples was integrally related to a personally significant and moving event in her earlier life—her mother's final illness and death. But more than that, towers and church steeples had come to represent and to bear the full emotional charge of those painful events, with the result that the patient's memory of her mother's actual death was pale, emotionless, and without importance to her. Thus focused and localized, the experiencing of these painful emotions could be escaped by avoiding the towers to which they had become attached—or, in clinical terms, the patient had developed a phobic neurosis. It should be noted that the creation of a phobia involves a series of ego defenses. Initially the emotional charge associated with the mother's death was *displaced* to a small, insignificant fragment of the totality of the imagery of the painful event itself; it was shifted from the naturally painful memory of the mother's death to the memory of the church tower bells, which in and by themselves alone had no inherent meaning or capacity to arouse feeling. Secondly, the emotional charge was *projected outward* from the mental imagery of towers to actual towers in the external environment. It was these real objects that were now capable of activating the emotional charge. The patient was thereby enabled to avoid the painful emotions by a final defensive maneuver of *avoiding* any form of contact with the towers in her environment.

Two aspects of this extended process of defense should be noted. In the first place, the form of the symptom (and of the neurotic syndrome that it defines) is determined by the nature of the defenses that underlie it. In Alice V's disorder, the primary defense was *repression,* which excluded from her consciousness an awareness of the totality of the conflictual material (her attachment to her father and the memories and fantasies associated with it). For many years the defense was successful and (abetted by a secondary avoidance of contact with her father) she remained symptom-free. When the defense of repression was weakened, the nuclear conflict itself emerged into consciousness without significant alteration of its content in the form of frightening sexual images of sexual activity with her father. In Prince's patient the conflictual material was processed by a *series* of defensive maneuvers that removed a large portion of it from consciousness, but left a fragment (the fear of towers) available to her awareness in the form of a chronic disabling phobia.

From these clinical considerations it becomes evident that the unconscious elements leading to psychopathological states include not only unacceptable drives and their derivatives, but ego defensive mechanisms that are opposed to them. In his earliest clinical writings Freud indicated an awareness of defense mechanisms and their role in determining the form and nature of psycho-pathological symptoms (1894, 1896b). And as analytic theory developed over the decades, Freud and others elaborated on the number and variety of defenses in clinical studies that culminated in the landmark monograph by Anna Freud, *The Ego and the Mechanisms of Defence* (1942)—a volume that summarized and firmly established the central role of unconscious ego defense mechanisms in normal and pathological psychic functioning.

Anxiety in Freud's Models of the Mind

Although in early psychoanalytic writings the role of defense mechanisms in controlling drives and contributing to symptom formation was clearly recognized, neither their specific localization in the psychic structure nor the mechanism for their activation was explicitly recognized or described. In particular, the central place of signal anxiety as a motivation for defensive action came later in the development of psychoanalysis (Freud, 1926). In Freud's first *topographic model* of psychic functioning, the mind was viewed as being divided into two parts—the Conscious and the Unconscious (Freud, 1900). The Unconscious essentially consisted of all that had been repressed—namely, the sexual drives and their derivatives, which, coming into conflict with the unconscious, ego self-preservative drives, were banished from conscious representation and awareness. In this conception, anxiety was seen as being the result of repression; it was, according to the theory, the product of the alteration of the repressed sexual drive (libido), which, barred from discharge in sexual behavior, was transformed directly into anxiety (Freud, 1895).

It was not until Freud arrived at his *structural model* of the mind that anxiety was conceived of as being a central activating force in the arousal of ego defenses. The tortuous pathway through his study of narcissism that led to Freud's revision of his notion of psychic structure is beyond our purview here. Suffice it to say that in his ultimate view the psyche was divided into the familiar three mental agencies of id, ego, and superego. In this theoretical model the id is the source of instinctual drives and their repressed derivatives, the superego is viewed as an agency that by internalization of environmental values and sanctions becomes the site of ego ideals and self-monitoring conscience, and the ego is conceived of as a set of functions, among which ego defences hold a prominent place. The Unconscious is no longer a division of the mind, as it was in the topographic model, but a *quality* of mental functioning characteristic of the id and of specific ego and superego operations. And finally, anxiety is viewed as being the motivator of repression (and other defense mechanisms), not its result. Anxiety is now seen (like depression) to be an *ego affect*. It is experienced by the ego when the psychic equilibrium is distorted and dangerous repressed drives threaten to escape from control. As a response to this danger, anxiety acts as a signal to the ego to strengthen its existing defenses and if necesary to call up auxiliary defensive mechanisms to aid in maintaining an intact psychic structure. In the patient to be examined in the section that follows, we shall find clinical observations that extend our knowledge of the nature of anxiety, ego defenses, and the drives to which they are set in opposition.

A Case of Anxiety and Depression

Cora P, aged 27, married, and with three small children (two boys, aged 4 and 2½, and a daughter who was just 3 weeks old) was admitted to the hospital for a mixture of anxiety and depression. Of the anxiety she could say little, except that she "had a fear to her that she would lose control," but, she protested, "I don't think I'd ever harm anybody or anything." She was more informative about her depression. She had been somewhat distressed when she became pregnant for the third time, with two demanding small boys already requiring hard work and constant attention. It was not, however, until she moved from one house to another that she began to feel really dispirited. The move had been a painful one for her, since she had left behind a number of good friends among her neighbors, while in her new home she knew no one and felt alone and lonely. Even more disturbing was the fact that her mother had previously lived a block away. She was closely attached to her mother and depended on her for almost daily help and support, and it was a sad loss to her when the move some distance away made it impossible for her to see her mother as often as she liked or was accustomed to. In this context she began to feel depressed and tired, lost interest in everything, felt "washed up," worthless, "a failure in life," and "wanted to die."

She was, she said, surprised at how she felt, for she had always been "happy-go-lucky. Nothing ever bothered me or anything. I always took everything in stride." There was, however, one thing that had always distressed her—she could not stand having anyone criticize or "yell" at her children. And yet, when it occurred she could do nothing about it. "If anybody yells at them, I don't say anything—I take it all to heart. I don't yell at the person that's yelling at them. I just take my children away.... If anybody says anything to my kids, it just hurts my feelings...I take everything to heart. I just don't let it brush off my shoulders. I think about it. But I'd never fight back, Doctor. I never did. My husband says that's why I'm here because I let everybody bother me."

In this brief and insightful bit of self-description we begin to see evidence of the ego defense mechanism of reaction formation against aggression. In situations of unpleasantness or strife, where one might expect her to retort angrily, she refrains from saying anything, controls herself, walks away, and though she may brood about the episode, she leans over backwards to be peaceful and unaggressive herself.

However, when the patient talked about her children, her problems with aggressiveness and her exaggerated defenses against it became strikingly apparent. In the course of a clinical interview the following interchange occurred between the patient and her doctor:

PT: I can't stand to see my kids abused, Doctor...I can't stand it.

DR: How does it bother you?

PT: It breaks my heart to see. I cry when I see anybody yell at them or hit them.

DR: Do you ever punish your kids?

PT: No, I can't punish them, Doctor. It hurts me to punish them. I just can't do it. I can't face up to hitting them. Even my husband—he'll tell you. Even my sisters say the same thing about me. I'm too good to them. I let them run my life, and yet I can't help it. They can do anything and I won't hit them. I know I should, but I can't. I can't go out unless I buy them a toy. Every Saturday when I would go out shopping I would usually buy them a truck or something.... But when we moved everything changed. I never got out or anything. That's when I lost my interest, when I moved down here.

DR: Had you wanted to move?

PT: I wanted to move because of the heating system—for the children. Not for myself, I didn't. I did it for my children.

DR: You make a lot of sacrifices for them.

Pt: I make too many. That's what my husband says. I never went out or anything. I never left them with anybody. I always stayed home. I've never had any time away from my children. Since I've had my first boy, I've never had no time away from them—no time at all.

As the patient talked, one could not help being impressed with her extreme solicitousness, concern, and care for her children. Unlike most mothers, she could not punish them, she felt compelled to do nice things for them, and what is more striking, she had never been able to leave them with anyone else in order to be by herself or to enjoy herself. Her husband and her sisters recognized that she was too good to her children, and even she herself had a suspicion that her behavior was a bit exaggerated. And finally, we should note that at great cost to herself she had moved for the children's sake. Suspecting that behind this saintlike goodness there lurked a hidden resentment toward the children, her doctor finally asked the patient, "Do you ever get mad at your children?"

Pt: No. No, I never get mad at them.
Dr: You never got angry at them?
Pt: Now that I'm thinking of it now, I might have got angry at my older boy—yelled at him, but that's all. Tell him to stop doing something—he'd go near the bassinet to look at the new baby. I'd start yelling at him because I didn't want him near her.
Dr: Why not?
Pt: I didn't want him to touch the new baby, you know. I was afraid that he might pinch her or go for her eyes. He had the blanket over the baby's head the day before I came in the hospital, and I thought I'd collapse, I got so nervous and upset over it. You know, every ten or fifteen minutes I'd go over and look at the new baby. When I saw the blanket over the baby's face, I started crying—I couldn't control myself. I figured if I didn't go over there to look at the baby, what would have happened to her?
Dr: What do you figure would have happened?
Pt: Well, she could have smothered to death!

Here we get hints from our glimpses behind the reaction formation that the patient harbored more aggression than she was aware of or was willing to admit to herself. Not only does she finally confess to yelling occasionally at her older son, but she brings forth fanciful thoughts (attributed to her boy) of damaging, even lethal actions directed at her baby.

Following this lead, her doctor asked, "Have you had any thoughts of hurting her?"

Pt: Oh, no! God, no!
Dr: Or about your boys?
Pt: Well, I wasn't happy while I was carrying the baby. I managed to call my

husband home from work and tell him I was going to kill myself. He was scared, you know, because I was so down in the dumps.

Dr: Did you ever have thoughts of hurting your boys?

Pt: I'd say I did, but I never did hurt them, Doctor. I used to say to my husband, "I'll kill them"—just like that. Like I'd say I'd kill myself.

Dr: What would put that thought in your mind?

Pt: I don't know. It just came out of me, just being so depressed. I didn't have no plan that I was going to put them in the bathtub or something.

Dr: To put them in the bathtub?

Pt: (becoming increasingly anxious) No! Like you said, did I have any plans of doing it? No! No! Like you were saying—if you want to plan something, say, like in the bathtub or something like that. No! I had no plans on what I was going to do. I was more disgusted with myself.

Dr: What were you thinking about with the bathtub? What would you do?

Pt: Who? Me?

Dr: Yes.

Pt: That was just a saying. I had no thought in my mind, Doctor, when I said "bathtub." I would think more of doing harm to myself than I would do to them. I would rather hurt myself than them.

In the evolution of this interview we find, as in the patients we have already examined, a significant psychological conflict behind the surface symptoms that brought her to the hospital. But, although the general form of the conflict is the same (that is, an opposition of drives and defenses leading to symptoms that are a vector of the conflicting psychological forces), the nature of the individual warring elements is different. In the first place, the central underlying drive was not, as in Alice V, sexual, but aggressive, and, as far as could be determined from the observations at hand, the patient had no conflict over her sexual drives. Second, we were able to observe two new defenses that appear to be specifically associated with and designed to control aggression. It will have been noted that toward the end of the interview, as the doctor pressed the patient to talk about her possible aggressive fantasies, she several times veered abruptly and immediately from talking about hurting others to hurting herself. As she said of her children, "I would rather hurt myself than them." In this reversal and turning inward of aggression against the self we see a common ego defense against the aggressive drive—one that in some patients can lead to serious, occasionally successful, suicidal acts.

We have already mentioned, in connection with the patient's exaggeratedly solicitous and protective attitude toward her children, a second defense commonly employed as a mechanism for controlling the aggressive drive—namely, reaction formation. It should be noted that the end result of the operation of this defense is different from that which we have observed in our examination of the other defense mechanisms. In those patients, defenses led to the formation of *symptoms*. In Prince's patient, for example, the effect of displacement and projection, while it protected the patient from an awareness of the painful affects connected with her mother's death, was to transpose these affects to external towers, which then became the object of phobic avoidance. The phobia was a neurotic *symptom,* which was the central feature of a chronic, disabling neurotic disorder. Cora P's defensive reaction formation did not result in a neurotic symptom or illness. Rather, it determined a *character trait*—a habitual pattern of behavior and relationships with other people that characterized her personality. Defenses, while serving the general purpose of controlling and canalizing the expression of drives and their derivatives, have different surface manifestations depending on their mechanism of action. They may, that is, produce pathological symptoms, or they may result in the formation of character traits that, superficially at least, appear normal.

Thus far in our consideration of Cora P and the other patients we have examined, we have been concerned primarily with elucidating the nature of drives and defenses and the compromise surface manifestations of the conflict between these two psychological forces. Before we leave Cora P we must focus our attention on her anxiety and the role it played as a motivating factor in the arousal of her defense—a process that we have touched on earlier in a more general, conceptual manner. It will be remembered that in addition to her depression, the patient complained of anxiety as one of her presenting symptoms. As one reviews the clinical material, it can be seen that her anxiety was closely associated with the aggressive drive. In the early part of the interview, for example, in direct association to mentioning her anxiety she introduced the idea of harming people; later she described her panic upon finding the covers over her baby's head, fearing (unrealistically) that the infant could have smothered to death. In these instances, the anxiety was a *consciously experienced ego affect* in response to *unconscious* aggressive thoughts and impulses threatening to emerge into conscious awareness. The anxiety, in other words, acted as a signal of internal danger. We should note further that when the doctor, guided by the aggressive quality of the patient's associations and imagery, directly asked the patient about her own hostile wishes and urges, a psychological process was set in motion. At first she admitted to having had thoughts of hurting her children, but as she began, with the doctor's encouragement, to elaborate on these fantasies, she became increasingly anxious, retracted what she had said, and began to talk about hurting herself. As the initially unconscious drive began to emerge into consciousness, her anxiety mounted, the defense of reversal and turning inward of aggression was activated, and her awareness of a wish to hurt others was removed, leaving her conscious only of the thought of hurting herself. To recapitulate the sequence, she experienced anxiety as the aggressive impulses emerged into consciousness, whereupon an *unconsciously* operating defense (reversal and turning inward) supervened and she was left with an awareness only of the thought of self-harm, a symptom of the depressive syndrome. What should be emphasized here is that the patient was *not* aware of the arousal and operation of the ego defense. It was a totally unconcious process. Defenses, as we have noted, are an important element in the contribution of the unconscious to psychopathology.

The Superego as a Source of Anxiety

Let us take a last look at Cora P's clinical history and psychological conflict to see what we can learn about the source of the anxiety experienced by her ego. One of her presenting symptoms, it will be recalled, was a feeling of worthlessness. In this component of her depressive syndrome we see the effects of the patient's superego. Measuring herself against her internalized standards for proper behavior, she judges herself to fall short of her ideal and accordingly experiences a guilty sense of worthlessness. We get a hint of her ideals in her striving to be good, kind, unaggressive, a loving, giving parent, and a person who sacrifices her own wants to those of others—an attitude that leads to a behavior pattern (exaggerated by reaction formation) determined by *internal* sanctions, not those imposed by others; indeed, we find that her family and friends think she is too good and, if anything, encourage her to be less demanding on herself. Her superego is, then, a harsh, exacting judge, which threatens her with punishment if she oversteps the strict bounds of the behavior it imposes. In the face of the aggressive drive impelling her to what she views as improper behavior, her ego reacts with anxiety in the face of the threatened superego sanctions and mobilizes the defenses against the forbidden drive to avoid the punishment anticipated from the superego. The latter, not only in Cora P, but in most human beings, is a central agency in the arousal of anxiety experienced by the ego. It should be emphasized that a significant portion of the processes associated with the functioning of the superego operates outside the realm of the individual's consciousness; one is not aware of the developmental roots of the standards it imposes nor of its role in the production of anxiety. Like the drives and defenses, the superego is yet another element in the unconscious production of psycho-pathology.

The Childhood Roots of Conflict—Miss Vé

In discussing Cora P's reaction formation, we pointed out that its effect was to produce personality characteristics rather than clearly defined psychopathological symptoms. In the history of Miss Vé, we shall see that there are other unconscious processes that similarly determine stable patterns of behavior and human relationships. Described by the Swiss psychologist, Théodore Flournoy (1915), in a document that rivals Schreber's autobiography (1903) for its poignant revelations of human suffering, Miss Vé's personal and clinical history was a long one. She was 47 when she first consulted Flournoy for a curious complaint. Although generally a staid, proper, and religious school mistress of considerable professional stature, she had been plagued for a number of years by a distressing cycle of events. Every few weeks she would notice a radical and disturbing change in her personality. Initially, at night she would have dreams of a frightful sort: of wild beasts attacking her, or of snakes charming and swallowing innocent birds, after which she would be flooded by dreams of lascivious sexual affairs. Sexual thoughts and preoccupations would gradually begin to invade her daytime hours, and she would give herself over to lurid sexual fantasies, intense sexual excitement, masturbation, and, she hints, on at least two occasions to sexual relations with men. During these periods she was bright, lively, flirtatious, and gay, and amazed her colleagues, who knew her usually as a sober, pious spinster. After a few days the attack would disappear, and she would revert to her proper self. Following a religious conversion at 30, the episodes became less frequent, but her failure to control them altogether led her ultimately to seek professional help.

The patient's past history added interesting details to the development of her clinical disorder. As a child she had lived much alone, indulging in vivid daydreams in which "gray reality ceased to exist, and I was transported into a fictitious world more colorful and captivating than my real existence" (p. 19). At the age of 7 she was introduced by a family maid to the practice of masturbation, which had, as she commented, "always instinctively represented for me the sin par excellence" (p. 19). During her adolescence, however, she had no recollection of this childhood sexual behavior, and until the age of 18 lived in "the most complete ignorance of sexual matters . . . I believe I realized once or twice that the other girls had secrets among themselves . . . but it aroused no curiosity in me. . . . Even my twin sisters developed more rapidly than I, and my ignorance was a subject of joking for them . . ." (p. 20). Her virginal innocence, however, was rudely shattered at 18, when at the hands of "an unscrupulous man I was precipitated all alone, without help, into the furnace of sexual emotions, and of brutal, filthy revelations" (p. 20). It was following this episode that her symptoms first appeared and that she "became convinced that I had no right to get married and that no respectable man could love me . . ." (p. 21).

The patient, as we have noted, had lived a solitary life as a child. She had had little contact with her mother and sisters, and had reserved all her affection and attention for her father. As she commented, "My father, who was a schoolmaster of considerable culture, and a rare intellectual cast, was alone able to win my heart" (p. 17). From childhood and throughout adolescence she had for him "an affection that was exclusive, passionate, and jealous. . . . From a very early period there developed between him and me a delicious intimacy—not very expansive or open, because he frightened me a bit, but very profound and intuitive" (pp. 19–20).

Although, as we have seen, the patient had never considered herself worthy to enter into marriage, she had, nonetheless, had a number of relationships with men, each of which followed a similar pattern of development. The men she was attracted to were much older, often reminded her of her father, and were frequently married and had children. At first the relationship would be platonic, based on a sharing of intellectual and artistic interests, but invariably, after a shorter or longer period of time, sexual feelings and desires would supervene, and with a sense of moral revulsion, the patient would break off the relationship—

only to start afresh on a similar path with someone else. She had never been able to make a long-lasting liaison, nor, as already mentioned, to marry and have a family of her own.

The most recent of these friendships was with a Mr. Y, like the others a married man, with whom she developed a "growing intimacy, founded on a sympathy so instinctive that it seemed to us that we had always known each other and belonged in some mysterious fashion to the same race. From the very start he pleased me because of that part of him that reminded me of my father, and because of the ardor of his idealism and his warm understanding for me" (pp. 33–34). Unfortunately, and inevitably, matters took their usual course, and as the relationship became increasingly sexualized, Miss Vé realized that she was getting deeper into a situation that (as Flournoy commented) "could not have an honorable outcome.... Twice already...she had allowed herself to be swept along much further than she ought to have, and only the most energetic starting up of her whole moral nature had enabled her to recover herself at the last moment" (p. 31). As the patient herself remarked, "I had to face the evidence that our relationship was not good for either one of us, and . . . I understood at last that for both of us to save ourselves, there had to be a total suppression of any connection between us" (p. 34).

In the midst of this moral crisis, Miss Vé asked Flournoy for his help in terminating the liaison. During the course of several therapeutic sessions, Flournoy hypnotized the patient and suggested calmness and firmness of resolve. The treatment worked. Miss Vé resisted her passionate desires to see Mr. Y and completely and permanently broke off the relationship.

As might have been predicted, although Mr. Y was banished, there was a successor—this time Professor Flournoy himself. As the patient wrote to Flournoy, "I came to see you...in great moral and physical distress; you cured me, or at least helped me to cure myself.... At your touch the moral atmosphere which I breathed was purified. You gave me confidence in myself and helped me to turn my back on all those unwholesome shadows which had haunted me for so long. In some measure you gave me what I experienced with my father" (p. 28). As she reflected on her relationship with Flournoy she recognized "the very great gratitude and the deep affection I have for you. There could be nothing else in it—I have analysed myself thoroughly and looked at myself in every possible way, and I do not believe I have discovered in what I experience anything whatever of morbid or unwholesome excitement" (p. 28).

Miss Vé spoke too soon. Not long afterward she found herself increasingly preoccupied with Flournoy's image; she would, for example, have long daydreams about him while attending church and sensed a growing possibility of a passionate attachment to him. "I realized," she wrote him later, "that I depended on you in a curious measure, that you had become strangely necessary to me, that I was restless, agitated, and uneasy away from you and contented in your presence. But it was a physical feeling in which I very soon saw danger, and which I vigorously suppressed with complete success" (p. 26). The "suppression" included a breaking off of her therapeutic visits to Flournoy. Though she continued to write copious and detailed letters, she never saw him again thereafter.

Instead Miss Vé found a new friend. Here is her account of their meeting, which occurred at night, in her bedroom:

> For several weeks the Friend ["l'Ami" in the original French] has been coming to see me. I see and hear nothing, but I know that he is there because of the calmness and delightful peace that runs through me. I do not know if he has a body; he is in no way perceived by my senses, with the exception that I think I hear him speak, but with a completely internal voice like my own thought. However, it is not I.... He comes to me from without, and he brings me something which is pure and clean. He speaks very little, and when he is there...I tell him everything that goes on in me.... He understands as no one else can understand, better than I understand myself. (p. 42)

From a clinical point of view we find that the patient has substituted a hysterically hallucinated "presence" endowed with all of the characteristics of the actual men with whom she had previously had relationships (including Flournoy), but without the danger of an entangling physical, sexual alliance. Or so it would have seemed, but gradually the character of the Friend took a more specific and personal form. One night the Friend appeared. "He spoke several words about inner peace, talking in a manner that reminded me of my father" (p. 42). On subsequent nights she discovered that increasingly, when she was waiting expectantly for the Friend, vivid images of her father would appear to her instead and when the Friend himself came, his character was increasingly intrusive and sexual. And then, after a period of intermingled images of her father and the Friend, suddenly the wild, lascivious sexual nightmares and daytime reveries (that as symptoms had first impelled her to seek Flournoy's help) recurred with all their frightening intensity.

Although this was not the end of the patient's troubles, we must leave her to her despairing turmoil and review the significance of that fragment of her history reported here. From a clinical point of view her symptoms were those of a dissociative hysterical disorder, and their genesis in a profound conflict over sexuality is evident both in her life's history and the imagery associated with her symptoms. It is also apparent from the close intermixture of the imagery of the Friend and her father, combined with intrusive sexual feelings and followed by the irruption of her sexually-toned symptoms, that her sexual drive had retained a strongly incestuous coloring that made it forbidden and the center of intense psychological conflict. Our concern here, however, is not primarily with the pathogenesis of the patient's neurotic illness but with the nature of her relationships with men and the factors that determined their inevitably troubled course.

In this regard we should take note of several facts. The men with whom the patient developed relationships were universally paternal in nature. They were older, strong, protecting, intellectual—all traits that applied to her father, and, indeed, the patient herself often recognized the fact that they reminded her of him. With each man the relationship ran into difficulties when it became sexualized, forcing the patient to terminate the liaison, only to start the whole process over again with a new partner. Central to the pattern of these relationships was the unresolved, largely unattenuated incestuous sexual tie to the patient's father. Her desire for him determined her choice of men who resembled him, and similarly the anxiety and conflict over the incestuous quality of her sexual feelings caused her to terminate each relationship when these sexual feelings emerged into consciousness. Although we can see the incestuous quality of the patient's sexuality from the rich associations of her fantasies, symptoms, and imagery, she herself remained unaware that her love for her father was in any way sexual in nature. This element remained unconscious, but at the same time was the central factor in her conflict over sexuality, in her symptoms, and in *determining the patterns of her adult relationships.* In this connection, further-more, we should note that the special therapeutic relationship with Flournoy was no different. He reminded her of her father, the relationship became increasingly sexualized, and had to be terminated. The fact that Flournoy was her therapist did not protect him from a *transference,* which, shaped by the patient's unconcious conflicts, eventually became disruptive to treatment. In summary, from our exploration of Miss Vé's emotional difficulties, we discover that unconscious mental elements play a central role not only in the formation of psychopathological symptoms and of character traits, but in the shaping of intimate human relationships, including that of *transference* in the therapeutic situation.

Ego Regression and Symptom Formation—Grace C

We now turn our attention to a final patient who will show us yet another way in which unconscious mental processes contribute to the formation of clinical psychopathology. Grace C, a married woman of 47, was brought to the hospital by her husband because of the recent outbreak of severe, disturbing, and disruptive psychotic symptoms and behavior. Initially she began to hear strange noises coming through the pipes and faucets in her sink. Next she heard the doorbell ringing in an odd and capricious way day and night. Shortly before coming to the hospital she had spent an entire night jumping out of bed to run downstairs to the door to admit what she thought was a host of angels sent to her house from heaven. On one occasion she heard "a heavy, strong flapping of wings on my kitchen screen," which she believed to be the Holy Ghost seeking entrance. As dawn broke, she noted a "blowing noise" coming from her radio, which she interpreted as being special messages for her, which she felt compelled to write down on scraps of paper. She was vague as to the nature of these communications and would comment only that they bade her "destroy this, destroy that, such as destroy the Vatican in Rome, do away with the Pope. It had a lot of religion in it."

Despite the patient's bizarre behavior and hallucinations, it was notable that during an evaluative interview her attention could be engaged and that she could give a relatively coherent account of her life and recent experiences. Her life had not been an easy one. When the patient was 5½, her mother had suddenly and unexpectedly died. The patient was at once put into an orphanage where she remained for two years. Thereafter she lived serially with a variety of relatives until her father remarried several years later and took her home to live with him and her stepmother. She remembered this period of her life as one of abuse and neglect, and her marriage at 22 did not improve matters, for her husband was a severe alcoholic with all the attendant difficulties of that condition. During all of these experiences the patient faced her troubles with stoical resignation. She lived a narrow, restricted life of doing her housework and daily chores with great thoroughness and conscientiousness, and had no interests or friends outside her home. She never complained and kept any feelings she may have had to herself. To an observer, she appeared to have lived a humdrum, routine existence, and to be a person with little depth and without interests.

The patient's own account of her life's course was vivid and poignant, and was presented to the interviewer with strong emotion:

All my life I've been alone. I lived an empty life, and I did things for the sake of doing them and tried the best I possibly could.... I lost my mother at age 5½, and you might say I went through Hell's kitchen the hard way.... I was put away in a home. My father remarried, and I was taken out, and I led one rotten life, in plain English—one abused, neglected, terrible, wicked life, and it went that way till my marriage.... The only person in my life that had any meaning in my life was my mother. She was always there in my mind...the sorrow for her I always had. I may not have showed it. I never showed feelings. I never had feelings—they may have been hidden without my knowledge; I only felt pain. So all through my life I was always alone. Alone through childhood, alone through the years after childhood, alone through marriage. I was married in name only, the way I look at it, and I had a husband who wasn't interested. He thought more of the bottle than he did of me. He never knew what it was to pay a gas bill. The responsibilities were always on my shoulders. I've done that all my life. That's how I ran my whole life. I never griped. I never looked for anything.... I never belonged anywhere. I never fitted anywhere. I never had a family—I had a family, but it was a family with no meaning. The only one that meant anything was my mother, and I never knew her. She was the only one that would have filled my life. It was a broken up family because of my mother's death—and then just nothing."

Against this background let us look at the events that took place in the months immediately preceding the outbreak of the patient's psychotic illness. About a year before her admission to the hospital, her husband had himself been admitted to another institution because of complications arising out of his alcoholism. To help Grace C deal with the problems of living with an alcoholic husband, she was assigned to a social worker, Miss M, who set up a regular schedule of three, hour-long therapeutic interviews a week. Miss M took a nondirective, inactive, listening stance with the patient, which initially left her in doubt as to what she was to talk about. Receiving no guidance or clues from Miss M, the patient at length decided to recount the history of her life, which she did in great detail as the hours progressed. Over the weeks and months the patient felt she had gained a great deal of help from her visits. As a result of them, she said, she had become "a new person in a new world. Great changes—spectacular—wonderful—words can't express it. I was rejuvenated, you might call it."

Miss M, however, was not so sanguine about the changes. She had, in fact, been urging the patient to seek psychiatric consultation and had encouraged her ultimate hospitalization. What particularly troubled Miss M was the patient's growing attachment and dependency upon her that developed during the course of therapy, as well as the gradual emergence of a delusional system involving Miss M. The presence of the latter was evident in the opening moments of the evaluation interview after her hospitalization. As the patient sat down in the doctor's office, she pulled from her pocket the following manifesto and proceeded to read it:

> I, Grace C, am in the hospital for one purpose and one purpose only. That purpose I speak about was, and is, to please one Miss M, my social worker. About two months ago I had concluded my talks in person with her. My continued correspondence with her since has been talking with her over the telephone and writing letters to her. My social worker, Miss M, kept insisting I talk with a psychiatrist when I had concluded my talks with her in person. I, in turn, kept insisting that I felt it was not necessary, and, therefore, I kept on refusing to do so. My feelings are still the same, but nevertheless, I am still trying to please my social worker. I, Grace C, want you, doctor, to remember and do not forget that it was and is Miss M, my social worker, who chose you. My social worker, Miss M, and Miss M alone can choose and do as she and she alone sees fit. Any further talks or any further information concerning myself, Grace C, will have to come from my social worker, Miss M. She, my social worker, Miss M, holds the key to all that has been known and all that can be known. I put myself in her hands, in the hands of Miss M, and in her hands only. In closing, doctor, I do hope you will stop being idiots and use your heads for a change. Good day, doctor. Signed Mrs. Grace C. That is all I intend to say.

Despite what appeared to be an inauspicious beginning, the interview proceeded apace as the patient talked readily about her life, her attitudes, and her recent experiences. As she indicates in her "manifesto," Miss M had become not only a central person in her existence, but was endowed with superhuman powers. "Through her," the patient said, "I could see the Blessed Virgin.... With her sitting there, talking with her...I could see the Blessed Mother. She was a beautiful woman, with beautiful hair...coaching me, telling me different things to say." Furthermore, Miss M was, in the patient's delusional system, the head of a far-flung organization of psychiatrists whose sole current purpose, at Miss M's direction, was to provide the care that the patient needed.

The patient, however, wanted only the attention and guidance of Miss M. Grace proclaimed:

> If I shared wherever she lived it would make me the happiest person in the world. That feeling of being alone would no longer be there. God sent her to me for a reason, because before I went there, I was neither her nor there. I was, you might say, a walking dead.... I have to be around her—included in her life. It would make me happier if, rather than go home, I could share living in her house. Just talking with Miss M made me feel wonderful. The oneness means there's a completion of the love and joy feeling—to work with here, to work around her, to be part of her life. And like I say, if she wants me to live with her, that's her business, but that's what I would like. That would give me completeness.... She is the only good thing that's happened to me in my life.... My feelings toward her are like that I would have, had I had a mother.... She was always patient and understanding just like a mother would be.... If I could be with her, I'd be the happiest woman in the world. It would be like as though I had a mother, if there was someone that was interested in me, someone I could sit down and talk with, someone that would help me. If there was any good that could come out of me, she'd sure ease the way. We'd work together. In other words, that's the only thing I never had in the past. I never had understanding. There was never any love. The only feeling I felt or knew was that of pain. Other things I did, it was without feeling. I did what was good. It gave me some satisfaction.

At that point the doctor commented, "You're picking up again where you were as a child?" The patient replied, "Like I say, it's starting off the same way, only now I'm an older person. Instead of 5½, I'm 47. All I can say, it was a wonderful experience."

Let us review the sequence of events in the patient's life and the processes that led to her eventual psychotic illness. At the age of 5½ she suddenly lost her mother and was sent off alone to an orphanage. Her entire little girl's world was turned upside down, with all the attendant pain, loneliness, sadness, longing, and fear that this could be expected to arouse. Her response appears to have been to repress all of her feelings, which since her childhood had remained unexpressed, undischarged and unresolved—especially those having to do with the loss of her mother. They remained subsequently buried in her unconscious throughout her adulthood, during which she led a dull, isolated, emotionally flat, and shallow life, dedicated to dutifully carrying out her limited responsibilities as a housewife. Then came her prolonged and intensive therapeutic contract with Miss M, a warm and sympathetic woman, who encouraged her to talk about her past and present troubles. In this setting, all of her old feelings for her mother and about her painful childhood, which had been unconscious for many years, began to emerge into conscious awareness. As they appeared, they were still the feelings of a little, 5½-year-old girl, which had remained unmodified in character and intensity during their long state of repression. There was, however, one important difference; instead of being experienced as feelings for her mother, they were transferred onto a person in her adult environment—her social worker,

Miss M. Despite this transposition, they remained qualitatively unchanged from what they had been 40-odd years before, and the patient developed the relationship of a little girl to Miss M, whom she saw as big, maternal, protecting, loving, and all powerful.

If we compare Grace C with the Swiss schoolmistress, Miss Vé, we find that both developed a transference to their therapists that reflected feelings and attitudes characteristic of an important childhood relationship—in Miss Vé with her father; in Mrs. C with her mother. But there the similarity ends. Although Miss Vé's incestuous ties to her father colored her adult relationships with men (including her therapist) in a manner that prevented her from making a satisfying and lasting marriage, and although her forbidden sexual drive resulted in distressing and often disabling neurotic symptoms, her basic personality and ego functions remained intact. In Mrs. C, on the other hand, as her early, infantile dependent longings for her mother emerged in the transference from their unconscious prison during the course of therapy, they were accompanied by devastating changes in her ego functions manifested clinically in her psychotic symptoms. Unlike Miss Vé, Mrs. C lost her capacity for reality testing; she projected her needs for nurturance onto the world around her in the form of a delusional system in which she was the focus of attention of a huge caretaking organization headed by her social worker, Miss M; with a totally unrealistic idealization, the patient transformed Miss M into an omnipotent, supernatural being; and throughout her sensorium was invaded by visual and auditory hallucinations. In short, her ego underwent a *regression* that altered its structure and function as developmentally primitive modes of thinking and feeling took command and distorted the more adaptive, reality-oriented ego that underlies mature, adult mental activity.

How are we to understand this difference in the kind of transference relationship each patient developed for her therapist—the one a neurotic, the other a psychotic transference? A partial answer, at least, is to be found in the nature of the unconscious elements that emerged in the transference relationship. In Miss Vé these were predominantly oedipal and libidinal in coloring, derived from disturbances arising during her oedipal phase of development. In Mrs. C, on the other hand, the primary issue was narcissistic in nature, deriving from the much earlier developmental phase of the dependent, dyadic relationship between infant and mother. When Mrs. C's long-repressed narcissistic dependent needs emerged from her unconscious in the intensity of her transference relationship with her therapist, they were accompanied by the *reactivation of pre-oedipal,* infantile modes of ego-functioning, which were clinically manifested as psychotic symptoms. Although both patients developed a transference stemming from childhood relationships, the character of the transference (as well as of the accompanying clinical symptoms) of each patient was determined by the developmental phase from which it was derived. Adult relationships and emotional disorders, in other words, not only rest ultimately on unconscious fixations and distortions in the processes of early growth and development; the *specific* form and nature of those adult relationships and disorders are further determined and differentiated by phase-specific disorders along the developmental time dimension.

THE CONCEPT OF PSYCHOLOGICAL STRUCTURE

If one takes a broader view of the clinical observations and the individual psychological processes they have illustrated, it becomes apparent that the human psyche is a richly variegated, complex, organized psychological structure. Drives and their related feelings and fantasies, ego defenses, ego affects (especially anxiety and depression), a variety of ego functions of greater or lesser developmental maturity, and processes referable to the superego are fitted together into an overall dynamic equilibrium that represents the not always completely stable resolution of conflicting psychological forces. Much of this psychic structure is observable to the individual who looks within himself, and he is able to describe to others the nature and variety of his inner experiences; but much of it is hidden from his view and beyond his voluntary recall. The psychological organization is, in other words, partly conscious, partly unconscious. When the individual is subjected to environmental emotional stress, all of the parts of the total structure, conscious and unconscious, are set in motion, often leading to a change in the equilibrium of the totality. To the person observing himself, changes may occur in his psychological functioning that are puzzling to him, since he is not aware of the underlying unconscious forces that have contributed to bringing about the surface alterations. It is only when the repressed unconscious elements are made conscious so that the previously hidden psychic structure can be observed in their relations and interactions with one another that the surface changes brought about by stress become intelligible. The psychic organization functions as an integrated whole without regard to whether the various contributing processes are conscious or unconscious from the self-observer's point of view.

Much of psychiatric interviewing is, of course, aimed at bringing the unconscious portion of the psychological structure into conscious awareness, partly to shed light on the mechanisms underlying surface manifestations (e.g., symptoms) and in part to help the individual overcome psychological distress as a result of the insight thus gained. In the course of such interviewing, especially when it is aimed at focusing the patient's attention on his inner life and encouraging his free association, one finds the patient disclosing a rich tapestry of experiential facts. In this setting he reports memories, fantasies, feelings, and urges, and in his associations, weaves these elements into a picture of current events and human relationships intermixed with those from the past from which they originate.

The Contribution of Psychosomatic Research

This summary of the nature of psychic structure of course states the obvious to anyone with knowledge of psychodynamic theory. So commonplace are psychodynamic concepts and so wide their dissemination that one tends to take it for granted that they refer to a basic and universal characteristic of human psychological functioning. The psychodynamic model, derived initially from patients with psychoneurotic disorders, has, indeed, been applied to a widening sphere of both normal and psychopathological behavior, always with the assumption that unconscious processes play a major role in the production of clinical symptoms and observable behavior, and that understanding these unconscious forces will lead to an expanded understanding of the origins of the surface phenomenon.

When, for example, psychiatrists turned their attention nearly half a century ago to a formal clinical study of patients with psychosomatic disorders, they initially invoked the mechanism of hysterical symptom formation as the model for explaining the psychogenesis of psychosomatic disorders (Deutsch, 1959; Eissler, 1943; Lorand, 1943). They viewed the somatic symptom as a symbolic representation of repressed, unconscious mental elements. And, indeed, their clinical observations gave reason for doing so in some of the patients whom they investigated. That this mechanism of symptom formation can occur is evident in the details of Janet's patient, Marie, whose history we reviewed earlier. Marie, it will be recalled, suffered from a total suppression of her menses followed by a traumatic experience in connection with her first period, and when her menses reappeared five years later, each episode was invariably abnormally shortened. Although many of the symptoms associated with her menstrual disorder were classically hysterical in nature, the abnormality in her periods itself was clearly psychosomatic—that is, it was mediated by the autonomic-endocrine rather than the sensory-motor nervous system. At the same time, it was evident from psychological exploration that the form that her menstrual symptoms took was determined by and plastically represented unconscious memories of the initial traumatic event; the disappearance of the somatic symptoms when the underlying psychological contents were therapeutically modified confirmed their role in the psychogenesis of those symptoms.

As clinical psychosomatic research continued, however, it was discovered that hysterical mechanisms were not universally to be found in psychosomatic symptom formation. From their intensive clinical studies of a large number of patients with a variety of common psychosomatic disorders (e.g., peptic ulcer, ulcerative colitis, rheumatoid arthritis, hypertension) Alexander and his colleagues (1943, 1948, 1950) proposed a revised theoretical formulation that took into account the fact that hysterical mechanisms were often absent in the patients they examined. Alexander (1943) wrote:

> It seems advisable to differentiate between hysterical conversion and vegetative neurosis (i.e., a psychosomatic condition). Their similarities are rather superficial: both conditions are psychogenic, that is to say, they are caused ultimately by a chronic repressed or at least unrelieved emotional tension. The mechanisms involved, however, are fundamentally different both psychodynamically and physiologically. The hysterical conversion symptom is an attempt to relieve an emotional tension in a symbolic way; it is a symbolic expression of a definite

emotional content. This mechanism is restricted to the voluntary neuromuscular or sensory perceptive systems whose function is to express and relieve emotions. A vegetative neurosis consists of a psychogenic dysfunction of a vegetative organ which is not under control of the voluntary neuromuscular system. The vegetative symptom is not a substitute expression of the emotion, but its normal physiological concomitant. (p. 208)

Alexander's formulation differs significantly from the classical explanation of hysterical symptom formation. In the latter, cognitive and affective elements *together* combine to produce symptoms. In psychosomatic disorders, as Alexander conceived of them, affect alone results in dysfunction; the cognitive element is not a factor. Behind the psychosomatic symptoms one finds no ideas (which in hysterical disorders determine the form of a symptom that symbolizes the underlying conflict); one finds only affect, which as a result of repression is unable to expend itself as an emotional discharge over the usual channels of emotional expression. This damming up of affect should be contrasted with the usual process of emotional discharge that normally occurs when an affect is aroused. Ordinarily, for example, when one is angry, although one may consciously exert self-control over aggressive behavior, one indulges in vivid fantasies of angry response to the anger-provoking stimulus; one may verbalize one's anger in a variety of ways, and one experiences the feeling of rage—all of which gradually allows for the discharge of the affect and the restoration of psychic calm. In Alexander's formulation none of these elaborate psychic processes is set in motion either consciously or unconsciously. All that occurs in response to an environmental stimulus is an arousal of the autonomic component of the affect, *without any accompanying psychic elaboration,* and, as the autonomic discharge persists over time, it leads to chronic, ultimately pathological changes in the end organ innervated, thus producing somatic symptoms.

A Case of Peptic Ulcer—John G

It is not entirely clear from his writings why Alexander made these modifications in the traditional psychodynamic theory when he applied it to an explanation of the psychogenesis of psychosomatic symptoms. One suspects that it was, in part at least, because he found that the responses of many patients with psychosomatic disorders to an exploration of their possible conflicts was different from that of psychoneurotic patients, and that they revealed a constellation of behavior and psychological functioning markedly dissimilar to that of individuals with neurotic illness. By way of illustration of this difference, let us review the highlights of an initial psychiatric interview with John G, a 26-year-old married man who was hospitalized for the evaluation of the recurrence of peptic ulcer disease.

At the beginning of the interview, when the patient was asked about the nature of his illness, he spoke readily, volubly, and in detail about the onset and course of his symptoms. They had started, he said, some three years before with a sudden unheralded episode of acute abdominal distress that had led to emergency surgery during which a perforated duodenal ulcer was found and repaired. Subsequently the patient had had bouts of typical epigastric ulcer pain relieved by food and antacids, for an exacerbation of which he had recently been hospitalized. In addition to his readily given history of his illness, the patient was able to recount fluently the external events of his recent life, from which it became evident that he had been under considerable stress. When his ulcer had perforated, the patient had been working full-time in a factory to support himself and his wife, while he was simultaneously engaged in a course of graduate studies aiming toward a Ph.D. The patient had been considerably pressured by his busy schedule, by his financial worries, and by chronic marital trouble with a wife who required and demanded more attention than he felt able to give her. In the course of things, his wife developed bronchial asthma, which had added to the life stresses besetting him. When she had finally been hospitalized some weeks previously, the patient's own ulcer symptoms had worsened.

The patient was able to describe these factual events precisely and freely in a ready flow of well-chosen and easily spoken words. When, however, attention in the interview was focused on his emotional reactions to the stressful troubles in his life, the patient suddenly and dramatically became almost wordless. The whole character of the interview changed from a lively conversation to an interchange in which the doctor could only listen expectantly, sympathetically, and quietly as the patient's flow of words ceased and long silences ensued. The patient could say only that he was somewhat "nervous," that he felt a "bit guilty" about not being able to do more for his wife, that sometimes he would get "a little mad" at his wife's demands, or that there were periods when he was slightly "upset" or "depressed" in the face of his difficulties. But beyond offering these labeling words, he could in no way describe his inner experiences, what the feelings were like, or what characterized them. When asked, for example, to describe the guilty feeling, he replied after a silence of a half minute or more, "I really couldn't tell you how it would manifest itself." After a considerable exploration of the patient's feelings, including an attempt to get him to describe where he experienced them in his body, he finally commented that when he felt guilty or sad, it was "a kind of nauseated feeling." Similarly, being "mad" led to nausea and an "upset stomach," and being "nervous" was a "stomach thing too." From his description of these variously named feelings, in other words, it was evident that he experienced them all in exactly the same restricted, somatic way, and that he could not distinguish one from another.

Similarly, any attempt to elicit fantasies from the patient in association with the reported feelings was totally unproductive. Although, as we have seen, he could talk volubly about external events, things, and people, he was at a loss to recount any related fantasies. When asked, for example, what thoughts he had when he was "mad," he was silent for many seconds and finally replied, "I just think about the situation" (i.e., about the surrounding external events). No fantasies could be elicited from which one could infer the qualitative coloring (e.g., hostile, apprehensive, self-derogating) of the feelings he named. It was clear that he was in some diffuse way upset inwardly in the face of stressful events, but he could make no qualitative differentiation of the nature of his emotional responses. This, it should be noted, is quite unlike what we have observed in the patients described earlier, each of whom, although there were gaps in their conscious mental contents, manifested, even in an initial interview, a rich network of associations—memories, fantasies, events, emotional responses— that gave the observer a vivid picture of the quality and details of their inner turmoil and psychological conflicts.

The Alexithymia Syndrome: Observations and Hypotheses

Recent clinical investigation indicates that the behavior of John G is character-istic of many patients with psychosomatic disorders (Nemiah, 1978; Sifneos, 1973). It constitutes a readily recognized behavioral syndrome to which the term "alexithymia" (from the Greek meaning "no words for feelings") has been applied (Sifneos, 1972, p. 81). The alexithymia syndrome is characterized by two main features: (1) an inability to describe a feeling beyond using a standard stereotyped word for it, combined with an incapacity to differentiate among feelings; (2) a striking absence of fantasies, that is, of imagery determined by inner drives and affects. Instead, the patient's thought content is preoccupied with external environmental events, objects, and people; it is concrete, mundane, unimaginative, and dominated by imagery supplied by the external world—a form of thinking to which the term *pensée opératoire* has been applied (Marty & de M'Uzan, 1963). To paraphrase, one may say that the patient's thoughts are objectively determined rather than drive-directed; they reflect adaptive environ-mental concerns rather than creative, inner, fanciful imaginations.

How is this psychological syndrome to be understood and explained? To return to Alexander's theoretical formulation of psychosomatic symptom formation, it will be recalled that he modified the traditional dynamic explanation of neurotic symptoms by eliminating the cognitive elements and focusing on unconscious affect alone as the etiological factor in psychogenesis. It should be emphasized that despite this significant modification in the concept of symptom formation, Alexander retained the basic notion of psychological conflict; in his theoretical model, repressed, unconscious affects were the basic driving force underlying the appearance of psychosomatic disorders.

The Conflict Model

Alexander's model provides us with a reasonable hypothesis for understanding and explaining alexithymic behavior and psychosomatic symptom formation. It does not strain psychodynamic theory or stretch credibility to suggest that a massive degree of repression has so thoroughly removed affect and its associated mental elements from John G's consciousness that he is totally unaware of any feelings or fantasies even in their most derivative and disguised forms. One might accordingly postulate that what differentiates him from psychoneurotic patients and explains the dissimilarity in the clinical, psychological behavior of these two groups of patients is a quantitatively stronger and more extensive degree of repression. In neurotic patients, repression allows some derivative mental elements (fantasies, specific feelings) to emerge into consciousness, keeping only the core of the conflict out of awareness. In John G the greater strength and extent of his repression excludes all the elements, resulting in what clinically appears as alexithymic behavior.

This is, as we have said, a reasonable hypothesis, but it is *only* a hypothesis. When we state that John G is repressing *all* affect and fantasy, we are predicting that given certain procedures, we should be able to alter his defenses and psychological structure so that the hypothesized underlying mental elements would ultimately emerge into consciousness, where, once available both to the patient and to those to whom he communicates them, they would provide substantiating evidence of the initial predictions. In the neurotic patients whom we examined earlier, we could readily observe the emergence of such confirming, originally unconscious mental elements during the course of a single interview. The fact that unconscious material did not issue forth so readily in John G (and other psychosomatic patients), it could be argued, is merely a reflection of the greater power of his repressing forces. Had he been given more time over a prolonged course of psychotherapy, his initially unconscious affects and fantasies would have been uncovered.

Unfortunately for this hypothesis, clinical experience indicates that in patients with psychosomatic symptoms who are at the same time alexithymic, insight-oriented psychodynamic psychotherapy is ineffective (Karush & Daniels, 1969; Nemiah, 1971; Sifneos, 1975). Despite a prolonged course of therapy (though many such patients seem unable to understand what is wanted of them and drop out of treatment), the patients remain psychologically unchanged and do not develop a capacity for describing their feelings or for experiencing fantasies. Consequently, the observer is unable to recover those predicted mental elements whose emergence into the open is required to substantiate the hypothesis of repression, psychological conflict, and the dynamic psychogenesis of psychosomatic symptoms.

The Deficit Model

The observation of this fact has led some clinical investigators to suggest that the conflict model is not applicable to alexithymic psychosomatic patients (McDougall, 1974; Nemiah, 1977). It has been suggested instead that either as the result of ego repressions or developmental deficits, such patients lack the ego functions necessary for describing affect and creating fantasy. In this *deficit model,* alexithymic behavior is understood as resulting not from the repression of mental elements, but as the direct manifestation of absent ego functions. Similarly, in the context of the deficit model, symptom formation itself is viewed as involving different mechanisms from those seen as being operative in the conflict model. It is not that alexithymic psychosomatic patients, like patients with neurotic disorders, are not reacting to environmental stress, for indeed they are. The difference lies in the processes by which the stress is tranformed into symptoms. In neurotic patients, a high degree of psychic elaboration involving defenses and unconscious forces leads ultimately to a highly structured symptom that represents the outcome of the underlying psychological conflict. On the other hand, in psychosomatic patients who lack the ego functions required for the psychic elaboration of internal arousal following stress, the internal arousal is directly transformed without any psychic elaboration into pathological somatic symptoms. As McDougall (1974) puts it, the deficit model

> comprises an economic theory of psychosomatic transformation and the concept of a psychosomatic personality structure (as opposed to neurotic...structures), ...emphasis being laid upon urgent instinctual discharge which escapes psychic elaboration because of deficient representation and diminished affective responses: in short, an impoverishment of the capacity to symbolize instinctual demands and their conflict with reality, and to elaborate fantasy. Instinctual energy, bypassing the psyche, thus affects the soma directly, with catastrophic results. This particular theoretical approach to psychosomatic formations is in complete opposition to the theory of hysterical formation; the latter being the result of repressed fantasy elaborations while the former would result precisely from the lack of such psychic activity. (p. 445)

What, then, are the consequences of and the inferences to be drawn from these varying clinical observations and the different conceptual models constructed to explain them? In the first place, the clinical and psychological findings from the study of patients with psychosomatic disorders suggest that unconscious mental processes are *not* universally involved in the genesis of stress-related symptoms and disorders. This is a conclusion that is hard for many psychodynamically oriented clinicians to accept, since the concept of psychological conflict has become so central to modern psychiatric thinking that one automatically assumes that defensive mechanisms are at work whenever specific mental elements (e.g., feelings and fantasies) normally found in response to stress are absent in a given individual. Yet, as we have seen, in many psychosomatic patients, the unconscious elements predicted by the conflict model cannot be detected despite thorough psychological exploration; one is consequently forced to conclude that in such patients the conflict hypothesis does not apply and that a deficit model is a better explanation of the observed facts.

TWO MODELS OF THE MIND

The Transformations of Stress

One is led by this conclusion to a further proposition about mental functioning and its role in the process of transforming environmental stress into pathological symptoms. It appears, in psychological terms, that there are two basic kinds of psychological structure. In many individuals, as we have noted in our extensive examination of neurotic symptom formation, one finds a complex psychic organization of drives, feelings, fantasies, memories of past experiences and relationships, and other mental functions, all of which are subject to defensive mechanisms that render many of the mental elements unconscious. However, even though unconscious, they continue to be active outside of the individual's awareness and stamp their imprint on consciously experienced and observable behavior patterns and symptoms. Stress, in other words, activates a richly elaborated set of psychic processes, partly conscious, partly unconscious, that determines the ultimate response to that stress—often in the form of a neurotic symptom. By contrast, however, there are many individuals in whom this elaborate structure of psychological functions and processes *does not exist.* Subjected to the arousal prompted by an environmental stress, they have no psychic apparatus over which to process, modulate, and shape that arousal, which is consequently short-circuited directly into the somatic symptoms that constitute a psychosomatic disorder. It must be emphasized that both types of individuals are reacting to stress; the difference lies in the internal processes of transformation that lead in each to a distinctly different form of response—that is, to either a neurotic or a psychosomatic disorder. In the former, unconscious factors play a psychopathological role in symptom production; in the latter they do not.

The Deficit Model and Brain Function

It should be emphasized that denying the role of unconscious psychological conflict in the formation of many psychosomatic symptoms does not necessarily mean abandoning an understanding of psychosomatic disorders within a theoretical psychological framework. Indeed the deficit model is couched in psychological terms that evoke the notion of the absence of ego functions and defects in the psychological structure—a conceptualization that is currently much in vogue in the extension of psychoanalytic thinking to include object-relations theory (Kohut, 1971; Kernberg, 1975; Balint, 1979). At the same time, it should be noted that structural psychological concepts are ideationally close to concepts involving *physiological* structure. And, indeed, psychosomatic investigations have proposed physiological explanations for psychosomatic symptom formation. MacLean (1949) many years ago suggested that such symptoms resulted from "disconnections" between the "visceral brain" (now called the limbic system) and the cerebral cortex—the assumption being that the visceral brain was central to the initial mediation of emotional arousal stemming from environmental stress and that the cortex, especially the frontal areas, underlay the processes of higher psychic elaboration. More recently it has been proposed that disturbances in the mesolimbic dopamine tracts or in the functional relations of the right and left hemispheres set the stage for the production of both the alexithymic syndrome and psychosomatic symptoms (Nemiah, 1975; Shipko, 1982). In this connection, the clinical observations of Hoppe and Bogen (1977) are of interest, indicating that following commissurotomy for intractable epilepsy, individuals develop the alexithymia syndrome. Similarly, the Heibergs' (1977) genetic studies revealing a statistically higher concordance for alexithymic characteristics in monozygous as compared with dizygous twin pairs points to the possible relevance of brain structures in this syndrome. And psychological investigations of Frankel et al. (1977) provide experimental evidence in favor of a dichotomy in the pattern of mental functioning. Using standard measures of hypnotizability, he and his colleagues have shown that individuals with alexithymic characteristics score at the lower end of the scale. This is, of course, in contrast to the known high degree of hypnotizability of neurotic patients, especially those with hysterical and phobic disorders. These findings indicate the presence in neurotic patients of the capacity for dissociation and the unconscious mental processes related to neurotic symptom formation and their absence in alexithymic patients, whose psychological structure (or lack of it) leads to stress-related psychosomatic disorders.

It is evident that the recent work cited here is preliminary and that although it is the subject of a growing body of investigation and literature, the concept of alexithymia and its relation to psychosomatic illness remain tentative and by no means completely elucidated. Not all patients with psychosomatic illness, as noted earlier, manifest the alexithymia syndrome; indeed some clearly have the capacity for the higher psychic elaboration of the arousal resulting from external stress and exhibit mechanisms of psychosomatic formation similar to those found in individuals with neurotic disorders. At the same time, the recognition that unconscious processes are not universal in the pathogenesis of stress-related illness not only focuses attention on alternate psychological mechanisms of symptom formation but paves the way for physiological investigations that will extend our understanding of the psychophysiological correlates of the processes involved in the transformation of stress into psychosomatic illnesses.

CONCLUSION

The systematic study of unconscious mental processes during the past hundred years has taught us a great deal about the nature of the human mind and the psychogenesis of emotional illness. In the limited space of this chapter we have been able to touch only briefly on the highlights of modern psychodynamic knowledge and theory. We have reviewed the nature of unconscious mentation, of psychic conflict, and of psychological growth and development, and we have seen how these result in the creation of a complex psychic structure which underlies the development of disturbed human relationships and the production of the symptoms of psychological disorders. We have also seen that more recent clinical investigation, especially of the psychosomatic process, suggests that some psychogenic disorders may result from a lack of psychic structure rather than being the product of psychological conflict.

In our preoccupation with the psychological understanding of emotional illness, we must not lose sight of the recent investigations into the biology of mental illnesses, which have led to striking advances in our knowledge of the etiology and in the effectiveness of our treatment of patients suffering from them. Indeed the enthusiasm over these biological discoveries has tended recently to overshadow our appreciation of the psychodynamic aspects of emotional disorder. While swings of the pendulum are perhaps inevitable in the world of human thought, clearly the ultimate explanation of psychiatric disease must come from a synthesis of both biological and psychological observations and theory, the creation of which is the central task immediately before us. In any such synthesis, the body of observations based on a thoroughgoing appreciation of the role of psychological conflict and unconscious mental processes must be a full and equal partner.

NOTE

1. Quotes from Janet and Flournoy translated by author.

REFERENCES

Alexander, F. Fundamental concepts of psychosomatic research, *Psychosomatic Medicine*, 1943, *5*, 205.

Alexander, F. *Psychosomatic medicine*. New York: Norton, 1950.

Alexander, F., & French, T. *Studies in psychosomatic medicine*. New York: Ronald Press, 1948.

Balint, M. *The basic fault*. New York: Brunner/Mazel, 1979.

Bonaparte, M., et al. *The origins of psychoanalysis*. New York: Basic Books, 1954.

Breuer, J., & Freud, S. On the psychical mechanism of hysterical phenomena. In J. Strachey (Ed.), *The standard edition of the complete psychological works of Sigmund Freud* (Vol. 2). London: Hogarth Press, 1955. (Originally published 1893.)

Breuer, J., & Freud, S. Studies on hysteria. In J. Strachey (Ed.), *The standard edition of the complete psychological works of Sigmund Freud* (Vol. 2). London: Hogarth Press, 1955. (Originally published 1895.)

Balint, M. *The basic fault: Therapeutic aspects of regression*. London: Tavistock, 1968.

Deutsch, F. (Ed.). *On the mysterious leap from the mind to the body*. New York: International Universities Press, 1959.

Eissler, K. Some psychiatric aspects of anorexia nervosa demonstrated by a case report. *Psychoanalytic Review*, 1943, *30*, 121.

Flournoy, T. Une mystique moderne. *Archives Psychologiques* (Génève), 1915, *15*, 1.

Frankel, F., et al. The relationship between hypnotizability and alexithymia. *Psychotherapy and Psychosomatics*, 1977, *23*, 172.

Freud, A. *The ego and the mechanisms of defence*. London: Hogarth Press, 1942.

Freud, S. The neuro-psychoses of defense. In J. Strachey (Ed.), *The standard edition of the complete psychological works of Sigmund Freud* (Vol. 3). London: Hogarth Press, 1962. (Originally published 1894.)

Freud, S. On the grounds for detaching a particular syndrome from neurasthenia under the description "Anxiety Neurosis." In J. Strachey (Ed.), *The standard edition of the complete psychological works of Sigmund Freud* (Vol. 3). London: Hogarth Press, 1962. (Originally published 1895.)

Freud, S. The aetiology of hysteria. In J. Strachey (Ed.), *The standard edition of the complete psychological works of Sigmund Freud* (Vol. 3). London: Hogarth Press, 1962. (Originally published 1896.)(a)

Freud, S. Further remarks on the neuro-psychoses of defence. In J. Strachey (Ed.), *The standard edition of the complete psychological works of Sigmund Freud* (Vol. 3). London: Hogarth Press, 1962. (Originally published 1896.)(b)

Freud, S. *The interpretation of dreams.* In J. Strachey (Ed.), *The standard edition of the complete psychological works of Sigmund Freud* (Vols. 4–5). London: Hogarth Press, 1953. (Originally published 1900.)

Freud, S. Three essays on the theory of sex. In J. Strachey (Ed.), *The standard edition of the complete psychological works of Sigmund Freud* (Vol. 7). London: Hogarth Press, 1953. (Originally published 1905.)

Freud, S. Inhibitions, symptoms and anxiety. In J. Strachey (Ed.), *The standard edition of the complete psychological works of Sigmund Freud* (Vol. 20). London: Hogarth Press, 1959. (Originally published 1926.)

Heiberg, A., & Heiberg, A. Alexithymia—an inherited trait? A study of twins. *Psychotherapy and Psychosomatics,* 1977, *28,* 221.

Hoppe, K., & Bogen, J. Alexithymia in twelve commissurotomized patients. *Psychotherapy and Psychosomatics,* 1977, *28,* 148.

Janet, P. *L'automatisme psychologique.* Paris: Alcan, 1889.

Janet, P., & Raymond, F. *Les obsessions et la psychasthénie.* Paris: Alcan, 1903.

Karush, A., & Daniels, G. The response to psychotherapy in chronic ulcerative colitis. *Psychosomatic Medicine,* 1969, *31,* 201.

Kernberg, O. *Borderline conditions and pathological narcissism.* New York: Jason Aronson, 1975.

Kohut, H. *The analysis of the self.* New York: International Universities Press, 1971.

Lorand, S. Anorexia nervosa: Report of a case. *Psychosomatic Medicine,* 1943, *5,* 282.

MacLean, P. Psychosomatic disease and the "visceral brain." *Psychosomatic Medicine,* 1949, *11,* 338.

Marty, P., & de M'Uzan, M. La pensée opératoire. *Revue Française de Psychoanalyse,* 1963, *27*(Supplement), 1345.

McDougall, J. The psychosoma and the psychoanalytic process. *International Review of Psychoanalysis,* 1974, *1,* 437.

Nemiah, J. The psychological management and treatment of patients with peptic ulcer. *Advances in Psychosomatic Medicine,* 1971, *6,* 169.

Nemiah, J. Denial revisited: Reflections on psychosomatic theory. *Psychotherapy and Psychosomatics,* 1975, *28,* 199.

Nemiah, J. Alexithymia: Theoretical considerations. *Psychotherapy and Psychosomatics,* 1977, *28,* 199.

Nemiah, J. Alexithymia and psychosomatic illness. *Journal of Continuing Education in Psychiatry,* 1978, October, 25.

Prince, M. *The unconscious.* New York: Macmillan, 1924.

Schreber, D. *Memoirs of my nervous illness.* (I. Macalpine and R. Hunter, trans.) London: Dawson, 1955. (Originally published 1903.)

Shipko, S. Further reflections on psychosomatic theory. *Psychotherapy and Psychosomatics,* 1982, *37,* 82.

Sifneos, P. *Short-term psychotherapy and emotional crisis.* Cambridge: Harvard University Press, 1972.

Sifneos, P. The prevalence of "alexithymic" characteristics in psychosomatic patients. *Psychotherapy and Psychosomatics,* 1973, *22,* 255.

Sifneos, P. Problems of psychotherapy of patients with alexithymic characteristics and physical disease. *Psychotherapy and Psychosomatics,* 1975, *26,* 65.

CHAPTER 3

Development of the Structures
of Unconscious Thought

KURT W. FISCHER AND SANDRA L. PIPP

When Freud put forth the psychodynamic concept of the unconscious, he placed it firmly within a developmental perspective. Unconscious processes are founded, he argued, on the developmentally primitive mind. A young infant functions in a fundamentally unconscious way, and unconscious processes in an older child or adult are to be traced back to the primitive functioning of the infant or young child. Indeed most psychopathology originates in traumatic experiences in infancy and childhood, when most of the mind is naturally unconscious (Freud, 1900/1953, 1911/1958, 1915/1957).

Within the traditional psychoanalytic framework, then, the unconscious is present at an early age and shows little or no development. Thus the unconscious thought of the 30 year old is said to be identical in many ways to that of the 3 year old or even to that of the young infant. This absence of development is especially characteristic of primary process, which is the standard mode of functioning of unconscious thought.

Since Freud formulated psychoanalysis, substantial progress has been made in cognitive psychology, and the newer conceptualizations would seem to merit integration with Freud's original insights. How should unconscious processes be conceptualized, and how does their development relate to the systematic cognitive changes that occur during childhood? Several investigators have called for an integration of Freud's work with cognitive-developmental approaches (e.g., Greenspan, 1979; Wolff, 1960, 1967). Their general argument has been that

We would like to thank the following people for many hours of discussion that have contributed directly to this chapter: Helen Hand, Susan Harter, Phillip Shaver, Louise Silvern, Michael Westerman, and Peter Wolff. In addition, we are thankful to several colleagues who have recently contributed to our thinking on unconscious processes: Donna Elmendorf, Melvin Feffer, Elaine Jackowitz, and Kathy Purcell. We also appreciate the assistance of Denise Hall and Marilyn Pelot in preparing this chapter. Preparation of the chapter was supported by a grant from the Carnegie Corporation of New York to the first author and a grant from the Foundation for Child Development to the second author. The statements made and views expressed are solely the responsibility of the authors.

Freud's model of the mind does not really mesh with his insights about the dynamic functioning of conscious and unconscious processes. Approaches such as those of Piaget (1946/1951, 1970), Werner (1957), and Dewey (1948) promise to help resolve the inconsistencies in Freud's model. Some progress has been made in reformulating psychoanalysis so that it is more consistent with the insights of cognitive-developmental psychology (e.g., A. Freud, 1966; Kernberg, 1976; Mahler, Pine, & Bergman, 1975), but integration of the two approaches has proceeded slowly.

In recent years, the pace of progress seems to have quickened, and major strides have been made toward a general integration of cognitive psychology and psychoanalysis (e.g., Feffer, 1982; Hilgard, 1977; Lester, 1983). The result has been fundamental change in both approaches. For example, the extreme rationalism of Piaget, with his emphasis on logic as the defining characteristic of intelligence, is giving way to a view of the mind as more dynamic, emotional, and fractionated. The traditional psychoanalytic equation of unconscious functioning with the developmentally primitive mind is giving way to the view that there are continuing developments in both conscious and unconscious processes throughout childhood and perhaps in adulthood as well.

In this chapter we sketch an approach that is intended both to incorporate insights such as these and to place them in a general framework for analyzing the development of conscious and unconscious processes. The framework must be considered preliminary and tentative: In a sense, it is a plan for approaching the integration of psychoanalysis and cognition, although it is articulated enough to allow us to make many specific, testable predictions. Many of the "new" ideas in the approach have been formulated in the neo-Freudian literature of the last 30 years, and others that are inconsistent with most psychodynamic theory seem to be consistent with the actual practices of mental health workers.

Indeed, even Freud's work contained many of the fundamental ideas that we are elaborating. For example, although his explicit theory of mental processes and his analysis of primary process assumed that unconscious functioning was developmentally primitive (Freud, 1911/1958, 1915/1957), his interpretations of particular phenomena and cases clearly demonstrated the existence of developmentally advanced forms of unconscious functioning (e.g., Freud, 1900/1953). We believe that the framework put forward in this article is more consistent with psychodynamic *practices* than the classical psychodynamic framework and most of its derivatives.

We argue that unconscious thought does not remain static during childhood but demonstrates systematic developments that are structurally parallel to the developments in conscious thought. With development, the capacity for integrating components of thought and behavior grows, and at the same time the capacity for active fractionation increases (e.g., dissociation and repression). The mind is therefore both fractionated and integrated; there is neither a unitary conscious system nor a unitary unconscious one, but there are conscious and unconscious components that can be coordinated or kept separate.

One key to understanding the fractionation and integration is the organization of a person's skills. The framework that we use for analyzing this organization is called skill theory (Fischer, 1980; Fischer & Pipp, 1984). The organization of a skill is affected by factors in both the person and the environment, including (1) the contexts in which a skill is acquired, (2) the developmental level of the skill, (3) the affective relation of the skill to the self, and (4) the functional support provided by the situation in which the skill is used. Within this transactional framework, primary-process thought occurs whenever there is a gap between the demands of the task or situation and the level of the skill that the person brings to bear upon it (Feffer, 1982). Such gaps commonly arise from many different sources, including (1) the natural fractionation of the mind, (2) dissociation that is motivated, and (3) the inability to deal with a task because it requires a higher level skill than the person is capable of.

THE CONSTRUCTED UNCONSCIOUS AND ITS DEVELOPMENT

What is the unconscious? For Freud, the unconscious is a section of the mind, a repository of drive impulses and memories (Holt, 1967, 1976; Wachtel, 1977).[1] The memories stored in the unconscious are like photographs or tape recordings —accurate copies of what was originally perceived. According to this doctrine of "immaculate perception" (Schimek, 1975), children passively record events that take place around them and lay down copies of these events in the mind. When the person tries to bring forth the memories, they are subject to distortion by impulses within the unconscious. But in their original, recorded state, they are perfect, "immaculate" copies.

This view of perception and memory was widely held when Freud was formulating psychoanalysis. In recent decades, however, it has been replaced as a result of advances in research on cognition and perception (Bruner, 1957; Dewey, 1948; Feffer, 1982; Loftus & Loftus, 1980; Neisser, 1976; Piaget, 1983; Wolff, 1967). The person is seen not as a passive recorder of events, but instead as an active constructor of them: An object is perceived through the processes by which the person can act upon it. Likewise for memory, a remembered event is a reconstruction.

The processes of construction and reconstruction exist in infants, children, and adults, but they vary systematically with age. How a person can construct objects or events changes dramatically with developmental level (see Case, 1980; Fischer, 1980; Piaget, 1970). At each successive level, the same event can be coded, remembered, and thought about differently.

Within the constructivist framework, what does the unconscious become? One of the main points of this chapter is that the unconscious is a process of thought, not a repository for memories and drive impulses. Components of thought that need to be coordinated, related, or differentiated for a specific task, issue, or situation remain separated or dissociated. As a result, some potential implications of the thoughts remain not created, not under the person's control, not in awareness, or unconscious. For Freud, the unconscious has processes associated with it: Veridically stored memories are *distorted* by impulse-driven processes that do not change with development. For the position we are presenting, the unconscious is a type of process—a way of *constructing* perceptions, memories and other kinds of cognition that changes systematically with development. It is not a portion of the mind. Indeed, instead of *the* unconscious, it is more appropriately referred to as "unconscious thought," since it is not a unitary entity but a way of processing information.

One key to understanding the type of process that produces unconscious thought, we will argue, is analysis of mental processes within a developmental perspective. Freud had an important insight when he identified unconscious structures as developmentally primitive (Freud, 1900/1953, 1911/1958, 1915/1957); but unconscious structures can both be developmentally primitive and show developmental change. Repression in a 5 year old, for example, will typically have a different form from repression in a 30 year old, even though both forms are developmentally primitive for a person of that age. This combination of developmental primitiveness with developmental change is fundamental to the argument put forth in this chapter.

Behavior shows unconscious structures whenever there is a gap between the developmental level of skill necessary for a particular task and the level that the person brings to bear upon the task (Feffer, 1982). Such a gap produces behavior that is developmentally primitive in that it is not advanced enough to deal with the task. This primitive behavior shows the characteristics of unconscious thought (primary process) as traditionally defined, such as condensation, displacement, and wish fulfillment, and consequently we label it "unconscious thought."

Developmental primitiveness need not be equated with functioning like an infant or young child, however: When the task requires a very high developmental level and the person can function only at a level slightly below what is required, the level of the person's behavior will be relatively high even though it involves an unconscious structure. Consequently, people can show developmental advances in unconscious structures at the same time that their behavior remains developmentally primitive in terms of the requirements of the task.

Our focus is on the set of behaviors that are classified as unconscious within psychoanalysis and other psychodynamic perspectives, behaviors that are not only primitive, confused, disorganized, or inadequate but also affect-laden. In traditional psychoanalysis, primitiveness or disorganization in the thought of older children and adults is inevitably tied to affective impulses. In the present framework, on the other hand, primitiveness or disorganization is characteristic of a wider range of thought, some of which is affect-laden and some of which is not: Unconscious thought can occur independently of affect. A 5 year old's conceptual confusion over the amount of water poured from one glass to another or a 30 year old's confusion over the nature of molecules will fit the most general meaning of unconscious thought as well as the fear-ridden delusions of a paranoid schizophrenic. Thus the joining of primitiveness with affect becomes a special case of unconscious processing. Before the relation of affect to unconscious thought can be explained, however, it is necessary to outline the theory we are using to analyze the organization of behavior.

A STRUCTURAL-DEVELOPMENTAL APPROACH: SKILL THEORY

The assumption that unconscious thought does not develop has been called into question by a number of neo-Freudians (e.g., Holt, 1967, 1976; Rapaport, 1951; Schimek, 1975; Wolff, 1960), but there has been less consensus about how to portray the development of unconscious thought. What seems to be needed is a framework that provides general tools for analyzing the structures of unconscious thought and how they change with development (Wolff, 1967). We propose a structural-developmental approach based on skill theory (Fischer, 1980; Fischer & Pipp, 1984) for analyzing how both conscious and unconscious thought develops. Many of the assumptions and arguments in this approach follow not only from skill theory but also from a number of other recent cognitive-developmental theories, including those of Biggs and Collis (1982), Case (1980), Halford and Wilson (1980), and Siegler (1981).

Skills: Natural Fractionation and Potential Integration

According to this framework, the mind is naturally fractionated, dissociated, or separated into pieces, because people always acquire specific skills in particular contexts and for distinct emotional states. Skills are organized in terms of context and state, and they do not automatically generalize to potentially related contexts and states. When a person learns to walk on the ground, he cannot automatically walk in snowshoes through deep snow. When a child comes to understand one situation where his mother acts nice to him and another situation where his mother acts mean to him, he does not automatically relate those two understandings.

As the latter example implies, the emotional state of the individual knower is a potent organizer of skills. When two experiences occur in similar situations but involve different emotions, they will be organized separately (Bower, 1981). The child whose mother acts first nice and then mean builds two distinct skills for understanding her behavior, as if there were two separate mothers—a good one and a bad one (Harter, 1983; Kernberg, 1976; Mahler et al., 1975; Sullivan, 1953). Such affective splitting leads to the acquisition of dissociated skills that could logically be integrated because they refer to one adult in one situation.

Specific skills can be generalized to additional contexts, and separate skills from different contexts can be integrated; but people must work to achieve generalization or integration: Skills are not automatically or easily generalized or integrated. Consequently, even when people have skills appropriate for a task, they frequently fail to use the skills and thereby function below the level required by the task. Because fractionation routinely produces such a gap between task and skill, unconscious functioning is common.

The capacity to integrate or generalize—and thus to move beyond the unconscious thought of the young child—develops through a series of hierarchically organized cognitive levels defined by specific types of skill structures. The structures of the levels provide tools for describing not only how conscious, rational thought develops, but also how unconscious, irrational thought develops. Indeed we propose that levels in the development of the structures of unconscious thought directly parallel levels in the development of the structures of conscious thought. Consequently, even when people develop beyond the types of unconscious thought characteristic of the young child, they still can demonstrate other types of unconscious thought, ones that are more complex.

The specificity of skills to particular domains and states means that the development of one skill to a certain level is typically independent of the development of a second skill from a different domain or state. Understanding mother's nice behavior at a certain level does not imply that mother's mean behavior will be understood at the same level. Across domains and states, unevenness is the rule in development (Biggs & Collis, 1982; Fischer, 1980; Flavell, 1971). This is what Piaget (1941) calls *décalage horizontal*. It is so pervasive that in scores of studies apparently minor changes in task or procedure have routinely changed a child's level in developmental assessments.

How, then, can behaviors be categorized in terms of developmental levels? In what sense do two behaviors belong to the same level if they do not develop at the same point in time? The answer we have proposed lies in the concept of *optimal level* (Fischer & Pipp, 1984): Children have an upper limit on the complexity of skills that they can construct and control. That limit is characterized in terms of one of the series of developmental levels. A task or issue that requires children to build a skill beyond their optimal level cannot be solved. Because this limit is general across domains, skills that are at optimal level will develop in close synchrony. When a child moves to a new optimal level, however, most skills will still exist below it. Gradually, the child will construct more and more skills at the upper limit until many behaviors will reflect that level, but a large number of skills will always remain at lower levels. A child's behaviors, therefore, can never be characterized in terms of a single developmental level. Instead, they vary across a range of levels below the optimal one.

According to this framework, the fractionation or dissociation that typifies unconscious thought is a fundamental characteristic of the mind: Skills are separate unless the person works to integrate them. Moreover, the distribution of an individual's skills across a range of levels and the splitting effect of emotions act to increase the degree of fractionation across domains. Because of this natural separateness of domains, the elimination of fractionation in one domain will not typically have an effect on fractionation in other domains.

Tiers

Developmental levels occur in cycles that are called "tiers," which capture the largest scale of reorganization in childhood. Between 3 months of age and adulthood, there are three successive tiers, each involving vastly different types of skills. In describing the tiers and levels, we will use examples of behaviors involving the categories of good and bad, as defined emotionally. These examples were chosen because they relate directly to the role of emotional organization in unconscious processes. We will use them throughout the chapter to illustrate unconscious development. The analyses of categories of good and bad are based on the research of Hand (1981a), Harter (1977, 1982), and Fischer, Hand, Watson, Van Parys, and Tucker (in press), as well as object relations theory (Kernberg, 1976; Mahler, Pine, & Bergman, 1975; Sullivan, 1953).

The first tier encompasses *sensorimotor actions* and develops in the first two years of life. Babies understand their world through the actions and perceptions they can perform on things—how they can grasp, touch, feel, look at, or hear something. Although cognitive-developmental research has primarily emphasized how infants learn to manipulate parts of the physical world, as in searching for hidden objects, there is an obvious affective component to infant experience, which has been captured in various psychodynamic descriptions. One of the main dimensions along which skills seem to be organized is whether they involve pleasure and comfort or pain and discomfort. This dimension is often described as involving separate categories of good and bad, such as good nipple and bad nipple in early infancy, good mother and bad mother or good self and bad self in later infancy (Kernberg, 1976; Sullivan, 1953).

In the second tier, which first emerges at approximately 1½ to 2 years of age, children develop *representations.* They can mentally evoke thoughts of concrete objects, events, or people instead of simply acting upon them or experiencing them. For example, children can pretend that a doll is carrying out an action such as walking or eating, which the doll cannot do on its own, of course. They can think about what a person might do surreptitiously to hide an object. In language they develop a large vocabulary, and they can begin to speak in simple sentences, which requires the structure of a representational skill (Fischer & Corrigan, 1981). In general, skills change from sensorimotor categories involving one's own actions and experiences to representational categories for concrete people or things. For the dimension of good and bad, the child can understand, among other things, how someone can be nice in a social interaction, or how they can be mean.

At 10 to 12 years of age, children enter the third tier as they develop the capacity for *abstractions,* which deal with intangible attributes for broad categories of objects, people, or events. Children and adolescents can understand concepts such as justice, honesty, kindness, responsibility, and conformity and can begin to construct the notion of an unconscious (Broughton, 1978; Chandler, Paget, & Koch, 1978; Selman, 1980). Along the dimension of good and bad, the individual moves from concrete representations to more general affect-laden abstractions, such as benevolent and malevolent. The developmental levels hypothesized for the abstract tier go far beyond Piaget's (1970) period of formal operations, which is said to emerge at 10 to 12 years and to end major cognitive-developmental change. The abstract tier involves a sequence of four developmental levels, the last of which emerges at 25 years of age and continues to develop for many years. Major cognitive change thus continues well into adulthood (Fischer, Hand, & Russell, 1983).

Levels

Within each of the three tiers, there are four developmental levels. Table 3.1 shows the levels and their grouping into tiers, and Figure 3.1 provides a geometric metaphor for the cycle of levels within a tier.

The levels describe a scale of reorganization that is smaller than that of the tiers but still substantial. The levels also explain how skills at one tier are gradually transformed to produce skills at the next tier. Movement from level to level occurs when the child can intercoordinate two or more skills at a prior level to form a skill at the next one, as shown for adjacent levels in Table 3.1 and Figure 3.1. To illustrate the levels within a tier, we will use as examples the development of the concepts of nice and mean in the representational tier, which will demonstrate how unconscious affective splitting occurs naturally in the course of development within a tier. As we use the term "splitting," it refers to building skills that are separated because of their affective content, especially "good" and "bad."[2] These examples are based primarily on the research of Hand (1981a), Harter (1977, 1982, 1983), and Harter and Buddin (1983) as well as the analyses of Fischer, Hand, Watson, Van Parys, & Tucker (in press).

At the first level, the person can control variations in only a *single set* at a time—one action, one representation, or one abstraction, as shown in Table 3.1. With the representational tier, for example, children can control single representations, such as a representation for a nice person, which typically develops at 1½ to 2 years of age. A minimal case of such a representation in pretend play involves the child making a doll perform a single nice action, such as kissing or saying "I like you." A more complex instance of a representation for a nice person at the same level includes two or more nice actions carried out together, as when a doll kisses another doll, gives it some candy, and says "I like you." In the minimal case for a single representation for a mean person, the doll carries out a single mean action, such as hitting. The more complex instance includes several mean actions carried out together, such as hitting, taking away candy, and saying "I hate you." Notice that in all these behaviors, there is a second doll or other agent toward which the nice or mean actions are directed, but it is merely a recipient of the actions. It plays no active role in the interaction.

Because children can control only a single representation at the first level, they are incapable of integrating or coordinating two representations. This incapacity means that they cannot, for example, compare the category of nice with that of mean. Consequently, when feelings are paramount, they are forced into what is sometimes called "affective splitting": Thoughts about nice and mean behaviors in the same person (self or other) cannot be integrated but are organized separately, almost as if two separate people were involved, such as a good mother and a bad mother, a fairy godmother and a witch (Kernberg, 1976; Mahler et al.,

TABLE 3.1. Ten Levels of Skill Structures

Level	Name of Structure	Sensorimotor[a] Tier	Representational[a] Tier	Abstract Tier	Estimated Age Region of Emergence
1	Single sensorimotor action	$[A]$ or $[\mathbf{B}]$			3–4 mo
2	Sensorimotor mapping	$[A \longrightarrow \mathbf{B}]$			7–8 mo
3	Sensorimotor system	$[A_{G,H} \longleftrightarrow \mathbf{B}_{G,H}]$			11–13 mo
4	System of sensorimotor systems, which is a single representation	$\begin{bmatrix} A \rightarrow \mathbf{B} \\ C \rightarrow \mathbf{D} \end{bmatrix} \equiv [R]$			20–24 mo
5	Representational mapping		$[R \longrightarrow T]$		4–5 yr
6	Representational system		$[R_{J,K} \longleftrightarrow T_{J,K}]$		6–7½ yr
7	System of representational systems, which is a single abstraction		$\begin{bmatrix} R \rightarrow T \\ V \rightarrow X \end{bmatrix} \equiv [\mathcal{E}]$		10–12 yr
8	Abstract mapping			$[\mathcal{E} \longrightarrow \mathcal{T}]$	14–16 yr
9	Abstract system			$[\mathcal{E}_{A,B} \longleftrightarrow \mathcal{T}_{A,B}]$	18–20 yr
10	System of abstract systems, which is a single principle			$\begin{bmatrix} \mathcal{E} \rightarrow \mathcal{T} \\ \mathcal{G} \rightarrow \mathcal{H} \end{bmatrix}$	24–26 yr[b]

Note: Boldface capital letters designate sensorimotor actions, italic capital letters designate representations, and script capital letters designate abstractions. Each action, representation, or abstraction is a set. Multiple subscripts designate differentiated components of a set; whenever there is a horizontal arrow, two or more subsets exist by definition, even when they are not expressly shown. Long straight lines and arrows designate a relation between sets or systems. Brackets designate a single skill.

[a] Sensorimotor structures continue after Level 4, and representational structures after Level 7, but the formulas become so complex that they have been omitted. To fill them in, simply replace each representation with the sensorimotor formula for Level 4 and replace each abstraction with the representational formula for Level 7.

[b] Since little research has been done on development at this level, this age region must be considered highly tentative.

LEVEL

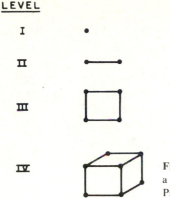

Figure 3.1.   A geometric metaphor for the cycle of levels within a tier (reprinted from Fischer, 1980). Copyright American Psychological Association.

1975)[2]. The next level constitutes a major step toward overcoming this limitation. (See also Case, 1984, concerning the importance of moving to the second level in a cycle.)

The second level of the representational tier emerges when the child can intercoordinate single representations to form a representational *mapping,* a relation between two or more representations. By approximately 3½ to 4 years, a representation of nice can be coordinated with a representation of mean to produce the understanding that nice and mean are opposites. Of course, children's emotions will reflect the opposition of nice and mean from an early age, because the dimension of good and bad is part of the human emotional makeup (Kernberg, 1976; Osgood, Suci, & Tannenbaum, 1957; Sullivan, 1953). Only after a mapping is constructed, however, will the child be able to represent the opposition; finally then, the opposition will be conscious.

Other types of relations can also be produced with representational mappings. For example, nice behavior in one doll can be related to nice behavior in a second doll, demonstrating what is called a reciprocal nice interaction. The first doll is nice to the second one, perhaps sharing a toy and saying something pleasant; and then expressly because of that action, the second doll is nice in return. Reciprocal mean interaction likewise requires a representational mapping. The general type of interaction embodied in these instances involves one-dimensional social influence, because the reciprocal interaction is based only on a single category such as niceness or meanness.

Although representational mappings mark a cognitive advance, affective splitting is still common at this level. In one-dimensional social influence, social interactions are organized in terms of a single affect: nice begets nice, or mean begets mean. Similarly, understanding the opposition of nice and mean maintains a split. Yet in the midst of the many mapping skills that show such splitting, integration of opposite emotions also begins. With a mapping, children can coordinate nice and mean (or other affective opposites) as joint characteristics of a single person. Mother can be both good and bad at the same time

(Mahler et al., 1975), and for the self too, positive and negative emotions can be integrated. Such integration is sometimes evident in the aftermath of strong negative emotions. One 4 year old had a temper tantrum in which he told his father, "I hate you!" Half an hour later, at a calmer time, he qualified what he had said, "Daddy, I love you even when I say, 'I hate you.'"

At the third level, the child can combine several mappings to produce a *system,* a relation between two or more subsets of two or more sets. Representational systems become common by 6 to 7 years of age, when children can, for example, relate both nice and mean behavior in one person to reciprocal nice and mean behavior in a second person. This type of interaction is called two-dimensional social influence. The first person is simultaneously both nice and mean to the second one, who reciprocates with appropriate nice and mean behaviors. For example, in pretend play with two boy dolls, a child can make the first doll try to initiate friendship with the second one by hitting him (as boys often do, in mock aggression) while at the same time saying "I like you. Let's be friends." The second one notes the discrepancy between hitting and liking and says that he would like to be the first one's friend but only if the hitting stops.

This third level marks another major step in being able to coordinate multiple contradictory emotions, since opposite emotions are now easily understood as coexisting in the same people during social interactions. At the previous level, children could relate nice and mean behavior in a single person, such as the good-and-bad mother; but they could not deal with both categories in two people at the same time, as when the self and the mother act both nice and mean simultaneously in an interaction with each other.

With the development of systems at the third level, similar changes in the complexity of relations between many types of physical and social categories besides emotions also occur. Children can understand intersections of social roles in which one agent fills two roles in interaction with a second agent appropriately filling two complementary roles. For instance, a married couple can each be both a parent and a spouse at the same time. At the previous level, children cannot deal with two roles simultaneously in two people. In the mapping between mother and father, therefore, children cannot mentally separate the roles of parent and spouse (Fischer & Watson, 1981). A father is not distinguished from a husband, nor a mother from a wife.

The fourth level marks not only a new level but also the beginning of a new tier. The child can coordinate two or more systems to form a *system of systems,* a relation between systems that produces a new single set beginning the next tier. This process is illustrated metaphorically in Figure 3.1 by the emergence of a cube at the fourth level—a new building block to start another tier.

As early as 10 to 11 years of age, children can combine two representational systems to form a system of representational systems, which is a single abstract set. They can compare two cases of two-dimensional social influence from the previous level in terms of some abstraction that coordinates two mean-and-nice interactions. That is, they can construct a general concept that goes beyond the concrete case.

This new capacity constitutes a major cognitive-emotional advance in at least two senses. First, complex combinations can be readily formed of representations of positive and negative emotions, such as comparisons of nice and mean behaviors in two pairs of people. Just as mother and father can be both nice and mean to each other, for example, self and friend can be both nice and mean to each other. Second, these combinations allow the child to construct an abstraction that integrates those combinations. For the comparison of mother and father with self and friend, both show inconsistency with each other: People that are close are sometimes emotionally inconsistent.

At the previous level, children used a category such as inconsistency in concrete cases, but they did not treat it as a general concept independent of the particular case. In defining it, these younger children will provide a concrete case as a definition: "Inconsistency is like you really want to be Jason's friend, but you get mad and hit him." With abstractions, on the other hand, older children can provide an appropriate definition of the general intangible concept: "Inconsistency is that people do two things that do not really belong together," and they can apply that definition to concrete cases.

The development of abstractions opens up a whole new mental world, because the individual can begin to conceive of self and other in general terms that go beyond the concrete. Concepts such as personality, anxiety, and unconscious can only be understood with the emergence and elaboration of abstractions. In general, social and emotional categories become less tangible and much more grand, as in concepts like benevolent and malevolent.

Despite the obvious advances resulting from abstractions, there is a major new limitation that also arises. Since this is only the first level of the abstract tier, children can understand only single abstractions; they are unable to coordinate two or more such concepts. Consequently, the affective splitting that was characteristic of single representations reappears, but for abstractions, not representations. When thinking of good and bad in abstract terms, such as benevolent and malevolent, children cannot relate them. This prediction of skill theory has important implications for developmental analyses of unconscious processes, which will be elaborated below. Such abstract splitting need not last, however, because single abstractions merely begin the abstract tier. The types of abstract skills that people can build change systematically through four levels, as shown in Table 3.1, and much of what is considered rational, secondary-process thought requires levels higher than single abstractions.

Unconscious Structures, Transformations, and Microdevelopment

Tiers and levels portray reorganizations on a broad scale, changes that occur over relatively long periods of time—what might be called "the big picture" of cognitive development. As children's optimal level increases, the complexity and sophistication of their skills advances, moving through the levels of sensorimotor actions, representations, and abstractions. Because of the limitations of specific levels, certain kinds of unconscious structures will emerge at particular levels.

With Level 4 single representations, for example, affective splitting is virtually inevitable, because Level 4 does not allow integration of representations in a mapping. Consequently, 2 and 3 year olds are incapable of integrating representations of nice and mean behavior in one person. When a situation requires such integration, there is a gap between what the children can do and what the situation demands, and affective splitting is inevitable. The emergence of optimal Level 5 representational mappings at 3½ or 4 years of age will allow children to move beyond Level 4 splitting because they can build skills that integrate nice and mean.

However, all cognitive development does not involve movement from level to level. Children show development within a level as well, which we call "microdevelopment." Indeed much everyday learning seems to involve such skill acquisition within a level. For example, once a 2 year old has constructed Level 4 single representations for nice and mean, he or she continues to learn new things about nice and mean by building more and more complex and diverse single representations for nice and mean. Analysis of such microdevelopment is important for understanding unconscious processes, because the gap between task and skill that produces unconscious structures can arise from deficiencies within a level as well as between levels.

Skill theory provides tools for analyzing microdevelopment, which can be used to illuminate the nature of within-level gaps and the resulting unconscious structures. According to skill theory, these small-scale changes occur through processes of transformation of skills. These processes are formally characterized in terms of algebraic rewrite rules for moving from the structure of one or two skills to a new, more complex skill structure. Four such transformation rules have been specified for within-level changes, and others may be discovered (Fischer, 1980). We will simply describe two of the rules—compounding and shift of focus—to provide a general sense of how microdevelopmental transformations function.

The compounding transformation involves the addition of two skills at a given level to produce a more complex skill that is still at the same level. For example, two mappings each composed of two representations can be added to produce a single mapping composed of three representations. Suppose a 5 year old girl has two Level 5 mapping skills for pretend stories with dolls, each composed of two representations. In one skill, a mapping for reciprocal nice interaction, she makes one doll act nicely to a second doll, and the second one is nice in return. The second mapping is reciprocal mean interaction between two dolls. One form of coordinating these two skills would produce a Level 6 system for characters being nice and mean simultaneously, but because the girl's optimal level is mappings, she cannot construct such a system. Nevertheless, she can coordinate the two skills via compounding at Level 5 to produce a complex mapping—one-dimensional social influence with three characters behaving in opposite ways: In a single story with three dolls, one character acts friendly to the other two, and a second one is nasty to the others. The third character responds with a nice action to the friendly one and a mean action to the nasty one. This complex Level 5 mapping thus is transitional to a Level 6 nice/mean integration, in that it has one character acting both nice and mean at the same time. The combination of nice and mean is possible at Level 5 because the nice and mean actions are directed to different characters.

The second transformation, shift of focus, provides a simpler means of combining the two original Level 5 skills, and the resulting skill typically forms an earlier step than the compounded mapping in the developmental sequence for integrating nice and mean. The child combines the two skills by juxtaposition, first doing one and then doing the other in sequence. That is, she makes two characters show a reciprocal nice interaction, and then she makes two characters show a reciprocal mean interaction; or vice versa. If she uses the same dolls for both stories, she will often do something to indicate a sharp separation between the two interactions, such as pausing after the first one and saying "And a long time later" as she starts the second one. Clearly, the child is not truly integrating the two skills but is merely juxtaposing them. Thus the two skills are kept separated or fractionated.

Shift of focus represents not only a transformation for predicting developmental sequences, but also a common mechanism children use to simplify complex tasks. When asked to reproduce a story that is difficult for them, such as the compounded mapping of nice and mean, children frequently simplify it into a shift of focus. Indeed many of the spontaneous errors that people show in a variety of tasks seem to employ this transformation (Fischer, Hand, & Russell, 1983; Fischer, Hand, Watson, Van Parys, & Tucker, in press). It is used both for within-level simplifications, as in the compounded mapping example, and for between-level ones, in which the person is functioning one level below what is required by the task. For instance, for a story that requires the integration of nice and mean in two characters, as in two-dimensional social influence, children often simplify the story to a shift of focus: First, the two characters show a reciprocal mean interaction, and then they show a reciprocal nice interaction, or vice versa. Presumably, shift of focus is also often used when emotional factors interfere with integration of components. Shift of focus is a naturally occurring unconscious process for dealing with tasks that are slightly beyond the person's reach.

With microdevelopmental transformations such as compounding and shift of focus, the structures specified in skill theory can be used to predict developmental sequences in detail for any domain. Note, however, that the sequence holds only within the domain. As soon as there is a change from one domain to another, developmental unevenness becomes an issue, and detailed sequences cannot be predicted. A switch from pretending about mean interactions between dolls to actual mean interactions between children, for example, involves a substantial change in domain, and no detailed sequences can be specified across the two domains. In this way, application of the transformation rules captures both the potential integration of skills and their natural fractionation: The rules specify how integration can occur; but they apply only for development within a narrowly defined domain, because skills do not develop in a broad form that automatically generalizes across domains.

A Developmental Sequence of Mean and Nice Social Interactions

The ability to integrate conflicting emotions is especially relevant to unconscious processes, since emotions seem to play a central role in much unconscious functioning. For example, when emotional opposites such as goodness and badness or niceness and meanness are not integrated in the understanding of self and other, the result will be unconscious exaggerations and distortions, such as those we have outlined for affective splitting (see also Harter, 1977, 1982, 1983). Skill theory provides tools for predicting in detail developmental sequences involving conflicting emotions, and research in our laboratory has tested one such sequence—development of the integration of nice and mean in social interactions. We will use this sequence to illustrate both the mechanisms of development in skill theory and some of the conditions that lead to unconscious processing. In addition, the sequence serves to demonstrate both the complexities of emotional concepts that children must master and the slow, gradual paths that children take in developing those concepts.

Table 3.2 presents an example of a detailed developmental sequence for the development of mean and nice social interactions for pretend stories with realistic cardboard figures. All the steps listed in Table 3.2 have been directly tested in research reported by Hand (1981a), Fischer, Hand, Watson, Van Parys, and Tucker (in press), and Fischer, Hand, and Russell (1983). Also a number of these steps were already introduced in the earlier descriptions of the developmental levels and transformations.

The twelve steps of the sequence encompass all four levels of the representational tier, and the second level of the abstract tier is also included to show how development continues after the emergence of abstractions. For each of the first four levels, several steps are described to illustrate how detailed, multistep sequences can be predicted and how tasks can be analyzed for assignment to levels and steps. Many more steps could be predicted by further applications of the transformation rules.

For each step, a story embodying the skill described in Table 3.2 was presented to the subject, who was asked to act out the story with the cardboard figures or to describe it. For young children, the children typically acted out each story with the figures. For older children and adolescents, the children usually described the story in their own words and answered a few questions about it. To pass the step, subjects did not need to reproduce the story verbatim, and they seldom tried to do so. They merely had to demonstrate that they understood the type of structure embodied in each story.

The first three steps constitute increasingly complex forms of Level 4 single representations. At Step 1, active agent, the child makes a doll carry out a single action which can fit a wide range of categories, including nice or mean. These are not true categories, however, because they have only one component and a true category must have at least two. The emergence of a true category awaits Step 2, the compounding of two or more actions to produce what is called a behavioral category, such as nice or mean. At Step 3, shifting behavioral categories, the child juxtaposes two categories but does not coordinate them. For example, one doll acts nice, and then another doll acts mean, with no integration of the two sets of behaviors.

Step 4 brings the integration of two categories in a Level 5 representational mapping. Two different forms of Step 4 are shown in Table 3.2 to demonstrate that there can be tasks that are roughly equivalent in structural complexity and therefore cannot be ordered as separate steps. In Step 4a, combination of opposite categories in a single person, one doll acts both nice and mean in one story to a second doll who is merely the passive recipient of the actions. Step 4b, one-dimensional social influence, coordinates two instances of the same category, as when one doll acts mean to another doll who responds in kind contingently. The one-dimensional social influence of Step 4b is extended to three characters via compounding in Step 5, where two dolls each act mean to the others, and the third doll responds meanly to both of them.

In Step 6, shifting one-dimensional social influence, two skills from Step 4b or 5 are juxtaposed, reciprocal nice interaction and reciprocal mean interaction. First, two or three dolls interact nicely, and then the child shifts to a different story in which two or three dolls interact meanly.

Sometimes tasks may fall between two levels, in the sense that they can be done at the earlier level but are much easier to do at the later level. Such a task was predicted at Step 7, one-dimensional social influence with three characters behaving in opposite ways, which was described earlier as an example of compounding. One doll acts nice to the others, while a second one acts mean, and the third doll responds differentially—nice to the first and mean to the second. Because of the separation of nice and mean in the behavior of two different dolls, this task can be performed with a Level 5 mapping. However, the combination of nice and mean in the behavior of the third doll makes the task much easier to perform with a Level 6 system, where such integrations of opposite behaviors in a single person are routine.

With the Level 6 capacity to integrate opposite behaviors in two people interacting, the child can perform Step 8, two-dimensional social influence. One doll acts nice and mean simultaneously to a second one who responds with appropriate nice and mean behaviors. Step 9, two-dimensional social influence with three characters, brings a compounded form of integration of opposites, in which a third doll joins the interaction and also acts both nice and mean, evoking appropriate responses from the other dolls.

The development of Level 7 abstractions at Step 10, integration of opposite behaviors in terms of a single abstraction, produces one coherent interpretation of the inconsistent behaviors in Steps 8 and 9. When characters act nice and mean to each other, the responses are determined by a general rule for dealing with such opposite behaviors, such as "People's intentions matter more than their

TABLE 3.2. A Developmental Sequence for Understanding Nice and Mean Social Interactions

Level	Step	Skill	Examples
4: Single Representations	1	*Active agent:* A person performs at least one behavior, which may or may not fit a social-interaction category.	Child pretends that one doll picks up a ball or hits another doll ("mean") or gives another doll candy ("nice").
	2	*Behavioral category:* A person performs at least two behaviors fitting an interaction category, such as "nice" or "mean."	Child has one doll act nice to another doll, giving it candy and saying, "I like you." The second doll can be passive.
	3	*Shifting behavior categories:* One person performs at least two behaviors fitting the category "nice," as in Step 2, and then a second person performs at least two behaviors fitting the category "mean."	Child has one doll act nice to a second doll, giving it candy and saying, "Let's play." A third doll enters and acts mean to the second one, hitting it and saying, "Give me your ball!" In both cases, the second doll can be passive.
5: Representational Mappings	4a[a]	*Combination of opposite categories in a single person:* One person performs behaviors fitting two opposing categories, such as "nice" and "mean."	Child has one doll act nice to a second doll, saying "Let's be friends" and giving the doll candy. The first doll then hits the second, saying "Since we're friends, you should give me your ball!" The second doll can be passive throughout.
	4b[a]	*One-dimensional social influence:* The mean behaviors of one person produce reciprocal mean behaviors in a second person. The same contingency can occur for nice behaviors.	Child has one doll say mean things and hit another doll, who responds by hitting and expressing dislike for the first one. The second one's behavior is clearly produced by the first one's behavior.
	5	*One-dimensional social influence with three characters behaving in similar ways:* Same as Step 4b, but with three people interacting reciprocally in a mean way (or a nice way).	With three dolls, child has one tease the others, while a second one hits the others. The third doll rejects both of the first two because they are mean.
	6	*Shifting one-dimensional social influence:* The nice behaviors of one person produce reciprocal nice behaviors in a second person. Then, in a separate story, the mean behaviors of a third person produce reciprocal mean behaviors in the second person. (Or a reciprocal mean interaction can occur first, and then a reciprocal nice interaction.)	With three dolls, child has one act friendly to a second one, who responds nicely. Then, a third doll hits the second one, who responds meanly.
	7[b]	*One-dimensional social influence with three characters behaving in opposite ways:* The nice behaviors of one person and the mean behaviors of a second person produce reciprocal nice and mean behaviors in the third person.	With three dolls, a child has one act friendly to others, while a second one hits the others. The third doll responds nicely to the first doll and meanly to the second.
6: Representational Systems	8	*Two-dimensional social influence:* Two people interact in ways fitting opposite categories, such that the first one acts both nice and mean, and the second one responds with reciprocal behaviors in the same categories.	Child has one doll initiate friendship with a second doll, but in a mean way. The second one, confused about the discrepancy, declines the friendship because of the meanness. The first then apologizes and makes another friendly gesture, which the second one responds to accordingly.

9	*Two-dimensional social influence with three characters:* Same as Step 7 but with three people interacting reciprocally according to opposite categories.	With three dolls, child has one doll act friendly to a second one, while a third one initiates play in a mean way. The second doll acts friendly to the first one and rejects the third, pointing out the latter's meanness. The third then apologizes for being mean, while the first one does something new that is mean. The second doll accepts the third one's apology and rejects the first one, pointing out the change in his or her behavior.
7: Single Abstractions		
10	*Single abstraction integrating opposite behaviors:* Two instances of interactions involving opposite behaviors take place as in Step 7, and the relations between the two interactions are explained in terms of some general abstraction, such as that intentions matter more than actions.	With three characters, child has one act friendly to a second, while a third initiates play in a mean way. The second character responds to each accordingly, but then learns that the nice one had mean intentions while the mean one had nice intentions. The second character then changes his or her behavior to each to match their intentions and explains that he or she cares more about people's intentions than their actions.
11	*Shifting abstractions, each integrating opposite behaviors:* First, two instances of interactions involving opposite behaviors are explained in terms of an abstraction such as intention (as in Step 9). Then two other instances of interactions involving opposite behaviors are explained in terms of a different abstraction, such as responsibility. What matters is whether people take responsibility for the harm they do.	First, child performs a story like that in Step 9. Then child shifts to a different story, as follows: With three characters, child has two of them act mean to a third. The first one takes responsibility for her behavior by admitting her blame and accepting the consequences of her action. The second one takes no such responsibility. The third one forgives the one who took responsibility and refuses to forgive the one who did not take responsibility, because, she says, she cares about whether people take responsibility for the harm they do.
8: Abstract Mappings		
12	*Relation of two abstractions integrating opposite behaviors:* Two instances of interactions involving opposite behaviors are explained in terms of the relation of two abstractions, such as intention and responsibility: People who have a deceitful intention can be forgiven if they take responsibility in a way that undoes the deceit.	With three dolls, child has two of them act nice on the surface to a third, both with the intention of deceiving him into doing their homework. When the deceit is discovered by the third character, the first one takes responsibility for his deceit by admitting his intention and thus reestablishing his honesty. But the second one does not show such responsibility. The third character forgives the first one, but not the second, because she cares about whether people take responsibility for their deceitful intention and undo the deceit.

Note: Portions of this table are adapted from Hand (1981a).

[a]Steps 4a and 4b develop at approximately the same time.

[b]Step 7 is transitional between Levels 5 and 6. Apparently it can be mastered at Level 5, but it is much easier to do at Level 6.

actions." Thus an overtly mean behavior that was intended to be nice is rewarded, but an overtly nice behavior that arises from a mean intention is punished.

Step 11, shifting abstractions, involves the juxtaposition of two abstractions without coordination. Both abstractions deal with the integration of nice and mean behaviors, but no connection is made between the two types of integration. For example, the first abstraction may involve the concept of intention, as in Step 10, while the second abstraction coordinates similar behaviors under a different concept, such as responsibility: "Taking responsibility means a person shows she really cares about the effects her actions have on other people."

With Step 12, relation of two abstractions, the two concepts are not merely juxtaposed but coordinated in a Level 8 mapping. In one such relation, for example, a person initially has a negative intention toward someone. He or she can take responsibility for undoing the consequences of that intention and thus absolve the self of blame. Although Table 3.2 ends with Step 12, development can continue with additional steps at Level 8, and also more advanced skills can be built at Levels 9 and 10.

In a similar way, developmental sequences can be predicted in any domain, including those dealing directly with unconscious structures, such as characteristics of primary process thought or mechanisms of defense. Some sequences for unconscious structures will be outlined below.

Both Person and Environment: The Range of Functional Levels

For developmental sequences, individual people cannot function beyond their optimal level—the most advanced level of skill that they can construct under ideal conditions (Fischer & Pipp, 1984). Equally important, people do not automatically function at their optimum, and the character of variation below optimum has fundamental implications for analysis of the development of unconscious structures. Most everyday performance is not at optimal level, and most cognitive-developmental assessments do not reflect optimal level (Biggs & Collis, 1982; Fischer, 1980, 1983; Fischer, Pipp, & Bullock, 1984). Because it is not legitimate to assume that people will function routinely at their optimal level, analysis of unconscious structures requires specification of the functional level for the particular domain of interest.

The occurrence of a wide range of functional levels arises from the transactional (Sameroff, 1975) nature of skills: A skill is neither a characteristic of a person nor a characteristic of a task or context; it emerges from the transaction of person with context and is therefore a characteristic of a "person in a context." A change in either the person or the context changes the skill. As a result, both functional level and developmental sequence can be predicted with confidence only within narrowly defined domains and for individuals with experience in the specific domain.

The ease with which developmental step and level can be altered by environmental changes has been abundantly documented (see, for example, Bullock, 1983; Feldman, 1980; Flavell, 1971, 1983; Jackson, Campos, & Fischer,

1978). Until recently, however, many researchers have either ignored these findings or used them to dismiss concepts such as developmental level. A recently discovered environmental effect both supports the concept of developmental level and specifies a new type of order in environmental variation. In several studies, children and adolescents were assessed in what most investigators would categorize as a single domain, but the degree of environmental support for high-level performance was varied. The variations in environmental support produced systematic changes in the children's highest performance, giving vastly different portraits of the capacities of particular age groups (Fischer & Lamborn, in press; Hand, 1981b; Rubin, Fein, & Vandenberg, 1983; Watson & Fischer, 1980).

To measure children's performance, a single developmental scale like that in Table 3.2 was used in all conditions. Stimulus materials and scoring procedures were also identical across conditions, but the degree of environmental support for high-level performance varied. In the first condition, which was highly structured and thus provided strong support, children were shown a series of stories to assess all the predicted developmental steps and asked to act out or explain each story immediately after they saw it. Then in one or two "spontaneous," low-support conditions, they were asked to use the same materials to make up stories of their own that were similar to those they had been shown.

For both types of conditions, children's performances fit the pattern required for a functional developmental level: They showed a highest step as well as a number of steps earlier in the sequence. However, the different conditions produced dramatic variation in the locus of the highest step. In the high-support condition, most children showed a much more advanced highest step than in the low-support conditions. In one study using the sequence in Table 3.2, for example, 9 year olds typically reached Step 8 for the structured condition but only Step 4 for the low-support conditions (Hand, 1981a).

These findings show how people's functional levels vary across a wide range below their optimal level (Fischer & Lamborn, in press): In each specific, narrowly defined domain, a person's performance shows a highest step (called the "functional level") as well as lower steps. Variations across domains in the degree of support for high-level performance produce vastly different functional levels, with the person's optimal level setting the upper limit on variation.

One important result of the natural variations in functional level is that for the same task, apparently minor changes in the situation will move a person from understanding the task to misunderstanding it, or vice versa. For a task at Step 8 in Table 3.2, for example, typical 9 year olds will demonstrate understanding of the task (two-dimensional social influence) in a high-support condition. With change to a low-support condition, however, they will not be able to perform the task correctly, and instead a gap will appear between the demands of the task and the level of skill they can bring to bear upon it. To deal with the task, they will have to transform it into something simpler, such as simple one-dimensional social influence (Step 4b) or a shift of focus from a reciprocal nice interaction to a reciprocal mean interaction (Step 6).

This variation in functional level means that the individual person will show a gap for a specific task in one situation and show no gap whatsoever for the same task in a slightly different situation. Consequently, unconscious structures will appear and disappear systematically as a function of the degree of support provided by the situation. For a single task, such as Step 8 in Table 3.2, the person will produce conscious, rational behavior in a high-support situation and unconscious, distorted behavior in a low-support one.

Emotional state seems to produce similar variation in functional level, with anxiety or high arousal producing a reduction in level, as in the classical Yerkes-Dodson law (Hebb, 1955; Yerkes & Dodson, 1908); but there has been little research examining the effect of emotions on developmental level (Fischer, 1979). To our knowledge, the main research documenting this effect is with young infants: State of arousal strongly affects the developmental level of their performance (Prechtl, 1982; Wolff, 1966). If the effect of emotional state applies to children and adults as well, as would be predicted from the Yerkes-Dodson law, then emotional state will produce unconscious functioning whenever it lowers a person's functional level below that required by a particular task.

In summary, skill theory provides a framework for analyzing the organization of behavior and the way this organization changes with development. As the person grows from infant to adult, skills move through 10 successive optimal levels grouped into three tiers. Within each level, skills develop more complex forms via transformation processes that specify how skill structures can be rewritten. Because of the transactional nature of behavior, variations in either the environment or the person change the nature of a skill, so that skills tend to be acquired for specific contexts by individual people. Even apparently minor variations in context can change the developmental step of a skill, especially when they alter the degree of environmental support for high-level performance. And changes in the person's emotional state can also affect the level of functioning. A natural fractionation arises from the fundamental contributions of person and environment to each skill. To overcome this fractionation, the person must generalize or integrate skills to form a more sophisticated ability.

The skill framework provides a set of tools for analyzing the development of both conscious and unconscious structures. In describing the framework, we have attempted to illustrate how it can be applied to the development of unconscious structures, including those driven by emotion; but our major focus has necessarily been exposition of skill theory itself. Now it is time to focus on unconscious processes and how they are recast within the present framework.

THE STRUCTURES OF UNCONSCIOUS THOUGHT

Within psychoanalysis, unconscious thought is defined in terms of specific structures or organizations: A behavior is recognized as unconsciously motivated because it demonstrates one or more of those structures. A central characteristic of all the structures is that they are developmentally primitive, and any sign of such primitiveness is considered to indicate probable unconscious functioning.

The general structure of unconscious thought is called *primary process,* which is contrasted with secondary process. While secondary process is organized logically and serves the reality principle and the ego, primary process is organized illogically and serves the pleasure principle and the id. Primary process is thus distorting, whereas secondary process reflects undistorted reality. In this contrast, primary-process thought is sometimes treated as if it is so primitive that it lacks any organization at all. As Holt (1967, 1976) points out, however, what it lacks is not organization in general, since its characteristic structures can be identified, but organization in terms of reality-based logic.

Primary process is traditionally defined as *the structure* of unconscious thought, as if it captured all components of the organization of things unconscious. There are, however, other structures or processes as well that are essentially unconscious, such as the mechanisms of defense and the superego; and they are not easily subsumed under primary process explained by the characteristics identified with it. In addition, these other unconscious structures are often considered to arise from a more advanced developmental stage than primary process, although they remain primitive relative to the adult mind. The superego, for example, is hypothesized to develop from the resolution of the Oedipus conflict at the end of the preschool period; and the mechanisms of defense are said to emerge at various points during childhood (A. Freud, 1966; Haan, 1977; Vaillant, 1977). To avoid confusions about the meanings of terms, we use "the structures of unconscious thought" to refer to all unconscious structures, and we reserve "primary process" for the particular structure that is traditionally contrasted with "secondary process."

To explicate the nature of the structures of unconscious thought, we will begin with two examples of primary-process thought. Besides illustrating the structural characteristics of primary process, the examples also illuminate some of the bases for our new formulation, particularly with respect to the relation between developmental immaturity and affective bizarreness in unconscious structures (see Holt, 1967). The new formulation of the nature of unconscious thought distinguishes between immaturity and bizarreness and in the process leads to a broadening of the scope of what is categorized as unconscious thought. Within this broadened range of behaviors, several distinct types of unconscious structures are distinguished that arise from different conditions and function differently.

A woman patient named C showed primary process in her description of her relationship with a male friend. This man, she said, makes her "excited but it's not even a taste, only a smell of a good meal.... [He] kissed me and I gave him a hug and a kiss and enjoyed it and wanted more. Ought I? I've sought desperately for so long and now I feel I must run away from it. I don't want to eat these days. I couldn't sleep. I felt I'd lost him; what if he or I had an accident and got killed. It's ridiculous but I'm in a constant furor of anxiety, I must see him: nothing else matters.... [I am afraid that he will get] killed, and I feel I'll have an accident too. I get desperately tired, and feel empty inside and have to buy sweet biscuits and gobble them up" (Guntrip, 1952).

A 3 year old boy named S demonstrated primary process in describing a drawing that he had just made: "This looks like a square. It's a Christmas tree. It says *A*. There's a circle. It's where we eat out. Then there's a big, long square. I want it to be a circle with some lines."

Both of these statements are clearly primitive, showing an apparently contradictory fractionation and mixing together of ideas, which characterizes primary process, but the statements also differ greatly in degree of complexity and abstraction. The woman is depicting a social relationship and explaining her own needs in the relationship and her own fears about events that might follow from the relationship. Her thought is primary process because in the midst of this complexity, she confuses eating with participation in the relationship.

The boy, on the other hand, is merely describing a series of simple objects that he sees in his drawing. His description is primary process because it is not coherent but fractionated, shifting from one element to another, mixing them together haphazardly; yet the form of the primary process is much simpler than that in the woman's statement. There is nothing so complex as an interpersonal relationship or a sequence of causally related events. His most complex statement is merely the expression of a wish: "I want it to be a circle with some lines."

The child's statement is thus developmentally more primitive than the adult's because it is less complex. In another sense, however, the woman's statement is more typical of primary process, because it is affectively bizarre. In clinical settings, where practitioners deal with pathological or disordered behavior, the label "primary process" is typically reserved for this kind of bizarre thought. That is, the woman's thoroughgoing confusion of eating with a social relationship seems to require more advanced reasoning than the child's confusion about what his drawing depicts. But despite the greater "maturity" of the woman's statement in terms of complexity, its bizarreness makes it more typical of behaviors that in practice are categorized as primary process.

These examples illustrate some of the differences between types of primary process that we believe must be captured by an analysis of the development of unconscious structures. What is needed is a way of characterizing (a) the similarities underlying the categorization of both of these passages as primary process, (b) the differences in the level of complexity of the processes evident in the two passages, and (c) the differences in the affective bizarreness of the passages. But before explicating these issues, we need to deal with one additional part of the foundation of our argument—the defining characteristics of primary process.

Characteristics of Primary Process

According to Holt (1967), primary process is a relatively undifferentiated concept as it is used in much of the psychoanalytic literature, but it can be specified and coded with some precision. Primary process has three fundamental characteristics: condensation, displacement, and wishful, magical, or autistic thinking (Gill, 1967; Holt, 1967). In condensation, the person combines two or more components that should be kept separate. One common form of condensation in dreams involves a character who seems to be several people at the same time, such as a man who is father, brother, and husband all mixed together. In the example of primary process from the woman C, she shows condensation in her confusion of eating with a close social relationship, freely mixing together attributes of the two: Her male friend makes her "excited but it's not even a taste, only a smell of a good meal. . . ." The 3 year old S seems to show condensation when he says that an object is a square, a Christmas tree, and an *A*.

In displacement, one component is substituted for another one. Displacement commonly occurs in dream symbols, as when a tower takes the place of a penis or a cave substitutes for a vagina. The woman C seems to show displacement when she wants to see her male friend and instead gobbles up sweet biscuits. (In S's statement, there is nothing that can clearly be categorized as displacement.)

With wishful, magical, or autistic thinking, thought is distorted by the person's wishes or fears. Dreams frequently show wish fulfillment in both straightforward and disguised forms. The wish to have sexual intercourse with someone, for example, is realized in disguised form when the dreamer and the person fly through the air together and feel excited and ecstatic. The woman C's fear that her friend will die is a form of wish fulfillment representing her negative feelings about him. The boy S shows a direct form of wish fulfillment when he states that he wants his drawing to be a circle with some lines.

These three characteristics of primary process are often complexly intertwined and difficult to separate. In C's statements about her friend, for example, it is sometimes hard to tell whether she is condensing eating and the relationship or displacing the relationship with eating. Also, wishes and fears strongly affect what she says about eating and the relationship: Because she fears the relationship, she does not want to eat, and she worries about whether she or her friend will die. Because she wants the relationship, she eats lots of biscuits. For behavior to show primary process, the three characteristics, condensation, displacement, and wish fulfillment, do not need to be separable.

According to the traditional psychoanalytic view, primary process is the original state of the mind in early infancy, and development proceeds toward secondary process (Freud, 1900/1953). That is, secondary process develops from primary process. The infant's thought demonstrates condensation, displacement, and wish fulfillment, and gradually with development the logical forms of secondary process replace these illogical structures.

A number of scholars have suggested, however, that the developmental process is not so simple (Holt, 1967, 1976; Rapaport, 1951; Schimek, 1975; Wolff, 1960, 1967). The most salient problem with the traditional formulation is that unrealistic abilities are attributed to young infants. Research shows consistently that young infants are not capable of any behavior resembling thought (e.g., Bertenthal & Fischer, 1978; Case, 1980; McCall, Eichorn, & Hogarty, 1977; Piaget, 1936/1952). Yet primary process is primitive *thought*. The standard solution to this problem has been to relocate the onset of primary process at the emergence of representation, the ability to think about objects, events, or actions that are not immediately present in action or perception (Level 4 in skill theory). According to Piaget (1946/1951) and most neo-Piagetian theorists, representation emerges at 1 to 2 years of age, and with representation, symbolic thought becomes possible. In addition, the child's first representations clearly show the characteristics of primary process—condensation, displacement, and wish fulfillment (Fischer, Hand, Watson, Van Parys, & Tucker, in press; Holt, 1967; Piaget, 1946/1951).

This revision of the traditional formulation eliminates the attribution of unrealistic abilities to the young infant, although the role of the infant's abilities before representation is not specified. The revised formulation, however, suffers from the same fundamental problem as the traditional one: Primary process in an older child or adult is treated as equivalent to the thought of the 2 year old. The best evidence indicates that primary process does not remain constant from age 2 onward but that there are gradations from primary to secondary process (Holt, 1967). The examples of primary process in the woman C and the 3 year old S illustrate this problem, because the woman's primary process is clearly more complex and developmentally advanced than that of the 3 year old, even though it is more bizarre affectively.

The revision also does not deal sufficiently with the difficulties in Freud's original model of "immaculate perception"—that the unconscious contains a repository of veridical memories that are distorted by the mechanisms of primary process. Merely moving the age of onset of primary process does not provide the needed active, structural-developmental framework for unconscious thought (Schimek, 1975).

A New Structural-Developmental Definition of Unconscious Thought

What is needed is a framework that integrates the psychodynamic insights about unconscious processes with the modern structural-developmental perspective. Such an integration follows straightforwardly from the approach we have outlined, but a major redefinition of the conditions for unconscious thought is required: Unconscious functioning is not equated with any particular age or developmental level, but instead appears whenever there is a relative gap between the level required by a task or issue and the level used by the person. That is, unconscious structures arise when the structure of the task demands skills that are more complex or advanced than those the person brings to bear on the task.

In his recent book *The Structure of Freudian Thought,* Feffer puts forth this novel analysis of unconscious thought, and Fischer and Watson (1981) also suggest it in their explanation of the cognitive-developmental bases of the Oedipus conflict. At any point in development, knowledge has both primitive qualities and developmentally advanced ones, depending upon whether the task being approached is within or beyond the individual's explanatory limits. When people face a task that is within the explanatory limits of their skills, they show secondary process, which Feffer calls "hierarchic understanding" because the components of the task are differentiated and hierarchically integrated in a manner appropriate to the demands of the task. When people face a task that is beyond their explanatory limits, they evidence primary process, which he calls *pars pro toto* understanding, confounding the part with the whole. For example, in Piaget's task for conservation of amount of liquid, the child must understand that when water is poured from a short, wide glass into a tall, thin one, the amount of water remains the same. Preschoolers typically misunderstand this task, arguing that there is more water in the tall glass because the water is higher there. They thus confound the part, the height of liquid, with the whole, the total amount of liquid. This distortion arises from their attempt to solve the task with a skill that is not sufficiently advanced to handle variations in height and width simultaneously. Any situation in which people face a task beyond their explanatory limits will produce primary process behavior, showing condensation, displacement, and wish fulfillment.

Feffer's analysis changes the conceptions of primary and secondary process in several important ways. First, the range of behaviors fitting the concepts is substantially altered. Primary process is no longer limited to primitive, affectively bizarre thought that is characteristic of young children, disturbed individuals, and Freudian thought in dreams. Instead, it is a characteristic of an overextended skill—any overextended skill, whether or not it involves bizarre affect. Likewise, secondary process is no longer the state of rational, adult thought, but is a characteristic of a skill that is functioning at a level appropriate to a given task, whatever the developmental level of the skill or the age of the child.

Second, primary and secondary process become transactional concepts: Whether a skill is overextended depends not only on the skill the person uses but also on the task the environment poses. In the traditional approach, primary and secondary process are essentially characteristics of the person, but in Feffer's approach, the task or situation also plays a central role. This change is consonant with the emphasis in skill theory on both child and environment. A change in the degree of environmental support for a high-level skill, for example, will lead to a change in functional level, producing movement from primary to secondary process, or vice versa.

Third, when primary and secondary process are conceptualized transactionally, they become developmentally relative concepts. At *any* developmental level, behavior shows primary process whenever there is a gap between the level of the skill used and the requirements of the task. Even at advanced levels, such gaps can occur. The woman C, for example, shows primary process because she mixes together having a relationship with eating, instead of differentiating the two and relating them as separate needs. Her behavior fits primary process even though it shows abilities far advanced beyond those of a 2 or 3 year old.

Although primary process is no longer limited to behavior at low developmental levels, the classic observation that primary process is common in young children still follows from this framework. Because so many of the tasks that young children face are beyond their explanatory limits, they necessarily show primary process structures frequently. Children come up with "wrong" solutions, errors, or distortions that represent the best they can do within the limitations of their cognitive levels (Fischer, Hand, & Russell, 1983; Fischer, Hand, Watson, Van Parys, & Tucker, in press; Roberts, 1981). Within a normal developmental progression, moreover, these inadequate solutions are gradually elaborated to form more advanced skills for which fewer tasks are beyond the children's explanatory limits. Still, at every level, there are some tasks that are beyond the person's explanatory limits, and consequently, there are more and less advanced forms of primary process.

Whenever a person does not control the concepts, distinctions, or relations necessary to fulfill the demands of a task, primary process behavior occurs. The structures of primary process are thus a characteristic of behavior in general, not just of emotion-laden thoughts such as those encountered in pathology. Bizarre thoughts such as the woman C's muddling of eating with a social relationship become a special case of an ordinary mental process.

Types of Unconscious Processes

Thought is conscious when the person can differentiate the components of a task and control them in relation to each other in a manner that allows him or her to deal effectively with the task. This meaning of consciousness fits nicely with the structural-developmental orientation and also is consistent in spirit, we believe, with psychodynamic perspectives. It happens also to capture the original Latin root of "conscious," which is "knowing together" (*Webster's New International Dictionary,* second edition).

Thought is unconscious when the person cannot differentiate and integrate the potential components and relations in the task. That is, the person is unaware of the potential integrations of the components and relations at higher levels of thought, although a trained observer can detect them implicitly in the person's behavior and in the task. In skill development in general, construction of a new skill involves a process of simultaneous differentiation and integration of components that the person did not previously control or understand. The components are typically present implicitly in the person's behavior, and they become explicit when the person has differentiated or integrated them (Fischer, 1980; Werner, 1957).

The woman C is unaware of the potential distinctions and relations between a social relationship and eating, although the clinical observer readily sees them as separate. To make them conscious, she would have to compare them and construct a higher-level skill that differentiated and integrated them. The boy S is likewise unaware of the potential distinctions and relations between the several things that he sees in succession in his drawing—a square, a Christmas tree, an *A,* and a circle. As he develops a higher-level skill, he will differentiate and integrate those things and thus make conscious the distinctions and relations among them. In both cases, the fractionation (lack of differentiation and integration) effectively hides the potential components from the self. When there is some affective reason for the lack of differentiation, as seems to be the case for the woman C, the hiding can be potent and difficult to overcome. For these unconscious matters to become conscious, the person must construct higher-level skills that will change the components from potential to actual.

From the structural-developmental perspective, unconscious thought is an ordinary mental process, not something particular to emotional impulses or bizarre thoughts. People routinely deal with tasks or issues that require more advanced skills than they can bring to bear, and so they evidence unconscious structures in performing those tasks. There are systematic variations, however, in the processes behind the unconscious structures and concomitant differences in the emotional bases of the structures. In the framework we have put forward, unconscious thought arises from three general types of processes: limitations in optimal and functional levels, passive dissociation, and active dissociation.

Limitations in Optimal and Functional Levels

Within the traditional psychoanalytic perspective, young children produce unconscious structures automatically because of their developmental limitations. The 3 year old S, for example, gave a primary-process description of his drawing because he was not yet able to construct a secondary-process description. The concepts of optimal and functional levels explain this phenomenon and provide mechanisms for predicting how they occur. People cannot construct or control any skill above their optimal level, and so any task that requires a skill beyond their optimum will necessarily evoke an unconscious structure. In particular contexts, people also do not produce skills beyond their functional level for each domain, and any task that requires a skill beyond that level will likewise evoke an unconscious structure.

The optimal level sets a rigid upper limit on the sophistication of a child's skills, and for each level, different unconscious distortions result. Some common distortions can be illustrated by the developmental sequence for nice and mean (see Fischer, Hand, Watson, Van Parys, & Tucker, in press). Consider a 3 year old girl whose optimum is Level 4 single representations. Because of the limits of her optimal level, she is incapable of dealing with nice and mean or good and bad at the same time, and so she necessarily demonstrates affective splitting in her representations. She builds Level 4 skills for nice and mean, such as the first three steps in Table 3.2: If she has had experience with nice and mean social interactions and if she is acting in a supportive environment, she can make a doll carry out one or more mean actions, or one or more nice actions. She may even be able to juxtapose nice and mean actions in a shift of focus from one to the other (Step 3). But faced with a situation where nice and mean behaviors occur together, she is limited to simplifying the situation and thus distorting it: Typically she will split nice and mean, dealing with either one or the other and not integrating the two in a single relation. She cannot understand that an individual doll can be both nice and mean at the same time.

By 5 years of age, the same girl will have advanced to an optimum of Level 5 representational mappings, where she will be able to overcome her Level 4 splitting. She can integrate nice and mean in the behavior of a single doll (Step 4a, combination of opposite categories in a single person). She can relate one doll's mean behavior to another doll's mean behavior and do the same for nice (Step 4b, one-dimensional social influence). She can even make three dolls act mean (or nice) to each other (Step 5). And at her best, she can first make some dolls interact nicely and then shift to making them interact meanly (Step 6).

At this new optimal level, she will also show a more advanced kind of splitting. Faced with a task that requires a Level 6 representational system, in which two or more dolls act nice and mean simultaneously to each other, she must resort to splitting because she must simplify the task to a Level 5 structure. For example, she can deal only with the nice interaction and ignore the mean one (Step 4b), or she can make the dolls first interact in a mean way with each other and then later act nice (Step 6).

Splitting results not only from the upper bound set by children's optimal level but also from the limits set by their functional levels in particular domains. A child's optimum may be Level 6 representational systems, which, when applied to social interactions, would allow her to integrate nice and mean. If, however, her functional level for the domain is Level 4 or 5, she will still show splitting. Harter (1977) describes the play therapy case of a 7 year old girl named K, who demonstrated splitting with another pair of affectively loaded categories, smart and dumb. She had done poorly on some tests at school and was upset because she saw herself as "all dumb." Although she recognized that she did well in some tests and so was smart there, she seemed unable to integrate the dumb and smart experiences. K's optimal level seemed to be Level 6 representational systems, which allow the integration of opposite characteristics such as smart and dumb in two characters interacting. Yet her functional level in this domain was below Level 6, and so she had difficulty seeing that she was simultaneously smart in some things and dumb in others (like everyone else).

Harter devised a technique that provided environmental support for higher-level functioning and helped K to move her skills to her optimum and thus eliminate her problem of feeling all dumb. K drew a circle to represent herself and how she felt, and Harter showed how if a line was drawn down the middle of the circle, "smart" could be written on one side of the circle and "dumb" on the other. The girl easily understood the meaning, and within a few sessions was drawing circles with a number of lines separating several cases of smart and dumb. The technique provided the environmental support she needed to function at her optimum, and thus it aided the integration of smart and dumb.

Optimal and functional levels set natural limits on the complexity of skills that people can build, and specific kinds of unconscious structures arise from those limits. In the course of development, children experience increases in optimal and functional levels, and this cognitive growth produces natural resolution of many of the unconscious distortions that children evidence early in development.

Passive Dissociation

Skills are naturally fractionated, and people must work to integrate them. This "passive dissociation" or "compartmentalization" arises from the nature of the organization of behavior, not from some Freudian process that actively motivates fractionation. As discussed earlier, at least two general characteristics of skills produce passive dissociation—their context specificity and the prepotency of emotional state in their organization.

Even when people are using skills at a high developmental level, they commonly show unconscious structures, because the skills are not appropriate to the task they are doing. Such application of inappropriate skills occurs routinely as a result of the way skills are naturally organized by domain. People are unaware of the potential connections or relations needed to deal effectively with the task in the particular domain they are now addressing. An inappropriate skill is effectively at a lower level than is needed despite the fact that it would be a high-level skill for a task where it was appropriate. Of course, the lack of awareness of potential connections can also arise from the person's having a skill that is at a low level by any criterion, but the occurrence of dissociation arises from the relation between the skill and the requirements of the particular task, not from the level of the skill considered by itself.

People's skills are acquired for some particular context, and when that context is different from the task at hand, they do not automatically know how to adapt their skills. Skills remain context-specific and fractionated until people actively integrate them across contexts. Such passive dissociation occurs even for emotionally neutral material, such as that studied by many cognitive scientists. For example, when college students learn information about the relative magnitude of various items, they can produce a skill integrating those items into a series. Items that are learned in different tasks, however, are almost never integrated spontaneously; there must be some environmental support that explicitly evokes the integration (Potts, 1980). With two separate skills, the same content is thus differentially accessible—conscious when one skill is activated but unconscious when the other one is activated.

The behavior of the 3 year old boy S illustrates how this passive dissociation can operate in a single task. His description of the drawing was primarily a list of separate ways the drawing or parts of it could be interpreted—a square, a Christmas tree, an A, a circle, a restaurant, a big, long square. These interpretations were fractionated, juxtaposed in a shift-of-focus organization. S's final description demonstrates, however, that he could achieve some integration of similar components: "I want it to be a circle with some lines." Given environmental support, he could presumably move from passive dissociation to integration of some of the components, although the limitations in his optimal and functional levels would prevent him from producing a sophisticated integration.

Passive dissociation operates at all ages, not just in childhood. A man may know that his daughter is acting moody, and he may also know that her best friend from high school is sick. But if he has learned these two facts in different contexts and if she has not explained the connection, the two skills will be passively dissociated, and he will have to build the connection between them—that she is upset about her friend's illness.

A special case of passive dissociation resulting from context specificity has attracted the attention of experimental psychologists since William James

(1890). In what is often called "automatization," people who master a complex skill are aware of the components of the skill only at the level at which the components are integrated. They tend to lose their awareness of the lower-level components of the behavior (Bruner, 1968, 1969; Hirst, Spelke, Reaves, Caharack, & Neisser, 1980; Mandler, 1962; Shiffrin & Schneider, 1977; Welford, 1968). For example, in using a typewriter, a skilled typist is aware of the component for typing a familiar word but cannot typically decompose that word into its lower-level component actions. In a sense, he or she is not aware of these lower-level components, which are said to occur automatically. The difficulty in decomposing component actions is not surprising, because the typist normally does not perform the decomposition task. Even though the components being decomposed are in some sense included in the normal typing task, the typist doing the decomposition is in fact faced with a new and unfamiliar task. With practice, this new task can be mastered, and the natural dissociation that occurs in the decomposition task can be overcome.

Such dissociation resulting from a change in level of analysis of the components of a familiar task is more than a laboratory curiosity. Overcoming this type of dissociation constitutes one of the major procedures in some forms of psychotherapy (Schafer, 1976; Wachtel, 1977). Patients must reconsider components of their behavior that are organized in certain automatized ways and recast them in different forms. If the reorganization is not blocked by some motivated dissociation, then the reorganization is a straightforward cognitive task. In psychodynamic therapy, constructions deriving from one's parents are often recast, and at times the recasting is straightforward and easy. For example, many male patients with loving but overly possessive mothers work to reinterpret the guilt they feel over having "abandoned" their mothers by growing up. They may come to see their mothers as, for example, having an inappropriate oedipal attraction to them and consequently having acted distressed at their sons' expression of interest in other women during adolescence and adulthood. When there is no motive to maintain the dissociation, such a reinterpretation can lead to a rapid improvement in understanding and behavior.

As this example illustrates, passive dissociation need not involve emotionally neutral material. Indeed emotions themselves produce an important type of passive dissociation because they are such potent determinants of the organization of skills (Bower, 1981; Kernberg, 1976; Sullivan, 1953). Affective splitting is, of course, one sign of the organizational potency of emotions. One girl performing a doll-play story that required the simultaneous integration of nice and mean behavior in two dolls (Step 8 in Table 3.2, two-dimensional social influence) showed a dramatic instance of dissociation arising from emotional content. After seeing a story in which two dolls were nice and mean to each other at the same time, she split the story into two separate parts and stated that they occurred at different times. First, she had the two dolls interact in a mean way, and then she announced, "And a long time later," and had them interact in a nice way (Hand, 1981a; Fischer, Hand, Watson, Van Parys, & Tucker, in press).

In other cases, the incompatibility of emotions can be more extreme, and one emotion skill can block the detection or use of another. Then the dissociation is no longer clearly passive and a diagnosis of active dissociation must be considered. When one boy bumps into another on the playground, for example, the first one will typically apologize for the accident—a mean action followed by a nice one. Research with hyperaggressive boys indicates, however, that if one of them is bumped in this manner, he will typically not even notice the apology and leap to an attribution about the mean intentions of the other boy (Dodge & Frame, 1982; Nasby, Hayden, & dePaulo, 1980). Such distortion does not arise straightforwardly from the separate emotional content of the skills, and so it begins to take on some of the properties of active dissociation.

Active Dissociation

Within the psychoanalytic tradition, the term "unconscious" refers primarily to the dynamic unconscious, in which components of behavior are actively dissociated, usually for affective reasons. The capacity to build separate skills and to actively keep them separate is clearly a general human capacity, at least for adults. Active dissociation occurs when a person is *motivated* to keep two or more skills or clusters of skills in a state of fractionation or dissociation. The motivation can arise from affect, as in the Freudian dynamic unconscious, or from nonaffective circumstances. In cases of obvious pathology or bizarre behavior, such as the condensation of eating and having a relationship by the woman C, the motivation is generally assumed to be affective.

The adult capacity to actively dissociate takes one of its most extreme forms when a person builds separate agents or co-consciousnesses in the mind (James, 1890), and in some instances the co-consciousnesses seem to arise from nonaffective motivation. For example, Hilgard (1977) has experimentally documented the existence of a co-consciousness that he calls the "hidden observer" in hypnosis, an agent that watches what the hypnotized person is experiencing and sees through the distortions induced by the hypnotic trance but has no control over the person's actions. Research by Hilgard and others (e.g., Orne, 1959) indicates that more than half of all adults are capable of being hypnotized and that a small percentage can construct such a hidden observer. Affect seems to play no fundamental role in the active dissociation induced by hypnosis, because the dissociation occurs even when all the events of the hypnosis are affectively neutral.

An everyday experience that often involves a phenomenon similar to the hidden observer is dreaming, which everyone experiences (Dement, 1974). In the dream itself, there is often an agent or co-consciousness that observes the self acting in the dream but does not control the self (Freud, 1900/1953; Fromm, 1949). Besides these normal co-consciousnesses, dissociated co-consciousnesses have been documented in many instances of extreme psychopathology, including schizophrenia (Freeman, Cameron, & McGhie, 1958; Modell, 1968), spirit possession (Mischel & Mischel, 1958), and multiple personality (Bliss, 1980; Putnam et al., 1983; Rosenbaum, 1980).

According to the structural-developmental approach, active dissociation involving co-consciousnesses develops through the same developmental levels as all other capacities: It is not possible early in development, it becomes possible at some particular developmental level, and it evolves to more complex forms at later levels. We will outline some of the evidence about this developmental progression in a later section.

The form of active dissociation emphasized most in the psychoanalytic view of the unconscious is *repression,* which is traditionally treated as a process in which a thought or action is actively removed from consciousness or prevented from attaining consciousness for affective reasons (Brenner, 1973; S. Freud, 1915/1957; A. Freud, 1966). Some cases of repression seem to involve a co-consciousness like those in hypnosis and dreaming, an agent that eliminates material from a part of consciousness; these will be referred to as "co-conscious repression." In general usage, however, the concept of repression refers to a broad range of phenomena involving affective isolation, in which material is isolated from consciousness to avoid negative affect; these will be called "isolating repression."

The central dimension of emotional organization in psychopathology involves the categorization of content as self-enhancing or self-threatening (Kernberg, 1976; Sullivan, 1953). Indeed this dimension seems to be important not only for psychopathology but for all human experience (see Osgood et al., 1957; Zajonc, 1980). Skills that are perceived as self-enhancing, or at least not self-threatening, can be brought to consciousness easily, while those that are perceived as self-threatening may be barred from consciousness.

In co-conscious repression, there is one agent barring an item from the experience of a second agent for affective reasons. If the two co-consciousnesses or agents can function independently at least some of the time without strong affective interference, then they can both develop to high levels of complexity, although they may "grow up strangely," showing unusual or pathological development. But potential differentiations and integrations across the co-consciousnesses will generally be lacking, especially in domains where one co-consciousness eliminates material from the experience of the other.

In isolating repression, an affective threat, sometimes called "signal anxiety," leads a person to avoid thinking about a content, so that the skills for that content can never grow up to attain higher levels of complexity (Wachtel, 1977). Because it hurts to think about this content, the person devises strategies to avoid it and thus never develops the potential differentiations and integrations with other domains that may seem obvious to an outside observer. As a result, the domain is fractionated in the extreme—dissociated. Therapeutic attempts to instigate the development of these differentiations and integrations lead to cognitive lability, including the forgetting of material that a person knew or experienced at an earlier time. One cause of the lability is the person's strategy for repression, and another is negative affect, which interferes with keeping content in mind long enough to integrate it with other contents. Isolating repression seems to be closely related to affective splitting, but splitting can be passive, arising from the psychological tendency to organize skills in terms of affective state. The repression is active, motivated by a major threat to self-esteem.

Within the structural-developmental framework, both types of repression arise from specific cognitive structures that develop through the same levels and transformations as other structures. There is no single dynamic unconscious, but there are a number of individual skills for repression of specific components of thought. Moreover, both types of repression are complex and sophisticated cognitive maneuvers that cannot be constructed at the earliest levels of development: For co-conscious repression, the person must develop the capacity to construct two distinct co-consciousnesses and relate them to each other. For isolating repression, a person must develop a sense of self, the capacity to detect that a certain content is threatening to that self, and the capacity to construct strategies for isolating the content.

In summary, three natural, everyday processes can produce a gap between the demands of a task and the level of the skill that the person can bring to bear on the task: limitations in level, passive dissociation, and active dissociation. Such gaps produce the structures of unconscious thought, which are a characteristic of a wide range of behaviors, not only of the Freudian dynamic unconscious. In the phenomena of the dynamic unconscious, gaps between task and skill are induced by affect, and consequently the unconscious behavior is more emotional and bizarre than that arising from more ordinary unconscious structures.

THE DEVELOPMENT OF UNCONSCIOUS STRUCTURES

Although psychological development can take an infinite variety of forms, the general outlines of specific developmental paths can be derived from the structural-developmental framework. To illustrate such derivations and to flesh out some of the particulars of the development of unconscious processes, we sketch developmental sequences for three psychodynamic domains: the emotional process of affective splitting, the primary process characteristic of condensation, and the defense mechanism of repression.

The sequences are described for the most part as simple progressions through the developmental levels and tiers. The movement from level to level can be readily elaborated with the prediction of multiple microdevelopmental steps at each level, as illustrated in Table 3.2. Sequences of this sort provide valuable descriptions of the general course of development in a domain, and they can serve as useful scales for measuring behavioral change.

It is important to remember, however, that children's real behavior varies widely within a portion or zone of the scale for a domain; children do not limit themselves to one step at a time. Developmental progress is reflected primarily by increases in the upper bound of the zone. Across domains, the upper bound varies too, as reflected by an individual's range of functional levels. Factors such as environmental support for high-level performance, social context, and emotional state strongly affect the developmental step that a person will actually demonstrate at any instant. Consequently, an individual may show an advanced step at one moment in a given task, and at another moment in the same task he or she may show a primitive step involving unconscious distortion.

In addition, the complexity of the particular task strongly affects developmental step. A person who is faced with a simple task may show an advanced step for that domain, but when given a complex task involving the same content, performance will "regress" to a lower step (Fischer, Hand, & Russell, 1983; Fischer, Hand, Watson, Van Parys, & Tucker, in press; Roberts, 1981). In the sequence for mean and nice in Table 3.2, for example, 5 year olds given the story for Step 4b (one-dimensional social influence) will typically understand it and repeat it appropriately. Faced with a much more complex story, such as that for step 10 (a single abstraction integrating opposite behaviors), they will not only usually fail to understand the story, but their behavior on the task will fall at a step below their Step 4b capability: They will regress to a more primitve behavior, such as Step 1 or 2. The developmental maturity of a person's behavior is strongly affected by the particular task he or she is facing.

As people's skills become more developmentally mature, their behavior typically becomes better adapted, more flexible, and healthier; but the correlation with adaptation, flexibility, and health is not a necessary one. Structural-developmental advance is defined by increases in complexity, not by health or adaptation. Higher-level thought cannot, therefore, be equated with better thought. People are capable of growing up strangely, constructing complex, developmentally advanced forms of pathological behavior (Mahlerstein & Ahern, 1982; Silvern, 1984). Paranoid delusional systems are an especially dramatic case illustrating the principle that higher levels of thinking can lead to more complex and sophisticated forms of distortion. Several studies have shown a similar pattern for other forms of pathology. For example, psychopaths evidenced higher stages of moral judgment than normal adults (Link, Scherer, & Byrne, 1977), and emotionally disturbed boys with more advanced perspective-taking skills produced greater antisocial behavior than those with less advanced skills (Waterman, Sobesky, Silvern, Aoki, & McCaulay, 1981). Some of our analyses of the development of unconscious structures will illustrate how pathology can progress to high levels of cognitive development.

Affective Splitting

Affective splitting is a pervasive phenomenon in both mental illness and normal development, and the research on children's use of emotion categories can be directly applied to analysis of the development of splitting, as was demonstrated earlier. In affective splitting, skills are organized primarily in terms of emotional categories of good versus bad instead of categories based on objects, events, or people. (As noted earlier, this meaning of "splitting" is more general than the technical meaning used in clinical work with borderline patients.) Splitting results from the prepotent effect of emotions on the organization of skills

(Bower, 1981; Sullivan, 1953), and it is also virtually inevitable at certain levels of development.

Representations

In our portrayal of the developmental sequence for nice and mean, the evolution of affective splitting for one domain in the representational tier was described in some detail, and therefore only a brief sketch of that sequence is necessary here. The tier begins with Level 4 single representations, which first emerge at about 2 years of age. Level 4 skills for emotions must be split because the child can control only one representation at a time and so cannot relate one representation of an emotion to another. People, including the self, are seen as either nice or mean, not as both simultaneously. Preschoolers act as if they are "all nice" or "all mean," with no blending of the opposing categories (Harter, 1982).

Level 5 representational mappings, which first appear at 3½ to 4 years of age, bring the first capacity to integrate opposite emotions (Step 4a in Table 3.2), as the child can understand that a person can be both nice and mean.[3] But there is a peculiar limitation to this understanding: When two people are interacting, the child cannot construct a skill for simultaneous nice and mean behavior in both of them in the interaction. This limitation places serious constraints on the child's understanding of nice and mean, because they are, of course, fundamentally social concepts. In a social situation where two people act nice and mean to each other at the same time, children who are limited to Level 5 skills must simplify the situation in order to understand it. In one form of simplification, they separate the people, dealing only with the behavior of one person, who is both nice and mean. In another form, they split the emotions, seeing either a nice interaction or a mean interaction—or at best one followed "a long time later" by the other. Each specific emotion tends to be attributed to a different situation.

With Level 6 representational systems, emerging at approximately 6 years, children can move beyond splitting of representations of emotions (Hand, 1981a; Harter, 1982; Harter & Buddin, 1983). Systems give children the capacity to integrate simultaneous nice and mean behavior in interactions between two or more people, which are called two-dimensional social influence (Step 8 in Table 3.2). The final level in the representational tier, Level 7 systems of representational systems (which are also single abstractions), first develops at 10 or 11 years. It constitutes a further advance in integrating opposite emotions, in that Level 7 skills allow the relation of different instances of two-dimensional interactions in terms of some general concept, such as that intentions matter more than actions. By the end of the representational tier, then, children have the capacity to integrate representations of opposite emotions and thus overcome splitting of concrete emotion categories.

Abstractions

Even while Level 7 capacities aid the integration of opposite concrete emotions, they produce a new kind of splitting—of abstractions. At this initial level of the abstract tier, people can build their first intangible categories for emotions, personality concepts, and so forth; but the limitations of the first level prevent them from relating those categories. Consequently, when they construct concepts like evil and benevolence, they are unable to relate them: People are seen as either evil or benevolent, not both. Personality concepts, such as treacherous, brave, virtuous, moral, and malicious, tend to be filled with emotional significance and are also split in terms of good and bad. In fact, research indicates that early abstractions are typically treated in all-or-none terms (e.g., Adelson, 1975; Kenny, 1983; Kitchener, 1983).

The progression of splitting through the abstract tier is generally parallel to that of representational splitting in the previous tier. Level 8 abstract mappings, which first appear at approximately 15 years of age, allow the first relations of opposite emotional and personality categories, but the integration tends to be incomplete. Positive and negative categories are often treated as simple opposites, even when their relation is more complex in reality. For instance, evil and benevolent may be reasonable opposites, but treacherous and brave do not really form an appropriate contrast. The simplistic treatment of abstract relations at this level thus produces some splitting, as it did with the second representational level.

Psychodynamic analyses of unconscious structures have generally failed to note the possibility that splitting and other unconscious processes can be characteristic of relatively high levels of development, such as Levels 7 and 8. Because the formal characteristics of these levels are similar to those of the early levels of sensorimotor and representational development, the assumption has generally been made that behavior showing these formal characteristics is fixated at levels in early childhood. The distinction between splitting of abstractions and splitting of representations may be helpful in explaining differences between more and less mature forms of splitting encountered in clincial practice and everyday life.

Understanding the subtleties of relations between positive and negative categories awaits the emergence of Level 9 abstract systems at about 20 years of age, and the integrations of these subtle relations in terms of general principles begins with the first appearance at about age 25 of Level 10 systems of abstract systems, which are general principles (see Table 3.1). Only with these most advanced levels can the person treat emotional and personality categories with the complexity that is seen in psychodynamic approaches to personality. Fischer, Hand, and Russell (1983), Harter (1983), Kitchener (1983), and Broughton (1978) elaborate upon some of these later developments beyond the abstract splitting of the first two levels.

Sensorimotor Actions

The focus of this chapter is on unconscious *thought,* and so we in general have had little to say about infancy. However, the striking correspondence between the skill-theory analysis of sensorimotor development and the treatments of infant affective development by Sullivan (1953) and Kernberg (1976) merit comment. The levels of the sensorimotor tier directly parallel those of the representational and abstract tiers, as shown in Table 3.1, and so infants are predicted to move through a sensorimotor progression from affective splitting to eventual integration of contradictory emotions.

Kernberg and Sullivan describe exactly such a sequence. Early in infancy, with Level 1 single sensorimotor actions, babies construct sensorimotor categories for good and bad based on positive and negative emotional experiences. Self and other are not separated within these categories. In the nursing situation, for example, there can be nursing the good breast or trying to nurse the bad breast, with no self or mother separate from the good and bad nursing actions. In the middle of the first year, with Level 2 sensorimotor mappings, infants can begin to relate good and bad as opposites but cannot integrate aspects of self and mother with good and bad. Starting at a year of age, Level 3 sensorimotor systems finally allow infants to put self and mother together with good and bad, so that they can coordinate and differentiate, for example, good and bad aspects of the nursing situation having to do with their own sucking and with problems with their mother's breast or bottle.[4] Further progress is made in this integration and differentiation with Level 4 single representations, in which self and mother can be represented as independent agents separate from the child's own actions at the moment (Fischer, Hand, Watson, Van Parys, & Tucker, in press; Pipp, Fischer, & Jennings, 1984; Watson & Fischer, 1977).

Across the three developmental tiers, then, people normally show both (a) steady progress across all levels from affective splitting toward integration and (b) a cyclical pattern of splitting of the component sets for each tier at the early levels of the tier followed by integration of those sets at the later levels. In the sensorimotor tier, the infant starts with a fundamental split between positive and negative emotional experiences and moves toward integration of those experiences with differentiated notions of self and other. With the emergence of the representational tier, the integration of positive and negative sensorimotor experiences culminates as the child builds representations for self and other as independent agents. The development of representations also brings with it the ability to represent emotions, and the early levels of the representational tier produce splitting between representations of good and bad. Progression through the representational levels allows the child to integrate representations for good and bad emotions, and the tier concludes with the ability to integrate good and bad in terms of abstractions about, for example, social interactions. The emergence of abstractions creates a new kind of affective splitting, because initially the young adolescent can control only single abstractions about emotions or affect-laden concepts. Finally, this type of splitting can be gradually eliminated as the person develops the capacity to integrate abstractions at the highest levels of development.

In normal development, progression through the levels thus seems to lead to the elimination of most affective splitting. Individuals need not take this developmental path, however: Splitting can continue even in people who have reached advanced developmental levels. The occurrence of such splitting seems to take two different forms. First, the person's affective skills can fail to grow up to advanced levels. Second, the person can follow a strange developmental path that results in the development of high-level splitting instead of affective integration.

Not Growing Up

The failure of affective skills to grow up fits the traditional Freudian analysis of unconscious structures, but the structural-developmental perspective provides a different portrait of *how* the skills fail to grow. First of all, affective splitting can occur not only when skills remain at the levels of infancy or early childhood, but also when they stay at the early levels of abstraction (Levels 7 and 8 in Table 3.1). Affective splitting can therefore develop in early adolescence and remain a part of the adult personality.

Second, affective skills can remain at low levels for a number of distinct reasons. Of course, there can be emotional blocking that prevents the person from constructing high-level skills, as in the traditional psychodynamic analysis. In addition, however, affective skills can remain at a low level for a broad array of reasons relating to environmental support for advanced functioning. If the person has never experienced an environment that induced movement toward a higher level of affective skills, then the skills will remain at a low functional level, and they will evidence splitting. If the person has constructed high-level skills but is now in a context that does not support high-level functioning, then the skills will usually occur at a low level despite the persons' capacity to function at a high level. Oddly, the need for support for high-level functioning has been generally neglected in theories of development in both the psychodynamic and cognitive-developmental traditions, except for the work of Vygotsky (1978).

In several recent studies in our laboratory, the effects of differences in environmental support have varied as a function of developmental level within a tier (Fischer & Lamborn, in press; Hand, 1981b; Watson & Fischer, 1980). This "tier effect" seems to have important implications for the development of unconscious structures. At the first level of a tier, people can easily sustain a behavior at or near their optimal level even without much environmental support. As their optimum moves to higher levels in the tier, however, they have more difficulty performing at their highest step without support. As a result, people who are capable of high-level functioning within a tier often fail to show that capacity in low-support situations. In the developmental sequence for nice and mean, for example, children who are capable of the steps at the first representational level (Steps 1 to 3 in Table 3.2) seem to produce those steps easily in spontaneous play. At the later representational levels, on the other hand, children seldom evidence their highest capacities in spontaneous play, but produce stories one or two levels below their optimum (Hand, 1981a).

This tier effect seems to be even more pronounced for the abstract tier than for the representational one (Fischer, Hand, & Russell, 1983; Hand & Fischer, 1981). Adults who can readily demonstrate high-level abstract skills in a supportive context have difficulty sustaining the high-level behavior in situations that do not directly support it. Consequently, abstract affective splitting should arise frequently when adults are acting in situations that lack support for high-level functioning. Perhaps one of the functions of psychotherapy is to help individuals raise their functional levels for abstract affective skills so that they can sustain high-level behavior without a great deal of environmental support.

Growing Up Strangely

Within psychodynamic theory, affective splitting seems to be treated uniformly as a primitive unconscious structure (e.g., Kernberg, 1976; Kohut, 1977), although psychotherapists sometimes encounter what seem to be more mature forms of splitting. Such mature splitting represents an alternative, pathological developmental path in which the person constructs high-level skills that maintain affective splitting.

In the normal path, positive and negative emotions are combined, and the person becomes the locus of the combination: A 4 year old boy, for example, uses Level 5 mappings to understand that his mother is a single person who happens to be sometimes nice and sometimes mean. In the strange path, on the other hand, the split between positive and negative is maintained, and mother is treated as two separate agents, similar to a fairy god mother and a wicked witch. The child can represent each of these split agents in Level 5 mappings, relating, for example, the behavior of his nice mother to his own nice actions (Step 4b in Table 3.2). At higher levels, this strange path results in continuing development of more complex skills that sustain the split of the mother into good and bad forms. The split can continue to the highest levels of abstraction, where the person can construct complex personality descriptions of the benevolent mother and the evil mother, thus treating the same person as two separate people. Borderline patients often demonstrate this sort of splitting, stating, for example, that the therapist they are talking with today is not the same person that they were talking with during the last session (Kernberg, 1976; Kohut, 1977).

The case of the woman C illustrates the attainment of relatively complex skills that sustain the split between good and bad in social relationships. She can discuss what a relationship is and describe social interactions in her relationship with her male friend and thus demonstrate skills that are at least at Level 6 or 7. Yet she vacillates between strongly positive and negative characterizations of the relationship, maintaining a split between feeling "all good" and "all bad" about it.

A number of scholars of psychotherapy are beginning to question the general assumption that psychopathology always involves functioniong at primitive developmental levels (e.g., Mahlerstein & Ahern, 1982; Silvern, 1984). In cases of "developmentally mature" mental illness, the source of psychopathology seems to be not the low cognitive level of the person's behavior, but its inappropriate and maladaptive nature. Description of the developmental course of growing up strangely is an important task for scholars of mental illness.

Condensation in the Oedipus Conflict

Primary process refers to the structural characteristics of unconscious thought, and we have argued that primary-process structures do not remain static but develop through the cognitive levels. Because there is no unitary unconscious, primary process is not a single entity; instead, it is a characteristic of behavior in situations where there is a gap between the level required by a task and the skill the person uses for the task. Early in development, young children necessarily show primary process frequently because their cognitive level is so limited. At later ages, more complex forms of primary process appear as the person acquires the capacity to misunderstand and distort in sophisticated ways.

This overview makes it clear that no single sequence can portray the development of primary process, because it is not a single process. What can be done is to describe sequences for the development of particular characteristics of primary process in specific domains. We have chosen to describe the development of condensation in the domain of the Oedipus conflict, based on the structural-developmental analysis proposed by Fischer and Watson (1981). Although they discuss a number of different components of the Oedipus conflict, we will focus here exclusively on condensation. The argument will be presented for boys in a nuclear family, in keeping with the Freudian tradition; but it applies as well to girls.

The basic thesis of the argument is that the Oedipus conflict results from developmental changes in preschool children's understanding of social roles in the family. In the Oedipus conflict, as in most real-life behavior, cognitions, emotions, and social interactions intermesh to form a common developmental pattern. The Oedipus conflict arises from the distortions caused by one level in that development, and it is resolved as a result of the elimination of those distortions at the next level. The developmental sequence of family role concepts required by this thesis has been empirically supported in several studies (Fischer, Hand, Watson, Van Parys, & Tucker, in press; Watson, 1981).

With Level 4 single representations, 2 and 3 year olds can construct concrete categories for roles in the family—mother, father, child, boy, girl, and so forth. Because of the limitations of single representations, however, each category is understood in isolation: The category of mother cannot be related cognitively to that of father, nor father to child, nor mother to girl. One result of this limitation is an extreme form of condensation: Whenever children are faced with a situation where several family roles occur together, they are unable to keep the roles separate. They regularly mix together the categories of mother and father when both parents take care of the child. They confuse boy and father when they must focus on being male. They blend girl and mother when they have to deal with being female. And in one of the most frequent and obvious examples of condensation encountered by parents, they condense all women (and sometimes a few men) into the category "mommy" and all men (and sometimes a few women) into the category "daddy."

Level 5 representational mappings provide the ability to understand the relation between two role categories, such as woman to man, wife to husband, Mommy to Daddy, boy to man, girl to woman, and so forth. Some of the relations among the categories in the real world are illustrated in Figure 3.2 and Table 3.3. The extreme condensation of the previous level dissipates as 4 and 5 year olds construct mappings for these various role relations and in this way differentiate the roles.

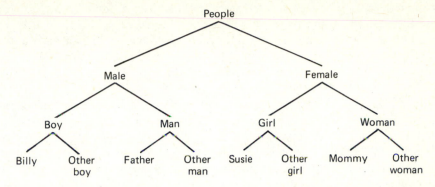

Figure 3.2.   Hierarchy of family roles (reprinted from Fischer & Watson, 1981, with permission).

A more sophisticated type of condensation arises with the new level, however, and that is what causes the Oedipus conflict. A 4 year old boy named Billy condenses the complex relations in Figure 3.2 and Table 3.3 into mappings, so that the mapping of mommy to daddy mixes together mother to father, wife to husband, and female to male. In Figure 3.2, he can construct a separate skill for each of the forks (such as *male-female, girl-woman, Mommy-other woman*), but he cannot move from one fork to another, up and down the classification hierarchy. In Table 3.3, he can construct the division *child versus parent* and the division *male versus female,* but he cannot integrate the two divisions. The result is the condensed, nondifferentiated understanding that Billy can substitute for Daddy and marry Mommy since he will some day become a daddy. "Children construct an understanding of social relationships in their families that allows them to realize they can become husbands or wives, but the limitations of mappings lead them to think they can actually take the place of their fathers or mothers" (Fischer & Watson, 1981, p. 86).

At approximately 6 years, the child develops Level 6 representational systems, which give him the ability to construct skills coordinating all the relations in Figure 3.2 and Table 3.3. With these skills, he can eliminate all the condensations from Level 5 that led him to Oedipal confusions. He can thus achieve a full understanding of complementary social roles, such as husband and wife, because he can differentiate the characteristics that distinguish husband and wife from other related role pairs, such as father and mother, male and female. For understanding his parents, he can construct a representational system in which

TABLE 3.3.   Intersection of Family Roles

	Child	Parent
Male	Boy	Father
Female	Girl	Mother

Source: Reprinted from Fischer and Watson (1981) with permission.

the parents carry on two role relations simultaneously: Daddy is both husband and father, and Mommy is both wife and mother. Comparing himself to his parents, he realizes that he is a male child, while his father is a male adult. Furthermore, as he grows to be a man, his mother will also grow older. He knows, then, that he cannot really substitute for Daddy in the marital relationship with Mommy.

In this way, the structural-developmental analysis explains the emergence and resolution of the Oedipus conflict in terms of (a) the unconscious distortions that characterize particular developmental levels and (b) the type of family environment in which children grow up. Contrary to Freud's (1909/1955) position, the Oedipus conflict is not universal, because children growing up in different family constellations do not experience the same role relations. For the roles they do experience, they will produce similar types of unconscious distortions, and the result will be not the Oedipus conflict but some other affect-laden confusion.

Of course, variations within the nuclear family environment also affect the course of the Oedipus conflict. If a 7 or 8 year old has not been given environmental support for constructing and using Level 6 relations between roles or if the roles are fraught with negative affect, he will continue to function at Level 5 and show the condensations typical of the Oedipus conflict. Or if the family encourages an Oedipal relation between a boy and his mother, then the role distinctions will be blurred, and he may develop along a strange developmental path, constructing Level 6 categories that do not produce resolution of the Oedipus conflict.

Although the traditional treatment specifies that the Oedipus conflict normally ends by age 6 or 7, some scholars have suggested that it reemerges and must be reworked in adolescence (see Blos, 1979). One effect of the sexual blossoming of puberty is to bring forth Oedipal issues once again. The emergence of the abstract tier at 10 to 12 years likewise implies that Oedipal issues will recur as adolescents rework their understanding of their parents in abstract terms. Adolescents can use Level 7 single abstractions to construct concepts of their parents' personalities that were not previously possible, but as with Level 4 representations, they are unable to relate two such constructions. Consequently, condensation of categories reigns supreme, and adolescents are unable to consider their parents' personalities in relationship to each other. With Level 8 abstract mappings, adolescents can compare and distinguish personality categories, thus substantially reducing condensation; and they can build understandings of how their parents' personalities fit together in a marital relationship. For example, Paul at age 15 began to ask questions about what his parents had been like as a young couple, as well as what his grandparents had been like. The answers to such questions inevitably have personal implications for growing adolescents' conceptions of their own personalities and the love relationships they will build. Level 9 abstract systems and Level 10 general principles provide the capacity to eliminate most condensation of categories and to develop a sophisticated understanding of one's parents and one's own relationship with them.

Condensation in the Oedipus conflict thus illustrates how a basic character-istic of primary process develops through the developmental levels, moving continually toward greater complexity and sophistication while at the same time demonstrating the recurrence of general types of distortion with the emergence of each new tier. Environmental variation and emotional state strongly affect the levels of skills and the resulting unconscious structures, so that a person can show wide fluctuations in level of functioning and degree of condensation.

Repression

An important component of normal development, according to psychoanalysis, is the acquisition of mechanisms of defense—mental maneuvers by which the ego defends itself against unconscious impulses and anxiety. A dozen or more specific defense mechanisms are usually described, including projection, intro-jection, reaction formation, regression, and repression, and several attempts have been made to describe when each mechanism first develops (see Chandler et al., 1978; A. Freud, 1966; Haan, 1977; Vaillant, 1977). Why the focus has been primarily on specifying the onset of each defense mechanism is not clear. Plainly, the development of a defense mechanism can go on after it has emerged. Indeed the structural-developmental framework predicts that defense mechanisms, like any other skill structure, will develop through a series of increasingly advanced forms. To illustrate the development of defense mechanisms, we have chosen to analyze repression, because it is often treated as the most fundamental of all defense mechanisms.

In active dissociation, the person actively tries to keep two or more skills separated or dissociated. Repression is a special case of active dissociation, in which a thought or content is kept out of awareness in order to avoid negative affect. Just as there is not a single dynamic unconscious, there is not a single mechanism of repression, but a class of mental maneuvers for keeping things out of awareness. Because of the variations in types of repression, it is not possible to give a unified account of the development of all repression, but it is possible to specify some of the boundaries on the class of repression mechanisms and to describe the developmental course of some specific types of repression.

Repression is a transitive process, in which one thought or agent acts on another. To repress something, the person must somehow use one thought to avoid experiencing another thought, which requires the ability to relate the first thought to the second. Based on such a global analysis, the earliest that children are capable of constructing a mechanism that clearly merits the label "repression" is 3½ to 4 years of age, when the ability develops to relate two representations in Level 5 mappings. For sophisticated forms of repression, involving relations of not only concrete thoughts (representations) but more general mental structures, the earliest age for the emergence of repression could be as late as about 15 years, when adolescents develop the ability to relate two abstractions in Level 8 mappings. One of the boundaries on the various forms of repression, then, is that they develop in middle childhood or adolescence, not in infancy or early childhood. Certain complex types may not appear until early adulthood. To illustrate both this boundary and the developmental course of repression, we will describe the development of two types of repression—co-consciousnesses and affective isolation.

Co-Consciousnesses

A common criticism of the classical Freudian concept of repression is that it requires warring parts of the psyche and that somehow one of these parts must remove content from the consciousness of some other part (Feffer, 1982; Wolff, 1960, 1967). That is, the mind must know something in order not to know it.

The empirical study of dissociative phenomena has clearly documented, however, that co-consciousnesses do exist. One of the most convincing demonstrations comes from research on hypnosis in adults: The experimenter can not only induce dissociation of conscious experience into two pieces, but also instruct one of the co-consciousnesses to prevent the other from experiencing something, such as hearing a certain word or seeing a certain event (Hilgard, 1977; Orne, 1959). This repression-like phenomenon is not caused by negative affect and so is not literally repression, but it nevertheless demonstrates the reality of active dissociation by co-consciousnesses.

The study of extreme pathological dissociation in schizophrenia, psychogenic amnesia, and multiple personality documents that co-conscious repression also occurs. Although multiple personality seems to be rare, it provides evidence on the limits of people's dissociative capacity. The co-consciousnesses in multiple personality are distinct and elaborate and can clearly produce repression (Bliss, 1980; Rosenbaum, 1980; Thigpen & Cleckley, 1954). A specific co-consciousness or personality controls the body (or most of it) at any one time, yet another co-consciousness can prevent the one in control from experiencing something or induce an experience that is not based in reality. Such co-conscious repression is frequently related to negative affect, especially fears that the repressing co-consciousness will somehow be harmed if the repressed co-consciousness experiences the content in question.

Recent research on the bases of the extreme dissociation of multiple personality suggest that it may be typically caused by extreme abuse in early childhood; in one study of 100 cases, 97 had experienced such abuse, and there was a significant correlation between the number of types of trauma in childhood and the number of alternate personalities (Putnam et al., 1983). A child who is subjected to extreme, repeated physical or sexual abuse will sometimes escape from that abuse by dividing his or her consciousness into separate personalities. Once this strategy for dealing with stress has been established, it can lead to a proliferation of distinct co-consciousnesses to deal with different situations. Interestingly, each co-consciousness seems to have a markedly different emotional makeup from the others (Bower, 1981).

We know of no research that directly traces development of the ability to form co-consciousnesses in multiple personality, but there is some research on the development of other relevant phenomena, including hypnosis (Hilgard, 1965,

1977), free association (Harter, 1982), dreams (Foulkes, 1982), and play (Fischer, Hand, Watson, Van Parys, & Tucker, in press). The findings regarding these phenomena to be described below are based on the references cited here, except where other citations are given. Combining these results with structural-developmental theory, we have constructed a developmental sequence for repression arising from co-consciousnesses. The sequence could be tested empirically in a number of ways. The simplest method would seem to be hypnotic induction of each developmental step in children of different ages, but naturally occurring dissociations could also be assessed in children of different ages suffering from multiple personality, schizophrenia, or other dissociative pathologies.

Not until approximately 2 years of age, with the emergence of Level 4 single representations, can children construct an independent agent, an actor who can carry out one or more actions. In pretend play, they begin to make dolls or other characters act on their own (Watson & Fischer, 1977; Wolf, 1982). Searching for objects hidden by an adult, they start to treat the adult as an independent agent who can carry out surreptitious hiding acts (Bertenthal & Fischer, 1983). When placed in front of a mirror, children represent the mirror image as themselves (Bertenthal & Fischer, 1978; Pipp et al., 1984). In reports of dreams, they begin to describe animals doing things, but interestingly they do not mention the participation of the self in their dreams.

With this capacity to represent independent agents, children should be able to build rudimentary co-consciousnesses, each of which is an agent characterized by a few concrete actions and characteristics fitting some single represented category. There can be no co-conscious repression because at Level 4 the child is unable to relate one represented agent to another.

The one type of experience that would seem likely to produce co-consciousnesses in a 2 or 3 year old is extreme splitting, where an ongoing traumatic experience leads a child to form an abused co-consciousness that is different from the normal co-consciousness. The prepotent effect of emotions in the organization of skills makes such dissociation especially likely when a parent or loved one is the abuser. The co-consciousnesses cannot relate to each other via repression, however, because of the child's inability to coordinate representations at this level. The child can only shift from one to the other by means of the shift-of-focus transformation.

Level 5 representational mappings bring the capacity to relate two agents. In pretend play, for example, 4 and 5 year olds can make one doll act in relation to the actions of another, as in one-dimensional social influence (Step 4b in Table 3.2). They can also make one doll have two related characteristics, such as nice and mean (Step 4a in Table 3.2), which are related as opposites. In dreams, children show a similar pattern: Characters interact socially or act out a meaningful sequence of events. People begin to appear in dreams too, especially family members.

The ability to relate two agents allows the first, primitive mechanisms of co-conscious repression. One co-consciousness embodying a few similar actions and concrete characteristics can relate to another co-consciousness embodied by different actions and characteristics, and so the one can act to repress some experience in the other. Although there has been no research directly testing the development of multiple personality, Bliss (1980) used information from assessment of 14 adult cases to reconstruct their developmental histories. His results strongly support the prediction that a Level 5 capacity is necessary for the construction and relating of co-consciousnesses: All 14 cases first developed multiple personality between 4 and 6 years of age. In addition, some psychotherapists report the first instances of repression at approximately 4 years (A. Freud, 1966; Vaillant, 1977). Repressions involving Level 5 mappings must necessarily be crude and simple, however, because the mapping relation between representations allows only the coordination of a single category for one agent with a single category for a second agent. There does not seem to be any solid data on the susceptibility to hypnosis during this period, at least in part because of the difficulties preschool children experience in following arbitrary instructions.

Level 6 brings the first capacity for flexible and stable mental structures, because representational systems allow the child to coordinate several aspects of two or more representations. Because of the complexity of such systems, the degrees of freedom of what can be coordinated expand greatly. In pretend play, children 6 years of age and older make characters interact in terms of several categories simultaneously, as in two-dimensional social influence (Step 8 in Table 3.2). In a wide array of domains, they also begin to be able to monitor and control some of their own mental products (Brown & DeLoache, 1978; Flavell & Wellman, 1977). For example, they can easily report what they are thinking, and they can monitor their own memories with some accuracy and adopt memory strategies to help them remember difficult items. A correlate is that their memories at later ages for events during this period improve sharply; indeed memory is so poor for infancy and the early preschool years that the young child is sometimes described as showing childhood amnesia (White & Pillemar, 1979).

The ability to construct and relate concrete co-consciousnesses is definitely present during this period. Children as a group show a spurt in susceptibility to concrete hypnotic suggestions, such as posthypnotic amnesia, with the highest susceptibility being reached by 8 or 9 years. It is doubtful, however, that children at this age can sustain some of the prolonged, complex hypnotic procedures that are often associated with hypnotic demonstrations. In dreams, the self becomes a major character for the first time, suggesting that the dreamer can now coordinate two concrete selves in the dream—the one experiencing the dream and the one acting in the dream. Co-conscious repression will show parallel growth: With representational systems, one co-consciousness (one representation composed of several subsets) can monitor several related aspects of another co-consciousness and thus repress concrete content much more effectively than at Level 5.

With Level 7, children 10 to 12 years of age can coordinate two or more representational systems into a system of systems, which also gives them the ability to understand single abstractions. In stories, they can coordinate several two-dimensional social interactions, which means they can handle great complexity in specific social exchanges. So many of the concrete abilities of the previous levels flower during this time that the period is sometimes called the culmination of concrete intelligence (Biggs & Collis, 1982; Flavell, 1971). The construction of co-consciousnesses shows the same flowering: Children can coordinate two or more representational systems to produce great richness in concrete detail, but they cannot yet deal effectively with abstractions because they can only deal with one at a time. Dreams include more details about physical events and concrete interactions between self and others than at any other age. Susceptibility to concrete hypnotic suggestions continues at the high level that it reached by age 8 or 9.

Level 7 is not only the culmination of the representational tier, but also the beginning of the abstract tier. The capacity for single abstractions means that children can move beyond concrete agents to the construction of agents with full personalities. In descriptions of self and others, they start to use personality constructs (Broughton, 1978; Harter, 1983), although the usage seems to be inconsistent and confused (Fischer, Hand, & Russell, 1983; Kitchener, 1983). The confusions engendered by this new ability seem to be reflected in dreams, where 13 to 15 year olds show a drop in references to the self.

Co-consciousnesses at Level 7 thus have two different faces. From the perspective of the representational tier, children can have co-consciousnesses of great complexity, because the coordination of representational systems allows each one to have a whole representational system to itself. The result is a great advance in the ability of one co-consciousness to monitor and repress experiences in the other. These co-consciousnesses are still based on concrete actions and characteristics, however. From the perspective of the abstract tier, children can build a new type of co-consciousness, in which sveral representational systems are coordinated around a single abstraction. This co-consciousness is severely limited by the child's inability to relate abstractions. In a manner analagous to Level 4, the co-consciousness based on a single abstraction cannot repress a parallel co-consciousness but can only exist separately from it. Strong, negative affective experiences may be the most likely factor to induce the formation of abstract co-consciousnesses at Level 7.

The development to higher levels in the abstract tier at age 15 and beyond should lead to the emergence of full-fledged co-consciousnesses similar to those evident in the best documented cases of hypnosis, schizophrenia, and multiple personality (e.g., Pattie, 1935; Thigpen & Cleckley, 1954). Based on abstractions, a co-consciousness can develop a rich personality that consists of more than a few concrete actions and characteristics. The capacity of one abstract co-consciousness to monitor and repress another begins with Level 8 abstract mappings, in which two or more abstractions are related. Unfortunately, there has been little research on the development of dissociative capacity during adolescence, although some scanty evidence does support the proposition of a major advance at about age 15. It seems that cases of multiple personality are likely to be detected starting then. Hypnotic susceptibility seems to converge on the adult pattern during this period. And apparently the ability to free associate—letting one's thoughts move freely and observing them—becomes possible at approximately this time (Harter, 1982).

Co-conscious repression, then, seems to first become possible with representational mappings at about age 4. The complexity of the co-consciousnesses and of the relations between them increases greatly throughout the childhood years, until single abstractions emerge in preadolescence. However, the rich personalities that populate case studies of co-consciousnesses in multiple personality, hypnosis, and schizophrenia do not seem to develop until approximately 15 years of age, when abstract mappings provide the capacity not only to build abstract co-conscious personalities but also to relate them, as in co-conscious repression. The schizoid reaction from which the woman C is suffering, for example, involves a dissociation in which the self withdraws to become something like the co-consciousness called a hidden observer in hypnosis; it watches the emotional reaction that the other co-consciousness is experiencing but remains detached. In that way, the emotional turmoil evident in the woman's confusion of eating and social relationships does not upset the co-conscious self. Such a sophisticated type of dissociation may only be possible at the highest levels of development, abstract mappings and beyond.

Isolating Repression and the Self

In many cases of repression, no co-consciousnesses seem to be involved, but instead a skill or content is isolated from consciousness because it evokes strong negative affect. The class of strategies for such affective isolation is diverse, and each strategy will produce a different developmental course. According to psychodynamic analyses, the various strategies nevertheless share a common thread: People affectively isolate material that threatens self-esteem (Kernberg, 1976). This thread provides a basis for a global analysis of the developmental foundations of isolating repression.

One component of isolating repression is that something is threatening to the self, and at different levels what is perceived as a threat changes systematically. A second component is the strategy used to isolate threatening material, which also changes with level. In our global analysis, the broad course of development in these two components is sketched. Harter (1983) has provided an excellent review of research and theory on the development of the self, which strongly influenced our analysis.

In the sensorimotor tier, infants cannot literally repress anything because they cannot control representations. They can, however, develop strategies for avoiding events that cause negative affect (Kernberg, 1976; Sullivan, 1953). At the first level of the tier, single sensorimotor actions, their ability to anticipate an aversive event is severely limited because they are not yet able to relate one action or perception to another. At 7 or 8 months of age, however, they can begin to relate two actions in a sensorimotor mapping and thus develop simple sensorimotor strategies for anticipating and avoiding negative affect. For example, when they see something "bad" approaching, they turn or crawl away. The third and fourth levels of the sensorimotor tier bring much greater sophistication in anticipating and avoiding such events.

Isolating repression requires the development of representations for at least two reasons. First, it arises from a threat to the self, and children do not have a definite self-concept until they can start to represent the self at age 2, the beginning of the representational tier. Second, thoughts that frighten the self also appear at the same point in development. It is at this age that children begin to be able to scare themselves with their own thoughts, as when they are afraid of an imaginary monster (Fischer, Hand, Watson, Van Parys, & Tucker, in press).

Level 4 single representations do not provide the capacity for isolating repression, however, because children cannot yet relate one representation to another. The best they can do is to stop thinking the frightening thought after it has begun. At times, children as young as 2 years of age do seem to be able to develop this stopping strategy and so demonstrate a skill approaching repression (A. Freud, 1966).

Level 4 single representations provide the capacity for only a weak form of isolating repression, because children cannot yet relate one representation to another. The best they can do is shift to another thought in order to stop thinking the frightening thought after it has begun. The minimum structure for this strategy seems to be the following: The child activates a representation that is frightening, and he or she then immediately shifts focus to another representation. At times, children as young as 2 years of age seem to be able to develop this weak form of repression (A. Freud, 1966). The capacity to switch to another representation is limited, however, by the child's inability at this level to relate one representation to another. Switching quickly from a frightening representation to a nonfrightening one is much easier when the child can relate the two representations, and the more efficient strategy of anticipating a frightening thought in order to prevent it from occurring would seem to be impossible until the next level.

A full form of isolating repression becomes possible with Level 5 representational mappings, where children can purposely use one representation to prevent themselves from thinking about another one. At 3½ or 4 years, children begin to show a capacity to monitor their own thoughts to some degree, anticipating what they know, how their own memories are limited, what simple strategies they can use to remember something, and so forth (Brown & DeLoache, 1978; Flavell & Wellman, 1977). Effective isolating repression seems to require such monitoring, which allows the child to anticipate a frightening thought instead of merely reacting to it after it has occurred. Because of this monitoring, as well as the increased ease in switching from one representation to another, this level provides the capacity to construct effective strategies for isolating repression.

In addition, the range of events that can motivate repression increases at this level because children develop a greater capacity to experience events as threatening to the self. With mappings, children can begin to compare a representation of the self with a representation of something else, such as a simple ideal or another person (Fischer et al., in press). These comparisons produce a whole new set of potential threats to the self.

The capacities that allow full forms of isolating repression to appear at Level 5 become more flexible and complex with Level 6 representational systems, and the result is further developments in isolating repression. Skills relating subsets of several representations provide more effective monitoring of thoughts and more powerful strategies for switching quickly from one representation to another. Comparisons of the self with others and with ideals also become more complex. As a result, isolating repression becomes commonplace in children 6 years and older.

The emergence of Level 7 at age 10 or 12 produces not only a further increase in the flexibility and complexity of concrete strategies for isolating repression and of concrete comparisons involving the self, but it also produces single abstractions. We have already illustrated some of the many ways that conceptions of self and others change at this level. In addition, strategies for isolating repression should show similar pervasive transformations, which will be elaborated and consolidated with development through the later levels of abstractions. Descriptions of mature mechanisms of defense, such as sublimation and humor (Haan, 1977; Vaillant, 1977), appear to provide some hints about the nature of these transformations. Yet clearly one of the major tasks that remains for the structural-developmental approach is analysis of the development of various strategies of isolating repression and their transformations at the highest developmental levels.

SUMMARY AND CONCLUSIONS

Many of the problems with psychodynamic approaches to the unconscious stem from difficulties with Freud's model of psychic processes and their development. A structural-developmental approach promises to provide a framework that will eliminate these problems and suggest new insights into the development of the structures of unconscious thought. The framework helps to explain both how unconscious structures can arise from developmentally primitive skills and also how they can develop to advanced, sophisticated levels.

The mind is naturally fractionated, and people must work to integrate its pieces. This property of the mind is the foundation for the existence of unconscious structures. Whenever a gap exists between the developmental level required for a task and the level of the skill a person brings to bear on the task, the result is an unconscious structure. Natural fractionation means that such gaps occur routinely even for adults functioning at advanced developmental levels. "Unconscious" thus refers to a fractionation process in thought that enables some implications of material to remain uncreated, or out of awareness. There is no unitary unconscious, no single repository of drives and memories, but, instead, a set of diverse structures arising from the natural fractionation of skills.

Skills are organized in terms of the context in which they are acquired and the person's emotional state. Changes in context or state lead to changes in skill, so that people must work to efficiently generalize a skill from one context or state to another or to integrate skills from different contexts or states.

Skills of all kinds develop through a series of ten hierarchical cognitive levels divided into three cycles or tiers—sensorimotor, representational, and abstract. Within each tier, skills progress through four levels: from single, separate sets to mappings (simple relations) to systems (relations with subcomponents) to systems of systems. The final level, systems of systems, generates a new type of skill, which is the single set starting the next tier: single sensorimotor actions, single representations, or single abstractions. In the first level of a tier, it is impossible to relate the single, separate sets, and one result is a type of fractionation, as in the splitting of good and bad emotions. At succeeding levels, the capacity for integration emerges and increases, with a concomitant decrease in the tendency for this type of fractionation. The recurrence of the cycle of levels in infancy, childhood, and adolescence means that mental processes with certain developmentally primitive properties reappear in each cycle. Such processes in childhood and adolescence can be confused with fixation or regression to infant structures.

With development, children's optimal level—the upper limit on the complexity of skills they can construct and control—moves through the ten levels. In everyday life, people seldom function at optimum, but instead for each domain they show a functional level, a step on a developmental scale that sets their ordinary limit for that domain. When a task requires a more advanced level than the child's functional level for the domain, the result is an unconscious structure, like what Freud called "primary process."

Besides this limitation of level, there are two other types of processes that produce unconscious structures—passive dissociation and active dissociation. Passive dissociation represents the natural fractionation arising from the effects of context and emotional state on skills. In active dissociation, the person is motivated to maintain a separation of skills. Repression is a special case of active dissociation in which the motivation comes from negative affect.

Both conscious and unconscious structures follow the same general progression through the skill levels, but the specifics of the developmental sequence differ with the particular type of structure and the domain. Also, people's behavior moves up and down in each sequence as a function of the degree of environmental support for high-level performance. Variations in environmental support can thus cause appearance or disappearance of an unconscious structure.

The structural-developmental framework provides tools for predicting development of specific types of unconscious structures in particular domains. To illustrate such predictions, we have outlined three such sequences: affective splitting, condensation, and repression.

Emotions are an important part of unconscious development, and affective splitting illustrates the roles emotions play. Affective splitting is characteristic of the first level of the representational tier, which emerges at about 2 years of age. At the second representational level, the first relations of opposite emotions can be constructed, but the relations are necessarily simple, and so a more sophisticated type of splitting occurs: Social interactions within a specific emotion category, such as mean, can be sustained, but coordinations across opposite categories, such as mean and nice, tend to be unconsciously distorted. The third and fourth representational levels allow effective integration of opposite emotions about concrete people and social interactions.

A new type of affective splitting occurs with the emergence of the fourth representational level at 10 to 12 years of age, because it produces the first single abstractions, which begin the abstract tier. Abstractions for emotions are necessarily split at this level. Movement through the second to fourth abstraction levels produces capacities to relate opposite abstractions for emotions in progressively more complex ways. Even after adults have developed the highest optimal levels of abstractions, however, they seem to normally function at lower levels, and so they demonstrate splitting.

Psychopathology has often been equated with functioning at a primitive developmental level, but people can also show developmentally advanced forms of pathology, which we call "growing up strangely." That is, they can develop along an alternative path, such as the construction of complex skills based on primary categorization in terms of affects rather than objects, events, or people.

Condensation in the Oedipus conflict illustrates how the characteristics of primary process develop. At the first representational level, children condense family roles such as mother and father and are unable to understand relations between roles. The development of the second level produces an understanding of role relations that leads to a new type of condensation: Children mix up, on the one hand, father, husband, and male and, on the other hand, mother, wife, and female, and they relate these two condensed categories to form a relationship between mommies and daddies. This condensation leads to the Oedipus conflict, in which children believe they can take the place of the same-sex parent. The conflict is resolved when the third representational level leads children to understand the complex relations of family roles. A similar pattern of condensation recurs in the abstract tier for the development of abstractions about family roles.

Repression, in which one skill is used to prevent another skill from becoming conscious, can take at least two forms—co-conscious repression and isolating repression. In co-conscious repression, one co-consciousness (mental agent) prevents another co-consciousness from experiencing some particular content. The capacity to construct concrete co-consciousnesses emerges at age 2 years with the first level of representations, and the capacity to relate co-consciousnesses to establish repression develops at the second level and is elaborated at later levels. The emergence of abstractions produces the capacity for a more sophisticated form of co-consciousness with more complex characteristics. Later levels of abstractions lead to skills for establishing repression between these abstract co-consciousnesses.

Isolating repression arises not from separate co-consciousnesses but from the development of strategies for keeping a content isolated from awareness. The content is isolated because the person's self-esteem is threatened by it. Changes in both self-concept and strategies for isolating a content therefore affect the development of this form of repression.

In general, then, unconscious structures can be both developmentally primitive *and* sophisticated. They are primitive in that they involve the fractionation of skills, so that potential knowledge remains unknown; but they can develop into highly sophisticated forms, including ones that produce active maintenance of fractionation or dissociation.

NOTES

1. Of course, the term "unconscious" has traditionally been employed in a number of different ways. Besides Freud's usage, one of the classic meanings has involved bodily processes over which people exercise no conscious control, such as the functioning of the liver. Related to this sense of unconscious is what Helmholz (1884) called "unconscious inference" in perception: The sense organs and the nervous system make apparent inferences about the nature of what is sensed, such as the existence of a line or an angle, but the observer has little or no conscious control over this inference process. We will not be dealing with these sorts of unconscious processes, although undoubtedly psychological development affects some of them.

2. This meaning is consonant with much clinical practice, but it is more general than the special type of splitting associated with borderline personalities, as described by Kernberg (1976) and Kohut (1975).

3. Some investigators have suggested that affective object constancy and Piagetian object permanence develop in parallel (for example, Decarie, 1965). The present analysis implies, however, that object constancy and object permanence should not develop at the same time. Children attain complete object permanence with single representations: By 1½ to 2 years they are able to represent an object as existing even when they cannot perceive or act upon it (Piaget, 1937/1954; see also Fischer & Jennings, 1981). Children do not attain affective object constancy until they attain representational mappings: According to object relations theory (e.g., Kernberg, 1976; Mahler et al., 1975) the integration of representations for good mother and bad mother occurs by 3½ years.

4. In sensorimotor development, babies cannot yet represent the self or the mother independently of their own actions and perceptions, but as they progress through the levels, they can gradually construct more complex actions and perceptions involving characteristics or components of self and mother (e.g., Bertenthal & Fischer, 1978; Pipp, Fischer, & Jennings, 1984).

REFERENCES

Adelson, J. The development of ideology in adolescence. In S.E. Dragastin & G.H. Elder, Jr. (Eds.), *Adolescence in the life cycle: Psychological change and social context.* New York: Wiley, 1975.

Bertenthal, B.I., & Fischer, K.W. The development of self-recognition in the infant. *Developmental Psychology,* 1978, *14,* 44–50.

Bertenthal, B.I., & Fischer, K.W. The development of representation in search: A social-cognitive analysis. *Child Development,* 1983, *54,* 846–857.

Biggs, J., & Collis, K. *Evaluating the quality of learning.* New York: Academic Press, 1982.

Bliss, E.L. Multiple personalities. *Archives of General Psychiatry,* 1980, *37,* 1388–1397.

Blos, P. *The adolescent passage.* New York: International Universities Press, 1979.

Bower, G.H. Mood and memory. *American Psychologist,* 1981, *36,* 129–148.

Brenner, C. *An elementary textbook of psychoanalysis.* New York: International Universities Press, 1973.

Broughton, J. Development of concepts of self, mind, reality, and knowledge. In W. Damon (Ed.), *Social cognition.* New Directions for Child Development No. 1. San Francisco: Jossey-Bass, 1978.

Brown, A.L., & DeLoache, J.S. Skills, plans, and self-regulation. In R.S. Siegler (Ed.), *Children's thinking: What develops?* Hillsdale, N.J.: Erlbaum, 1978.

Bruner, J.S. Going beyond the information given. In H. Gruber (Ed.), *Contemporary approaches to cognition.* Cambridge, Mass.: Harvard University Press, 1957.

Bruner, J.S. *Processes of cognitive growth: Infancy.* Worcester, Mass.: Clark University Press, 1968.

Bruner, J.S. *The origins of problem solving strategies in skill acquisition.* Paper presented at the 19th International Congress of Psychology, London, July 1969.

Bullock, D. Seeking relations between cognitive and social-interactive transitions. In K.W. Fischer (Ed.), *Levels and transitions in children's development.* New Directions for Child Development No. 21. San Francisco: Jossey-Bass, 1983.

Case, R. The underlying mechanism of intellectual development. In J.R. Kirby & J.B. Biggs (Eds.), *Cognition, development, and instruction.* New York: Academic Press, 1980.

Case, R. *Intellectual development: A systematic reinterpretation.* New York: Academic Press, in press.

Chandler, M.J., Paget, K.F., & Koch, D.A. The child's mystification of psychological defense mechanisms: A structural and developmental analysis. *Developmental Psychology,* 1978, *14,* 197–205.

Corrigan, R. The development of representational skills. In K.W. Fischer (Ed.), *Levels and transitions in children's development.* New Directions for Child Development No. 21. San Francisco: Jossey-Bass, 1983.

Décarie, T.G. *Intelligence and affectivity in early childhood* (E.P. Brandt & L.W. Brandt, trans.). New York: International Universities Press, 1965.

Dement, W.C. *Some must watch while some must sleep.* San Francisco: Freeman, 1974.

Dewey, J. *Reconstruction in philosophy.* Boston: Beacon Press, 1948.

Dodge, K.A., & Frame, C.L. Social cognitive biases and deficits in aggressive boys. *Child Development,* 1982, *53,* 620–635.

Feffer, M. *The structure of Freudian thought.* New York: International Universities Press, 1982.

Feldman, D.H. *Beyond universals in cognitive development.* Norwood, N.J.: Ablex, 1980.

Fischer, K.W. Towards a method for assessing continuities and discontinuities in development. Paper presented at the Fifth Biennial Conference of the International Society for the Study of Behavioral Development, Lund, Sweden, June 1969.

Fischer, K.W. A theory of cognitive development: The control and construction of hierarchies of skills. *Psychological Review,* 1980, *87,* 477–531.

Fischer, K.W. Developmental levels as periods of discontinuity. In K.W. Fischer (Ed.), *Levels and transitions in children's development.* New Directions for Child Development, No. 21. San Francisco: Jossey-Bass, 1983.

Fischer, K.W., & Corrigan, R. A skill approach to language development. In R. Stark (Ed.), *Language behavior in infancy and early childhood.* Amsterdam: Elsevier-North Holland, 1981.

Fischer, K.W., Hand, H.H., & Russell, S.L. The development of abstractions in adolescence and adulthood. In M. Commons, F.A. Richards, & C. Armon (Eds.), *Beyond formal operations.* New York: Praeger, 1983.

Fischer, K.W., Hand, H.H., Watson, M.W., Van Parys, M., & Tucker, J. Putting the child into socialization: The development of social categories in the preschool years. In L. Katz (Ed.), *Current topics in early childhood education* (Vol. 6). Norwood, N.J.: Ablex, in press.

Fischer, K.W., & Jennings, S. The emergence of representation in search: Understanding the hider as an independent agent. *Developmental Review,* 1981, *1,* 18–30.

Fischer, K.W., & Lamborn, S. The collaboration of child and environment in cognitive development. *Newsletter of the International Society for the Study of Behavioral Development,* in press.

Fischer, K.W., & Pipp, S.L. Processes of cognitive development: Optimal level and skill acquisition. In R.J. Sternberg (Ed.), *Mechanisms of cognitive development.* San Francisco: Freeman, 1984.

Fischer, K.W., Pipp, S.L., & Bullock, D. Detecting discontinuities in development: Method and measurement. In R.N. Emde & R. Harmon (Eds.), *Continuities and discontinuities in development.* New York: Plenum, 1984.

Fischer, K.W., & Watson, M.W. Explaining the Oedipus conflict. In K.W. Fischer (Ed.), *Cognitive development.* New Directions for Child Development No. 12. San Francisco: Jossey-Bass, 1981.

Flavell, J.H. Stage-related properties of cognitive development. *Cognitive Psychology,* 1971, *2,* 421–453.

Flavell, J.H. Structures, stages, and sequences in cognitive development. In W.A. Collins (Eds.), *Minnesota symposium on child psychology.* Hillsdale, N.J.: Erlbaum, 1983.

Flavell, J.H., & Wellman, H. Metamemory. In R.V. Kail, Jr., & J.W. Hagen (Eds.), *Perspectives on the development of memory and cognition.* Hillsdale, N.J.: Erlbaum, 1977.

Foulkes, D. *Children's dreams: Longitudinal studies.* New York: Wiley, 1982.

Freeman, T., Cameron, J.L., & McGhie, A. *Chronic schizophrenia.* New York: International Universities Press, 1958.

Freud, A. *The ego and the mechanisms of defense.* New York: International Universities Press, 1966.

Freud, A. *Normality and pathology in childhood.* New York: International Universities Press, 1965.

Freud, S. The interpretation of dreams. *Standard Edition* (Vols. 4 and 5). London: Hogarth Press, 1953. (Originally published 1900.)

Freud, S. Analysis of a phobia in a five-year-old boy. *Standard Edition* (Vol. 10). London: Hogarth Press, 1955. (Originally published 1909.)

Freud, S. Formulation on the two principles of mental functioning. *Standard Edition* (Vol. 12). London: Hogarth Press, 1958. (Originally published 1911.)

Freud, S. Papers on meta-psychology. *Standard Edition* (Vol. 14). London: Hogarth Press, 1957. (Originally published 1915.)

Fromm, E. The nature of dreams. *Scientific American,* May 1949, *180,* 44–47.

Gill, M.M. The primary process. In R.R. Holt (Ed.), *Motives and thought: Psychoanalytic essays in honor of David Rapaport. Psychological Issues,* 1967, *5* (2–3, Serial No. 18–19). New York: International Universities Press.

Greenspan, S.I. *Intelligence and adaptation.* New York: International Universities Press, 1979.

Guntrip, H. A study of Fairbairn's theory of schizoid reactions. *British Journal of Medical Psychology,* 1952, *25,* 86–103.

Haan, N. *Coping and defending.* New York: Academic Press, 1977.

Halford, G.S., & Wilson, W.H. A category theory approach to cognitive development. *Cognitive Psychology,* 1980, *12,* 356–411.

Hand, H.H. *The development of concepts of social interaction: Children's understanding of nice and mean.* Unpublished doctoral dissertation, University of Denver, 1981. (a)

Hand, H.H. The relation between developmental level and spontaneous behavior: The importance of sampling contexts. In K.W. Fischer (Ed.), *Cognitive development.* New Directions for Child Development No. 12. San Francisco: Jossey-Bass, 1981. (b)

Hand, H.H., & Fischer, K.W. The development of concepts of intentionality and responsibility in adolescence. Paper presented at the Sixth Biennial Meetings of the International Society for the Study of Behavioral Development. Toronto, Canada, August 1981.

Harter, S. A cognitive-developmental approach to children's expression of conflicting feelings and a technique to facilitate such expression in play therapy. *Journal of Consulting and Clinical Psychology,* 1977, *45,* 417–432.

Harter, S. Cognitive-developmental considerations in the conduct of the play therapy. In C.E. Schaefer & K.H. O'Connor (Eds.), *Handbook of play therapy,* New York: Wiley, 1982.

Harter, S.H. Developmental perspectives on the self system. In E.M. Hetherington (Ed.), *Socialization, personality, and social behavior.* Vol. 4 in P.H. Mussen (Ed.), *Handbook of child psychology* (4th ed.). New York: Wiley, 1983.

Harter, S.H., & Buddin, B.J. Children's understanding of the simultaneity of two emotions: A developmental acquisition sequence. Paper presented at the meetings of the Society for Research in Child Development. Detroit, April 1983.

Hebb, D.O. Drives and the C.N.S. (Conceptual Nervous System). *Psychological Review,* 1955, *62,* 243–253.

Helmholtz, H. von. Über das Sehen des Menschen. *Vortrage und Reden*, 1894, *1*, 365–396.

Hilgard, E.R. *Hypnotic susceptibility*. New York: Harcourt, Brace, & World, 1965.

Hilgard, E.R. *Divided consciousness*. New York: Wiley, 1977.

Hirst, W., Spelke, E.S., Reaves, C.C., Caharack, G., & Neisser, U. Dividing attention without alternation or automaticity. *Journal of Experimental Psychology: General*, 1980, *109*, 98–117.

Holt, R.R. The development of the primary process: A structural view. In R.R. Holt (Ed.), *Motives and thought: Psychoanalytic essays in honor of David Rapaport, Psychological Issues*, 1967, *5*, (2–3, Serial No. 18–19). New York: International Universities Press.

Holt, R.R. Freud's theory of the primary process. *Psychoanalysis and Contemporary Science*, 1976, *5*, 61–99.

Jackson, E., Campos, J.J., & Fischer, K.W. The question of decalage between object permanence and person permanence. *Developmental Psychology*, 1978, *14*, 1–10.

James, W. *Principles of psychology*. New York: Holt, 1890.

Kenny, S.L. Developmental discontinuities in childhood and adolescence. In K.W. Fischer (Ed.), *Levels and transitions in children's development*. New Directions for Child Development No. 21. San Francisco: Jossey-Bass, 1983.

Kernberg, O. *Object relations theory and clinical psychoanalysis*. New York: Jason Aronson, 1976.

Kitchener, K.S. Human development and the college campus: Sequences and tasks. In G. Hanson (Ed.), *Assessing student development*. New Directions for Student Services. San Francisco: Jossey-Bass, 1983.

Kohut, H. *The restoration of the self*. New York: International Universities Press, 1977.

Link, N.F., Scherer, S.E., & Byrne, P.N. Moral judgment and moral conduct in the psychopath. *Canadian Psychiatric Association Journal*, 1977, *22*, 341–346.

Lester, E.P. Separation-individuation and cognition. *Journal of the American Psychoanalytic Association*, 1983, *31*, 127–156.

Loftus, E.F., & Loftus, G.R. On the permanence of stored information in the human brain. *American Psychologist*, 1980, *35*, 409–420.

Mahler, M.S., Pine, F., & Bergman, A. *The psychological birth of the human infant: Symbiosis and individuation*. New York: Basic Books, 1975.

Mahlerstein, A.J., & Ahern, M. *A Piagetian model of character structure*. New York: Human Sciences Press, 1982.

Mandler, G. From association to structure. *Psychological Review*. 1962, *69*, 415–427.

McCall, R.B., Eichorn, D.H., & Hogarty, P.S. Transitions in early mental development. *Monographs of the Society for Research in Child Development*, 1977, *42* (3, Serial No. 171).

Mischel, W., & Mischel, F. Psychological aspects of spirit possession. *American Anthropologist*, 1958, *60*, 249–260.

Modell, A.H. *Object love and reality*. New York: International Universities Press, 1968.

Nasby, W., Hayden, B., & dePaulo, B.M. Attributional bias among aggressive boys to interpret unambiguous social stimuli as displays of hostility. *Journal of Abnormal Psychology*, 1980, *89*, 459–468.

Neisser, U. *Cognition and reality*. San Francisco: Freeman, 1976.

Orne, M.T. The nature of hypnosis: Artifact and essence. *Journal of Abnormal and Social Psychology*, 1959, *58*, 277–299.

Osgood, C.E., Suci, G.J., & Tannenbaum, P.H. *The measurement of meaning*. Urbana: University of Illinois Press, 1957.

Pattie, F.A. A report of attempts to produce uniocular blindness by hypnotic suggestion. *British Journal of Medical Psychology*, 1935, *15*, 230–241.

Piaget, J. *The origins of intelligence in children* (M. Cook, trans.). New York: International Universities Press, 1952. (Originally published 1936.)

Piaget, J. *The construction of reality in the child* (M. Cook, trans.). New York: Basic Books, 1954. (Originally published 1937.)

Piaget, J. Le mécanisme du développement mental et les lois du groupement des opérations. *Archives de Psychologie, Genève*, 1941, *28*, 215–285.

Piaget, J. *Play, dreams, and imitation in childhood* (C. Gattegno and F.M. Hodgson, trans.). New York: Norton, 1951. (Originally published 1946.)

Piaget, J. Piaget's theory. In J.H. Flavell & E. Markman (Eds.), *Cognitive development*. Vol. 3 in P.H. Mussen (Ed.), *Handbook of child psychology* (4th ed.). New York: Wiley, 1983.

Pipp, S.L., Fischer, K.W., & Jennings, S. Self and mother knowledge in infancy. Manuscript submitted for publication, 1984.

Potts, G.R. Memory for text: Integration versus compartmentalization. Paper presented at the meetings of the Midwestern Psychological Association, St. Louis, May 1980.

Prechtl, H.F.R. Regressions and transformations during neurological development. In T.G. Bever (Ed.), *Regressions in mental development: Basic phenomena and theories*. Hillsdale, N.J.: Erlbaum, 1982.

Putnam, F.W., Jr., Post, R., Guroff, J., & Silberman, E. One-hundred cases of multiple personality disorder. Paper presented at the American Psychological Association Convention, New York City, April 1983.

Rapaport, D. *Organization and pathology of thought*. New York: Columbia University Press, 1951.

Roberts, R.J. Errors and the assessment of cognitive development. In K.W. Fischer (Ed.), *Cognitive development*. New Directions for Child Development No. 12. San Francisco: Jossey-Bass, 1981.

Rosenbaum, M. The role of the term schizophrenia in the decline of diagnoses of multiple personality. *Archives of General Psychiatry*, 1980, *37*, 1383–1385.

Rubin, K.H., Fein, G.G., & Vandenberg, B. Play. In E.M. Hetherington (Ed.), *Socialization, personality, and social behavior*. Vol. 4 in P.H. Mussen (Ed.), *Handbook of child psychology* (4th ed.). New York: Wiley, 1983.

Ruble, D.N. The development of social comparison processes and their role in achievement-related self-socialization. In E.T. Higgins, D.N. Ruble, & W.W. Hartup (Eds.), *Social cognition and social development: A socio-cultural perspective*. New York: Cambridge University Press, in press.

Sameroff, A. Transactional models in early social relations. *Human Development*, 1975, *18*, 65–79.

Schafer, R. *A new language for psychoanalysis*. New Haven, Conn.: Yale University Press, 1976.

Schimek, J.G. A critical examination of Freud's concept of unconscious mental representation. *International Review of Psychoanalysis,* 1975, *2,* 171–187.

Selman, R.L. *The growth of interpersonal understanding.* New York: Academic Press, 1980.

Shiffrin, R.M., & Schneider, W. Controlled and automatic human information processing: II. Perceptual learning, automatic attending, and a general theory. *Psychological Review,* 1977, *84,* 127–190.

Siegler, R.S. Developmental sequences within and between concepts. *Monographs of the Society for Research in Child Development,* 1981, *46* (2, Serial No. 189).

Silvern, L. Traditional descriptions of childhood emotional-behavioral disorders and an alternative: Disorder as a failure of system functions. In G. Gollin (Ed.), *Developmental plasticity.* New York: Academic Press, 1984.

Sullivan, H.S. *The interpersonal theory of psychiatry.* New York: Norton, 1953.

Thigpen, C.H., & Cleckley, H. A case of multiple personality. *Journal of Abnormal and Social Psychology,* 1954, *49,* 135–151.

Vaillant, G.E. *Adaptation to life.* Boston: Little, Brown, 1977.

Vygotsky, L. *Mind in society* (M. Cole, V. John-Steiner, S. Scribner, & E. Souberman, Eds.). Cambridge, Mass.: Harvard University Press, 1978.

Wachtel, P.L. *Psychoanalysis and behavior therapy.* New York: Basic Books, 1977.

Waterman, J.M., Sobesky, W.E., Silvern, L., Aoki, B., & McCaulay, M. Social perspective-taking and adjustment in emotionally disturbed, learning-disabled, and normal children. *Journal of Abnormal Child Psychology,* 1981, *9,* 133–148.

Watson, M.W. The development of social roles: A sequence of social-cognitive development. In K.W. Fischer (Ed.), *Cognitive development.* New Directions for Child Development No. 12. San Francisco: Jossey-Bass, 1981.

Watson, M.W., & Fischer, K.W. A developmental sequence of agent use in late infancy. *Child Development,* 1977, *48,* 828–835.

Watson, M.W., & Fischer, K.W. Development of social roles in elicited and spontaneous behavior during the preschool years. *Developmental Psychology,* 1980, *16,* 483–494.

Welford, A.T. *Fundamentals of skill.* London: Methuen, 1968.

Werner, H. The concept of development from a comparative and organismic point of view. In D.B. Harris (Ed.), *The concept of development.* Minneapolis: University of Minnesota Press, 1957.

White, S.H., & Pillemer, D.B. Childhood amnesia and the development of a socially accessible memory system. In J. Kohlstrom & F. Evans (Eds.), *Functional disorders of memory.* Hillsdale, N.J.: Erlbaum, 1979.

Wolf, D. Understanding others: A longitudinal case study of the concept of independent agency. In G.E. Forman (Ed.), *Action and thought.* New York: Academic Press, 1982.

Wolff, P.H. The developmental psychologies of Jean Piaget and psychoanalysis. *Psychological Issues,* 1960, *2* (1, Serial No. 5). New York: International Universities Press.

Wolff, P.H. The causes, controls, and organization of behavior in the neonate. *Psychological Issues,* 1966, *5* (1, Serial No. 17). New York: International Universities Press.

Wolff, P.H. Cognitive considerations for a psychoanalytic theory of language acquisition.

In R.R. Holt (Ed.), *Motives and thought: Psychoanalytic essays in honor of David Rapaport. Psychological Issues,* 1967, *5* (2–3, Serial No. 18/19). New York: International Universities Press.

Yerkes, R.M., & Dodson, J.D. The relation of strength of stimulus to rapidity of habit formation. *Journal of Comparative Neurology and Psychology,* 1908, *18,* 459–482.

Zajonc, R.B. Feeling and thinking: Preferences need no inferences. *American Psychologist,* 1980, *35,* 151–175.

CHAPTER 4

Conscious, Subconscious, Unconscious: A Cognitive Perspective

JOHN F. KIHLSTROM

I cannot but think that the most important step forward that has occurred in psychology since I have been a student of that science is the discovery . . . that, in certain subjects at least, there is not only the consciousness of the ordinary field, with its usual center and margin, but an addition thereto in the shape of a set of memories, thoughts, and feelings which are extra-marginal and outside of the primary consciousness altogether, but yet must be classed as conscious facts of some sort, able to reveal their presence by unmistakable signs. I call this the most important step forward because, unlike the other advances which psychology has made, this discovery has revealed to us an entirely unsuspected peculiarity in the constitution of human nature.

WILLIAM JAMES, *Varieties of Religious Experience* (1902, p. 233)

The study of consciousness has had a checkered past in the history of psychology. It was almost the whole of the field for James and Wundt, but declined to virtual nonentity status with the onslaught of the behaviorist movement. Thereafter, interest in *unconscious* mental states persisted in the hands of the psychoanalysts, and was revived twice within the living memory of academic psychology: once with the debate over subliminal perception and learning without awareness, and again with the discovery of psychological deficits among medical patients who have undergone cerebral commissurotomy. The purpose of this chapter is to analyze various concepts related to conscious, subconscious, and unconscious mental contents and processes. It begins with a consideration of the features of conscious mental life, and of the way in which various special states of consciousness may be diagnosed through the logic of converging operations.

Preparation of this paper was supported in part by Grant MH-35856 from the National Institute of Mental Health, United States Public Health Service. Work was begun while the author was a Visiting Scholar at the Center for Cognitive Science, University of Michigan, supported by a grant from the Sloan Foundation. I thank Kenneth S. Bowers, Nancy Cantor, Reid Hastie, William Heindel, Irene P. Hoyt, Pamela S. Ludolph, Don Meichenbaum, Richard E. Nisbett, Mary A. Peterson, Patricia A. Register, Howard Shevrin, Jeanne Sumi, and Leanne Wilson for their comments at various stages of the preparation of this paper. Portions of this paper previously appeared in Kihlstrom (1982).

Concepts related to consciousness are then analyzed from the perspective of classic cognitive approaches to the mind. While these theories have plenty to say about conscious and unconscious mental contents and processes, they appear to leave little room for the kind of subconscious mental contents and processes inherent in the concept of dissociation. Nevertheless, a wide variety of phenomena encountered in the clinic, laboratory, and everyday life appear to invite such a concept. These phenomena are briefly and selectively reviewed. Finally, a tentative view of divided consciousness, dissociation, and subconscious thought and action is offered within the context of resource theories of attention and network models of memory.

ON CONSCIOUSNESS AND SPECIAL STATES OF IT

What gives us the impression that we are conscious? What kind of evidence would convince us that a machine such as a computer, or a nonhuman animal, or (for that matter) another human being, was conscious? Scientists and philosophers disagree violently on the answers, and even on whether these are sensible questions. But nobody doubts that we humans at least, possess consciousness. The facts that erase any doubt are the facts of experience. "The first fact for us, then, as psychologists, is that thinking of some sort goes on" (James, 1890, p. 224). With the coming of the cognitive revolution, psychologists have given increasing recognition to this "first fact" (Hilgard, 1977a, 1980a; Hochberg, 1970; Mandler, 1975a; Sperry, 1968, 1969). Consciousness, in the form of attention, perception, memory, imagery, and thought, is once again at the center of things—with the difference that mental contents and processes are approached with the same commitment to publicly verifiable, quantitative observation that characterized the behaviorist paradigm of Watson and Skinner. Still, there is evidently some lingering uncertainty as to just what consciousness is.

One way to gain conceptual clarity is to turn to the dictionary. Natsoulas (1978), following Dewey (1906), has recently offered an exegesis of the word *consciousness* as defined in the 1933 *Oxford English Dictionary*. At the other extreme, James (1890) and Jaynes (1976) have provided extremely articulate introspective analyses of the phenomenal experience of consciousness. We say that we are conscious when we register distal and proxmimal events in phenomenal awareness; reflect on our past experiences, categorical knowledge, and rules of judgment, inference, and problem solving; direct our attention selectively to some stimuli rather than others; and deliberately select and execute some action in response to environmental conditions and personal goals. In short, consciousness has to do with two things:

1. *Monitoring* ourselves and our environment, so that percepts, memories, and thoughts come to be accurately represented in phenomenal awareness.
2. *Controlling* ourselves and our environment, so that we are able to voluntarily initiate and terminate behavioral and cognitive activities.

The key to the experience of consciousness, as James (1890, p. 226) noted, is self reference, as experiencer or agent: "The universal conscious fact is not 'feelings exist' and 'thoughts exist' but 'I think' and 'I feel.'" The two functions are obviously interrelated: It is hard to think of deliberately initiating a response to, or making a judgment about, some event which has not entered our awareness; and many of our deliberate actions seem precisely geared to bringing new stimuli into our awareness and exploring them more closely (Powers, 1973). It is by means of consciousness that we become aware of events, interpret them, and plan and execute strategies for dealing with them. It is also consciousness that permits us to communicate our ideas, experiences, intentions, and expectations to other people. Consciousness, coupled with language, thus forms the basis for the development and evolution of culture, and opens up the possibility of learning by precept as well as by direct experience and example (Bandura, 1977).

This much seems clear enough. It seems clear enough, too, that under some circumstances we experience profound alterations in the monitoring and/or controlling functions of consciousness. Ingesting drugs such as marijuana or LSD, practicing a meditative discipline such as yoga or Zen, falling asleep, and becoming hypnotized all seem to lead to such alterations; so do certain syndromes of psychopathology such as acute schizophrenia and hysteria. Ludwig (1966) has provided a list of the features of various states in which consciousness is ostensibly "special" or "altered." Ludwig's list offers a useful characterization of the kinds of phenomena observed in various special states of consciousness, but it is important to realize that it is *only* a list; there is no reason to think that it is exhaustive. More important, these features themselves have additional attributes which may be important in deciding whether a particular condition qualifies as a "special" or "altered" state of consciousness. For example, we might want to include the conditon that the state be temporary, so that eventually the person reverts to baseline conditions; otherwise, a "special state" becomes a "normal trait." This would eliminate as a special state of consciousness such conditions as chronic coma, as well as the various stages of cognitive development proposed by Piaget and the "raising" of consciousness discussed in Marxist theory. It is debatable whether falling in love and out of it would qualify. We might also want to specify that the change from "normal" to "altered" consciousness and back be relatively abrupt; or that some threshold of significance and pervasiveness be crossed, so that a special state represents some dramatic departure from the individual's usual manner of relating to the world as a whole. This would eliminate learning some specific item of new information from the category of alterations in consciousness.

Finally, whatever list is employed, we do not know how many features must be present before some mental condition may qualify as a special state of consciousness. Following contemporary analyses of categorization (e.g., Rosch & Lloyd, 1978; Smith & Medin, 1981), it seems best to think of the notion of "special state of consciousness" as a natural concept represented by a prototype or one or more exemplars consisting of features which are correlated with category membership. No such feature is singly necessary, and no set of features

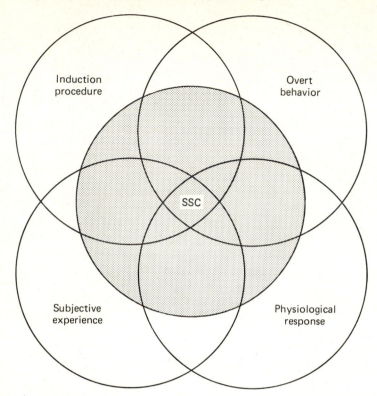

Figure 4.1. Converging operations contributing to the diagnosis of a special state of consciousness (after Stoyva & Kamiya, 1968).

is jointly sufficient, to define a state as special, so that there are no clear boundaries between one special state of consciousness and another, or between altered and normal consciousness. The situation with special states, then, is similar to that which obtains in psychiatric diagnosis (e.g., Cantor & Genero, in press; Orne, 1977).

If special states of consciousness represent natural concepts, they also represent *hypothetical constructs*. Because we can never have direct knowledge of another mind, judgments about one's state of consciousness (and often our own; see Nisbett & Wilson, 1977) must be the work of informed imagination, inferred from a network of relationships among variables that are directly observable. Four sorts of observables are described below: none is necessary, and under certain circumstances knowledge of only one might be sufficient to index the presence of a special state of consciousness. The diagnosis of a special state can be made with confidence to the extent that there is convergence among the four kinds of variables, as in Figure 4.1 (Campbell & Fiske, 1959; Garner, Hake, & Ericksen, 1956; Stoyva & Kamiya, 1968).

Induction Technique

One way to define a special state of consciousness is as the output resulting from a particular input: this sort of operational definition is a residue of radical behaviorism. In this case, the presence of a special state is defined by the means employed to induce it: a psychedelic state follows the ingestion of LSD or marijuana, and hypnosis follows from receiving a hypnotic induction. Although there has been at least one attempt to employ such an input-output definition as the sole index of a special state (in the case of hypnosis; Barber, 1969), there are reasons for thinking that sole reliance on it is a mistake, and that some sort of manipulation check is also required. Obviously, the induction of a state does not necessarily follow from the performance of an ostensibly state-inducing ritual. As parents, lovers, and insomniacs know, sleep does not necessarily follow from crawling into bed and turning out the light; nor are these acts sufficient for sleep to occur. There may be resistance to the induction; or there may be individual differences which constrain response to the induction even when the situation is congenial and the individual has the proper set. Individual differences are important in another way: a person may be so disposed to enter the state (as in narcolepsy) as to require no induction at all.

Subject Report

Another approach is to define the state in terms of the person's subjective report that his or her consciousness is different from normal. Introspections such as these provided the data for much early psychological research, but the unreliability of the results led the behaviorists to reject subjective reports as proper data for psychology. With the cognitive revolution, introspections are permissible once again (Ericsson & Simon, 1980), but not without an appreciation of their limitations (Nisbett & Wilson, 1977). For example, sometimes subjects simply do not tell the truth. The good will which characterizes the experimental subject may lead him or her to say what the investigator wants to hear (Orne, 1962, 1977)—although, if the research is characterized in terms of open inquiry, the same good will should lead the subject to be candid. There are also familiar problems from the literature on eyewitness testimony stemming from the impact of leading questions (Barber, Spanos, & Chaves, 1974). Moreover, subjects may not recognize that they are in a special state until after it has terminated—as in the case of concussion or alcoholic blackout, in which the change in state is recognized only retrospectively by virtue of an amnesic gap.

Overt Behavior

"Objective" behavioral evidence is often preferred to "subjective" self-reports—though why this is so is a little puzzling, insofar as subjects can fake behavior as easily as they can lie (Orne, 1970, 1979). However, given the subject's good will and an experimental atmosphere of open inquiry, there are numerous behavioral indices available to the investigator who wishes to test for changes in the monitoring and controlling functions of consciousness. The number of possible behavioral measures is limited only by the ingenuity of the experimenter. Measures of accuracy, organizational structure, and response latencies have proved especially useful elsewhere in cognitive psychology for gaining a view of various mental processes, and are likely to be promising in the investigation of special states of consciousness as well.

Psychophysiological Responses

Because overt behaviors and subject reports are under voluntary control and thus subject to distortion through motivated compliance and other social-influence processes, many investigators have turned to the covert, involuntary responses measured by psychophysiologists. This seems to be predicated on the perfectly reasonable assumption that because the brain is the body of mind, changes in consciousness should be associated with changes in nervous system activity. The best example is the correlation of rapid eye movements with dreaming, and the use of EEG criteria to mark the onset of sleep and to break it down into separate stages. It should be said, however, that these psychophysiological indices bring with them their own problems, not the least of which is the apparent fact that whether the question is distinguishing sleep from wakefulness (Johnson, 1970), or one emotion from another (Mandler, 1975b; Leventhal, 1983), psychophysiology alone is of no use. Even if there were specific patterns of psychophysiological response that were uniquely associated with various mental states, there would remain the fact that such indices have been validated against subjective report and overt behavior; and that a correlate cannot, logically, substitute for a criterion. As Malcolm (1959) points out, psychological concepts demand psychological referents. While psychophysiological correlates of mental activity are interesting in their own right (Hillyard & Kutas, 1983), to study them is not the same as to study consciousness. Subjective report and overt behavior, then, will serve as windows on the mind in a special state of consciousness.

States as Causes Versus States as Categories

In speaking of special states of consciousness, it is important to guard against the tendency to assign them a causal function—as, for example, in the statement that sleep causes dreams, or hypnosis causes hallucinations (Hilgard, 1969a). It may be the case that certain phenomena are more likely to occur in a particular special state, but that is not to say that the state is responsible for the phenomenon. To assign a causal function to a state risks tautology (Spanos, 1970a): How does one know that a subject is hypnotized? Because the subject is hallucinating. Why is the subject hallucinating? Because he or she is hypnotized. In fact, however, the risk of tautology is not particularly great, as Tellegen (1970) has argued in a response to Spanos (for a rejoinder, see Spanos, 1970b). While it may be possible to define, as Tellegen (1978–79) does, hypnosis as an organismic state (or states) that enables or facilitates response to hypnotic suggestions—that is, as something which causes hypnotic behavior—it seems preferable to follow Hilgard (1973a, 1977b) and Orne (1977), by defining hypnosis as a state in which certain phenomena are known to occur. If a hypnotizable individual has volunteered for hypnosis and received a hypnotic induction procedure, and then proceeds to respond positively to suggestions offered by the experimenter for hallucinations, anesthesias, paralyses, amnesia, and the like, then we may say with some confidence that he or she has been hypnotized. Similar diagnoses could be made in the case of other possible special states, such as sleep, dreaming, and so forth. Our principal objection to assigning a causal function to a special state is that it does nothing to promote scientific understanding. We want to determine the cognitive (or psychobiological, or social) processes responsible for the phenomena categorized under the rubric of a particular special state of consciousness.

STEPS TOWARD A TAXONOMY OF MENTAL STATES

This chapter is concerned with unconscious mental processes—a topic which may strike many readers, as it did James (1890), as involving a contradiction in terms. James vigorously argued against the notion of unconscious thought, although he did agree that there are brain processes associated with mental activity of which we might not be aware. As if in warning to Freud and the psychoanalysts who were shortly to follow, James asserted that the concept of unconscious states of mind "is the sovereign means of believing what one likes in psychology, and of turning what might become a science into a tumbling-ground for whimsies" (1890, p. 163). But the Freudian psychology which was to come shared the force of James's critique with other trends in the psychology of his time, such as those which implicated unconscious inference in perception and judgment. He argued that the allegedly unconscious thought was rapidly forgotten; that it represented a revision of an earlier thought; or that it was not a *thought* at all, but merely an innate or habitual brain process. For James, clearly, thought and consciousness were identical.

The Concept of Unconscious

Arguably a person who is unconscious, as for example a victim of concussion or coma, has no mental processes at all: there is virtually no electrical activity recorded rrom the cortex, little or no response to environmental stimulation, and no memory of events occurring during the state if the patient should be so fortunate as to recover. Something else, then, must be meant by the concept of unconscious mental processes. Useful coverage of the various meanings assigned to the term "unconscious" are provided elsewhere (English & English, 1958; Klein, 1977; Whyte, 1960), and there is no need to review this material here. Evidently what the editors of this book, and most other psychologists as well, have in mind when they use the term are those cognitive contents and processes, existing in the cognitive system at some point in time and actively influencing ongoing cognition and action, of which the person is not aware. But in the final analysis even this is too broad: there are many objects and events available in the perceptual field and in memory storage of which we are not presently aware, but which we could bring into awareness by the simple expedient of turning our attention to them. It seems inappropriate to label these as unconscious.

It was for just such cases that Freud (1900–1901) developed his tripartite division of the mind into the conscious, preconscious, and unconscious systems.

> Thus there are two kinds of unconscious, which have not yet been distinguished by psychologists. Both of these are unconscious in the sense used by psychology; but in our sense one of them, which we term the *Ucs,* is also inadmissible to consciousness, while we term the other the *Pcs* because its excitations...are able to reach consciousness. (pp. 614–615)

Unfortunately, as Chomsky (1980) has noted, Freud's use of the distinction between Psc and Ucs was inconsistent. At times he asserted that material in the Ucs was inaccessible in principle; at other times he conceded that the material might be accessible under certain special conditions. Chomsky, like many other contemporary cognitive psychologists (e.g., Anderson, 1982a; Nisbett & Wilson, 1977; Pylyshyn, 1981; Rozin, 1976), appears to identify unconscious mental contents and processes with those that are inaccessible *in principle*. We can acquire knowledge of their presence and activity by inference, but not by means of direct, immediate introspective awareness. This definition is preserved in the present essay: the term "unavailable" is used to characterize knowledge that is not represented in the cognitive system at all; by contrast, the term "unconscious" is used to characterize knowledge which resides in the mental system, and is actively employed in the service of ongoing cognitive processing, but which is incapable of being brought into phenomenal awareness and placed under voluntary control. We know the unconscious contents of the mind only by inference, never through direct introspection.

Far from rejecting the possibility, as James did, cognitive psychologists now believe that such unconscious contents compose a large portion of the mental system. Even the notion of unconscious inference, so scorned by James, appears to be necessary in order to account for elementary perceptual phenomena (Kaufman, 1974; Rock, 1975). Shevrin and Dickman (1980) have attempted to reconcile the conception of the unconscious offered by contemporary cognitive psychology with that held by Freudian psychoanalysis. They are able to show that the two conceptions have two features in common at the abstract level: in both cases, the unconscious is active rather than latent; and in both cases, unconscious mental processes operate on different principles than conscious ones. The attempt ultimately fails, however, because the nature of these unconscious contents, and the principles of their operation, are so radically divergent from the proposals of psychoanalysis. The information represented in the unconscious knowledge structures of cognitive psychology is very different from that conceived by Freud, who restricted it to primitive sexual and aggressive impulses, and those repressed memories and ideas which are associated with them. Nor do the unconscious contents of cognitive psychology operate according to the irrational "primary process" principles associated with the Freudian unconscious, as opposed to the rational "secondary process" principles of the Freudian ego. Moreover, the contents of the cognitive unconscious do not achieve their status by virtue of defensive maneuvers motivated by anxiety, as the contents of the Freudian unconscious do.

The Concept of Subconscious

While rejecting the concept of *unconscious* thought, James did admit that under some circumstances "the total possible consciousness may be split into parts which coexist but mutually ignore each other, and share the objects of knowledge between them" (1890, p. 206; see also Hilgard, 1969b). Following Janet and Binet, from whom he drew his examples, James referred to this phenomenon as representing "secondary" consciousness, rather than "unconsciousness." Prince (1939), in the same vein, referred to "co-consciousness." This phenomenon, which Janet, Prince, and their associates referred to as "dissociation," was a cornerstone of an important but almost-forgotten school of thought within turn-of-the-century psychology and psychiatry.

It is commonly thought that the concepts of nonconscious mental processes and of the psychological causation of mental illness both trace their origins to Freud and the theory of psychoanalysis. To the contrary, as Ellenberger (1970; see also Hilgard, 1973a) has shown, both ideas have a long history before Freud. In 1775, with the appearance of Mesmer on the European medical scene, speculation about nonconscious states combined with rationalized, materialistic versions of primitive psychotherapeutic procedures to form the First Dynamic Psychiatry, whose inspiration came from such French neurologists and psychiatrists as Charcot, Liebeault, and Bernheim. This psychiatry was concerned with demonstrable "functional," as opposed to "organic," mental illnesses—that is, those pathological syndromes which appeared not to be associated with brain insult, injury, or disease. It attempted to account for a wide range of phenomena, including hysteria, fugue (then called ambulatory automatism), and multiple personality; the "magnetic diseases" of catalepsy, lethargy, and somnambulism (so named because of their resemblance to certain phenomena of animal magnetism, a precursor of hypnosis); spiritistic practices such as automatic writing and crystal-gazing; hypnosis; and suggestibility in the normal waking state. Each of these phenomena, the school held, represented the power of ideas to engender action (one of the meanings of "dynamic" in the psychological sense); and each seemed to reflect a change in consciousness, as thoughts and actions occurred outside of phenomenal awareness and voluntary control.

The First Dynamic Psychiatry, with its emphasis on unconscious mental processes, invoked one or the other of two explicit models of the mind (Ellenberger, 1970). The point of view known as *dipsychism* held that the mind consisted of two layers, each of which in turn consisted of chains of associations. The "upper consciousness" was active in the normal waking state, while the "lower consciousness" was active in such phenomena as dreams, hysteria, and hypnosis. According to *polypsychism,* each segment of the anatomy was served by its own mental structures, called *egos,* each of which was capable of perception, memory, and thought. These structures, in turn, were subject to the control of a superordinate structure which was identified with normal consciousness. When the link between subordinate and superordinate egos was broken, certain aspects of cognition and action were carried out subconsciously.

The issues confronted by the First Dynamic Psychiatry were subsequently taken up by another French psychiatrist, Pierre Janet (1889, 1907; see also Perry & Laurence, this book). Following the principle of analysis-then-synthesis familiar in physiology, Janet began by considering the elementary parts of the mental system. Instead of following the lead of the earlier faculty psychology or the chemical analogies of the structuralists, he argued that the elementary structures of the mind were *psychological automatisms:* complex acts, tuned to environmental and intrapsychic circumstances, preceded by an idea and accompanied by an emotion. Each of these psychological automatisms, by combining cognition, conation, and emotion (Hilgard, 1980b) with action, represented a rudimentary consciousness. According to Janet, all of these elementary automatisms were bound together into a single, united stream of consciousness, and normally operated both in awareness and under voluntary control. Under certain circumstances, however, one or more of these automatisms could be split off—Janet's term was *disaggregation*—from the rest, functioning outside awareness, voluntary control, or both. Janet's concept of psychological automatism appears to anticipate Bartlett's (1932) appropriation of the schema concept to refer to organized knowledge structures containing both declarative and procedural information (Hastie, 1981; Neisser, 1976).

This dissociation view of the unconscious, as distinct from the repression view elaborated by Freud and his followers, was further developed by the American psychologist and psychiatrist Morton Prince (1906, 1914, 1939). Prince, following the practice of his day as exemplified by James's (1890) ten arguments against the existence of unconscious thoughts, reserved the term "unconscious" for the dormant traces of forgotten memories and unattended perceptual inputs as well as the strictly neurophysiological processes associated with mental activity. Instead, he offered the term *co-conscious,* referring to mental activity which takes place outside phenomenal awareness. Prince preferred this term because it connoted mental activity rather than the lack of mentation (as in the standard conception of unconsciousness associated with concussion or coma); and because it permitted the division of consciousness into parallel streams without one or more of these being outside of awareness. Co-conscious mental activities performed outside awareness, together with unconscious mental contents and brain processes, form the *subconscious.*

This conceptualization of consciousness was very popular on both sides of the Atlantic, featured prominently in the pages of the new *Journal of Abnormal and Social Psychology* (founded and edited by Prince), and was the chief alternative within dynamic psychiatry to Freudian psychoanalysis. However, it was a conceptualization that was short-lived (Hilgard, 1973a, 1977a, 1980a). The eventual dominance of psychoanalysis in clinical psychology and scientific personology led investigators to be interested in different syndromes and phenomena, a different model of the mind, and the eventual replacement of dissociation by repression as the hypothetical mechanism for rendering mental contents unconscious. At the same time, the behaviorist revolution in academic psychology removed consciousness (not to mention *the unconscious*) from the vocabulary of the science. At fault as well were the dissociation theorists themselves, who often made extravagant claims for the centrality of the phenomenon and whose investigations were often methodologically flawed. The final blow to the concept stemmed from the interpretation that dissociated streams of consciousness, because they were ignorant (Janet's term) of each other, should not influence each other. Numerous demonstrations of mutual interference between ostensibly dissociated tasks (e.g., White & Shevack, 1941) showed the contrary, and reference to dissociation gradually disappeared. The following taxonomic exercise shows that the phenomena of mental life include subconscious as well as conscious and unconscious mental processes, and call for a revival of the concept of dissociation.

Brain Processes

In an attempt at a rough, tentative classification of mental states, we begin with the observation that we are not aware of the activity of the central nervous system that forms their biological substrate. We do not perceive the firing of individual neurons, or even masses of them, in the same way that we perceive heartbeat, muscle tension, and bladder distension. Nor do we have voluntary control over the activity of individual neurons or larger brain structures. However, results apparently contradicting this conclusion have been described in a literature emerging over the past few years on EEG biofeedback. For example, Kamiya (1969) reported that subjects apparently could learn to identify periods of high-density EEG alpha activity, and that such periods were associated with a distinctive mental state; and he and others (e.g., Mulholland, 1968) reported that subjects apparently could learn to increase or decrease alpha activity at will. Both claims have aroused considerable controversy (for reviews see Black, Cott, & Pavlovski, 1977; Hardt & Kamiya, 1976; Orne & Wilson, 1978; Plotkin, 1976a, 1976b, 1981). In general, however, it appears that the phenomenon of "discriminative awareness" is largely an artifact of response bias, and that there is no mental state uniquely or probabilistically associated with a high density of alpha in the EEG. Furthermore, the changes in alpha density observed in biofeedback appear to reflect either disinhibition of alpha blocking (rather than a genuine increment of alpha above baseline), or else an artifact or adventitious consequence of voluntary oculomotor activity. Awareness and/or control of other EEG patterns has been reported in the literature from time to time, but these phenomena have not yet been studied with the same rigor as the alpha phenomenon. For the present then, brain activity can remain classified as unavailable, in the sense that it is not represented in the cognitive system, is inaccessible to phenomenal awareness, and is not amenable to voluntary control.

The Right Hemisphere

Perhaps the most dramatic and compelling demonstration of nonconscious mental processes is provided by patients who have undergone cerebral commissurotomy for treatment of severe epilepsy (Gazzaniga, 1970, 1972; Gazzaniga & LeDoux, 1978; Sperry, 1968, 1969). While most of the research on the "split brain" syndrome has been devoted to the topic of hemispheric specialization (Segalowitz, 1983; Springer & Deutsch, 1981), some of the experiments have dealt with the problem of interhemispheric communication. These studies take advantage of the fact of contralteral projection, whereby stimuli occurring in the right sensory field are first represented in the left hemisphere, and vice versa; the anterior commissure and corpus callosum then transfer information held in one hemisphere to the other, so that each contains a complete representation of the perceptual field. When the commissures are severed, this communication no longer takes place, so that patients are typically unable to verbally describe objects presented to the left visual half-field (which projects to the right hemisphere). Nor, when responding to stimuli presented to their right hemisphere, are they able to give an account of their own behavior. Under appropriate testing conditions, these relationships can be reversed, so that neither hemisphere seems to know what the other one is doing.

Although Sperry himself was quite careful to speak of this phenomenon in terms of a disruption in the unity of consciousness, some others have tended to identify consciousness with the linguistic processing of the left hemisphere (e.g., Eccles, 1965, 1973; Popper & Eccles, 1977). Galin (1974), drawing on studies of hemispheric specialization in intact subjects as well as commissurotomy patients, identified the right hemisphere with the Freudian *System Ucs* and primary-process thinking. This suggestion received additional support when Galin and his colleagues (Galin, Diamond, & Braff, 1977) found a statistical tendency for hysterical hemianesthesias and hemiparalyses to be located on the left side—that is, with processing controlled by the right hemisphere. With respect to the commissurotomy data, it should be noted, with Corballis (1980), that a more parsimonious explanation is that the right hemisphere is fully conscious in its own way, except that its disconnection from the left hemisphere precludes verbal expression. All the other requirements for consciousness—attention, perception, memory, judgment, categorization, and action planning—are shown by the right hemisphere. The hysteria data are interesting, but the effect is weak in a highly selected sample: there were also many patients with symptoms isolated on the right side, and even more with bilateral symptoms. A more parsimonious explanation, one considered and rejected by Galin et al. (1977), is that the symptoms are lateralized where they will do the least harm. Commissurotomy may represent a division in consciousness, somewhat along the lines of an organic (as opposed to functional) dissociation, but this is not the same as restricting awareness and voluntary control to the dominant, verbal hemisphere.

Consciousness in the Multistore Model of Memory

Cognitive psychologists have proposed a number of different conceptualizations of the memory system. The most popular of these has been a multistore model consisting of a variety of different storage structures and a number of control processes which transfer information from one storage structure to another, transforming it variously along the way (e.g., Atkinson & Shiffrin, 1968; Bower, 1975; Newell & Simon, 1972; Waugh & Norman, 1965). A generic representation of such a system is presented in Figure 4.2. A pattern of energy radiating from stimuli in the external or internal environment impinges on sensory surfaces, and is transduced into a neural impulse which is carried along a tract of sensory nerves to a particular projection area in the brain. According to the theory, incoming sensory information first makes contact with the higher mental processes involved in perception, memory, thought, and language when it is encoded in memory structures known as the sensory registers. From this point on, the type of processing received by the stimulus information determines whether it will become conscious.

According to classic information-processing theory, the sensory registers contain a complete, veridical representation of the physical characteristics of the stimulus—for instance, its shape or pitch—but nothing of its meaning. Although

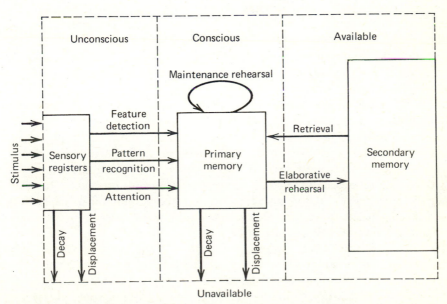

Figure 4.2.   Conscious and unconscious mental contents and processes viewed within the framework of a multistore model of memory (after Atkinson & Shiffrin, 1968).

in principle there is one register for each sensory modality, only the visual and auditory registers—the *icon* and the *echo* respectively (Neisser, 1967)—have been studied in any detail (for reviews see Crowder, 1976). Information held in these registers is subject to extremely rapid decay; alternatively it can be effectively erased by newly arriving information—the phenomenon of backward masking. Until it decays or is displaced, the information is subject to analysis by a variety of feature-detection and pattern-recognition processes, which endow the preattentive representation with some measure of meaning.

Once there has been some preliminary analysis of the meaning of the pattern held in iconic memory, another control process, attention, selects some of the material for further processing. By virtue of paying attention, some information is copied into the next storage structure, variously called primary or short-term memory. Following James (1890) and Crowder (1976), we may identify primary memory as that structure which contains the psychological present, including the very recent past. Primary memory is different from sensory memory in that the information represented therein can be extracted from either the perceptual field (via the sensory registers) or retrieved from records of the distant past stored in secondary (long-term) memory. Primary memory is commonly identified as the major workspace of the memory system: it is here that information is maintained in an active state while further perceptual-cognitive operations take place. This occurs by means of yet another control process, maintenance rehearsal. Unrehearsed material may be lost through decay over time, but the most important factor determining forgetting appears to be interference. Primary memory is a limited-capacity structure, and newly arriving information, if it is to be maintained, must displace older material. If the information is not encoded into secondary memory before decay or displacement takes place, it will be permanently lost. Once new information has been copied into secondary memory, information-processing theory holds that it is permanently retained; but, of course, it must be retrieved, and copied back into primary memory, before it can be put to any use.

New information is copied into secondary memory by means of elaborative rehearsal. According to Anderson's (1976, 1982b) ACT model of memory, for example, encoding an episode involves activating nodes in a preexisting associative network representing particular concepts related to the event, linking them together associatively to form a proposition, and linking this proposition with others representing the context in which the event took place. Retrieval begins with a query to the memory system. Nodes corresponding to information provided by the query are activated, and activation spreads out along the various associative pathways. Where activated pathways intersect, the proposition (or part thereof) is checked against the specifications of the query. Where there is a match between cue and trace information, the proposition (or part thereof) is retrieved. The retrieval process is held to be highly dependent on the presence of a rich associational structure uniting the various propositions stored in memory, sufficient cue information in the query to guide the search, the nature of the search plan employed, and the availability of a suitable point of entry into the memory network. The matching process involves testing the various properties and contextual features of a candidate item against criteria specified in the original query to the memory system.

The classic multistore, information-processing view of memory, as represented by the generic version outlined above, generally identifies consciousness with focal attention and primary memory. Anything that is not in focal attention and/or primary memory, then, is almost by definition not conscious. Similarly, what is being attended to is conscious, by virtue of the fact that it resides in primary memory. Obviously, stimulus information which fails to fall on the sensory surfaces never has the opportunity to be processed within the cognitive system. Less obviously, the cognitive system is oblivious to stimulation which falls on the sensory surfaces, but which fails to be transformed by the preattentive processes of feature detection and pattern recognition. While such information is represented in the sensory registers, it is unconscious; if it decays or is displaced before receiving any preattentive processing, it becomes permanently unavailable. Even if it has been subject to some preattentive processing, the information remains unconscious until it has been processed further and brought into primary memory by means of attention. Once in primary memory, items that decay or are displaced from this storage structure before they can be encoded in secondary memory are rendered permanently unavailable. While the model is not expressly clear concerning the status of the control processes themselves, later developments in the theory (e.g., Schneider & Shiffrin, 1977; Shiffrin & Schneider, 1977) suggest that they are unconscious, unless the processing task is very demanding.

Items that are held in primary memory are conscious by definition, and this holds for information which has been retrieved from secondary memory as well as that which arrives from the sensory registers. What is retrieved is a copy of the trace in secondary memory, so when decay or displacement occurs, as it ultimately must, it is only the item as *reconstructed* that becomes unavailable—unless, of course, this new version is also encoded in secondary memory by means of elaborative rehearsal. According to the classic theory, information is not lost from secondary memory, although various processes such as decay and interference can impair its retrieval. Nevertheless, such items are not themselves conscious unless they have been retrieved; but it will not do to call them unconscious, because they are in principle accessible to phenomenal awareness and voluntary retrieval. Following Tulving and Pearlstone (1966), it seems best to characterize these permanently stored traces as *available* to consciousness. Freud's concept of *preconscious* may also serve to describe this material.

Consciousness in a Unistore Model of Memory

According to the classic theory, unattended inputs do not become conscious. At this point a serious question arises: *are* there any unattended inputs? Since the earliest theories of attention posited by Cherry (1953) and Broadbent (1958), it has been common to describe attention as a filter which screens out information on the basis of criteria set by higher mental processes. From the beginning, however, it has been clear that this filter was very leaky indeed. Thus Cherry and Broadbent found that certain physical attributes of unattended inputs, but not their meaning, could be represented in consciousness. Later, Moray (1959) and Triesman (1960) found that more abstract features, such as meaning, could also be processed through to primary memory under certain conditions. Triesman (1969) characterized attention as an attenuator, rather than a filter, which could be tuned to various properties of the stimulus depending on the goals and intentions of the perceiver. Unattended inputs were apparently analyzed outside of consciousness, and were brought into awareness if they met criteria relevant to the ongoing cognitive task. Later Deutsch and Deutsch (1963) and Norman (1968) argued that all inputs were analyzed to some degree along all dimensions, regardless of task demands, before attention is directed to them. This processing is performed automatically as the information enters the cognitive system. Attention is not so much a matter of passing inputs further into the cognitive system for deeper or more complicated analysis as it is a matter of selecting those inputs, after they have been processed, according to their pertinence to the task at hand. In the course of perceptual processing, all inputs make contact with their corresponding preexisting representations in secondary memory. Those that are pertinent become conscious; the others do not. Thus consciousness is still identified with attention, although the scope of preattentive processing has been expanded considerably and attention is now located late rather than early in the cognitive sequence. All active traces which are not in focal attention may be thought of as *preconscious* (Dixon, 1981); as before, the perceptual processes themselves are *unconscious*. The situation is represented schematically in Figure 4.3.

The fact that all inputs activate corresponding representations in secondary memory raises the possibility that even unattended inputs can affect ongoing cognition and action outside of awareness. At stake here, of course, are the kinds of effects variously known as subliminal perception, perceptual defense and vigilance, and the like (for reviews see Dixon, 1971, 1981; Erdelyi, 1974; Erdelyi & Goldberg, 1979; Hilgard, 1962). Despite shortcomings in the early demonstrations of these effects (e.g., Eriksen, 1960, 1962), the case for them seems now to have been made. Even if the empirical support remained weak, the revisionist conception of attention, which permits stimuli to be analyzed for meaning preattentively, and with the focus of attention determined by such considerations as pertinence, *predicts* such effects. We can look forward to a resurgence of the New Look in perception, as a mainstream rather than a vanguard enterprise (Bruner & Klein, 1960; Bruner & Postman, 1949). We are not conscious of all that we perceive. And information that has never reached consciousness can still have observable effects on cognition and action. When activated, preconscious representations may serve to bias the meaning given to a percept, the choice among possible responses, and the like.

The evolution of theories of attention has seriously undercut the multistore model of the cognitive system with which we began. Apparently perceptual

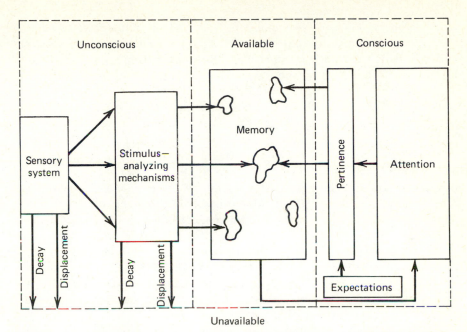

Figure 4.3. Conscious and unconscious mental contents and processes viewed within the framework of a unistore model of memory (after Norman, 1968).

inputs can make contact with secondary memory, the permanent repository of knowledge, without first going through primary memory. In fact, there has long been a dispute in the literature over whether there is a meaningful distinction between primary and secondary memory structures (e.g., Craik & Lockhart, 1972; Melton, 1963; Tulving, 1968; Wickelgren, 1973). Lately, even the existence of the sensory registers as separate storage structures has been questioned (Haber, 1983). In fact, it is possible to postulate a single, unitary memory store. For example, the levels of processing theory of Craik and Lockhart (1972; see also Cermak & Craik, 1979) begins by characterizing the memory trace as the residue of the cognitive processes involved in perceiving and interpreting a stimulus event (see also Bartlett, 1932; Neisser, 1967). This processing naturally involves activating preexisting information stored in memory. At this point, it seems preferable to abandon the terms *primary* and *secondary* memory, and refer instead to *memory* and those portions of it that are active at any particular time. The distinction between primary and secondary memory becomes not one of separate structures, but rather of degree of activation: those memories which are active at any given moment may be said to be represented in consciousness, or potentially so; those that are dormant are not, although they are available to consciousness (Anderson, 1982b).

While items lost from the sensory registers are forever consigned to oblivion, items lost from active memory may be restored to consciousness through the process of reactivation during memory retrieval. This raises the question of whether information can be truly forgotten from memory, and thus rendered unavailable in this way. One point of view, which actually antedates the multistore, information-processing model, holds that all memories are subject to decay and/or interference (Keppel, 1968; Postman & Underwood, 1973). The other view is that these memories remain permanently available in storage, although they may be inaccessible under certain conditions (Tulving, 1974). Implicit in this latter view is the possibility that all material available in memory is potentially accessible, if only the right cues were used. Levels of processing theory, as elaborated by Craik and his colleagues (Craik & Lockhart, 1972; Jacoby & Craik, 1979; Lockhart, Craik, & Jacoby, 1976), holds that the accessibility of a memory is determined principally by the degree to which it was elaborated with respect to preexisting memories at the time of perception (see also Anderson & Reder, 1979). Memories that have been subject to much elaboration, and which thus have been rendered distinctive, are more easily retrievable compared to impoverished memories. However, even very impoverished memories are retrievable under the right conditions: soon after encoding has occurred, for example, while the trace is still relatively active; or if the query or cue which initiates the retrieval process is rich enough to compensate for the poverty of the trace. However, sheer quantity of trace or cue information is not enough to guarantee retrieval. According to the encoding specificity principle of Tulving and Thomson (1973), the most important factor determining the success of a retrieval attempt is the amount of *overlap* between information supplied by the query and information contained in the trace. Even a very rich cue will not contact a memory unless it contains the right type of information.

If, as Tulving (1974) holds, retrieval is more dependent on the nature of the cue than on the nature of the trace, forgetting is not permanent. Given the proper cues, any memory can be retrieved and be brought into consciousness. It has long been recognized, for example, that the results of a single query may not fairly represent all the items that are available in a subject's memory (Brown, 1923; Buschke, 1973; Tulving, 1967). Cued recall and recognition procedures may produce items that were inaccessible to free recall. Even without a change in the type of memory test, once-forgotten memories may be recovered. When subjects are allowed repeated recall attempts, as in the Recall-Test-Test (RTT) paradigm, they will often remember on later trials items that appeared to be forgotten on earlier ones. Often such recovered items are traded for others that are recalled on earlier trials but forgotten on later ones, so that overall levels of recall remain fairly stable. Under other circumstances, however, intertrial recovery can exceed intertrial forgetting, so that there occurs a net increment in recall over time (Ballard, 1913; Erdelyi & Kleinbard, 1979). Presumably this effect represents the spreading of activation from those items which were strong enough to be recalled on earlier trials, available in memory, to others that were too weak to cross the threshold for conscious representation.

The view that information is permanently stored in the brain, while popular, has recently been criticized by Loftus and Loftus (1980). Their review shows that much of the most dramatic evidence for memory permanence—Penfield's activation of long-forgotten memories by brain stimulation, the forensic use of hypnosis to enhance the memories of witnesses and victims to crimes, the recovery of forgotten events through fantasy and free association, and so on—has been vastly overstated. While they do not doubt the shifts in accessibility that are obtained under carefully controlled laboratory conditions by shifting from free recall to cued recall or recognition tests, or by allowing reminiscence to occur, they correctly argue that these effects do not prove that all memories are permanently stored. Moreover, some memories, known to have been adequately encoded at some earlier time, are not retrievable despite the use of extremely rich, appropriate cues.

Perhaps their most telling argument is based on studies of leading questions and eyewitness reports (e.g., Loftus, 1975, 1979). In a typical experiment, a subject who has viewed some event is led by a biased interrogation to testify to something that he or she did not actually witness. Later testing under unbiased conditions shows that memory favors the biased reconstruction over the original perception, and even careful, systematic inquiry typically fails to yield any recollection of the veridical memory. The problem is the classic one of the locus of interference, as in paired-associate learning. One possibility is that traces of both the original percept and the reconstructed event are available in memory, but that retrieval favors the latter over the former (Hintzman, 1972). Loftus and Loftus (1980) suggest that the newly reconstructed version of the event is written over the older version, so that the former is permanently lost. It seems, then, that even well-encoded "permanent" memories may be subject to decay or displacement, so that they become completely inaccessible (functionally unavailable) to retrieval, if not actually unavailable in storage.

The memories classified as functionally unavailable, if indeed they exist at all, are not unconscious in the sense used in this chapter, because they do not interact with other ongoing cognitive processes. Those memory elements activated during perceptual processing, but not brought into focal attention by virtue of their pertinence for the task at hand, also do not classify as unconscious because in principle they can be brought into awareness by a simple redeployment of attention. From a narrow view of memory, the only mental contents that can be characterized as unconscious are the products of early, automatic phases of perceptual processing. From a wider view, however, memory contains much more than this (Hastie & Carlston, 1980). Memory contains stored representations of knowledge, and cognitive psychologists find it useful to maintain two somewhat independent distinctions within the memory system: between declarative and procedural knowledge (Winograd, 1975), and between episodic and semantic memory (Tulving, 1972). Declarative knowledge consists of facts concerning the nature of the physical and social world; procedural knowledge consists of cognitive skills by which the person manipulates and transforms declarative knowledge. Episodic memory concerns specific personal experiences, and is marked by self-reference and the spatiotemporal context in which the event occurred; semantic memory comprises the "mental lexicon" of abstract, categorical information. Roughly speaking, all episodic knowledge is declarative in nature; semantic knowledge may be either declarative or procedural.

From this point of view, fully processed traces of perceived objects and events—declarative knowledge—are available to consciousness, in the sense that they can be brought into awareness by an appropriate deployment of attention. We can define the words in our vocabularies, describe, name, and categorize the objects and events that we perceive, tell the stories of our lives, express our ideas, emotions, and goals, and reflect on our experiences. However, it appears that a great deal of procedural knowledge is unconscious, in the strict sense that we have no awareness of or control over it. Procedures are instantiated by appropriate inputs, run themselves off, and deliver appropriate outputs automatically. A case in point is the knowledge by which we generate and interpret linguistic utterances (Chomsky, 1980). We have no introspective access to the rules of transformational grammar that yield surface structures from deep structures. Other examples may be found in the procedures involved in skilled motor routines, such as touch typing, piano playing, and (for sailors and scouts) knot tying. Novices perform these tasks consciously, and with a great deal of cognitive effort; experts perform them automatically and effortlessly. Similarly, we have no access to the basic processes involved in feature detection, pattern recognition, perceptual recoding, and meaning analysis (Mandler, 1975b; Neisser, 1967), or to the kinds of rules and strategies involved in perceptual inference and problem solving (Hochberg, 1978; Kaufman, 1974; Rock, 1975). We know these processes only indirectly, by inference. This principle, which seems to apply broadly to the kinds of cognitive skills involved in perception, memory processing, communication, and motor response, has recently been extended to the higher mental processes involved in thinking and judgment. Based on the results of a series of studies, Nisbett and Wilson (1977) have argued that people are largely unaware of stimuli that have influenced their behavior, that their appraisal of some situation, or of the considerations that led them to respond as they did to some situation, has changed. People may *think* that they know these things, but in fact they do not. The Nisbett-Wilson position is a strong one, perhaps excessively so (see Bowers, this book). Certainly, it seems a mistake to reject the possibility of a person having any privileged self-knowledge (Cantor & Kihlstrom, 1983; Kihlstrom & Cantor, 1983). But insofar as it applies to procedural knowledge, their position is consistent with observations in other cognitive domains such as reading and speech perception. We have no direct introspective access to the skills by which declarative knowledge is acquired, organized, stored, retrieved, manipulated, and transformed.

Thus in the final analysis, the taxonomy of cognitive contents may be represented as in Figure 4.4. Incoming stimuli are first processed by the sensory-perceptual system. The operation of this system is unconscious, in the sense that it is involuntary and the perceiver has no direct introspective access to it. Similarly, the stored procedural knowledge which guides this perceptual processing is unconscious. The physical and semantic attributes produced by feature analysis activate their corresponding representations in the preexisting network which comprises the storehouse of declarative knowledge. In a similar manner, some elements in the network are activated by attentional processes,

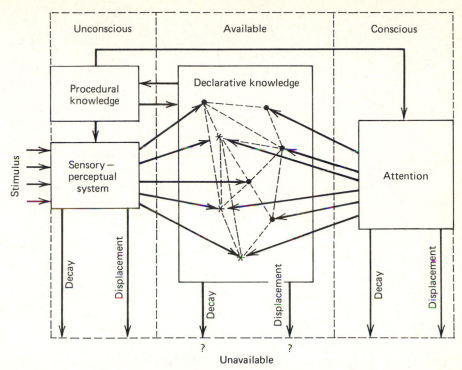

Figure 4.4. Conscious and unconscious mental contents and processes viewed within a revised unistore model of memory, permitting activation to spread within an associative network.

corresponding to the perceiver's expectations. Activation spreads out from both types of nodes, and those concepts and propositions which cross a threshold of activation form the full perceptual construction (or memorial reconstruction) of the object or event. This conscious percept is the product of the interaction between data driven ("bottom-up") and conceptually driven ("top-down") cognitive activity. Not all of the declarative knowledge available in memory is activated and thus represented in consciousness; but what is accessed and brought into consciousness is determined by contributions from both the perceiver and the perceptual world. Again, however, the procedures guiding this (re)constructive activity are unconscious, unless the cognitive task is especially demanding.

Note that the final conscious product of cognitive processing may be influenced by declarative (as well as procedural) structures that are not themselves represented in phenomenal awareness. Ordinarily action is determined by what is consciously perceived. However, in a manner analogous to sensory signal detection, there may be (within broad limits) no absolute threshold that activation must cross before cognition and action occur. If this is so, then there may be some circumstances—such as highly ambiguous stimulus situations—where action is determined by mental structures that are themselves not represented in awareness. Under these circumstances, perceivers may very well not know what stimulus they are responding to, or why they acted as they did. Thus this model of the mind affords the possibility of the sorts of preconscious influences on thought and action considered so important by New Look theorists, old (Bruner & Postman, 1949) and new (Nisbett & Wilson, 1977) alike.

The model also suggests a mechanism for repression, in the psychodynamic sense of a motivated failure to perceive or remember unpleasant or threatening objects or events. In classic psychoanalytic theory, Freud made a distinction between primal repression—the blocking of such stimuli from ever entering consciousness—and repression proper—the afterexpulsion of memories of events that had been consciously perceived. The classic theory confined repression to ideas and memories associated with primitive sexual and aggressive impulses, but there seems no reason not to liberate the concept from the theory of infantile sexuality and other Freudian trappings (Kihlstrom, 1981a). In princi- ple, it would seem an easy matter to assimilate repression to contemporary cognitive theory by construing it as a special instance of selective attention and retrieval (Erdelyi & Goldberg, 1979; Mandler, 1975b). Conceptually, however, repression differs from suppression in that the former is an unconscious process, so that repressors are not aware of their selective cognitive processing. It might be possible to solve this problem by postulating that repressors selectively attend to the fact that they are selectively attending, but the possibility of infinite regression is an unattractive one. Another tact, however, is offered by recent analyses of the development of procedural knowledge. Anderson (1982a), working within the ACT model, has proposed that all procedures begin as declarative structures—as facts *about* the procedures. This factual knowledge permits the individual to enact the desired process—deliberately, consciously, and crudely. As the person practices the activity, Anderson suggests that a process of "knowledge compilation" takes place, in which the declarative knowledge is converted into procedural form. At this point, the activity is highly skilled; but it is also performed automatically and unconsciously. In this way, repressors may begin by deliberately avoiding unpleasant material, and after much practice develop a repressive cognitive style that is "natural," unconscious, and difficult to modify.

PHENOMENA INVITING A CONCEPT OF DISSOCIATION

The evolution of thinking in cognitive psychology has gradually led to a theoretical conception of the mind that has a place for both conscious and unconscious knowledge and mental processes. However, conspicuously absent from these models is any place for *subconscious* mental processes of the sort that concerned the proponents of the First Dynamic Psychiatry. At first glance, this does not seem so bad. After all, the models do provide a decent theoretical account of most of the phenomena observed in the psychological laboratory, and doubtless many that occur in the ordinary course of everyday living as well. The phenomena that interested Charcot, Janet, and Prince were mostly observed in disturbed individuals, were not subject to rigorous empirical scrutiny, and in any case are rarely observed today. Reasonable people could conclude that these phenomena are somehow beyond the pale, and that cognitive theory need not take them seriously. Thus it seems important to reexamine the phenomena of dissociation, in order to determine how much consideration they actually warrant. Space permits only brief and selective coverage (for another review, see Hilgard, 1977b).

"Hysteria," Fugue, and Multiple Personality

Among the syndromes of neurosis are a variety of patterns that center around dramatic symptoms paralleling those of organic brain syndrome (Abse, 1959; Nemiah, 1967, 1969, 1979; West, 1967). These subsume motor disturbances of various sorts, including paralyses in the extremities (limpness or sustained contracture), astasia and abasia, and aphonia; sensory disturbances, including anesthesia (often accompanied by paralysis), blindness, and deafness; and amnesia for specific events, experiences, or periods of time. While the presenting symptoms typically represent the apparent loss of normal cognitive and behavioral functions, positive symptoms are also occasionally reported, in the form of hallucinations (typically visual), or "somnambulistic" states in which the person is observed to carry out complex activities over an extended period of time, with no concurrent responsiveness to environmental events and no subsequent recollection of the episode. As noted by Davison and Neale (1982), these syndromes differ from the other neuroses in that anxiety is not a prominent part of the clinical picture. However, the symptoms often seem to be precipitated by traumatic events, or emerge after a period of acute emotional stress. Neurological examination yields no compelling evidence of organic brain syndrome—or, at least, no insult, injury, or disease sufficient to account for the symptoms.

Interestingly, patients who complain of these symptoms typically display behavior which is inconsistent with their claims, and which demonstrates that the affected subsystem is in fact operating properly. For example, the hysterical patient who walks with a staggering gait rarely falls, and if the person is bilingual, the aphonia may be restricted to one language. The patients may also display *la belle indifference,* a complacent and unconcerned attitude toward both their ostensibly debilitating symptoms and their apparently paradoxical behavior.

These functional disturbances were diagnosed quite frequently around the turn of the century, and Janet (1907) has left us with a classic account of their clinical picture. Although such cases are still seen with some frequency (Templer & Lester, 1974), especially by general practitioners and neurologists, almost none have been subjected to any kind of laboratory investigation. Hilgard (cited in Hilgard & Marquis, 1940) showed that a patient with anesthesia and paralysis in one arm could acquire a conditioned finger-withdrawal response, and used such a procedure in an early form of behavior therapy. Perhaps the most controversial case is one of functional blindness reported by Brady and Lind (1961), and subsequently reanalyzed by Grosz and Zimmerman (1965). In an elegant study employing the technology of instrumental conditioning, Brady and Lind showed that the person was responsive to visual stimulation despite his denial of the experience of sight; like Hilgard, they used their procedure as the basis for a successful therapeutic regime. Grosz and Zimmerman extended these findings by showing that response to a visual stimulus reverted to baseline levels when the patient was informed of how a truly blind person would perform on the task. They suggested that the case was one of malingering rather than functional blindness, but Brady (1966) offered additional evidence favoring the original diagnosis. Occasionally, other case studies of a similar nature have appeared, again pointing out the contradictions between the deficit claimed and objective performance on laboratory tasks (for a review see Sackeim, Nordlie, & Gur, 1979).

Fugue

A dramatic, generalized form of functional amnesia appears to cover the individual's entire personal history: the victim has no knowledge of his or her identity or autobiography, or even any access to relevant clues; however, the general fund of information about impersonal matters is retained. Such losses of personal identity are often accompanied by wandering, which feature gives the syndrome its name. The state ends either with a sudden awakening to one's original identity, or to an awareness that identity has been lost. Recovery of normal identity often is followed by an amnesia for the period of the fugue. The corpus of published case histories is very large (e.g., Berrington, Liddell, & Foulds, 1956). Recently Schacter and his colleagues (Schacter, Wang, Tulving, & Freedman, 1982) reported the only known experimental study of a case of functional amnesia. The patient, P.N., complained of a failure to remember any personal information. When tested for his knowledge of public figures (semantic memories), he performed as well as a nonamnesic control subject both before and after the fugue. When asked to retrieve specific personal experiences related to verbal cues (episodic memories), however, those recovered were primarily drawn from the period since the onset of the fugue, whereas after recovery the memories spanned a much longer period of time, comparable to that shown by the control patient on both test and retest.

Multiple Personality

This syndrome is diagnosed when two or more distinct patterns of personality appear to coexist, alternating in their influence over overt behavior and subjective experience. Typically there is some measure of autonomy between the personalities, and some degree of amnesia separating them. A large number of such cases have been reported in the clinical literature (for reviews see Greaves, 1980; Sutcliffe & Jones, 1962; Taylor & Martin, 1944), mostly in the nineteenth century—although the incidence appears to be on the upswing again. Interestingly, there is no clear pattern of normality and pathology in these cases:

sometimes the subconscious personality—that is, the personality which departs from the usual way in which the patient identifies himself or herself, and is identified by others—is better adjusted than the conscious one. Sometimes the various personalities "cooperate" with each other, when one has a resource that another one needs (e.g., Ludwig, Brandsma, Wilbur, Bendfeldt, & Jameson, 1972). The majority of cases are of dual personality, and in most of these the amnesia is mutual, with each personality ignorant of the existence and operation of the other. Especially in cases of more than two coexisting personalities, the amnesic barrier is often asymmetrical.

Only a few cases of multiple personality have been subjected to rigorous clinical and experimental analysis and only one of these—Jonah—has included systematic tests of cognitive function that bear on the problem of dissociation (Ludwig et al., 1972). Jonah presented five personalities: Jonah ("the square"; primary), Sammy ("the lawyer"), King Young ("the lover"), Usoffa Abdullah, the Son of Omega ("the warrior"), and De Nova, a newly developing personality. Jonah had no knowledge whatsoever of Sammy, King Young, and Usoffa Abdullah; and he alone had knowledge of De Nova. Sammy, King Young, and Usoffa all had knowledge of Jonah, in that they had access to his thoughts and feelings; but while these three personalities knew of each others' existence, they had no access to each other's mental life. This pattern of symmetrical and asymmetrical amnesia was largely confirmed with a series of laboratory tests involving transfer of training. Interestingly, tests of semantic (as opposed to episodic) memory and skill learning showed no differences, and even some evidence of practice effects.

Depersonalization, Derealization, and Other Anomalies of Memory

The cardinal symptom of these disorders is a subjective awareness or feeling of change in oneself—depersonalization—or in the surrounding world—derealization (Roth, 1960; Sedman, 1970). Surveys of college students indicate that depersonalization and derealization occur spontaneously in one-third to one-half of normal subjects, during periods of fatigue, illness, anxiety, or sadness; it can also be induced by looking in a mirror. It has been experimentally induced by marijuana, sensory deprivation, and LSD, and is frequently reported as a response to life-threatening danger (Noyes & Kletti, 1977). These last experiences are particularly remarkable for their reports of panoramic memory and out-of-body experiences. While not strictly an amnesia, depersonalization is certainly an anomaly of memory functioning, consisting at base of a failure to recognize oneself or one's environment (Reed, 1972, 1979). Apparently, affected individuals retain an unimpaired ability to remember factual knowledge about themselves and their world, but are not able to match their current experience to these memories. The result is a sense of unreality similar to that which occurs when one encounters a familiar room whose decor has been changed. The functional isolation of preexisting memories from encodings of current experience marks depersonalization and derealization as essentially dissociative in nature.

Depersonalization and derealization represent a transition between the frank amnesias of hysteria, fugue, and multiple personality, and other disorders of memory which do not properly classify as amnesia: *déjà vu,* the compelling sense of having been in a place before, coexisting with the knowledge that this is not the case; *jamais vu,* perhaps a less generalized form of derealization, in which there is no feeling of familiarity despite the knowledge that the situation has been experienced many times in the past; and cryptomnesia, unconscious plagiarism, in which an idea or a memory is attributed to oneself when in fact its origins lie elsewhere. Of these phenomena and their close relatives, only *déjà vu* has been the subject of systematic inquiry. A study of medical patients, interestingly, indicates that *déjà vu* is most common in those individuals who have had at least a secondary education, and infrequent in those who have never travelled far from home. Like depersonalization, *déjà vu* also appears to involve some disruption of the recognition process (Reed, 1972, 1979).

> In July 1976, while attending a scientific meeting, I visited the Philadelphia Museum of Art with Ken and Pat Bowers to view its Bicentennial exhibit of American painting and sculpture. While standing in one of the galleries I had the strong impression that I had been there before. Of course, I had been in the room before, many times, in the five years that I had lived in Philadelphia as a graduate student; but my feeling was that this particular room, with the exhibit in place, was familiar. It was not until November of 1977, sitting in the Stanford medical library preparing a lecture on the anomalies of memory, that I solved the puzzle: in fact I had seen the entire exhibit the previous May, when I had visited Philadelphia to witness the marriage of some friends. I knew this even in July, because I had encouraged the Bowerses to see the show on the basis of my previous visit; but for those moments in the gallery, and for the 16 months thereafter, I never made the connection.

While the clinical and subclinical phenomena of hysteria, fugue, and multiple personality originally gave rise to the concept of dissociation, they are so rare that few cases have been subjected to rigorous scrutiny even in the clinic, let alone the psychological laboratory. Moreover, the cases are contaminated by possible organic brain syndrome and—equally important—clear secondary gains from the "sick role" (Sarbin & Coe, 1979; Szasz, 1961). Accordingly, it seems important to search for other instances of dissociation manifested by normal subjects in the ordinary course of everyday living, or under controlled laboratory conditions. Such phenomena are often found in individuals who are asleep, drugged, or hypnotized.

Cognitive Activity During Sleep

Superficially, sleep may seem to represent an interruption of waking consciousness: the sleeper is typically hard to arouse, and he or she typically remembers little or nothing about the events of the past night's sleep. However, we also know that appearances in this case are deceiving: sleep is characterized by a continuous flow of many types of mental activity (Arkin, Antrobus, & Ellman, 1978). This activity qualifies as dissociated because it is not under voluntary control, and because it is not represented in memories accessible to the person during the normal waking state.

Dreams

Of course, the most familiar form of mental activity during sleep is the dream. Given the unusual content of most dreams, the apparent frequency with which they occur during the night, and their vivid hallucinatory quality, it is somewhat surprising that the typical person recalls at best only a single dream the next morning. A number of factors may contribute to this forgetting (Cohen, 1974, 1976, 1979; Goodenough, 1967, 1978; Koulack & Goodenough, 1976). From the point of view of the multistore model of memory, for example, it has been suggested that the dream is never consolidated in secondary memory, and is lost from primary memory shortly after the REM state ends. We remember a dream in the morning, according to this hypothesis, only if we awaken out of REM, permitting us to retrieve the dream directly from primary memory. A similar account can be constructed from the point of view of levels-of-processing theory, assuming a unitary memory system: because very little attentional effort is devoted to the dream as it occurs, the dream is not encoded in memory in such a way as to permit it to be accessible at a later time. From either point of view, upon awakening then, the dream is either not represented in the cognitive system at all (unavailable), or it is represented in such a way as to be inaccessible under ordinary conditions (functionally unavailable).

Another point of view holds that the dream is accessible in memory, but that various factors familiar in normal memory, such as salience and interference, diminish its retrievability. Repression is probably not a factor in dream recall: there is no recall disadvantage for dreams dreamt after viewing a highly threatening presleep film. It is possible, of course, that dream-recall failure represents an instance of state-dependent retention: that the dream is fully encoded and available in memory, but only when the person is in Stage REM. Unfortunately, difficulties in interviewing sleeping subjects preclude rigorous testing of this hypothesis. It may be possible to approach the problem of the availability of dream content in another way, however. REM awakenings typically yield a dream report, but not all of these dreams are remembered by the subject in the morning upon final awakening. This raises the possibility of conducting a recognition test for unrecalled dreams, by presenting each subject with a set of his or her own dreams, collected on line, along with distractor dreams contributed by a control subject. Provided that obvious identifying information has been removed, successful recognition would constitute evidence that dreams were encoded in memory—available in storage, but not usually accessible (Johnson & Raye, 1981).

Sleepwalking, Sleeptalking, and Sleeplearning

Dreams, and the thoughtlike mentation that accompanies Stage NREM, may be characterized as endogenous mental activities, in the sense that there is no direct, sustained interaction with the external environment at the time that the thoughts occur. Thus it might be said that if sleepers are not strictly unconscious, at least they are not conscious of events in the outside world. In fact, however, both REM and NREM mentation can be affected by stimuli presented during sleep (Arkin & Antrobus, 1978; Williams, 1973), and a little reflection on ordinary experience shows that this characterization of sleepers as cognitively isolated from their environment is incorrect. For example, we do not typically fall out of our beds, even unfamiliar ones, despite a considerable amount of body motility during the night. Moreover, many sleepers show selective arousal from sleep in response to their names or other significant stimuli; this appears to be especially true of the parents of infants. Finally, some people appear to be able to awaken at a predetermined time, without benefit of alarm clocks. While this evidence is largely anecdotal at present, rigorous laboratory studies confirm that people continue to respond to environmental events even while asleep.

Somnambulism is a prototypical example of dissociation, whether it occurs in hysteria or normal sleep. The sleeper rises from bed and engages in some activity resembling that of waking life, such as wandering around the room, the house, or even outside, turning lights or household appliances on and off, fumbling with objects, sometimes accompanied by incoherent talking or mumbling (Kales, Paulson, Jacobson, & Kales, 1966; Jacobson & Kales, 1967). The phenomenon is fairly common among children, and is reportedly common among campers, military recruits, and others who are under conditions of stress. The behavior seems purposeless, and not very dextrous. It can be induced in children with a prior history of sleepwalking by the simple procedure of gently sitting the subject up in bed. Similarly, in somniloquy the sleeper utters speech or other psychologically meaningful sound during sleep—in extreme cases a rambling monologue or one side of an extended conversation will ensue (Arkin, 1966, 1978, 1982). Whereas episodes of sleepwalking can last for 15 to 30 minutes, bouts of sleeptalking are typically brief. The phenomenon is so common that it can be difficult to find people who have *not* been told that they talk in their sleep, although again it is more prominent in children than adults. It is sometimes possible for an observer to enter into conversation with a sleeptalker, once the episode has begun. The topics of sleepspeech mostly revolve around everyday concerns, though very few secrets have been betrayed in this way. Both sleepwalking and sleeptalking have been studied in the laboratory—in the former case, with the aid of very long and light electrode leads or radiotelemetry; there is no doubt that the individuals involved are asleep at the time of the episode. Since sleepwalking and sleeptalking are typically observed in Stage NREM, they do not appear to represent acting out, or talking about, dreams.

Unlike somnambulism and somniloquy, hypnopaedia has proved difficult to document in the laboratory (Aarons, 1976; Evans, 1979a; Simon & Emmons, 1955). The overwhelming evidence for cognitive activity during sleep, as indicated by the phenomena discussed earlier, suggests that people may be able to acquire new information while asleep, and retrieve it in the morning, but the evidence is unconvincing. The most dramatic claims have come from the Soviet Union and Eastern Europe, where sleep is typically diagnosed by overt behavior and autonomic activity rather than the EEG (Hoskovec, 1966; Hoskovec & Cooper, 1967, 1969). When the EEG is used, the outcome of sleeplearning appears directly related to the density of EEG alpha activity—that is, to the degree that the subject is still awake. There have been some well-documented successes when subjects have been selected for high hypnotizability or given a presleep set that learning will occur, and when the material is presented in Stage REM as opposed to NREM. Of special interest are indications in the Soviet studies that information successfully retained from sleeplearning sessions pops into the mind when appropriate questions are asked, with the subjects unable to account for their knowledge of the answers. Nevertheless, the conclusion seems inescapable that sleeplearning, while perhaps possible, is not particularly efficient. As is the case with dreams, it is not yet clear why this is so. Perhaps the failure of sleeplearning reflects a failure to encode the items deeply enough to be retrieved (functionally unavailable). On the other hand, the amnesia may be an instance of state-dependent retention, with the memories accessible only during sleep. Some data collected by Evans (1979a), discussed below, support this possibility—although the hypothesis, if confirmed, would not lead people to be particularly optimistic about the utility of sleeplearning procedures.

State-Dependent Retention

State-dependent retention is said to occur when the memorability of an event is controlled by the congruence between the organismic state in which the memory was initially encoded and that in which retrieval is attempted. In the apocryphal example, an event that occurred while an individual was intoxicated is forgotten while sober, but accessible during a later drinking bout. The phenomenon was originally documented in nonhuman animals (Overton, 1964, 1968); but it has been produced in human subjects as well, by substances as diverse as alcohol, amphetamine, general anesthetics, barbiturates, marijuana, and physostygmine (for reviews, see Eich, 1977, 1980). Analogous congruence effects have been observed with shifts in mood state (e.g., Bower, 1981), and environmental context (Godden & Baddeley, 1975; Smith, Glenberg, & Bjork, 1978). In animals given sublethal doses of barbiturate, state-dependency can be substantial indeed, resulting in a complete failure of transfer from one state to the other. In humans, however, the effects are typically weak, and can be abolished by the use of rich retrieval cues such as those found in recognition as opposed to recall tasks. Perhaps this is because the manipulations are also relatively weak: in animals, state-dependency shows a clear dose-response curve.

Nevertheless, the literature does contain several examples of complete state-dependent retention in humans, or virtually so. Swanson and Kinsbourne (1976), for example, found a strong congruence effect of amphetamine on paired-associate learning (cued recall) in hyperactive, but not normal, children. Something closer to complete dissociation has been observed in the phenomenon of sleep suggestion (Evans, 1979a). Evans and his colleagues administered simple motor suggestions to subjects during alpha-free Stage REM sleep. Appropriate responses to the cues were elicited in about half the subjects, although the overall response rate was low. Responding persisted during subsequent REM periods the same night, the next night, and on six-month followup, without any further reinforcement of the suggestion. However, when interviewed in the waking state, the subjects typically were unaware that suggestions had been given; nor did they respond appropriately to the cues embedded in a word-association test.

A number of theories have been offered concerning state-dependent retention in humans and other animals (for reviews see Eich, 1980; Overton, 1977). Within the animal-learning community, so influenced by the behaviorist ethos, it is common to construe the drug state as a discriminative stimulus for a particular response. The major evidence for this hypothesis is that animals can discriminate among dosages of the drugs in question, making the classic phenomenon appear to be an extreme example of drug-discrimination learning. A more dissociative hypothesis, such as that suggested by the sleep-suggestion studies, is hard to test in nonhuman animals, because they cannot report on their thoughts; and in humans, too, because the effects of drug manipulations are necessarily weak. So far as nonverbal animals are concerned, consider an experiment in which rats are trained in a sunburst maze to enter one arm when drugged, and another when in the normal waking state. If subsequent testing reveals no generalization across states (i.e., state-dependent retention), then the alley appropriate to the animal's current drug state is blocked, preventing it from making its preferred response. A stimulus-generalization theory might predict that the animal would show a bias to enter the arm learned in the opposite state: if the animal is aware of both options and making a choice between them, then the other arm may be its best guess. On the other hand, if the animal is aware of only the response learned in its current state, its subsequent behavior might be more random. Turning to humans, the current results appear to exemplify the encoding specificity principle: without appropriate retrieval cues, items available in memory may be inaccessible to attempts at retrieval (Eich, 1980). This principle may form the basis for a cognitive approach to dissociative phenomena in general.

Phenomena of Hypnosis

The proponents of the First Dynamic Psychiatry studied hypnosis both clinically and experimentally because of the apparent parallels between the phenomena of hypnosis and the symptoms of hysteria. The phenotypic similarities were taken to imply genotypic similarities, resulting in the development of psychogenic theories of the etiology of psychopathology as correctives to the somatogenic theories that prevailed at the time. The analogy should not be pressed too far, because individuals who can experience hypnosis do not show the impairments in general functioning that are characteristic of mental patients. Nevertheless, the phenomena of hypnosis do seem to involve divisions in consciousness of the type associated with the concept of dissociation. Because these alterations in thought and action can be easily and reliably induced in normal individuals under controlled conditions without any trauma or hazard, the phenomena of hypnosis may serve as convenient laboratory models for the study of basic psychological processes highly relevant to psychopathology (Kihlstrom, 1979).

Posthypnotic Suggestion

Since the time of Freud, posthypnotic behavior has served as a prime example of nonconscious mental processes at work (Sheehan & Orne, 1968). The central feature of posthypnotic behavior is the eruption of an irresistible, compulsive act, whose motivational source is unknown to the subject. The action appears to break into the usual stream of behavior: the subject suddenly does something that is not integrated with the rest of his or her action; and it appears to be outside of the subject's volitional control. In the classic case, the individual is unaware that he or she is, in fact, doing anything unusual; in any event, the hypnotic origins of the behavior are often obscure for the subject. If his or her attention is drawn to the unusual behavior, and the subject is pressed for an explanation, he or she may infer its hypnotic origins—but this is far from direct, personal recollection. Posthypnotic suggestions have been reported to persist for well over a year in both experimental and clinical situations.

The compulsive, quasiautomatic, involuntary nature of posthypnotic behavior has been demonstrated in a number of experiments. For example, Nace and Orne (1970) showed that hypnotizable subjects who failed to respond to a posthypnotic suggestion at its initial test manifested a persisting tendency to perform the behavior at a later time. On the other hand, Fisher (1954) showed that posthypnotic suggestions were not acted upon outside the experimental context in which the subject expected them to be tested. However, a better designed experiment by Orne, Sheehan, and Evans (1968) did demonstrate a high level of response even when the cues were offered in a situation that was clearly perceived by the subjects to be outside the experimental context; simulators did not give posthypnotic responses under these conditions. Two other studies on the persistence of posthypnotic behavior make the same point in a different and superficially paradoxical way. In an experiment by Bowers (1975), subjects received a posthypnotic suggestion to express a preference for a style of painting that had previously been nonpreferred, covered by amnesia; then half the subjects were placed in a verbal-conditioning procedure where the experimenter additionally shaped this preference by means of appropriate contingencies of reinforcement. Then the reinforcement contingencies were eliminated, and the subjects in both groups were tested again by a new experimenter. The subjects who received only the posthypnotic suggestion continued to express their new preference, while those who had also received the verbal-conditioning regime reverted to their original preference. Two motivational sources, one internal and the other external, were not better than one. Finally, Damaser (1964; see Orne, 1970) asked hypnotizable subjects to mail the experimenter one postcard per day, and were dismissed from the experiment with a stack of cards to take home. One group received the request as a posthypnotic suggestion, covered by amnesia; for another group, the request was made in the normal waking state; a third group received both the posthypnotic suggestion and the waking request. This time, the behavior persisted longer for those who received the waking request and those who received both conditions, compared to those who received only the posthypnotic suggestion.

Despite the apparently conflicting results, all of this research converges on the conclusion that posthypnotic behavior represents a subjectively compelling, intrapsychic urge to carry out certain actions. For example, the subjects in the Orne et al. (1968) experiment were clearly responding to something besides the demand characteristics of the testing situation; and in the study by Nace and Orne (1970), it would have been much easier for highly motivated, compliant subjects to execute the suggestion at their first opportunity and be done with it. The case is strengthened by an analysis of posthypnotic persistence in terms of attribution theory (Bowers, 1973). According to attribution theory, subjects who perceive that their behavior is controlled and constrained by external environmental contingencies will show a diminution in that behavior if the contingencies disappear; by contrast, those who perceive their behavior as self-determined will show persistence despite changes in the situational context (Harackiewicz, 1979; Lepper, Greene, & Nisbett, 1973). In the Bowers (1975) and Damaser (1964) studies, the subjects behaved as if intrinsically rather than extrinsically motivated. This is clear enough in Bowers, but interpretation of the Damaser experiment is more conjectural. Apparently, those who agreed to the waking request felt committed to carrying it out; those who received the suggestion acted on it only so long as they felt inclined to do so. Interestingly, those who received both suggestion and request behaved like Lepper et al.'s (1973) overjustification subjects, discounting the internal sources of their own behavior.

Posthypnotic Amnesia

Following the termination of hypnosis, many subjects find that they cannot remember the events and experiences that transpired while they were hypnotized (for reviews, see Kihlstrom, 1977, 1978, 1982, 1983; Kihlstrom & Evans, 1979). Later, after the hypnotist has administered a prearranged cue, these memories seem to flood back into awareness, and the same subjects who showed such difficulty in remembering a few moments before now are able to remember the events of hypnosis vividly and clearly. This amnesia does not occur unless it has been explicitly or implicitly suggested, and it may be reversed by administration of a prearranged cue (although some measure of residual amnesia may persist for at least a time), thus distinguishing posthypnotic amnesia from state-dependent retention.

The dissociation of episodic memory occurring during posthypnotic amnesia seems to involve both the monitoring and controlling aspects of consciousness. In the first place, there is a frank failure of memory, as seen in the subject's inability to recall, or even to recognize, events that occurred or items that were learned while he or she was hypnotized (Kihlstrom, 1980). In the most dramatic display of this failure yet, McConkey and Sheehan (1981; McConkey, Sheehan, & Cross, 1980) found that the amnesia remained robust in some subjects even when they were shown videotapes of themselves taken during the hypnotic session; simulating subjects behaved rather differently. Even when hypnotizable subjects are able to successfully remember some of the critical material, a loss of control over the processes of retrieval and reconstruction may be observed in their failure to strategically organize recall around normally salient structural features of the material. In one set of studies, for example, partially amnesic subjects often listed those few events which they were able to recall in an order which did not reflect the actual chronological sequence of events, even when they were specifically instructed to do so (Kihlstrom & Evans, 1979). Moreover, subjects who have successfully recalled a fragment of an experience may not be able to flesh out their recollection, by adding other relevant features, so that it forms a full and complete representation of the event.

Despite these difficulties with awareness and control, there is abundant evidence that these memories remain available and active within the cognitive system. For example, relearning of a skill whose acquisition is covered by posthypnotic amnesia takes place more rapidly than if that skill had never been acquired at all (Hull, 1933); retroactive inhibition is not eliminated by a suggestion for amnesia for the interpolated list in the ABA paradigm; and the priming received by underlying semantic representations during learning is not diminished by amnesia. In the phenomenon of posthypnotic source amnesia (Evans, 1979b; Evans & Thorn, 1966), some subjects, otherwise densely amnesic for their hypnotic experiences, are able to answer questions concerning new factual material acquired during hypnosis; however, they are unable to give a satisfactory account of the circumstances under which they learned this information. Subjects simulating hypnosis and amnesia do not produce this effect. The paradox of posthypnotic amnesia—one which reveals its essentially dissociative quality—is that amnesic subjects make use of memories that they do not know they have.

Posthypnotic amnesia qualifies as dissociative because the person cannot retrieve memories that are available and, under normal conditions, would be accessible. Nevertheless these memories continue to influence ongoing thought and action, outside awareness, and can be recovered upon administration of the reversibility cue. In this case, the dissociative split occurs between the episodic and semantic components of memory. According to models such as ACT, learning a list of familiar words involves activating a preexisting semantic representation of the item and then linking it associatively with other concepts specifying the spatiotemporal context in which the item was encoded. In amnesia it appears that the underlying semantic memory remains active and linked to the remainder of the organized mental lexicon, but becomes detached from its contextual features and, correspondingly, the continuous record of autobiographical memory. This results in partial or full failure on episodic memory tasks, which ultimately demand reconstruction of the spatiotemporal context in which the event occurred, but spares performance on semantic memory tasks, which have no such requirement (Kihlstrom, 1980). Similar accounts can be given for a wide variety of amnesic states, including the organic amnesic syndrome (Schacter & Tulving, 1982) and infantile amnesia (Schacter &

Moscovitch, 1983; White & Pillemer, 1979). The hypnotic case is somewhat different from these, however, in that the amnesia is temporary and reversible, implying that the connection between semantic and episodic components remains somehow represented.

Perceptual Alterations and Trance Logic

Various changes in perceptual experience also offer an opportunity to study dissociative processes in hypnosis. In the positive hallucinations, for example, the person perceives objects and events that are not actually present in the environment; and in negative hallucinations, the person fails to perceive objects and events that are present. In age-regression, the person takes on a childlike demeanor and appears to relive an experience associated with some period in his or her past life. Superficially, all of these experiences involve changes in phenomenal awareness and control of the kind that raise the question of dissociation. In the negative hallucinations, there is a loss of normal awareness; in the positive hallucinations, the subjects do not perceive that they are constructing mental images for themselves (Hilgard, 1977b; Jaynes, 1976; Johnson & Raye, 1981; Kihlstrom, 1981b; Neisser, 1976); age-regression combines both features, in that the individual loses awareness of his or her true age, and does not realize that he or she is actively constructing a hallucinatory experience of being younger (Kihlstrom, 1982; Orne, 1951).

These changes in perceptual experience are subjectively compelling: for example, Spanos and Barber (1968) found that reports of visual hallucinations were not diminished when the subjects were administered strong honesty demands (see also Bowers, 1966, 1967; Hilgard, Macdonald, Morgan, & Johnson, 1978). Nevertheless, subjects experiencing these phenomena display paradoxical features conceptually similar to those seen in amnesia (and, as described below, analgesia). For example, hypnotically deaf subjects continue to manifest speech dysfluencies when subjected to delayed auditory feedback (Scheibe, Gray, & Keim, 1968; Sutcliffe, 1961); and when shadowing in a dichotic listening paradigm, they show substantial numbers of intrusions from material presented to their deaf ear (Spanos, Jones, & Malfara, 1982). And age-regressed subjects may continue to display their normal adult skills, as in the case of a subject who, when regressed to preschool age, took dictation of a complicated sentence, in a childlike scrawl, without misspelling a single word (O'Connell, Shor, & Orne, 1970; Orne, 1951).

In a classic paper, Orne (1959) pointed to other such inconsistencies and anomalies of response during hypnosis. In the case of the double hallucination, for example, it is suggested that the subject will see, and interact with, a confederate sitting in a chair which is actually empty. After the hallucination is established, the subject's attention is drawn to the real confederate, who has been quietly sitting outside his or her view. Orne reported that hypnotized subjects typically exhibited confusion as to which was the real confederate, but maintained both the perception of the real confederate and the hallucination. Similarly, many reported that they could see through the hallucinated confederate to the back of the chair. Subjects simulating hypnosis typically manifested neither effect. Orne dubbed this response "trance logic," and indicated that it represented a simultaneous awareness of two mutually contradictory states of affairs without attempting to resolve the contradictions inherent in the experience—a "peaceful coexistence" of illusion and reality.

Orne's original report was impressionistic in nature, and later investigators have attempted to study the effect quantitatively. The first study, by Johnson, Maher, and Barber (1972), reported a failure to confirm Orne's observations. However, a critique and reanalysis by Hilgard (1972; for a reply, see Johnson, 1972) indicated that their results were actually somewhat supportive of Orne's claims. Later experiments have also been supportive, although the magnitude of the effect has not been large (McDonald & Smith, 1975; Obstoj & Sheehan, 1977; Perry & Walsh, 1978; Peters, 1973; Sheehan, 1977; Sheehan, Obstoj, & McConkey, 1976). While most studies have confined themselves to the two canonical tasks described by Orne (1959), Peters (1973) employed a battery of tasks designed to elicit trance logic. When an overall score was calculated by summing the number of items on which trance logic was shown, the difference between reals and simulators was highly significant. Similarly, Obstoj and Sheehan (1977; see also Sheehan, 1977) and Perry and Walsh (1978) found that scores on a battery of trance logic items administered during hypnosis significantly differentiated hypnotizable from insusceptible subjects. The current situation seems to be that trance logic and other incongruities and anomalies of behavior and experience are not defining characteristics of hypnosis, as Orne originally thought them to be. They do not occur in all hypnotized subjects; and they also may occur in states other than hypnosis, such as when hypnotizable subjects are given imagination instructions (Obstoj & Sheehan, 1977). It should be recalled, however, that states such as hypnosis, as natural categories, are not defined in terms of such necessary and sufficient features.

In the present context, trance logic is of particular interest because it seems to represent co-consciousness, or a simultaneous representation in awareness of two independent streams of mental activity—the one involved in constructing the hallucinated experience, the other involved in perceiving reality. In all of the other instances of dissociation discussed in this paper, one such stream of mental activity is denied to conscious awareness, so that the subject does not become aware of his or her contradictory experiences and actions. The experience of multiple simultaneous, mutually contradictory perceptions can be expected to be rather difficult to maintain; it is not surprising that the phenomenon is rare and has been difficult to tame and bring into the laboratory for rigorous study under controlled conditions.

The Hidden Observer

Along with trance logic, the most controversial demonstrations of dissociation within hypnosis have involved the phenomenon of the "hidden observer" (Hilgard, 1973c, 1977b, 1979). The first formal demonstration of the hidden observer effect was provided by Knox, Morgan, and Hilgard (1974) in hypnotic analgesia. Analgesia is another of those paradoxical hypnotic phenomena, in that hypnotizable subjects who are given appropriate suggestions may report feeling no pain when exposed to normally painful stimulation. Despite their denial of pain, however, analgesic subjects may show normal psychophysiological responses to the pain stimulus. Thus the pain stimulus is registering in the cognitive system, although it is not represented in the subject's phenomenal awareness (Hilgard & Hilgard, 1974). The hidden observer is a metaphor for this continuing subconscious perception of pain, and the method by which it is accessed. After analgesia has been successfully established, the experimenter attempts to communicate with a "hidden part" of the person which may have recorded the true state of affairs. Under these circumstances, many (but not all) subjects give pain reports comparable to those collected under normal waking conditions (Hilgard, Hilgard, Macdonald, Morgan, & Johnson, 1978; Hilgard, Morgan, & Macdonald, 1975; Knox et al., 1974). Later, these findings were extended to hypnotic deafness (Crawford, Macdonald, & Hilgard, 1979). Other laboratories have replicated this effect in analgesia (Laurence & Perry, 1981; Nogrady, McConkey, Laurence, & Perry, 1983; Spanos, Gwynn, & Stam, 1983; Spanos & Hewitt, 1980).

Reports of the hidden observer have been criticized by those who analyze hypnosis in social-psychological terms as a kind of motivated compliance with the expectations and demands imposed on the subject by the hypnotic situation. For example, Coe and Sarbin (1977) have suggested that the hidden observer instructions give the subject permission to report pain that has been actually felt all along. However, the success of hypnotic analgesia in clinical situations argues against this hypothesis (Bowers, 1976; Hilgard & Hilgard, 1974). Similarly, Spanos and his associates have found that the direction of covert pain reports is influenced by the wording of instructions, leading them to conclude that the hidden observer is a product of social influence rather than a reflection of dissociation (Spanos et al., 1983; Spanos & Hewitt, 1980). These studies may be criticized on both conceptual and methodological grounds (e.g., Laurence, Perry, & Kihlstrom, 1983; for a reply, see Spanos, 1983).

Hypnosis, as an interpersonal phenomenon, is of course not immune to social influence processes such as compliance and impression management. However, there are reasons for thinking that the effect is not entirely a product of them. For example, the hidden observer is typically obtained in only about 50% of the subjects tested, despite the fact that they have all been preselected on the basis of their very high level of response to other hypnotic suggestions. Moreover, a study by Hilgard, Hilgard, et al. (1978) found that the occurrence of the hidden observer was not strongly associated with the subject's expectations following administration of the suggestion. The surprise of many subjects upon discovering that they had a hidden observer, and the disappointment of others when they failed to find one, are inconsistent with an account based solely on strategic social compliance. Perhaps most telling in this respect is the behavior of subjects who have been instructed to simulate hypnosis. Under instructional conditions that explicitly stated that there was such a subconscious registration of sense data,

Hilgard, Hilgard, et al. (1978) obtained hidden observer reports in 50% of their hypnotic subjects, and 75% of their simulators. The difference is nonsignificant, but overreaction to the suggestion is characteristic of simulating subjects, and again argues against hypnosis as merely a case of response to social cues and demands. In a later study employing a weaker suggestion, which indicated only that there might be such covert registration, Nogrady et al. (1983) obtained hidden observers in 42% of their hypnotic subjects and 0% of their simulators. Following the logic of the real-simulator design (Orne, 1979), the research shows that the demand characteristics of the experimental situation are not sufficient to produce the hidden observer response.

Added lawfulness has been brought to the phenomenon by recent successes in predicting which of a selected group of highly hypnotizable subjects will show the hidden observer effect. The two studies yielding the highest incidence of hidden observers (Knox et al., 1974, and Spanos & Hewitt, 1980—both 87.5%; see also Spanos, 1983) employed additional criteria of amnesia and/or automatic writing or talking, presumably insuring a sample of hypnotizable subjects with a talent for dissociation. The remaining studies employed high hypnotizability as the sole criterion, yielding an incidence averaging 45%. Laurence and Perry (1981) found that the occurrence of a hidden observer in less stringently selected samples could be predicted almost perfectly by the occurrence of duality response on age regression, in which subjects experience themselves simultaneously as child participants and adult observers—a finding strongly confirmed by Nogrady et al. (1983). This inconsistency in response, somewhat reminiscent of trance logic, again suggests a marked capacity for dissociation distinguishing these hypnotic virtuosos from other subjects who may achieve hypnotic experiences via other routes. In any event, the hidden observer, with its covert registration of pain or sound outside of awareness, is a prime example of dissociative processes at work. The stimulus is represented in the cognitive system, but not accessible to phenomenal awareness except under extraordinary conditions.

The Problem of Interference

Amnesia, trance logic, the hidden observer, analgesia, deafness, and other hypnotic phenomena are prime examples of dissociation in the laboratory, but they have also carried the seeds of the concept's destruction by showing that percepts and memories supposedly denied to conscious awareness continue to interact with ongoing cognition and action. Consider, for example, the studies of relearning, retroactive inhibition, and priming during posthypnotic amnesia; the psychophysiological responses to pain stimulation in analgesia; and the effects of delayed auditory feedback in deafness. In each case, the subject denies awareness of a percept or memory that nevertheless has a demonstrable influence on his or her behavior. Such evidence has long been taken as discrediting the concept of dissociation (e.g., White & Shevach, 1942). The argument is that since the ostensibly dissociated percepts and memories continue to interact with other cognitive and behavioral processes, there is no sense in which they have been split off and isolated from the rest of the system. Hilgard (1973a, 1977b) has persuasively argued, however, that noninteraction is a later importation into the theory, and not an essential property of the original concept of dissociation. Only lack of awareness of adequately registered inputs or adequately encoded memories, and perhaps perceived involuntariness, is essential.

The insistence of both early and late critics on noninterference as well as nonawareness seems to stem from a misunderstanding of James's (1890) metaphor of the stream of consciousness. Following the metaphor superficially, it is held that two streams of water, running parallel to each other but separated by tall banks, should not affect each other. However, if the two streams originate from the same source, each will certainly draw off some of the flow from the other. Interference will also occur if the streams flow into a common outlet. Given a model of attention such as Kahneman's (1973), in which a single source of attentional capacity may be deployed in multiple directions, James's metaphor would certainly lead one to predict some degree of mutual interference between simultaneous, dissociated tasks. This interference would be even more dramatic, of course, if the two streams of mental activity were competing for the same output channel at the response end of the cognitive cycle. Thus some degree of mutual interference among dissociated cognitive tasks is to be predicted.

Only three experiments have studied the mutual interference between simultaneous, dissociated tasks using concepts and methods current in the psychology of attention. In one experiment, Stevenson (1976) compared color naming, always a conscious task, with written arithmetic performed either consciously or subconsciously, by highly hypnotizable subjects. There were actually two arithmetic tasks: counting from one to ten, an easy task; and adding serial 7s to a two-digit seed number, a more difficult one. When the tasks were performed simultaneously they interfered with one another, compared to a baseline condition, with more interference during the more difficult arithmetic task. For both arithmetic tasks, subconscious performance actually created more interference than conscious performance. Similar results were obtained by Knox and her colleagues (Knox, Crutchfield, & Hilgard, 1975), comparing color naming with rhythmic key pressing: there was more interference when the key pressing was subconscious. Bowers and Brenneman (1981) asked their subjects to touch their noses in response to a signal presented during a shadowing task: this time, there was less interference on shadowing when nose touching was subconscious than when it was conscious, but interference still occurred. The results of the three experiments may be arrayed along a continuum representing the attentional demands of the simultaneous tasks. Arguably, serial addition is the hardest, and nose touching the easiest (many of us do this routinely outside of awareness, and without conscious intent), and the counting and tapping tasks fall in between. Thus given the assumption of a single attentional resource, divided according to the demands made by the tasks, the interference results are just what they should be.

But what of the finding that subconscious performance creates more interference than conscious performance does? Stevenson (1976) argued that it consumes more attentional resources to keep something out of consciousness than to permit it to be represented in awareness. While this may well be true, the argument does not necessarily apply to the cases described here. Consider once more the phenomenon of the hidden observer in hypnotic analgesia and deafness, and reversibility in posthypnotic amnesia. These all entail the creation of two streams of mental activity: one representing phenomenal awareness (or, rather, the lack of awareness) of the stimulus; and the other representing the subconscious monitoring of the true state of affairs; as tapped by the hidden observer procedure or memory reports after the reversibility cue has been administered. Applying this organization to the simultaneous tasks, we see that conscious simultaneous tasks require two streams (one for each task), but subconscious simultaneous tasks require three—the additional stream being required to monitor the subconscious task, and to serve as a potential later link between the two streams of thought and action. With three streams drawing on a single attentional resource, the degree of interference is likely to be increased. The contrary finding by Bowers and Brenneman (1981)—that subconscious nose touching produced less interference—appears to contradict this hypothesis, of course, and poses an interesting problem. Perhaps this anomaly reflects the special nature of their task: because even unhypnotized subjects routinely perform nose touching maneuvers automatically, outside of awareness, it may require extra attentional effort to bring this behavior into awareness. If so, then the subconscious condition restores the normal state of affairs, and reduces interference caused by the instruction to perform both tasks simultaneously.

A MECHANISM FOR DISSOCIATION

The case for dissociation rests on phenomena such as these, plus others observed in the clinic, laboratory, and ordinary life. Each of these instances, viewed in isolation, is somehow problematic. The phenomena of hysteria, fugue, and multiple personality are admittedly rare, and are complicated by the frequent presence of brain damage and the possibility of malingering. Depersonalization, *déjà vu,* and other anomalies of memory have not yet been studied in enough detail to permit us to draw conclusions about their nature. In the case of mental activity occurring during sleep, since subjects are not able to report on their subjective experiences, an important source of data is lost; and the predominance of psychobiological and psychoanalytic thinking in the area of sleep research has effectively inhibited investigations oriented toward theoretical issues in cognitive psychology. Finally, the phenomena of hypnosis present many of the same difficulties as do the syndromes of hysteria: hypnotic virtuosos, those most likely to achieve hypnotic effects by means of dissociation, constitute at best 10% of the population (Hilgard, 1965); and the interpersonal setting in which hypnosis occurs creates certain difficulties of inference.

Compelling experimental results favorable to the concept of dissociation in any one of these domains would be sufficient to require revision of our concept of the mind in such a way as to permit the possibility of divisions in consciousness and subconscious mental processing. At present, such documentation is lacking, in large part because research in these topics has typically been conducted within other theoretical frameworks. At the same time, however, the strong family resemblance which these phenomena bear to each other should not be ignored. All of the instances involve deliberate, intelligent, behavioral and cognitive activities of such complexity and extent as to require representation in phenomenal awareness, if not the full commitment of the person's attentional resources, given the assumptions of conventional models of the mind. Yet these very activities appear to occur involuntarily; or the person has little awareness of having engaged in them; or, if the person is aware of them, they are not integrated into the other activities and experiences of which he or she is also aware. These resemblances allow the phenomena, somewhat weak as separate instances, to form a strong case when taken together.

This argument is strengthened further by the observation of dissociative phenomena in the normal waking state, under tightly controlled laboratory conditions. Spelke, Hirst, and Neisser (1976) trained subjects to read a prose passage and take dictation simultaneously; performance was measured in terms of transcription accuracy and scores on a comprehension test. Although the task was difficult at first, with practice the subjects were able to perform it with a high degree of accuracy. While the subjects had good memory for the prose passages, enabling them to pass the comprehension test at a high level, they showed poor recall of the dictated words—despite the fact that during dictation they made rather complicated decisions concerning the semantic and syntactic relationships among the items. (Recognition levels were superior to chance, but not perfect, paralleling findings in posthypnotic amnesia.) A subsequent experiment (Hirst, Spelke, Reaves, Caharack, & Neisser, 1980) substantially replicated these findings. That the subjects were engaged in parallel processing, rather than rapid serial alternation between tasks, was demonstrated by their maintenance of reading speed at control levels, and by their success when reading both redundant and dense prose (see also Neisser, Hirst, & Spelke, 1981). With these kinds of demanding cognitive tasks, parallel processing amounts to Prince's notion of co-conscious mental states; when one stream of consciousness is accessible to recall and the other is not, that is what the concept of subconscious mental activity is all about. Similarly, it has been found that normal subjects can show considerable savings in relearning, even though they cannot consciously remember the original learning experience (Kolers, 1976; Nelson, 1978); and that previous experience can facilitate performance on a subsequent cognitive task even though subjects do not consciously remember what the earlier experience was (Jacoby & Dallas, 1981; Scarborough, Cortese, & Scarborough, 1977). These phenomena are phenotypically similar to those of the dissociative states described earlier, with the difference that the pathological and experimental dissociations can be created with overlearned material, and over short retention intervals. Even so, the underlying mechanisms may prove to be the same.

A Neodissociation Theory of Divided Consciousness

Recently, Hilgard has revived the concept of dissociation under the rubric of neodissociation theory, which acknowledges links to earlier approaches but seeks to free itself from the excesses and errors of previous formulations. The theory was originally stated as an interpretation of a single phenomenon—hypnotic analgesia (Hilgard, 1973c); later, it was expanded to cover a broad range of phenomena including the clinical syndromes of hysteria, fugue, and multiple personality, dreaming and other everyday experiences, and the whole range of hypnotic phenomena (Hilgard, 1977b, 1979). Neodissociation theory begins with the assumption that the mental apparatus consists of a set of cognitive structures similar to Janet's automatisms and Bartlett's schemata, which monitor, organize, and control thought and action in different domains. Each of these structures can seek or avoid inputs and facilitate or inhibit outputs. The structures are organized hierarchically, so that under ordinary circumstances each is in communication with the others. At the top of the hierarchy is a cognitive structure which exercises executive functions of monitoring and control. As the ultimate end point for all inputs to the system and the ultimate starting point for all outputs, the executive control structure provides the basis for phenomenal awareness and intentionality. Figure 4.5 shows the system in schematic outline.

According to the theory, certain conditions can constrain the operation of the central executive, disrupting the integration and hierarchical organization of the subordinate control structures. For example, the lines of communication

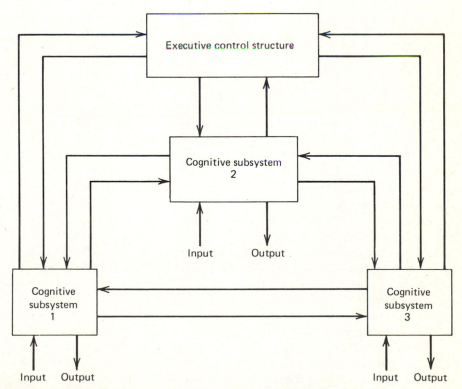

Figure 4.5.   A hierarchical system of cognitive controls, with all lines of communication intact (after Hilgard, 1973).

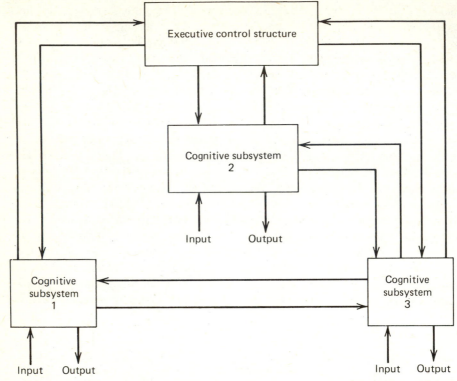

Figure 4.6. A hierarchical system of cognitive controls, with broken lines of communication between two cognitive subsystems.

between two subordinate controls might be cut, so that each performs its functions (receiving inputs and generating outputs) in the absence of any direct integration between them (Figure 4.6). Alternatively, the communication links between a subordinate control structure and the executive structure might be broken, resulting in a reduction of the normal degree of voluntary control over particular subordinate structures, or a reduction in the normal degree of awareness of what is being processed through them (Figure 4.7). Either case would represent a state of divided consciousness. The latter case, in which percepts, thoughts, and memories fail to be represented in phenomenal awareness, and/or actions are perceived as involuntary, is a classic instance of dissociation. When the constraining conditions are reversed, the reversion to the original integrated hierarchical structure will reinstate normal awareness and voluntary control.

It is important to recognize that in this theory, dissociated control systems need not be completely independent of each other. There may be indirect links between dissociated control structures, passing through other structures with which communication has been preserved. Or, the input or output of dissociated structures may be through a common channel. Finally, each control structure draws from a common attentional resource (e.g., Kahneman, 1973; Neisser,

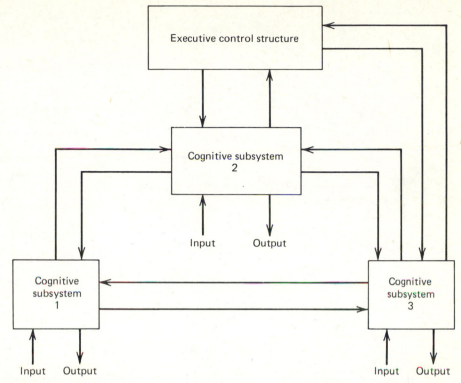

Figure 4.7. A hierarchical system of cognitive controls, with broken lines of communication between a cognitive subsystem and the executive control structure.

1967, 1976). Thus there is no implication that dissociation will reduce interference among the cognitive and behavioral tasks performed by the affected control structures. This is the most salient difference between neodissociation and the interpretation commonly given to older versions: the extent of interference is an empirical question, rather than a theoretical prediction. The phenomena central to the dissociation concept are awareness and voluntary control, not interference.

Dissociation and Cognitive Theory

In presenting the outlines of neodissociation theory, Hilgard (1977b) noted the relevance of the Deutsch-Norman model of the cognitive system—with a single memory store, automatic semantic analysis, and attention positioned late rather than early in the sequence of cognitive operations—to the phenomena of dissociation. The model is attractive, of course, because it permits information to be processed quite thoroughly before it is brought into awareness—thus allowing for various sorts of preconscious and subconscious influences on thought and action. According to the model, for example, the attentional process is responsible for selecting and integrating activated knowledge structures to form

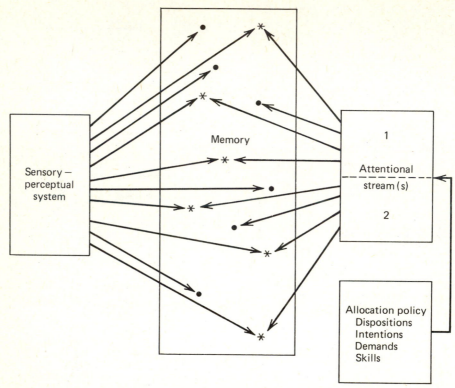

Figure 4.8.   Schematic conceptualization of a memory system permitting the division of attention and co-conscious mental processes (after Norman, 1968, and Kahneman, 1973).

conscious representations of percepts and memories, and to plan and execute actions in accordance with both short-term and long-term personal goals and situational demands. But apparently consciousness can be divided, permitting multiple streams of thought and action to be performed simultaneously. Accordingly, the Deutsch-Norman model needs to be supplemented with a notion such as Kahneman's (1973), which allows the total attentional resource available to be allocated among several tasks at once. In addition to the factors listed by Kahneman as determining allocation policy—enduring dispositions, momentary intentions, and task demands—the Hirst-Neisser-Spelke experiments indicate that the policy is also constrained by the individual's acquired skill at dividing attention. The modified model, then, might look something like Figure 4.8.

Such an arrangement permits activation of multiple simultaneous schemata organizing perception, memory, and action, and thus co-conscious streams of mental activity, but still has no room for subconscious streams. The principal problem for a neodissociation theory of divided consciousness is to indicate how such mental activities can proceed apparently involuntarily, and outside of phenomenal awareness. One possibility is suggested by the intrinsically episodic nature of consciousness. To paraphrase James: Conscious awareness does not

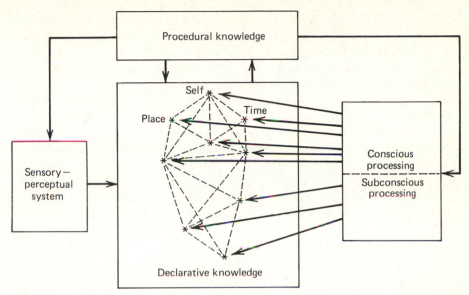

Figure 4.9.   Schematic model of memory permitting the division of attention and subconscious mental processes.

consist in the recognition that "This is happening"; but, rather, "I am doing this, or experiencing this, here and now." Central to the experience of consciousness, then, is linking activated concepts representing percepts, memories, thoughts, and actions with others representing the self as agent and experiencer on the one hand, and the spatiotemporal context of the event on the other. Those encodings that contain self-referential and contextual features become conscious; those that do not remain subconscious, regardless of how much processing is devoted to them. The outlines of such a system are presented in Figure 4.9.

Such a system appears to afford the possibility of all the major phenomena for which dissociation theory must account. The simultaneous allocation of attentional capacity to two or more tasks results in multiple co-conscious streams of mental activity, both represented in phenomenal awareness and perceived as voluntary, as described earlier. The implications of the model for subconscious streams of mental activity are manifold. The items processed in the conscious stream of mental activity will be associated with each other, but also with concepts representing self and context; those processed in the subconscious stream will be associated only with each other. Conceptually, reports of the contents of consciousness are elicited by the query, "What are you doing mentally, here and now?" According to network models of memory such as ACT, the query will activate preexisting concepts corresponding to self, time, location, and whatever other information is available (directly or by inference) from the cue. Activation spreads out along associative pathways, and when these intersect, an item will be retrieved. Such a process, applied to the present instance, will only contact the material processed consciously. Material processed subconsciously will remain available in the memory system, and even activated, but inaccessible to retrieval because the critical associative pathways have not been formed. A similar argument applies to queries about the past as well as the present—after all, perception simply involves accessing the most recent events stored in memory. The retrieval cue supplies information about the context of the prior event, but the matching contextual features are only to be found in memories for experiences processed consciously. Thus recall, in which activation spreads from the self and context nodes to associated items, and recognition, in which activation spreads from both items and self and context nodes, will succeed for items processed consciously, but not for those processed subconsciously. In cases of retrograde dissociations, as in functional or posthypnotic amnesia, the episodic links are established during encoding but subsequently broken. Such a pathway must remain available in the memory system, however, even if it is temporarily inaccessible, because episodic memory can be subsequently restored.

The fact that subconscious mental contents are not tied into the episodic memory system does not mean that they cannot influence ongoing thought and action. Each stream of mental processing, whether conscious or subconscious, is capable of organizing and executing actions, provided that the limits on processing skills are not exceeded. This state of affairs may lead to some of the inconsistencies and paradoxes observed in both hysterical and hypnotic phenomena. And even if there is no output channel available to contents being processed subconsciously, the items may still influence ongoing cognitive activity, and so indirectly affect behavior. So, for example, if a subject is run in the A-B, A-C retroactive inhibition paradigm, with the latter list covered by amnesia suggestions, the A-C associations may well remain intact, and interfere with reproduction of the A-B list. Moreover, when underlying semantic representations are activated during list learning, they will retain that activation even if they have been separated from the contextual features that mark the event as an item in episodic memory. Thus priming effects will facilitate perceptual recognition and similar tasks even though the subject does not remember what he or she learned. Finally, skills acquired during hypnosis, with the learning covered by amnesia, will still remain accessible in declarative memory, or procedural memory if knowledge compilation has begun, even though the loss of reference to self and context will mean that the person is unaware that he or she possesses them (i.e., lacks metaknowledge) and—if persuaded by events to acknowledge this fact—of the circumstances under which they were acquired.

The sparing of semantic memory representations may also lead to above-chance performance on certain *episodic* memory tasks. In recognition, for example, subjects are asked to indicate whether a test item has been presented before—clearly an episodic task requiring recovery of the spatiotemporal context in which the item occurred. In terms of a network model such as ACT, episodic retrieval activates nodes corresponding to item and context information provided by the query, activation spreads out from each node along associative pathways, and cognitive units formed by intersecting pathways are checked. If, as suggested earlier, dissociation is mediated by a disruption in the links between semantic representations and their contextual features, then recognition should fail: the critical item-to-context link cannot be formed. However, subjects may base their recognition decisions on feelings of familiarity as well as on direct reconstruction of episodic context: under appropriate conditions the mere fact that a test item "rings a bell" may be sufficient to lead a subject to call an item old rather than new. Such guessing strategies are found in sensory-perceptual tasks, and are familiar in the literature on signal detection theory. In memory, this effect can come about when the retrieval process adds activation to nodes that have already been activated (primed) during acquisition. A guessing strategy based solely on level of activation will, therefore, lead to a great many hits and very few false alarms. The failure to recover the item's episodic context, however, may be manifested in poor performance on tasks involving list differentiation, in which test items come from several lists, and the subject must assign recognized items to their correct contexts. In much the same way, residual activation may lead to savings in relearning, and the guessing strategy may lead to successful cued recall. However, free recall—in which activation must flow from context nodes to item nodes, should always be impaired.

Neither available space, nor available knowledge, permit systematic application of these ideas to the phenomena of dissociation. The theory is stated as a guide to, rather than a summary of, research. Most of the examples cited deal with posthypnotic amnesia, both because it is the most thoroughly investigated dissociative phenomenon and because the conceptual model, being a theory of memory, most easily addresses itself to problems of remembering and forgetting. Because the memory system supplies the knowledge base for perception and action, however, it seems reasonable to expect that the interpretative framework advanced here will be applicable to the other dissociative effects on perception and memory as well. And as research accumulates on other hypnotic phenomena, and on other special states of consciousness, the opportunity will arise to explore the model's generalizability. In principle, the network model of memory outlined here shows how dissociative phenomena can be construed in a familiar artificial intelligence system. While it very well may be possible to program a computer to dissociate, and determine if its behavior resembles dissociation as it occurs in patients and normals, the more important justification for the modeling enterprise is that it forces the theorist to define concepts and principles more clearly and rigorously than otherwise.

The model of dissociation tentatively advanced here centers on the weakening, fracturing, or breaking of the associative links between semantic representations of percepts and memories, and episodic representations of the self in spatiotemporal context. As such, it is placed within the framework of a model of the manner in which declarative knowledge is organized in memory. However, memory contains cognitive skills as well as factual information. The nature of this procedural knowledge, and the manner in which it is organized and brought to bear on ongoing cognition and action, is equally important. First, it is clear that dissociative processes such as those described here affect declarative but not procedural knowledge, and only those declarative knowledge structures that are episodic in nature. Like semantic knowledge, procedural knowledge does not contain reference to the episodic context in which it was acquired—thus adding support to the hypothesis that episodic features are critically involved in dissociation. More important, it is clear that the dissociative processes themselves—the processes by which episodic features are separated from, and later returned to, semantic representations—form part of the individual's repertoire of procedural knowledge. Thus once the declarative aspects of dissociation have been mapped out satisfactorily, inquiry should move to a different set of questions: What is the nature of dissociative procedures? How are these skills distributed in the population? Are individual differences in these skills innate or acquired?

Some preliminary answers to these questions are available from what we already know about the special states of consciousness involving dissociation. For example, all of us appear to have the capacity to dissociate, as in the case of dreams and other aspects of sleep. This level of dissociative skill appears to be innate, much like certain perceptual-cognitive and linguistic capacities. At the same time, however, some of us are more prone to dissociate than others, perhaps rendering us vulnerable to hysteria, fugue, multiple personality, obsessions, and compulsions at times of stress. And some of us have voluntary control over dissociative processes, an attribute that may differentiate hypnotic virtuosos from the rest of the population. The ultimate problem of dissociation concerns the nature of these cognitive skills, how they interact with declarative knowledge, how we acquire them, and how some of us gain access to and voluntary control over them.

THE PROMISE—AND CHALLENGE—OF DISSOCIATION

Understanding the nature of dissociation is important because the subconscious of neodissociation theory is rather different from the unconscious as it is conceptualized by other schools within psychology. Neodissociation theory differs from psychoanalysis, for example, because the subconscious is not restricted to primitive sexual and aggressive impulses and those memories and ideas associated with them. Nor do subconscious mental processes operate according to the irrational "primary process" principles associated with the Freudian unconscious. If anything, they seem to follow the rational, "secondary process" rules of the System Cs. Dissociated percepts and memories can be closely tied to objective reality; and dissociated ideas can be rational and even creative. Equally important, rendering something subconscious is not necessarily motivated by defense against anxiety, as is the case with Freudian repression. It can simply happen, as is the case in hysteria, fugue, or multiple personality (or, for that matter, in sleep); or it can be done for entirely adaptive purposes, voluntarily, as in the case of subjects who enter hypnosis or people who go to a movie precisely because they know that they will temporarily lose themselves in the action on the screen.

The subconscious of neodissociation theory also differs in important ways from the manner in which unconscious mental contents and processes are construed, implicitly or explicitly, in classical theories of human information processing. Thus the subconscious of neodissociation theory is not restricted to the procedural knowledge by which we detect features of perceptual stimuli, encode and decode language, retrieve memories, make elementary judgments, perform routine motor tasks, and so forth. It can also involve complex factual knowledge, both semantic and episodic in nature, concerning the existence of certain objects and the occurrence of past events; and it can include an extensive and organized autobiographical record. Nor is it restricted to the simple, automatic, and routine: complex cognitive and behavioral activities apparently can be performed outside awareness. Linguistic contents can be rendered subconscious, and percepts and memories can be subconscious even though the person's linguistic abilities remain intact. Nor, within the realm of declarative knowledge, is the subconscious simply the repository, if that is the word, for unattended perceptual inputs, weak memory traces, and the products of early, simple, and automatic cognitive operations.

Neodissociation theory links a diverse set of real-world and laboratory phenomena under a descriptive rubric and challenges cognitive science to account for them. It comes as no surprise that attention can be divided, though that fact in itself poses problems for conventional models of information processing that are predicated on the existence of limited-capacity channels and discrete storage structures. But if attention can be divided, with one stream of complex, deliberate cognitive activity proceeding outside awareness, this seems to cause some problems for the way we usually think about things. The empirical basis for the theory is sometimes problematic, but as in the case of "subliminal perception" all that is needed is one solid finding to change the way we think about the mind. The purpose of the present essay is to argue that current models of the mind do contain the raw materials—in the form of representational and procedural principles—of a plausible account of dissociation. James may have overstated the importance of the discovery of subconscious mental processing. Psychological research has turned up other surprises since the turn of the century. But while these findings have been largely incorporated into emerging theoretical developments, the phenomena of dissociation have not. If we do not take these phenomena seriously, and consider their implications for our understanding of the cognitive system, our evolving model of the mind may be led seriously astray. This is reason enough to continue to pursue neodissociation theory, and the phenomena it tries to comprehend, and to incorporate it and its insights into larger theories in order to produce a comprehensive view of the mind in order and disorder.

REFERENCES

Aarons, L. Sleep-assisted instruction. *Psychological Bulletin,* 1976, *83,* 1–40.

Abse, D.W. Hysteria. In S. Arieti (Ed.), *American handbook of psychiatry* (Vol. 1). New York: Basic, 1959.

Anderson, J.R. *Language, memory, and thought*. Hillsdale, N.J.: Erlbaum, 1976.

Anderson, J.R. Acquisition of cognitive skill. *Psychological Review*, 1982, *89*, 369–406. (a)

Anderson, J.R. *Cognitive psychology and its implications*. San Francisco: Freeman, 1982. (b)

Anderson, J.R., & Reder, L.M. Elaborative processing of prose material. In L.S. Cermak & F.I.M. Craik (Eds.), *Levels of processing in human memory*. Hillsdale, N.J.: Erlbaum, 1979.

Arkin, A.M. Sleep talking: A review. *Journal of Nervous and Mental Disease*, 1966, *143*, 101–122.

Arkin, A.M. Sleeptalking. In A.M. Arkin, J.S. Antrobus, & S.J. Ellman (Eds.), *The mind in sleep: Psychology and psychophysiology*. Hillsdale, N.J.: Erlbaum, 1978.

Arkin, A.M. *Sleeptalking: Psychology and psychophysiology*. Hillsdale, N.J.: Erlbaum, 1982.

Arkin, A.M., & Antrobus, J.S. The effects of external stimuli applied prior to and during sleep on sleep experience. In A.M. Arkin, J.S. Antrobus, & S.J. Ellman (Eds.), *The mind in sleep: Psychology and psychophysiology*. Hillsdale, N.J.: Erlbaum, 1978.

Arkin, A.M., Antrobus, J.S., & Ellman, S.J. *The mind in sleep: Psychology and psychophysiology*. Hillsdale, N.J.: Erlbaum, 1978.

Atkinson, R.C., & Shiffrin, R.M. Human memory: A proposed system and its control processes. In K.W. Spence & J.T. Spence (Eds.), *The psychology of learning and motivation* (Vol. 2). New York: Academic Press, 1968.

Ballard, P.B. Oblivescence and reminiscence. *British Journal of Psychology Monograph Supplement*, 1913, *1*, (No. 2).

Bandura, A. *Social learning theory*. Englewood Cliffs, N.J.: Prentice-Hall, 1977.

Barber, T.X. *Hypnosis: A scientific approach*. New York: Van Nostrand Reinhold, 1969.

Barber, T.X., Spanos, N.P., & Chaves, J.F. *Hypnotism, imagination, and human potentialities*. New York: Pergamon, 1974.

Bartlett, F.C. *Remembering: A study in experimental and social psychology*. Cambridge: Cambridge University Press, 1932.

Berrington, W.P., Liddell, D.W., & Foulds, G.A. A re-evaluation of the fugue. *Journal of Mental Science*, 1956, *102*, 280–286.

Black, A.H., Cott, A., & Pavlovski, A.P. The operant learning theory approach to biofeedback training. In G. Schwartz & J. Beatty (Eds.), *Biofeedback: Theory and research*. New York: Academic Press, 1977.

Blum, G.S., & Graef, J.R. The detection over time of subjects simulating hypnosis. *International Journal of Clinical and Experimental Hypnosis*, 1971, *19*, 211–224.

Bower, G.H. A multicomponent theory of the memory trace. In K.W. Spence & J.T. Spence (Eds.), *The psychology of learning and motivation* (Vol. 1). New York: Academic Press, 1967.

Bower, G.H. Cognitive psychology: An introduction. In W.K. Estes (Ed.), *Handbook of learning and cognitive processes* (Vol. 1). Hillsdale, N.J.: Erlbaum, 1975.

Bower, G.H. Mood and memory. *American Psychologist*, 1981, *36*, 129–148.

Bowers, K.S. Hypnotic behavior: The differentiation of trance and demand characteristic variables. *Journal of Abnormal Psychology*, 1966, *71*, 42–51.

Bowers, K.S. The effects of demands for honesty on reports of visual and auditory hallucinations. *International Journal of Clinical and Experimental Hypnosis*, 1967, *15*, 31–36.

Bowers, K.S. Hypnosis, attribution, and demand characteristics. *International Journal of Clinical and Experimental Hypnosis*, 1973, *21*, 226–238.

Bowers, K.S. The psychology of subtle control: An attributional analysis of behavioral persistence. *Canadian Journal of Behavioral Science*, 1975, *7*, 78–95.

Bowers, K.S. *Hypnosis for the seriously curious.* Monterey, Ca.: Brooks/Cole, 1976.

Bowers, K.S. Unconscious processes in social cognition and science. In K.S. Bowers & D.M. Meichenbaum, (Eds.), *Unconscious processes: Several perspectives.* New York: Wiley, 1983.

Bowers, K.S., & Brenneman, H.A. Hypnotic dissociation, dichotic listening, and active versus passive modes of attention. *Journal of Abnormal Psychology*, 1981, *90*, 55–67.

Brady, J.P. Hysteria versus malingering: A response to Grosz and Zimmerman. *Behavior Research and Therapy*, 1966, *4*, 321–322.

Brady, J.P., & Lind, D.L. Experimental analysis of hysterical blindness. *Archives of General Psychiatry*, 1961, *4*, 331–339.

Broadbent, D.E. *Perception and communication.* London: Pergamon, 1958.

Brown, J.A. Some tests of the decay theory of immediate memory. *Quarterly Journal of Experimental Psychology*, 1958, *10*, 12–21.

Brown, W. To what extent is memory measured by a single recall? *Journal of Experimental Psychology*, 1923, *6*, 337–382.

Bruner, J.S., & Klein, G.S. The function of perceiving: New Look retrospect. In S. Wapner & B. Kaplan (Eds.), *Perspectives in psychological theory.* New York: International Universities Press, 1960.

Bruner, J.S., & Postman, L. Perception, cognition, and personality. *Journal of Personality*, 1949, *18*, 14–31.

Buschke, H. Selective reminding in the analysis of learning and memory. *Journal of Verbal Learning and Verbal Behavior*, 1973, *12*, 543–550.

Campbell, D.T., & Fiske, D.W. Convergent and discriminant validation by the multitrait-multimethod matrix. *Psychological Bulletin*, 1959, *56*, 82–105.

Cantor, N., & Genero, N. Psychiatric diagnosis and natural categorization: A close analogy. In T. Millon & G. Klerman (Eds.), *Contemporary issues in psychopathology.* New York: Guilford, in press.

Cantor, N., & Kohlstrom, J.F. *Social intelligence: The cognitive basis of personality.* Technical Report #60. Ann Arbor: Center for Cognitive Science, University of Michigan, 1983.

Cermak, L.S., & Craik, F.I.M. *Levels of processing in human memory.* Hillsdale, N.J.: Erlbaum, 1979.

Cherry, E.C. Some experiments on the recognition of speech, with one and with two years. *Journal of the Acoustical Society of America*, 1953, *25*, 975–979.

Chomsky, N. Language and unconscious knowledge. In N. Chomsky, *Rules and representations.* New York: Columbia University Press, 1980.

Coe, W.C., & Sarbin, T.R. Hypnosis from the standpoint of a contextualist. In W.E.

Edmonston (Ed.), *Conceptual and investigative approaches to hypnosis and hypnotic phenomena. Annals of the New York Academy of Sciences,* 1977, *296,* 2–13.

Cohen, D.B. Toward a theory of dream recall. *Psychological Bulletin,* 1974, *81,* 138–154.

Cohen, D.B. Dreaming: Experimental investigations of representational and adaptive properties. In G.E. Schwartz & D. Shapiro (Eds.), *Consciousness and self-regulation: Advances in research* (Vol. 1). New York: Plenum, 1976.

Cohen, D.B. Remembering and forgetting dreaming. In J.F. Kihlstrom & F.J. Evans (Eds.), *Functional disorders of memory.* Hillsdale, N.J.: Erlbaum, 1979.

Corballis, M.C. Laterality and myth. *American Psychologist,* 1980, *35,* 284–295.

Craik, F.I.M., & Lockhart, R.S. Levels of processing: A framework for memory research. *Journal of Verbal Learning and Verbal Behavior,* 1972, *11,* 671–684.

Crawford, H.J., Macdonald, H., & Hilgard, E.R. Hypnotic deafness: A psychophysical study of responses to tone intensity as modified by hypnosis. *American Journal of Psychology,* 1979, *92,* 193–214.

Crowder, R.G. *Principles of learning and memory.* Hillsdale, N.J.: Erlbaum, 1976.

Damaser, E.C. *An experimental study of long term posthypnotic suggestion.* Unpublished doctoral dissertation, Harvard University, 1964.

Davison, G.C., & Neale, J.M. *Abnormal psychology: An experimental clinical approach.* New York: Wiley, 1982.

Deutsch, J.A., & Deutsch, D. Attention: Some theoretical considerations. *Psychological Review,* 1963, *70,* 80–90.

Dewey, J. The terms "conscious" and "consciousness." *Journal of Philosophy, Psychology, and Scientific Methods,* 1906, *3,* 39–41.

Dixon, N.F. *Subliminal perception: The nature of a controversy.* London: McGraw-Hill, 1971.

Dixon, N.F. *Preconscious processing.* Chichester: Wiley, 1981.

Eccles, J.C. *The brain and the unity of conscious experience.* Cambridge: Cambridge University Press, 1965.

Eccles, J.C. *The understanding of the brain.* New York: McGraw-Hill, 1973.

Eich, J.E. State-dependent retrieval of information in human episodic memory. In I.M. Birnbaum & E.S. Parker (Eds.), *Alcohol and human memory.* Hillsdale, N.J.: Erlbaum, 1977.

Eich, J.E. The cue-dependent nature of state-dependent retrieval. *Memory and Cognition,* 1980, *8,* 157–173.

Ellenberger, H.F. *The discovery of the unconscious: The history and evolution of dynamic psychiatry.* New York: Basic Books, 1970.

English, H.B., & English, A.C. *A comprehensive dictionary of psychological and psychoanalytical terms.* New York: Longmans, Green, 1958.

Erdelyi, M.H. A new look at The New Look: Perceptual defense and vigilance. *Psychological Review,* 1974, *81,* 1–25.

Erdelyi, M.H., & Goldberg, B. Let's not sweep repression under the rug: Toward a cognitive psychology of repression. In J.F. Kihlstrom & F.J. Evans (Eds.), *Functional disorders of memory.* Hillsdale, N.J.: Erlbaum, 1979.

Erdelyi, M.H., & Kleinbard, J. Has Ebbinghaus decayed with time? The growth of recall (hypermnesia) over days. *Journal of Experimental Psychology: General,* 1978, *4,* 275–289.

Ericsson, K.A., & Simon, H.A. Verbal reports as data. *Psychological Review,* 1980, *87,* 215–251.

Eriksen, C.W. Discrimination and learning without awareness: A methodological survey and evaluation. *Psychological Review,* 1960, *67,* 279–300.

Eriksen, C.W. (Ed.). *Behavior and awareness: A symposium of research and interpretation.* Durham, N.C.: Duke University Press, 1962.

Evans, F.J. Hypnosis and sleep: Techniques for exploring cognitive activity during sleep. In E. Fromm & R.E. Shor (Eds.), *Hypnosis: Developments in research and new perspectives.* New York: Aldine, 1979. (a)

Evans, F.J. Contextual forgetting: Posthypnotic source amnesia. *Journal of Abnormal Psychology,* 1979, *88,* 556–563. (b)

Evans, F.J., & Thorn, W.A.F. Two types of posthypnotic amnesia: Recall amnesia and source amnesia. *International Journal of Clinical and Experimental Hypnosis,* 1966, *14,* 162–179.

Fisher, S. The role of expectancy in the performance of posthypnotic behavior. *Journal of Abnormal and Social Psychology,* 1954, *49,* 503–507.

Freud, S. *The interpretation of dreams.* In J. Strachey (Ed.), *The standard edition of the complete psychological works of Sigmund Freud* (Vols. 4–5). London: Hogarth, 1900–1901.

Galin, D. Implications for psychiatry of left and right cerebral specialization: A neurophysiological context for unconscious processes. *Archives of General Psychiatry,* 1974, *31,* 572–582.

Galin, D., Diamond, R., & Braff, D. Lateralization of conversion syndromes: More frequent on the left. *Archives of General Psychiatry,* 1977, *134,* 578–580.

Garner, W.R., Hake, H.W., & Eriksen, C.W. Operationism and the concept of perception. *Psychological Review,* 1956, *63,* 149–159.

Gazzaniga, M.S. *The bisected brain.* New York: Appleton-Century-Crofts, 1970.

Gazzaniga, M.S. One brain—two minds? *American Scientist,* 1972, *60,* 311–317.

Gazzaniga, M.S., & LeDoux, J.E. *The integrated mind.* New York: Plenum, 1978.

Godden, D.R., & Baddeley, A.D. Context-dependent memory in two natural environments: On land and underwater. *British Journal of Psychology,* 1975, *66,* 325–332.

Goodenough, D.R. Some recent studies of dream recall. In H.A. Witkin & H.B. Lewis (Eds.), *Experimental studies of dreaming.* New York: Random House, 1967.

Goodenough, D.R. Dream recall: History and current status of the field. In A.M. Arkin, J.S. Antrobus, & S.J. Ellman (Eds.), *The mind in sleep: Psychology and psychophysiology.* Hillsdale, N.J.: Erlbaum, 1978.

Greaves, G.B. Multiple personality: 165 years after Mary Reynolds. *Journal of Nervous and Mental Disease,* 1980, *168,* 577–596.

Grosz, H.J., & Zimmerman, J.A. Experimental analysis of hysterical blindness: A follow-up report and new experimental data. *Archives of General Psychiatry,* 1965, *13,* 255–260.

Haber, R.N. The impending demise of the icon: A critique of the concept of iconic storage in visual information processing. *Behavioral and Brain Sciences,* 1983, *6,* 1–11.

Harackiewicz, J.M. The effects of reward contingency and performance feedback on intrinsic motivation. *Journal of Personality and Social Psychology,* 1979, *37,* 1352–1363.

Hardt, J.V., & Kamiya, J. Some comments on Plotkin's self-regulation of electro-encephalographic alpha. *Journal of Experimental Psychology: General,* 1976, *105,* 100–108.

Hastie, R. Schematic principles in human memory. In E.T. Higgins, P. Herman, & M.P. Zanna (Eds.), *Social cognition: The Ontario symposium.* Hillsdale, N.J.: Erlbaum, 1981.

Hastie, R., & Carlston, D.L. Theoretical issues in person memory. In R. Hastie, T.M. Ostrom, E.B. Ebbesen, R.S. Wyer, D.L. Hamilton, & D.L. Carlston (Eds.), *Person memory: The cognitive basis of social perception.* Hillsdale, N.J.: Erlbaum, 1980.

Hilgard, E.R. What becomes of the input from the stimulus: In C.W. Eriksen (Ed.), *Behavior and awareness: A symposium of research and interpretation.* Durham, N.C.: Duke University Press, 1962.

Hilgard, E.R. *Hypnotic susceptibility.* New York: Harcourt, Brace, & World, 1965.

Hilgard, E.R. Altered states of awareness. *Journal of Nervous and Mental Disease,* 1969, *149,* 68–79. (a)

Hilgard, E.R. Levels of awareness: Second thoughts on some of William James' ideas. In R.B. MacLeod (Ed.), *William James: Unfinished business.* Washington, D.C.: American Psychological Association, 1969. (b)

Hilgard, E.R. A critique of Johnson, Maher, and Barber's "Artifact in the 'essense of hypnosis': An evaluation of trance logic", with a recomputation of their findings. *Journal of Abnormal Psychology,* 1972, *79,* 221–233.

Hilgard, E.R. Dissociation revisited. In M. Henle, J. Janes, & J. Sullivan (Eds.), *Historical conceptions of psychology.* New York: Springer, 1973. (a)

Hilgard, E.R. The domain of hypnosis: With some comments on alternative paradigms. *American Psychologist,* 1973, *28,* 972–982. (b)

Hilgard, E.R. A neodissociation theory of pain reduction in hypnosis. *Psychological Review,* 1973, *80,* 396–411. (c)

Hilgard, E.R. Controversies over consciousness and the rise of cognitive psychology. Australian Psychologist, 1977, *12,* 7–26. (a)

Hilgard, E.R. *Divided consciousness: Multiple controls in human thought and action.* New York: Wiley-Interscience, 1977. (b)

Hilgard, E.R. States of consciousness in hypnosis: Divisions or levels? In F.H. Frankel & H.S. Zamansky (Eds.), *Hypnosis at its bicentennial.* New York: Plenum, 1978.

Hilgard, E.R. Divided consciousness in hypnosis: The implications of the hidden observer. In E. Fromm & R.E. Shor (Eds.), *Hypnosis: Developments in research and new perspectives.* New York: Aldine, 1979.

Hilgard, E.R. Consciousness in contemporary psychology. *Annual Review of Psychology,* 1980, *31,* 1–26. (a)

Hilgard, E.R. The trilogy of mind: Cognition, affection, and conation. *Journal for the History of the Behavioral Sciences,* 1980, *16,* 107–117. (b)

Hilgard, E.R., & Hilgard, J.R. *Hypnosis in the relief of pain.* Los Altos, Ca.: Kaufman, 1974.

Hilgard, E.R., Hilgard, J.R., Macdonald, H., Morgan, A.H., & Johnson, L.S. Covert pain in hypnotic analgesia: Its reality as tested by the real-simulator design. *Journal of Abnormal Psychology,* 1978, *87,* 655–663.

Hilgard, E.R., & Marquis, D.G. *Conditioning and learning.* New York: Appleton-Century-Crofts, 1940.

Hilgard, E.R., Macdonald, H., Morgan, A.H., & Johnson, L.S. The reality of hypnotic analgesia: A comparison of highly hypnotizables with simulators. *Journal of Abnormal Psychology,* 1978, *87,* 239–246.

Hilgard, E.R., Morgan, A.H., & Macdonald, H. Pain and dissociation in the cold pressor test: A study of hypnotic analgesia with "hidden reports" through automatic keypressing and automatic talking. *Journal of Abnormal Psychology,* 1975, *84,* 280–289.

Hillyard, S.A., & Kutas, M. Electrophysiology of cognitive processing. *Annual Review of Psychology,* 1983, *34,* 33–61.

Hintzman, D.L. On testing the independence of associations. *Psychological Review,* 1972, *79,* 261–264.

Hirst, W., Spelke, E.S., Reeves, C.S., Caharack, G., & Neisser, U. Dividing attention without alternation or automaticity. *Journal of Experimental Psychology: General,* 1980, *109,* 98–117.

Hochberg, J. Attention, organization, and consciousness. In D.I. Mostofsky (Ed.), *Attention: Contemporary theory and analysis.* New York: Appleton-Century-Crofts, 1970.

Hochberg, J. *Perception* (2nd ed.). Englewood Cliffs, N.J.: Prentice-Hall, 1978.

Hoskovec, J. Hypnopaedia in the Soviet Union: A critical review of recent major experiments. *International Journal of Clinical and Experimental Hypnosis,* 1966, *14,* 308–315.

Hoskovec, J., & Cooper, L.M. Comparison of recent experimental trends concerning sleep learning in the U.S.A. and the Soviet Union. *Activitas Nervosa Superior,* 1967, *9,* 93–96.

Hoskovec, J., & Cooper, L.M. A critical review of methodology of sleep learning experiments. *Activitas Nervosa Superior,* 1969, *11,* 161–164.

Hull, C.L. *Hypnosis and suggestibility: An experimental approach.* New York: Appleton-Century-Crofts, 1933.

Jacobson, E., & Kales, A. Somnambulism: All night EEG and related studies. In S.S. Kety, E.V. Evarts, & H.L. Williams (Eds.), *Sleep and altered states of consciousness.* Baltimore: Williams & Wilkins, 1967.

Jacoby, L.L., & Craik, F.I.M. Effects of elaboration of processing at encoding and retrieval: Trace distinctiveness and recovery of initial context. In L.S. Cermak & F.I.M. Craik (Eds.), *Levels of processing in human memory.* Hillsdale, N.J.: Erlbaum, 1979.

Jacoby, L.L., & Dallas, M. On the relationship between autobiographical memory and perceptual learning. *Journal of Experimental Psychology: General,* 1981, *110,* 306–310.

James, W. *Principles of psychology.* New York: Holt, 1890.

Janet, P. *Psychological automatisms.* Paris: Alcan, 1889.

Janet, P. *The major symptoms of hysteria.* New York: Macmillan, 1907.

Jaynes, J. *The origin of consciousness in the breakdown of the bicameral mind.* Boston: Houghton Mifflin, 1976.

Johnson, L.C. A psychophysiology for all states. *Psychophysiology,* 1970, *6,* 501–516.

Johnson, M.K., & Raye, C.L. Reality monitoring. *Psychological Review,* 1981, *88,* 67–85.

Johnson, R.F.Q. Trance logic revisited: A reply to Hilgard's critique. *Journal of Abnormal Psychology,* 1972, *79,* 234–238.

Johnson, R.F.Q., Maher, B.A., & Barber, T.X. Artifact in the "Essence of hypnosis": An evaluation of trance logic. *Journal of Abnormal Psychology,* 1972, *79,* 212–220.

Kahneman, D. *Attention and effort.* Englewood Cliffs, N.J.: Prentice-Hall, 1973.

Kales, A., Paulson, M.J., Jacobson, A., & Kales, J.D. Somnambulism: Psychophysiological correlates: I. All-night EEG studies. II. Psychiatric interviews, psychological testing, and discussion. *Archives of General Psychiatry,* 1966, *14,* 586–604.

Kamiya, J. Operant control of the EEG alpha rhythm and some of its reported effects on consciousness. In C.T. Tart (Ed.), *Altered states of consciousness.* New York: Wiley, 1969.

Kaufman, L. *Sight and mind: An introduction to visual perception.* New York: Oxford University Press, 1974.

Keppel, G. Retroactive and proactive inhibition. In T.R. Dixon & D.L. Horton (Eds.), *Verbal behavior and general behavior theory.* Englewood Cliffs, N.J.: Prentice-Hall, 1968.

Kihlstrom, J.F. Models of posthypnotic amnesia. In W.E. Edmonston (Ed.), *Conceptual and investigative approaches to hypnosis and hypnotic phenomena. Annals of the New York Academy of Sciences,* 1977, *296,* 284–301.

Kihlstrom, J.F. Context and cognition in posthypnotic amnesia. *International Journal of Clinical and Experimental Hypnosis,* 1978, *26,* 246–257.

Kihlstrom, J.F. Hypnosis and psychopathology: Retrospect and prospect. *Journal of Abnormal Psychology,* 1979, *88,* 459–473.

Kihlstrom, J.F. Posthypnotic amnesia for recently learned material: Interactions with "episodic" and "semantic" memory. *Cognitive Psychology,* 1980, *12,* 227–251.

Kihlstrom, J.F. On personality and memory. In N. Cantor & J.F. Kihlstrom (Eds.), *Personality, cognition, and social interaction.* Hillsdale, N.J.: Erlbaum, 1981. (a)

Kihlstrom, J.F. Puzzles of imagery. *Journal of Mental Imagery,* 1981, *5,* 42–44. (b)

Kihlstrom, J.F. Hypnosis and the dissociation of memory, with special reference to posthypnotic amnesia. *Research Communications in Psychology, Psychiatry, and Behavior,* 1982, *7,* 181–197.

Kihlstrom, J.F. Instructed forgetting: Hypnotic and nonhypnotic. *Journal of Experimental Psychology: General,* 1983, *112,* 73–79.

Kihlstrom, J.F., & Cantor, N. Mental representations of the self. In L. Berkowitz (Ed.), *Advances in Experimental Social Psychology* (Vol. 17). New York: Academic Press, 1983.

Kihlstrom, J.F., & Evans, F.J. Memory retrieval processes in posthypnotic amnesia. In J.F. Kihlstrom & F.J. Evans (Eds.), *Functional disorders of memory*. Hillsdale, N.J.: Erlbaum, 1979.

Klein, D.B. *The unconscious: Invention or discovery? A historico-critical inquiry*. Santa Monica, Ca.: Goodyear, 1977.

Knox, V.J., Crutchfield, L., & Hilgard, E.R. The nature of task interference in hypnotic dissociation: An investigation of hypnotic behavior. *International Journal of Clinical and Experimental Hypnosis*, 1975, *23*, 305–323.

Knox, V.J., Morgan, A.H., & Hilgard, E.R. Pain and suffering in ischemia: The paradox of hypnotically suggested anesthesia as contradicted by reports from the "hidden observer." *Archives of General Psychiatry*, 1974, *30*, 840–847.

Kolers, P.A. Reading a year later. *Journal of Experimental Psychology: Human Learning and Memory*, 1976, *2*, 554–565.

Koulack, D., & Goodenough, D.R. Dream recall and dream-recall failure: An arousal-retrieval model. *Psychological Bulletin*, 1976, *83*, 975–984.

Lachman, R., Lachman, J.L., & Butterfield, E.C. *Cognitive psychology and information processing: An introduction*. Hillsdale, N.J.: Erlbaum, 1979.

Laurence, J.-R., & Perry, C. The "hidden observer" phenomenon in hypnosis: Some additional findings. *Journal of Abnormal Psychology*, 1981, *90*, 334–344.

Laurence, J.-R., Perry, C., & Kihlstrom, J. "Hidden observer" phenomena in hypnosis: An experimental creation? *Journal of Personality and Social Psychology*, 1983, *44*, 163–169.

Lepper, M., Greene, D., & Nisbett, R. Undermining children's interest with extrinsic rewards: A test of the "overjustification hypothesis." *Journal of Personality and Social Psychology*, 1973, *28*, 129–137.

Leventhal, H. A perceptual-motor theory of emotion. In L. Berkowitz (Ed.), *Advances in experimental social psychology*. (Vol. 16). New York: Academic Press, 1983.

Lockhart, R.S., Craik, F.I.M., & Jacoby, L.L. Depth of processing, recognition, and recall: Some aspects of a general memory system. In J. Brown (Ed.), *Recall and recognition*. London: Wiley, 1976.

Loftus, E.F. Leading questions and eyewitness report. *Cognitive Psychology*, 1975, *7*, 560–572.

Loftus, E.F. *Eyewitness testimony*. Cambridge, Mass.: Harvard University Press, 1979.

Loftus, E.F., & Loftus, G.R. On the permanence of stored information in the human brain. *American Psychologist*, 1980, *35*, 409–420.

Ludwig, A.M. Altered states of awareness. *Archives of General Psychiatry*, 1966, *15*, 225–234.

Ludwig, A.M., Brandsma, J.M., Wilbur, C.B., Bendfeldt, F., & Jameson, D.H. The objective study of a multiple personality: Or, are four heads better than one? *Archives of General Psychiatry*, 1972, *26*, 298–310.

McConkey, K.M., & Sheehan, P.W. The impact of videotape playback of posthypnotic events on hypnotic amnesia. *Journal of Abnormal Psychology*, 1981, *90*, 46–54.

McConkey, K.M., Sheehan, P.W., & Cross, D.G. Posthypnotic amnesia: Seeing is not remembering. *British Journal of Social and Clinical Psychology*, 1980, *19*, 99–107.

McDonald, R.D., & Smith, J.R. Trance logic in tranceable and simulating subjects. *International Journal of Clinical and Experimental Hypnosis,* 1975, *23,* 80–89.

Malcolm, N. *Dreaming.* London: Routledge & Kegan Paul, 1959.

Mandler, G. Consciousness: Respectable, useful, and probably necessary. In R. Solso (Ed.), *Information processing and cognition: The Loyola symposium.* Hillsdale, N.J.: Erlbaum, 1975. (a)

Mandler, G. *Mind and emotion.* New York: Wiley, 1975. (b)

Melges, F.T., Tinklenberg, J.R., & Hollister, L.E. Temporal disorganization and depersonalization during marijuana intoxication. *Archives of General Psychiatry,* 1970, *23,* 204–210.

Melton, A.W. Implications of short-term memory for a general theory of memory. *Journal of Verbal Learning and Verbal Behavior,* 1963, *2,* 1–21.

Moray, N. Attention in dichotic listening: Affective cues and the influence of instructions. *Quarterly Journal of Experimental Psychology,* 1959, *11,* 56–60.

Mulholland, T.B. Feedback electroencephalography. *Activitas Nervosa Superior,* 1968, *10,* 410–438.

Nace, E.P., & Orne, M.T. Fate of an uncompleted posthypnotic suggestion. *Journal of Abnormal Psychology,* 1970, *75,* 275–285.

Natsoulas, T. Consciousness. *American Psychologist,* 1978, *33,* 906–914.

Neisser, U. *Cognitive psychology.* New York: Appleton-Century-Crofts, 1967.

Neisser, U. *Cognition and reality: Principles and implications of cognitive psychology.* San Francisco: Freeman, 1976.

Neisser, U., Hirst, W., & Spelke, E.S. Limited capacity theories and the notion of automaticity: Reply to Lucas and Bub. *Journal of Experimental Psychology: General,* 1981, *110,* 499–500.

Nelson, T.O. Detecting small amounts of information in memory: Savings for nonrecognized items. *Journal of Experimental Psychology: Human Learning and Memory,* 1978, *4,* 453–468.

Nemiah, J.C. Conversion reaction. In A. Freedman & H. Kaplan (Eds.), *Comprehensive textbook of psychiatry.* Baltimore: Williams & Wilkins, 1967.

Nemiah, J.C. Hysterical amnesia. In G.A. Talland & N.C. Waugh (Eds.), *The pathology of memory.* New York: Academic Press, 1969.

Nemiah, J.C. Dissociative amnesia: A clinical and theoretical reconsideration. In J.F. Kihlstrom & F.J. Evans (Eds.), *Functional disorders of memory.* Hillsdale, N.J.: Erlbaum, 1979.

Newell, A., & Simon, H.A. *Human problem solving.* Englewood Cliffs, N.J.: Prentice-Hall, 1972.

Nisbett, R.E., & Wilson, T.D. Telling more than we can know: Verbal reports on mental processes. *Psychological Review,* 1977, *84,* 231–259.

Nogrady, H., McConkey, K.M., Laurence, J.-R., & Perry, C. Dissociation, duality, and demand characteristics in hypnosis. *Journal of Abnormal Psychology,* 1983, *92,* 223–235.

Norman, D.A. Toward a theory of memory and attention. *Psychological Review,* 1968, *75,* 522–536.

Norman, D.A., & Bobrow, D.G. On data limited and resource limited processes.

Cognitive Psychology, 1975, *7,* 44–64.

Noyes, R., & Kletti, R. Depersonalization in response to life-threatening danger. *Comprehensive Psychiatry,* 1977, *18,* 375–384.

Obstoj, I., & Sheehan, P.W. Aptitude for trance, task generalizability, and incongruity response in hypnosis. *Journal of Abnormal Psychology,* 1977, *86,* 543–552.

O'Connell, D.N., Shor, R.E., & Orne, M.T. Hypnotic age regression: An empirical and methodological analysis. *Journal of Abnormal Psychology Monograph,* 1970, *76,* (3 Pt. 2).

Orne, M.T. The mechanisms of hypnotic age regression: An experimental study. *Journal of Abnormal and Social Psychology,* 1951, *46,* 213–225.

Orne, M.T. The nature of hypnosis: Artifact and essense. *Journal of Abnormal and Social Psychology,* 1959, *58,* 277–299.

Orne, M.T. On the social psychology of the psychological experiment: With particular reference to demand characteristics and their implications. *American Psychologist,* 1962, *17,* 776–783.

Orne, M.T. Hypnosis, motivation, and the ecological validity of the psychological experiment. In W.J. Arnold & M.M. Page (Eds.), *Nebraska symposium on motivation.* Lincoln: University of Nebraska Press, 1970.

Orne, M.T. The construct of hypnosis: Implications of the definition for research and practice. In W.E. Edmonston (Ed.), *Conceptual and investigative approaches to hypnosis and hypnotic phenomena. Annals of the New York Academy of Sciences,* 1977, *296,* 14–33.

Orne, M.T. On the simulating subject as a quasi-control group in hypnosis research: What, why, and how. In E. Fromm & R.E. Shor (Eds.), *Hypnosis: Developments in research and new perspectives.* New York: Aldine, 1979.

Orne, M.T., Sheehan, P.W., & Evans, F.J. Occurrence of posthypnotic behavior outside the experimental setting. *Journal of Personality and Social Psychology,* 1968, *9,* 189–196.

Orne, M.T., & Wilson, S.K. On the nature of alpha feedback training. In G.E. Schwartz & D. Shapiro (Eds.), *Consciousness and self-regulation: Advances in research* (Vol. 2). New York: Plenum, 1978.

Overton, D.A. State-dependent or "dissociated" learning produced with Pentobarbitol. *Journal of Comparative and Physiological Psychology,* 1964, *57,* 3–12.

Overton, D.A. Dissociated learning in drug states (state-dependent learning). In D.H. Efron, J.O. Cole, J. Levine, & R. Wittenborn (Eds.), *Psychopharmacology: A review of progress, 1957–1967.* Washington, D.C.: U.S. Government Printing Office, 1968.

Overton, D.A. Major theories of state-dependent learning. In B. Ho, D. Chute, & D. Richards (Eds.), *Drug discrimination and state-dependent learning.* New York: Academic Press, 1977.

Perry, C., & Walsh, B. Inconsistencies and anomalies of response as a defining characteristic of hypnosis. *Journal of Abnormal Psychology,* 1978, *87,* 574–577.

Peters, J.E. *Trance logic: Artifact or essence of hypnosis?* Unpublished doctoral dissertation, Pennsylvania State University, 1973.

Plotkin, W.B. On the self-regulation of the occipetal alpha rhythm: Control strategies, states of consciousness, and the role of physiological feedback. *Journal of Experimental Psychology: General,* 1976, *105,* 66–99. (a)

Plotkin, W.B. Appraising the ephemeral "alpha phenomenon": A reply to Hardt and Kamiya. *Journal of Experimental Psychology: General,* 1976, *105,* 109–121. (b)

Plotkin, W.B. A rapprochement of the operant-conditioning and awareness views of biofeedback training: The role of discrimination in voluntary control. *Journal of Experimental Psychology: General,* 1981, *110,* 415–428.

Popper, K., & Eccles, J.C. *The self and its brain.* Berlin: Springer, 1977.

Postman, L., & Underwood, B.J. Critical issues in interference theory. *Memory and Cognition,* 1973, *1,* 19–40.

Powers, W.T. *Behavior: The control of perception.* Chicago: Aldine, 1973.

Prince, M. *The dissociation of a personality.* New York: Longmans, Green, 1906.

Prince, M. *The unconscious.* New York: Macmillan, 1914.

Prince, M. *Clinical and experimental studies of personality* (rev. ed.). Cambridge, Mass.: Sci-Art, 1939.

Pylyshyn, Z. The imagery debate: Analogue media versus tacit knowledge. *Psychological Review,* 1981, *88,* 16–45.

Reed, G. *The psychology of anomalous experience: A cognitive approach.* London: Hutchinson University Library, 1972.

Reed, G. Everyday anomalies of recall and recognition. In J.F. Kihlstrom & F.J. Evans (Eds.), *Functional disorders of memory.* Hillsdale, N.J.: Erlbaum, 1979.

Richardson, T.F. Deja vu in psychiatric and neurosurgical patients. *Archives of General Psychiatry,* 1967, *17,* 622–625.

Rock, I. *An introduction to perception.* New York: Macmillan, 1975.

Rosch, E., & Lloyd, B.B. (Eds.). *Cognition and categorization.* Hillsdale, N.J.: Erlbaum, 1978.

Roth, M. The phobic anxiety-depersonalization syndrome. *Proceedings of the Royal Society of Medicine,* 1960, *52,* 587–595.

Rozin, P. The evolution of intelligence and access to the cognitive unconscious. In E. Stellar and J.M. Sprague (Eds.), *Progress in psychobiology and physiological psychology* (Vol. 6). New York Academic Press, 1976.

Sackeim, H.A., Nordlie, J.W., & Gur, R.C. A model of hysterical and hypnotic blindness: Cognition, motivation, and awareness. *Journal of Abnormal Psychology,* 1979, *88,* 474–489.

Sarbin, T.R., & Coe, W.C. Hypnosis and psychopathology: Replacing old myths with fresh metaphors. *Journal of Abnormal Psychology,* 1979, *88,* 506–526.

Scarborough, D., Cortese, C., & Scarborough, H. Frequency and repetition effects in lexical memory. *Journal of Experimental Psychology: Human Perception and Performance,* 1977, *3,* 1–17.

Schacter, D.L., & Moscovitch, M. Infants, amnesics, and dissociable memory systems. In M. Moscovitch (Ed.), *Infant memory.* New York: Plenum, 1983.

Schacter, D.L., & Tulving, E. Memory, amnesia, and the episodic/semantic distinction. In R.L. Isaacson & N.E. Spear (Eds.), *The expression of knowledge.* New York: Plenum, 1982.

Schacter, D.L., Wang, P.L., Tulving, E., & Freedman, M. Functional retrograde amnesia: A quantitative case study. *Neuropsychologia,* 1982, *20,* 523–532.

Scheibe, K.E., Gray, A.L., & Keim, C.S. Hypnotically induced deafness and delayed auditory feedback: A comparison of real and simulating subjects. *International Journal of Clinical and Experimental Hypnosis*, 1968, *16*, 158–164.

Schneider, W., & Shiffrin, R.M. Controlled and automatic human information processing: I. Detection, search, and attention. *Psychological Review*, 1977, *84*, 1–66.

Sedman, G. Theories of depersonalization: A reappraisal. *British Journal of Psychiatry*, 1970, *117*, 1–14.

Segalowitz, S.J. *Two sides of the brain: Brain lateralization explored.* Englewood Cliffs, N.J.: Prentice-Hall, 1983.

Sheehan, P.W. Incongruity in trance behavior: A defining property of hypnosis? In W.E. Edmonston (Ed.), *Conceptual and investigative approaches to hypnosis and hypnotic phenomena. Annals of the New York Academy of Sciences*, 1977, *296*, 194–207.

Sheehan, P.W., Obstoj, I., & McConkey, K. Trance logic and cue structure as supplied by the hypnotist. *Journal of Abnormal Psychology*, 1976, *85*, 459–472.

Sheehan, P.W., & Orne, M.T. Some comments on the nature of posthypnotic behavior. *Journal of Nervous and Mental Disease*, 1968, *146*, 209–220.

Shevrin, H., & Dickman, D. The psychological unconscious: A necessary assumption for all psychological theory? *American Psychologist*, 1980, *35*, 421–434.

Shiffrin, R.M., & Schneider, W. Controlled and automatic human information processing: II. Perceptual learning, automatic attending, and a general theory. *Psychological Review*, 1977, *84*, 127–190.

Simon, C.W., & Emmons, W.H. Learning during sleep? *Psychological Bulletin*, 1955, *52*, 328–342.

Smith, E.E. Theories of semantic memory. In W.K. Estes (Ed.), *Handbook of learning and cognitive processes.* Potomac, Md.: Erlbaum, 1978.

Smith, E.E., & Medin, D.L. *Categories and concepts.* Cambridge, Mass.: Harvard University Press, 1981.

Smith, S.M., Glenberg, A.M., & Bjork, R.A. Environmental context and human memory. *Memory and Cognition*, 1978, *6*, 342–353.

Spanos, N.P. Barber's reconceptualization of hypnosis: An evaluation of criticisms. *Journal of Experimental Research in Personality*, 1970, *4*, 241–258. (a)

Spanos, N.P. A reply to Tellegen's "Comments on 'Barber's reconceptualization of hypnosis.'" *Journal of Experimental Research in Personality*, 1970, *4*, 268–269. (b)

Spanos, N.P. The hidden observer as an experimental creation. *Journal of Personality and Social Psychology*, 1983, *44*, 170–176.

Spanos, N.P., & Barber, T.X. "Hypnotic" experiences as inferred from auditory and visual hallucinations. *Journal of Experimental Research in Personality*, 1968, *3*, 136–150.

Spanos, N.P., Gwynn, M.I., & Stam, H.J. Instructional demands and ratings of overt and hidden pain during hypnotic analgesia. *Journal of Abnormal Psychology*, 1983, in press.

Spanos, N.P., & Hewitt, E.C. The hidden observer in hypnotic analgesia: Discovery or experimental creation? *Journal of Abnormal Psychology*, 1980, *39*, 1201–1214.

Spanos, N.P., Jones, B., & Malfara, A. Hypnotic deafness: Now you hear it—Now you still hear it. *Journal of Abnormal Psychology,* 1982, *91,* 75–77.

Spanos, N.P., Radtke, H.L., & Dubreuil, D.L. Episodic and semantic memory in posthypnotic amnesia: A re-evaluation. *Journal of Personality and Social Psychology,* 1982, *43,* 565–573.

Spelke, E.S., Hirst, W., & Neisser, U. Skills of divided attention. *Cognition,* 1976, *4,* 215–230.

Sperry, R.W. Hemisphere deconnection and unity in conscious awareness. *American Psychologist,* 1968, *23,* 723–733.

Sperry, R.W. A modified concept of consciousness. *Psychological Review,* 1969, *76,* 532–536.

Springer, S.P., & Deutsch, G. *Left brain, right brain.* San Francisco: Freeman, 1981.

Stevenson, J.A. Effect of posthypnotic dissociation on the performance of interfering tasks. *Journal of Abnormal Psychology,* 1976, *85,* 398–407.

Stoyva, J., & Kamiya, J. Electrophysiological studies of dreaming as the prototype of a new strategy in the study of consciousness. *Psychological Review,* 1968, *75,* 192–205.

Sutcliffe, J.P. "Credulous" and "skeptical" views of hypnotic phenomena: Experiments on esthesia, hallucination, and delusion. *Journal of Abnormal and Social Psychology,* 1961, *62,* 189–200.

Sutcliffe, J.P., & Jones, J. Personal identity, multiple personality, and hypnosis. *International Journal of Clinical and Experimental Hypnosis,* 1962, *10,* 231–269.

Swanson, J.M., & Kinsbourne, M. Stimulant-related state-dependent learning in hyperactive children. *Science,* 1976, *192,* 1354–1357.

Szasz, T.S. *The myth of mental illness: Foundations of a theory of personal conduct.* New York: Harper & Row, 1961.

Taylor, W.S., & Martin, M.F. Multiple personality. *Journal of Abnormal and Social Psychology,* 1944, *39,* 281–300.

Tellegen, A. Some comments on Barber's "reconceptualization" of hypnosis. *Journal of Experimental Research in Personality,* 1970, *4,* 259–267.

Tellegen, A. On measures and conceptions of hypnosis. *American Journal of Clinical Hypnosis,* 1978–1979, *21,* 219–237.

Templer, D.I., & Lester, D. Conversion disorders: A review of research findings. *Comprehensive Psychiatry,* 1974, *15,* 285–293.

Triesman, A.M. Contextual cues in selective listening. *Quarterly Journal of Experimental Psychology,* 1960, *12,* 242–248.

Triesman, A.M. Strategies and models of selective attention. *Psychological Review,* 1969, *76,* 282–299.

Tulving, E. The effects of presentation and recall of material in verbal learning. *Journal of Verbal Learning and Verbal Behavior,* 1967, *6,* 175–184.

Tulving, E. Episodic and semantic memory. In E. Tulving & W. Donaldson (Eds.), *Organization of memory.* New York: Academic Press, 1972.

Tulving, E. Theoretical issues in free recall. In T.R. Dixon & D.L. Horton (Eds.), *Verbal behavior and general behavior theory.* Englewood Cliffs, N.J.: Prentice-Hall, 1968.

Tulving, E. Cue-dependent forgetting. *American Scientist,* 1974, *62,* 74–82.

Tulving, E., & Pearlstone, Z. Availability and accessibility of information in memory for words. *Journal of Verbal Learning and Verbal Behavior,* 1966, *5,* 381–391.

Tulving, E., & Thomson, D.M. Encoding specificity and retrieval processes in episodic memory. *Psychological Review,* 1973, *80,* 352–373.

Tulving, E., & Watkins, M.J. Structure of memory traces. *Psychological Review,* 1975, *82,* 261–275.

Waugh, N.C., & Norman, D.A. Primary memory. *Psychological Review,* 1965, *72,* 89–104.

West, L.J. Dissociative reaction. In A. Freedman & H. Kaplan (Eds.), *Comprehensive textbook of psychiatry.* Baltimore: Williams & Wilkins, 1967.

White, R.W., & Shevach, B.J. Hypnosis and the concept of dissociation. *Journal of Abnormal and Social Psychology,* 1942, *37,* 309–328.

White, S.H., & Pillemer, D.B. Childhood amnesia and the development of a socially accessible memory system. In J.F. Kihlstrom & F.J. Evans (Eds.), *Functional disorders of memory.* Hillsdale, N.J.: Erlbaum, 1979.

Whyte, L.L. *The unconscious before Freud.* New York: Basic Books, 1960.

Wickelgren, W.A. The long and short of memory. Psychological Bulletin, 1973, *80,* 425–438.

Williams, H.L. Information processing during sleep. In W.P. Koella & P. Levin (Eds.), *Sleep: Physiology, biochemistry, psychology, pharmacology, and implications.* Basel: Karger, 1973.

Winograd, T. Computer memories: A metaphor for memory organization. In C.N. Cofer (Ed.), *The structure of human memory.* San Francisco: Freeman, 1975.

CHAPTER 5

Psychobiology and
the Unconscious

DANIEL N. ROBINSON

The essential character of psychobiology is *correlative* rather than theoretical or even systematic. Its numerous and ever increasing contributions to general psychology are chiefly confined to reliable coincidences between, on the one hand, measureable aspects of learning, memory, perception, attention, motivation, and emotionality and, on the other, the structural and functional integrity of the nervous system. Accordingly, what is taken to be the proper mission of psychobiology cannot begin, or at least cannot proceed very far, until the relevant dependent variable has submitted to quantification and control. Traditionally and currently, the psychobiologist has been more or less content to entrust others with the psychological side of the psychobiological equation. What psychology at large accepts as "learning," "memory," "motivation," and so forth is thus uncritically absorbed into psychobiological research, which thereupon seeks to establish its physiological and chemical conditions ("correlates"). What distinguishes the specialty from such disciplines as neurophysiology and neurochemistry is just this focus on *psychological* dependent variables.

In light of this orientation, it should be clear that the *unconscious* presents psychobiology with special problems apart from those it offers to the whole of psychology. The most fundamental of these is the *ontological* problem of establishing the real existence of unconscious processes and events. That this may sound heretical is merely a measure of the extent to which what has never been more than a theoretical construct has come to be taken as an unimpeachable fact. Note that the ontological problem of the unconscious is not simply part of a Wittgensteinian "private language" problem, nor is it a version of the problem of introspection. Psychobiology has strong historical and current ties to psychophysics and has worked out any number of lawful relationships between introspective reports and neural events.

The psychophysicist does not consider it to be within his or her province to answer questions such as "Do Smith and Jones see the *same* red?" but, rather,

212

answers questions like "Over what range of physical changes in a stimulus do responses remain invariant?" (Graham, 1950). The most psychophysics can establish in such contexts is that the behavior (verbal reports, reaction times, color namings) of Smith and the behavior of Jones are both functionally dependent upon specific and quantitative features of the stimulus. This does not settle the *epistemic* issue of whether they both see what is "actually there" or the private-language problem of whether both of their "reds" are the same. But psychophysics is not plagued by ontological doubts as to whether or not Smith and Jones *have* experiences. And it is just this doubt that the psychobiologist must entertain when faced with an alleged state that cannot be rendered public *even introspectively*.

It is useful to pause over the epistemic dimensions of this matter, again by contrasting psychophysical reports with presumed states of unconscious processes. The word *consciousness* derives its first-person meaning from the sorts of events that give rise to psychophysical ("introspective") reports. As an attribution assigned by others, the word stands for an ensemble of actions ordinarily performed only by those having the first-person evidence as well. Note, however, that the epistemic grounds on which *I* claim to be conscious are not identical to the grounds on which others might claim that I am conscious. The first-person claim arises out of direct experience, whereas second- and third-person claims are inferential. In cases of conflict or contradiction between claims of this sort, epistemic authority is typically (if only implicitly) reserved for the first-person account. Thus we can have a phenomenon such as somnambulism only by accepting the somnambulist's claim that he or she is utterly unaware of having done any of the things we observed the person doing while in the "somnambulistic state." Unlike assertions that person might make about any event in the external world, assertions about his or her own experiences enjoy epistemically protected status.

It is at this point that the problem of the unconscious creates both conceptual and scientific difficulties of a unique nature. If it is taken to be a mental state or attribute belonging to Smith, we cannot use Smith's first-person reports at all, since whatever Smith is able to report about his mental states is ipso facto not unconscious. If, however, we adopt the third-person stance—and thus treat Smith's "unconscious" as the sort of empirical event over which Smith can claim no special epistemic authority—we are left with no more than Smith's observable behavior. This is enough for us to use the term "unconscious" in the ordinary sense of "lacking consciousness," but not in the theoretical sense of "an active and dynamic principle causally related to Smith's feelings, perceptions, and actions."

A variety of psychoanalytic gambits can be tested in order to find a way out of the bind. By and large, however, each of them pertains to the theoretical rather than the ontological standing of the concept of the unconscious. We can take *repression* illustratively. Suppose, for example, we discover that each time Smith is called upon to visit Aunt Edna (who always embarrassed him when he was a child), he forgets where he laid the keys to his car. After interviewing Smith at length, we learn that he is (consciously) very fond of Aunt Edna and that, like everyone else, Smith has a less than perfect memory. According to certain very popular theory, the best *explanation* of Smith's forgetting is that his *repressed* hostility toward Aunt Edna comes to the surface in the form of *active forgetting,* and that we now have additional evidence in support of the theory that unconscious processes influence conscious behavior.

To the extent that this is a scientific theory, it must lend itself to empirical modes of confirmation and refutation. We cannot, however, proceed in psychophysical fashion because Smith is not *conscious* of his hostility toward Aunt Edna; his (alleged) hostility has been *repressed.* Nor do we have a general theory of memory, empirically supported, which ties forgetting lawfully to measurable degrees of enmity. To have a scale for the latter we would need first-person psychophysical data, the very data rendered inaccessible by "repression." This leaves us with third-person accounts, but these are largely exhausted by the *fact* of Smith's forgetting—and a veritable infinity of theories can find confirmation in a single fact. The point of this discussion is not so much to cast doubt on the concept of the unconscious as to alert the reader to the incompatibility between concepts of this sort and the methods and perspectives characteristic of psychobiology.

Yet even the assertion that the "repressed hostility" account is not a scientific theory, but the best *explanation* of the fact, is unsatisfactory. In the end, what makes any explanation a good one is, among other considerations, the contact it makes with our direct and unbiased observations and experiences. This is not to say that observation and experience will turn up evidence for every term in an explanation; we do not "see" gravity or quanta or positive charges. But although the theoretical terms are not themselves of an empirical nature, the *events* they attempt to explain are. It is important, therefore, to make clear distinctions between the unconscious as a theoretical term and as an empirical claim. Psychobiology can make contact with the unconscious solely in its latter manifestation, if only because a fact cannot be correlated with a theory, but only with another fact. Thus as a purely theoretical construct, the unconscious cannot be dealt with in a psychobiological context. And as an empirical claim it is self-contradictory, for to report it is to show that it is not unconscious.

The remaining possibility for a "psychobiology of the unconscious" is one that takes "unconscious" as a code word for a collection of processes that manifest themselves behaviorally, but whose contents are unavailable to the otherwise fully conscious actor. To qualify for inclusion here, the processes must be distinguishable from such *passive* processes as fatigue and forms of forgetting, and must make nonaccidental contact with the actor's conscious motives, reasons, and perceptions. By "nonaccidental," I mean that the relationship between the (alleged) unconscious processes and the actor's conscious life must be akin to that obtaining between a plot and the actions of the characters; or, perhaps to beg the question: The relationship must be *psychological.* It must join overt actions or expressed sentiments, thoughts, or dispositions with equivalently psychological states and processes that are neither public nor accessible to the percipient (or actor) himself. Psychobiology may enter at this point as a specialty able to detect physiological correlates or signs of these inaccessible and otherwise nonpublic processes, and may thereby provide loosely corroborative evidence for them.

This is an admittedly modest role, and one that surely will be judged by some to be far too modest. Freud, after all, required far more than this in his famous "Project," and encouraged an entire generation of psychologists and psycho-analysts to look to the neutral sciences for the mechanisms causally associated with psychodynamic processes. But Freud, for all his literary fecundity and polemical exhortations, did not pause long enough to assess the deeper and inescapably *metaphysical* foundations of his "Project." As a member of the confidently physicalistic medical establishment of his day—and, perhaps to defend his standing against challenges coming from this same establishment—Freud extolled the virtues of reductive materialism without heeding the demands of *verificationism*. Nearly a century has passed since his earliest psychoanalytic writings, but what was something of a not too veiled ideology with him has by now sunk to mere sloth. Almost any interesting finding served up by psychobiology—such as the revival of memories through direct cortical stimulation, the (alleged) "two minds" of commissurotomized patients, drug-induced hallucinatory flights, biofeedback—will be used to affirm that "Freud was right!" The tendency, such innocent affirmations aside, is to look to psychobiology for confirmation rather than correlates, to find in psychobiology a more "objective" foundation than is provided by psychoanalytic theory, to use psychobiology the way anatomists use microscopes.

This search for objective confirmation is a mistake which must be exposed if the somewhat thin literature on "psychobiology and the unconscious" is to be of any value. Quite simply, psychobiology *cannot* turn up any more "objective" data than the psychoanalytic formulations, since the unconscious derives its ontological status exclusively from these formulations. It is an irreducibly psychoanalytic construct in the same way that "God" is an irreducibly theological construct. Again, *repression* is a useful exemplum. Let us suppose that in every instance of repression a specific pool of cells in the amygdala were to become hyperactive; moreover, that when this pool was directly activated, the patient committed frequent slips of the tongue and misplaced any number of personal possessions. Have we found the (or at least a) "repression center"? The answer is, of course, *yes,* if we define repression as tendencies to forget, to misplace psychologically significant items, to commit slips of the tongue in a revealing way, and so forth. But the activity of the amygdala is neither more nor less "objective" than these psychological signs, because the activity of the amygdala is utterly irrelevant to the very concept of repression. It is only after we have satisfied ourselves that the signs or symptoms just noted constitute repression that it becomes possible to search for correlates. The latter cannot *confirm* repression, objectively or otherwise.

It might be that although the psychobiological findings do not *confirm* repression, they are at least less vulnerable to the interpretive nuances that characterize psychoanalytic accounts of the process and its incidence. But this argument clearly fails, and on precisely the same grounds—it is only after we have the psychoanalytic account that we can search for physical correlates and recognize them should they appear. Neuronal activity within the amygdala, as with all purely physical events, is utterly neutral with respect to psychological formulations. Such activity *derives* its psychological significance from these formulations, and not vice versa. We see, then, that there is only one account of the unconscious, and that is the psychological account. That there may be psychobiological correlates of those states psychologically defined as "unconscious" is a possibility explored in the balance of this chapter. But these stand as correlates only on the hypothesis that what we have taken psychologically to mean "the unconscious" is, in fact, what we have taken it to be. Reductive materialism can only fail here because the events we try to reduce receive their psychological standing from psychoanalytic interpretations. A successful reduction would not, therefore, explain psychoanalytic concepts. It would dissolve them.

TWO MODES OF UNCONSCIOUSNESS

For purposes of psychobiological inquiry, I have defined the unconscious as a collection of processes that manifest themselves behaviorally but whose contents are unavailable to the otherwise fully conscious actor. Defined in this way, however, the unconscious is not restricted to psychoanalytically relevant processes. Rather, it includes certain aspects of human *information processing* in which material otherwise inaccessible to consciousness has been registered and "stored," and can be subsequently retrieved by the observer under appropriate experimental conditions. There are still other instances in which information has been registered—at least at a measurable sensory level of processing—but remains ever inaccessible to the observer at the level of conscious experience. The following illustrations indicate the mode of unconsciousness disclosed by studies of human information processing.

At present there is no persuasive evidence to support the view that the unconscious a là Freud, is merely a passive and essentially uniformly expressed aspect of cortical information processing. The closest the psychoanalytic tradition comes to this view is Janet's studies of hystericals (Janet, 1901/1978), in which neurosis is explained in terms of the narrowing of the field of consciousness. It is likely that Janet's notions will be resurrected, for his theory of hysteria is strikingly compatible with much of contemporary cognitive psychology. Yet a revival of Janetian thought would be at the expense of the unconscious itself, since Janet's cognitive-attentional theory is at variance with the more orthodox (Freudian) conception of unconscious processes.

There are, however, grounds for a reconciliation. As Janet understood the neuroses, the patient's symptoms arise from an abnormal constriction of attention leading to the formation of the *fixed idea* (*ideé fixe*) that renders the patient inaccessible to the normal flow of information. A Freudian theory of the origin of the fixed idea would not be difficult to fashion. But a psychobiological approach to neurosis would proceed more directly from Janetian than from Freudian hypotheses, since the former are already compatible with the information-processing (cognitive) model. If the Janetian therapeutic goal is the widening of the "field of consciousness," it is surely within the province of psychobiology to provide measures of just this sort of process. Whether one would take firm correlations between, for example, AER signs of widened attention and clinical signs of symptom relief as confirming Janet's theory would depend, of course, on just what one means by "confirmation." In uncharted territory, it is wise to take correlations wherever they can be found in anticipation of better days.

NEUROCHEMISTRY AND THE UNCONSCIOUS

At the level of purely circumstantial evidence (and metaphorical reasoning), recent studies of the *endorphins* provide a common base for psychobiological and psychoanalytic approaches to the unconscious. It is now known that the brain itself possesses specific neuronal "opiate" receptors; units with a special chemical affinity to opiate like molecules. Moreover, areas of the brain—notably the hypothalamus—are known to produce such substances (endorphins) which have powerful inhibiting effects and can therefore attenuate responses to painful stimulation.

The endorphins are most reliably associated with structures of the limbic system, the system whose activity is most directly tied to the emotional expressions of the organism. By untroubled inference, it is tempting to conclude that psychologically "painful" thoughts are removed from consciousness through a neurochemical mechanism that manufactures opiate like palliatives and delivers them to troubled areas of the brain. Indeed, it is not at all uncommon in current literature to discover suggestions to the effect that basic mechanisms of inhibition in neural circuits are somehow psychoanalytically relevant. Again, however, there is a difference between evidence and metaphor. Even on the showing of some gross relationship between, for example, depression and the relative concentration of some "brain opiate," the task of scientific interpretation remains formidable; when a process such as *repression* is substituted, the once formidable task becomes virtually impossible. With depression, there are only the behavioral or subjective reports needed by a correlative science, whereas it is in the nature of repression that the sufferer is totally unaware and the diagnostician is totally at sea.

Because some tend to regard certain patterns of behavior or clusters of symptoms as "ego defending," and thus assume a quasi-evolutionary mechanism for the defense of the ego's "strength," the recent discoveries in neurochemistry have enjoyed something of a charmed reception. The chain of reasoning is all too obvious: Just as, at the mental (unconscious) level there are modes of self-defense, so too (causally?) the biochemistry of the brain protects the system against overloading. And if additional "proof" is required, we need only recognize the extraordinary strides that have been made in chemotherapeutic approaches to psychiatric disorders. The implication is that the salutary effects of aspirin arise from the fact that headache is produced by too little aspirin in the brain!

If a small foveal stimulus is presented briefly (20 msec) and is followed by a larger, longer, and more intense stimulus falling on concentric regions of the retina, the first stimulus can be effectively masked. This "backward masking" of a target stimulus by one occurring later in time can extend over interstimulus intervals of 200 msec or longer. If, however, instead of requiring observers to report verbally whether or not they *see* the target, we require them to react as quickly as they can (by pressing a reaction-time key, for example) when they see any flash, we discover that they respond as quickly to the flash they did not "see" as they do to the target when it is presented alone (Raab, 1963). Without going into detail, it is enough to say that the neutral processing associated with reaction time is different from (and more efficient than) the processing associated with verbal (conscious) reports of the presence of a stimulus (Robinson, 1966).

In another example, subjects are called upon to report as many letters as they can recall after an array of letters has been briefly presented. Figure 5.1 illustrates a typical array. Under ordinary circumstances, observers recall no more than four or five items in an array that is briefly exposed, and their performance is remarkably unaffected by the size of the array. Here we have the familiar "span of apprehension" which received experimental attention as early as the nineteenth century. It has long been known that this "span" can be significantly extended under conditions of *cued retrieval* (Sperling, 1960). When a cue marker is placed over one of the positions occupied earlier by a member of the array, the observer is able to "recall" that member. Improvements in recall occur only over a range of several hundred milliseconds, however, and are attributable to short-term or "buffer" storage mechanisms of perception. Under such circumstances, it is plausible to describe the subject as being able to recall with the aid of a cue marker any number of stimuli of which the subject was "unconscious" initially.

Physiological correlates of such nuances in information processing have been chiefly confined to measures of the cortical responses to transient stimuli. The preferred measure is that of the *averaged evoked response* (AER). Unlike the electroencephalogram (EEG), which is a record of the intrinsic electrical activity of the brain, the AER is a record of the evoked or elicited activity of the brain

▌

F   J   D   G   L   T

M   C   K   V   B   X

Figure 5.1.   An array of 12 letters is presented for 20 msec, after which subjects are asked to report as many of the letters as they can recall. In a matching experiment, a bar marker (placed above G in this example) is presented 50 msec after the array is removed.

(cerebral cortex) occasioned by the arrival of a discrete stimulus. Because the background EEG activity is a thousand times stronger than electrical changes evoked by a single stimulus, the evoked response on any one trial is not readily detected against the "noisy" background of the ongoing EEG. However, through a computer-assisted averaging procedure, it is possible over a run of trials to "average out" or cancel the background EEG, and thus to accentuate the evoked responses of the brain—hence the averaged or average evoked response (AER).

When observers are distracted by the requirement of keeping track of information delivered to one sensory channel (e.g., a message delivered to one ear through headphones), they are largely oblivious to information presented simultaneously to a different channel (e.g., signals delivered to the other ear). There are distinct cortical correlates of this obliviousness: where recognition of the extraneous signal is poor, cortical AERs are diminished, and where recognition is entirely absent, the cortical AERs are nearly or totally absent (Robinson & Sabat, 1977). Thus within the nonpsychoanalytic context of ordinary information processing, there is close correspondence between conscious awareness of stimulation and cortical responses to that stimulation. It would be interesting to extend such basic research into psychoanalytically suggestive areas such as "repression." Is the brain (as revealed by AER measures) less responsive to emotionally unacceptable or negative information than to neutral or positive stimuli?

Studies of the AER in the context of information processing also indicate that the *variance* of cortical activity is affected by attention, and that the usual interhemispheric differences in responsivity tend to shrink under conditions of sustained attentiveness (Robinson & Sabat, 1977). Such findings lend themselves to the usual pleasures of speculation. If we think of the "continuum of consciousness" as a reflection of an underlying continuum of intracortical and intercortical organization, we can hypothesize that the degree of concert among cortical neurons determines the accessibility of consciousness to stimulation. Those entries not processed in concerted fashion would be relegated to the unconscious. The problem of unconscious processes in such an account is simply a signal-to-noise problem, with "neurotics" and "psychotics" so vulnerable to "unconscious" influences due to the intrinsic "noise" of their cortical receiving channels. Note how rich the metaphorical nervous system is as a source of theoretical fancy!

It is important, even as advances in neurochemistry proceed apace, to recognize the complex and probably innumerable factors participating in the formation of bona fide psychiatric problems. The ambulatory patient typically suffers not only from the well-known anguish that fills the therapist's notebooks, but also from the *behavior* arising from the anguished state. In important respects, psychological difficulties are self-sustaining. Into them are poured distortions of perception, attention, cognition, motivation, and even memory. And out of these interdependent states of distortion there arise patterns of counterproductive conduct leading to still greater distortions of thought and affect. When a chemical mode of therapy is found to "work," as it were, serious theoretical efforts may be said to have just begun, not ended. The depressive patient who responds to lithium has not provided telling evidence in favor of a "lithium theory" of depression—whatever that might mean—but evidence that, somewhere in that closed chain whose external manifestations include depression, lithium has positively disrupting or moderating effects. It is worth recalling that in the dim past, *some* depressives benefited from the ice bath. Does hypothermia then cause increases in the lithium concentration in the cerebral circulation? (The frivolousness of a question reflects the queerness of theories that cause it to be raised.)

ELECTROGRAPHIC CORRELATES

The most reliable and most frequently employed measure or sign of variations along "the continuum of consciousness" is, of course, the electroencephalogram (EEG). From behavioral states of arousal and alertness to those of deep coma, the EEG record undergoes specific alterations, culminating in the isopotential "flat" record of the brain-dead patient. The layman's vocabulary now includes such entries as "REM sleep" and "sleep spindles," not to mention that internal Guru, the "alpha rhythm."

For purposes of investigating psychobiologically the *psychoanalytic* "unconscious," however, even the orderliness of the EEG record is but marginally useful. On the assumption that REM sleep reliably reflects the duration and frequency of periods of dreaming, and on the additional assumption that dreams are, in Freud's words, the *via reggia* to the unconscious, it follows that EEG methods can provide added precision to clinical estimations of unconscious states. It is not too bold to suggest that a rough measure of therapeutic progress might be yielded by assessments of the patient's dream time. There are, to be sure, practical limitations, particularly when the ambulatory patient is the subject of study. Yet, with people spending hundreds and even thousands of dollars for personal computers and video games, perhaps it is not out of the question to consider continuous EEG recordings at home during various phases of psychotherapy. In light of the theoretical anarchy prevailing among psychotherapists, one cannot state a priori which EEG changes are to be taken as signs of progress, but at least with the benefit of data the theorists will be able to discuss the same facts.

The EEG is not, however, the only electrographic correlate of psychological states. Electromyography (EMG) provides a record of muscle tension and is a reliable sign of states of agitation. Even electrooculography (EOG) provides a measure of attentiveness and vigilance and may profitably be employed in settings in which distractability is clinically relevant. However, while it is a fact of statistics that in any large matrix of correlations, some will be significant, presumably there is a limit to the amount of "hardware" that can be strapped to a patient while still preserving an atmosphere congenial to candor, reflection, and introspective calm.

THE SELF (SELVES?) IN THE BRAIN

Even an all too brief chapter on the psychobiology of the unconscious cannot ignore the celebrated issues thought to arise from "split-brain" studies. Although no two are quite alike and the claims made about such patients become less dramatic as the seasons pass, what survives is the fact that the commissurotomized patient does not report verbally stimuli delivered to the nondominant (left) hemisphere. Wild speculation has grown from this and related findings—for example, that the dominant hemisphere, "like Western civilization," is verbal, analytical, Aristotelian; the nondominant, "like the East," is pictorial, intuitive, and Platonic. (Tests to determine if, for example, Orientals tend more toward left-handedness than do Occidentals have not been conclusive.)

As regards the psychobiology of the unconscious, the "split-brain" studies are routinely taken as confirming the notion that much of mental life occurs in those cerebral processes of some "other self." However, there is nothing in the actual data to warrant such conclusions (Robinson, 1976; 1982), since the same states of *epistemic contradiction* displayed by split-brain patients can be found in ordinary psychophysical settings—in vigiambulism, in automatic writing, in "multiple personality," and (see below) in blind sight. In all these contexts, observers provide competing or contradictory claims as to the contents of consciousness. In ordinary psychophysical settings, for example, the observer may be totally oblivious—as determined from verbal report data—to stimuli to which the same observer nonetheless emits reliable nonverbal responses. The subject in a backward masking study, for example, will provide reaction times to a perceptually "masked" stimulus that are as quick as those emitted in the presence of flashes verbally reported and consciously seen. Similarly, under conditions of cued retrieval, observers will report many more items from short-term memory than are recalled in the absence of post-stimulus cueing. Again, there is a contradiction in the knowledge claims in that, under one set of conditions, the observer's nonreport indicates nonrecall, whereas, under cueing conditions, his or her report indicates substantial recall.

The willingness to take the findings from "split-brain" patients as evidence favoring two selves is rooted in a fallacious conflation of the terms *self, self-identity,* and *personal identity.* An amnesic patient, totally unaware of *who* he is, is certain without the benefit of a moment's reflection *that* he is. What we can say of such a person is that, although he lacks a self-identity, he clearly is in possession of a self, that is, the immediate awareness of a continuing personal existence. In yet another vein, the case of the stranger is comparable. Here we have a person who is immediately aware of both *who* he is and *that* he is, although *we* have no knowledge about the facts of his life. Here then there is both self and self-identity, but not personal identity.

To avoid confusion it would be useful to confine the term *self* to this immediate, nonreflective awareness that every conscious being has of being conscious, and to reserve the terms *self-identity* and *personal identity* to settings in which evidence is relevant to the identification of, alas, selves. Using these definitions, we can describe commissurotomized patients as having more than one *personal identity* if, under certain conditions, the patient simultaneously claims to know and not to know whether, for example, a specific stimulus had been presented or a specific action had just been committed. We might say, for example, that there is a person—Person X—identifiable as having pointed to and having reported seeing the apple, and a simultaneously and differently identifiable person—Person Y—identifiable as having denied seeing the apple. We might refer to the apple-affirming observer as P_A and the apple-denying observer as P_D, thus giving some legitimacy to the claim that there are *two P*. This would not sustain the claim that there are two selves, however, nor even two self-identities. The latter would require not only epistemically contradictory utterances, but also contradictory self-attributions; one attribution being of the sort "I am partly identifiable as one who has seen an apple" and the other being of the sort "I am partly identifiable as one who has not seen an apple." These can be symbolized as affirmations and denials making up part of one's *self-identity: S-I*$_A$ and *S-I*$_D$.

Note, however, that conditions yielding P_A need not yield $S\text{-}I_A$. If verbal reports are employed, the observer in a backward masking study can be identified as one who has not seen the flash, and will identify himself in the same terms. Here there is a match between P_D and $S\text{-}I_D$. But if reaction time is employed, we will have an instance in which there is affirmation of perception of the P_A variety but denial of perception of the $S\text{-}I_D$ variety. That is, *we* will identify the observer with a phrase of the sort "who responded to the flash" whereas the observer will identify himself with a phrase of the sort "didn't see a flash."

Within the context of "split-brain" findings, distinctions such as these clearly establish that nothing relevantly new is contributed by studies of the commissurotomized patient. There are numerous nonsurgical conditions capable of yielding multiple *P* and multiple *S-I* and contradictions between the two classes. Moreover, the multiples exceed *two*—a fact not comfortably absorbed by a theory resting on the anatomical coincidence of there being two hemispheres. That much of what people do in the daily affairs of life proceeds from central (cortical) processes not within the "consciousness loop" is obvious; one doesn't "consciously" ride a bicycle. And that linguistic and other functions are lateralized in the cerebrum ceased to be news in the second half of the nineteenth century.

"BLIND SIGHT"

A literature has grown over the past decade or so on the subject of "blind sight" (Weiskrantz, 1980), the term that refers to the residual visual experiences available to persons and to experimental animals stripped of their primary (cortical) visual projection areas. Without this literature, the more or less official position regarding the neurophysiology of vision has been that an intact geniculostriate system is necessary for any and all visual functions in the advanced species. Historically, both the clinic and the laboratory have shown that profound and irreversible blindness ensues when the striate cortex—the primary cortical region receiving inputs from the visual radiations—is destroyed. Since the retina is topographically represented within the striate cortex, selective and circumscribed lesions within the latter produce specific scotomata in the visual field. Thus an area or "hole" of blindness can be created in specific visual fields by choosing specific regions of the striate cortex and introducing lesions of the appropriate extent.

It has been known since the nineteenth century that some visual sensitivity can survive even the massive destruction of the striate cortex, but such sensitivity as might remain has been thought to be confined to the grossest discriminations of brightness. Recent research, however, has successfully challenged this official view by showing a surprising degree of competent visual *performance* by patients otherwise "blind." Such a patient, required by a forced-choice discrimination task to "guess" which of two presentations contains a stimulus of a given geometric form, will provide highly accurate discriminations *while insisting that he or she has not seen anything!*

Theoretical attempts to account for "blind sight" are still unfolding and need not be examined here. There is good reason to believe that detection and recognition in vision are mediated by different cortical regions—detection by the classical geniculostriate system and recognition by areas of the peristriatal and parietal cortex. This anatomical separation of functions would allow in principle not only the clinically familiar detection in the absence of recognition, but also that "blind sight" by which the observer recognizes what he or she has failed to detect. This seems paradoxical until we appreciate the different *neural* criteria that must be met for the observer's awareness to be triggered. The keenest detections are, after all, available to animals so low in the phylogenetic series as to make attributions of self-conscious awareness implausible. Then, too, hallucinatory phenomena and dreams indicate quite dramatically that rich visual experiences occur in which there is no stimulus to be detected. Even in the developed cerebral cortex of man, it is necessary for arriving signals to exceed some threshold level of activation for the observer consciously to report sensations (Libet, Alberts, Wright, & Feinstein, 1967). And, as Sternberg has shown (1975), observers in a reaction time task will respond discriminatively to previously memorized items at a rate far in excess of *conscious* processing. Together this assortment of findings helps to dissolve the paradox of recognition without detection and recognition without awareness.

Many other studies support the same general principle; studies indicating activation of the supplementary motor area (SMA) just prior to the initiation of *intended* movements, but with no such SMA activity associated with passively elicited movements; studies of *subliminal* influences on conscious perceptions. All such research underscores the fact that central mechanisms have variable thresholds and undertake processing at various levels. In order to sample activity occurring at different levels, the experimenter must choose response indicators appropriate to the levels in question. It is enough to mention a few such indicators in order to convey the need for making careful choices if theory is not to be a hostage to accident: evoked responses, EEG wave forms, sensory potentials (such as the electroretinogram), gross motor response time (both simple and discriminative), binary ("Yes"—"No") verbal reports, detailed introspective reports, rudimentary and complex problem solving. Knowing, for example, that a fair number of stimuli—all of which evoke electrical events in the directly stimulated somatosensory cortex—are required for the subjective report of sensation, we are more cautious in accepting any cortical signal as a sign of conscious experience. Knowing that subjects will accurately locate visual signals in space by pointing, though the subjects deny having *seen* anything, we are less apt to take verbal reports as the last word on matters of visual sensitivity. The soundest option for today's investigator is to employ as large a variety of response indicators as is practical, in an attempt to identify the levels of processing engaged by stimulation and available to the observer.

A PRELIMINARY TAXONOMY OF THE UNCONSCIOUS

The term "unconscious" is now so generously applied to qualitatively different states and processes as to nurture confusion and ambiguity. Perhaps the following terms, if adopted by scholars and researchers in the various areas, would make communication more facile and experimental-theoretical matters clearer.

1. *Unarousable unconsciousness.*   The subject is comatose, unresponsive to intense stimulation and devoid of activity.

2. *Arousable unconsciousness.*   The subject *reacts* to intense stimulation but displays no self-initiated activity and is otherwise comatose in the absence of intense stimulation.

3. *Sleep.*   During various stages, the subject (a) is accessible to moderate stimulation and even to suggestion and (b) is capable of *active* responses of a nonreflexive nature. This term covers, therefore, vigiambulism

4. *Conscious sleep.*   As intended here, the term refers to dream-sleep of which the subject is either aware at the time or on awakening.

5. *Conscious unawareness.*   Here the conscious subject is otherwise unaware of certain stimuli which affect the course of conscious thoughts or actions. Included here are "blind sight" and other phenomena discussed earlier. Characteristic of this level is the subject's inability ever to be aware of these effective stimuli, even under prompting. The stimuli are *subthreshold,* though able to influence perception and/or behavior.

6. *Conscious inattentiveness.*   Unlike conscious unawareness, the subject at this level is unaware of certain stimuli because he or she is *inattentive* to them, though they too affect perception and conduct. With appropriate prompting, however, the subject does perceive these stimuli.

These six levels are admittedly too coarse to embrace the rich diversity of clinical and experimental observations. It is, however, in the nature of taxonomies to ignore any number of subtle features in order to set forth the most obvious *species* and *genera*. According to this scheme, the psychoanalytic "unconscious" comes close to *conscious inattentiveness* or, perhaps, *conscious unawareness* than to unconsciousness proper. The compatibility between this classification and Janet's theory is quite strong.

Apart from its possible heuristic value, the proposed scheme would also help to clarify the reported suddenness of psychoanalytic "insights" as reported by patients, not to mention the pivotal "breakthroughs" reported by therapists. Granting that the deep mysteries of repression and unconscious motivation are more intriguing than the other prosaic processes of inattention and unawareness, it can still be argued that, at the root of allegedly "unconscious" phenomena, we will find aspects of information processing, no less "psychological" for being nonpsychoanalytic. The anxiety of the neurotic patient is typically "irrational" in the sense that the patient cannot *state* the stimuli eliciting the anxiety reactions. As we have now seen, there is nothing special about such phenomena except, of course, for the distress caused to the patient. But once room is left for the possibility that the anxiety is not irrational—that it is produced by complex stimuli processed at a level that bypasses conscious awareness—the therapeutic goal may shift from convincing the patient that the anxiety is unfounded to encouraging the patient to make use of a larger ensemble of response indicators.

This is not the occasion to mint yet another theory of therapy (and, if it were, it would not be within the province of this author's competence). It is enough to note that psychiatric problems befall eminently reasonable and rational persons, and that attempts to solve such problems on the assumption of irrationality become less plausible the longer they are considered. Such success as has been reported by specialists in behavior modification, like that occurring in more traditional therapeutic settings, may be best understood not as vindications of Skinnerian or Freudian views of human beings, but as cumbersome ways of altering the manner in which patients *select* environmental events for processing and the agility they develop in processing them.

CONCLUSION

Given the nature of psychobiological methods and theory, the psychoanalytic unconscious poses special difficulties. As a largely correlative discipline, psychobiology brings special methods and pleasures to bear on observable psychological phenomena; phenomena that are either behavioral or plausibly inferred from the facts of behavior.

The integration of psychobiological methods with those traditionally employed in studies of the unconscious requires a somewhat diluted version of the unconscious itself; a version that is less beholden to established psychoanalytic notions and more in keeping with information-processing models of mental life.

At the more practical level, psychobiology addresses unconscious phenomena neurochemically and electrographically by establishing reliable correlations between certain signs of unconscious processes (e.g., dreams) and specific biochemical or electrophysiological events. It is lamentable that the point of common contact between students of the brain and students of the unconscious is marked by unnecessary imprecision and the relative absence of programmatic research organized around a set of elementary questions. Part of the difficulty is the wide extension given to the term "unconscious" and the absence of a serviceable taxonomy. Another part of the overall problem arises from the artificial constriction of the domain of response indicators needed to determine the levels at which processing is taking place.

As matters now stand, the psychobiology of the unconscious is more promise than reality, in which the illusion of reality is forged out of a penchant for metaphorical modes of explanation.

REFERENCES

Graham, C.H. Behavior, perception, and the psychophysical methods. *Psychological Review*, 1950, *57*, 108–120.

Janet, P. *The mental state of hystericals* (Caroline Corson, trans.). In D.N. Robinson (Ed.), *Significant Contributions to the History of Psychology* (Series C, Vol. II). Washington, D.C.: University Publications of America, 1978. (Originally published 1901).

Libet, B., Alberts, W.W., Wright, E.W., & Feinstein, B. Responses of human somatosensory cortex to stimuli below threshold for conscious experience. *Science*, 1967, *158*, 1597–1600.

Raab, D. Backward masking. *Psychological Bulletin*, 1963, *60*, 118–129.

Robinson, D.N. What sort of persons are hemispheres? Another look at the "split-brain" man. *British Journal for the Philosophy of Science*, 1976, *27*, 73–78.

Robinson, D.N. Cerebral plurality and the unity of self. *American Psychologist*, 1982, *37*, 904–910.

Robinson, D.N. Visual reaction time and the human alpha rhythm. *Journal of Experimental Psychology*, 1966, *71*, 16–25.

Robinson, D.N., & Sabat, S. Neuroelectric aspects of information-processing by the brain. *Neuropsychologia*, 1977, *15*, 625–641.

Sperling, G. The information available in brief visual presentations. *Psychological Monographs*, 1960, *74*, (11, Whole No. 498).

Sternberg, S. Memory scanning: New findings and current controversies. *Quarterly Journal of Experimental Psychology*, 1975, *27*, 1–32.

Weiskrantz, L. Varieties of residual experience. *Quarterly Journal of Experimental Psychology*, 1980, *32*, 365–386.

CHAPTER 6

On Being Unconsciously
Influenced and Informed

KENNETH S. BOWERS

There is a distinct tendency for the ordinary person to link "the unconscious" with psychoanalytic formulations of it. This connection is surely unsurprising, since historically, the very notion of unconscious influence was for the most part elaborated and detailed by investigators of a psychoanalytic persuasion.

There is, however, no need to identify concepts of unconscious influence with psychoanalysis, and part of the burden of this chapter is to disengage the unconscious from its Freudian connection. This decoupling is not done in the spirit of dismissing or discrediting psychoanalytic theory, to which I am by and large favorably disposed. Rather, it is done in the interests of conceptual clarity, since it is my contention that unconscious influences are logically prior to any particular theory about them. In other words, unconscious influences on human thought and action precede particular theories of "unconsciousness" in somewhat the same way that thinking precedes any particular theory of thought. While this claim may presently seem nonobvious and overstated, this chapter aims to clarify why unconscious influences on thought and action are logically necessary, and therefore do not depend on or derive from the warrant or validity of psychoanalysis or any other theory of mind.

This paper has benefitted immeasurably from the input and comment of many people. Several extended conversations with Richard Nisbett, including an APA debate, were particularly important in giving my ideas some form and impetus. The upshot of these interchanges is particularly evident in the second major section of this chapter. A number of people read and commented on the first draft of the manuscript. They include William Abbott, John Ellard, Michael Ross, Auke Tellegen, Paul Wachtel, and Mark Zanna. Helpful comments on a second draft were received from Derek Besner, Roy Cameron, Allan Cheyne, Thomas Davidson, Jane Dywan, Sid Segalowitz, Gary Waller, and Erik Woody. Claude Balthazard, Barney Gilmore, and Donald Meichenbaum each read two drafts of the chapter. Thank you all. I would like to extend a special appreciation to my wife Patricia, who read all the drafts, and lots more in between, and who frequently offered her encouragement and approval of what I was trying to do despite the awkwardness of initial and interim attempts to formulate my ideas.

The writing of this chapter and the research reported in the final section of it were supported by a Social Sciences and Humanities Research Council Grant No. 410-81-0278-R1.

We can begin, then, with a simple assertion: Determinants of thought and action that are not noticed or appreciated as such constitute unconscious influences. Surely this rather broad and descriptive formulation does not commit us to any particular theory of unconsciousness, or even to any particular locus of unconscious influence. Indeed, our descriptive formulation is consistent with a Freudian notion of unconscious influence that is largely intrapsychic (the repressed unconscious); but as well, it is consistent with more contemporary (e.g., social cognition) accounts which emphasize how external conditions exercise unconscious influence over thought and behavior (e.g., Nisbett & Wilson, 1977; Nisbett & Ross, 1980). Moreover, either psychoanalysis or social cognition could be wrong in small or major ways without in the least detracting from the basic proposition that thought and action have unconscious determinants. Indeed, as already indicated, I wish to argue that such a claim is *necessarily* true, and is therefore not subject to empirical refutation.

Even though I argue that unconscious influences are logically presupposed by human thought and action, this does not make such influences psychologically uninteresting; it simply means that we must turn investigative attention from questions about whether unconscious influences exist to their modus operandi. With this goal in mind, I argue that there are two generic modes of unconscious influence: Influences that go unnoticed, and influences that are unappreciated as such. Accordingly, the first section of the chapter introduces a critical distinction between perceiving and noticing, whereby important determinants of thought and action can be unconscious by virtue of being perceived without being noticed. The relevance of this perceiving-noticing distinction will then be indicated for experimental investigations of subliminal perception and memory on the one hand, and for clinical notions of dissociation and repression on the other.

The second section of the chapter indicates how actual determinants of thinking and behavior can be noticed, but nevertheless remain unappreciated as influential. Such uncomprehended influences are in effect unconscious, and the close relationship between comprehension and consciousness will be drawn out at some length. It is in this section that we will confront an epistemological dilemma, the upshot of which is that unconscious determinants of thought and action are not merely an empirical possibility, but a logical necessity.

Implicit in this epistemological dilemma is the insufficiency of introspection and even of controlled experiment to render an indisputable account of human thought and action. Recognition of these insufficiencies segues into the third and final section of the chapter, which considers the role of intuition in comprehension and the growth of knowledge. Among other things, I argue that intuition implies perception of an emerging coherence which is not yet noticed, but which nevertheless informs thought in productive and occasionally profound ways. In effect, the section on intuition will bring us around full circle to the possibilities for perceiving and responding to things tacitly, that is, without consciously noticing the basis for thought and action.

One final introductory comment is in order. There are clearly a plethora of processes that guide and regulate our behavior—processes such as synaptic transmission, pupillary dilation, and underlying mechanisms of perception and memory—that are unconscious while nevertheless contributing importantly to our conduct and welfare. For the most part, however, this chapter is less concerned with the unconscious mechanisms of information processing than with the information that is unconsciously processed. Still, it is sometimes difficult to make such hard and fast distinctions in practice, and we will have occasion to consider the processing of information insofar as it is pertinent to understanding how information can be both influential and unconscious.

THE UNCONSCIOUS AS THE UNNOTICED

Even the most unreconstructed behaviorist would readily concede that a stimulus has to be perceived in order to reinforce and shape behavior. But such a person would steadfastly reject the claim that a perceived stimulus has to be consciously represented in order to be an effective mover and shaper of behavior. In other words, for an arch behaviorist, consciousness of a stimulus is not implied by the perception of it. Rather, consciousness of a stimulus is considered to be only one possible effect of perceiving it, and is in no way necessary for the environmental control over behavior. In more contemporary terms, there is an important distinction to be made between the information processed, and awareness or consciousness of the processed information.

In an especially helpful and integrative article, Lars-Gunnar Lundh (1979) recognized this fact by arguing that "the failure to distinguish clearly between perceptions, thoughts and feelings, on the one hand, and introspective awareness of these perceptions, thoughts and feelings on the other hand is a major source of confusion in psychology" (p. 227). Implicit in this distinction is the notion that perception is not a singular, either/or event, but a multistage process that takes place over time (Erdelyi, 1974). One stage of this process involves selectively attending a perceived stimulus, and it is selective attention that transforms a perception into consciousness of what is perceived (Lundh, 1979). To facilitate exposition, I will henceforth use the term "perceived" when referring to information that is registered and influential, and reserve the term "noticed" for perceived information that is, in addition, selectively attended (i.e., consciously perceived).

The distinction between perceived and noticed information has several implications and consequences. First of all, it is clear that perceived information is logically prior to noticed information. It does not make sense to talk of information that is noticed without being perceived, whereas the whole point of the perception-noticing distinction is to acknowledge and emphasize the possibility that information can be perceived without being noticed. Second, the distinction at issue is clearly warranted on evolutionary grounds. Surely lower forms of life must in some sense perceive their environment in order to survive; yet it seems unwarranted to assume that ants and flatworms, say, notice (i.e., consciously perceive) the environment to which they respond.

Third, in addition to being logically and evolutionarily prior to noticing, perceiving is temporally prior as well. There is both phenomenological and experimental evidence to support the temporal priority of perceiving over noticing. At the phenomenological level, perhaps the reader has had the same experience as I have—of repeatedly checking the time on an unfamiliar clock before noticing that the clock face was inscribed with roman numerals rather than arabic numbers. Moreover, we often notice a headache or hunger after it has taken hold, for example, after the end of an exciting football game. Experimentally, there is ample evidence that consciousness of a stimulus requires its prior storage in short-term memory, which is itself something that occurs after initial registration of the stimulus in the nervous system. We briefly examine some of this experimental evidence relating consciousness and short-term memory below.

Fourth, the distinction between perceiving and noticing implies some functional independence of these two stages of information processing. In particular, it has been argued that the threshold for noticing a stimulus is higher than the threshold for perceiving it (Lundh, 1979; Simonton, 1980), and that the noticing threshold is more (or at least more obviously) influenced by motivational (Erdelyi, 1974; Sackeim, Nordlie, & Gur, 1979) and expectational (Neisser, 1976) factors, and by the extent and depth of a person's involvement in alternate activities (Triesman & Geffen, 1967).

Fifth, there is no reason to believe that information must be noticed before it can influence thought and conduct. At least some information can be influential when it is merely perceived. Indeed, what it means to perceive a stimulus without noticing it is that the stimulus has some measurable impact on the organism, even though it is not consciously experienced. Nevertheless, as we shall later see, information often needs to be noticed before it can fully inform thought and action (Lundh, 1979).

Finally, there are different criteria for classifying information that is perceived on the one hand, and noticed on the other. Noticed information is something that can generally be verbally reported; this is of course not the case for perceived information that is not noticed. As Lundh (1979) phrased it, "Introspective reports do not tell us about what the subject perceives, but only about what the subject is introspectively aware of having perceived. The criterion of what is perceived is not introspective, but behavioral in a wider sense" (p. 228–229). Some behavioral criteria for perceived but unnoticed stimuli have been reaction times (Posner & Snyder, 1975), word associations (Spence, 1964), dreams (Poetzl, 1917/1960), affective responses (Zajonc, 1980), physiological measures (Corteen and Wood, 1972; Shevrin & Fritzler, 1968), and so on.

Modes of Unconscious Influence

Having introduced the possibility that information can be perceived without being noticed, it is appropriate to explore more fully some of the complexities of this perceiving-noticing distinction. One way of pursuing this issue is to document its importance in several different investigative domains. Hence I discuss the perceiving-noticing distinction as it emerges in four different contexts: (1) subliminal perception, (2) memory, (3) dissociation, and (4) repression. I address each of these modes of unconscious influence in turn, but I am especially concerned with the issue of subliminal perception. One reason for this concentration of effort is that subliminal perception has a prototypic but highly controversial status as *the* unconscious influence par excellence (Dixon, 1971, 1981). Perhaps an even more important reason for focusing on subliminal perception is that many critical investigations of it have not been informed by the perceiving-noticing distinction. The consequence of this conceptual oversight is that empirical work on subliminal perception has been curiously inconclusive—thereby perpetrating a 30-year controversy that is still being waged.

Subliminal Perception

What is unusual about the literature on subliminal perception is that it has continuously debated whether or not such a phenomenon even exists—with some protagonists to the debate arguing vociferously that there is as yet no convincing evidence that it does (Eriksen, 1959, 1960; Merikle, 1982), and others arguing that the evidence in favor of subliminal perception is overwhelming (e.g., Dixon, 1971, 1981; Wolitsky & Wachtel, 1973). I have no intention of reviewing the reams of empirical evidence that are relevant to this issue; rather I attempt to indicate how evidence has had less to do with the hardened positions on this debate than is generally assumed. My position is that the debate has been fueled for the most part by conceptual and definitional disagreements, and that progress must be made at this level before subliminal perception can even be sensibly addressed as an empirical issue. It is convenient for this purpose to take a somewhat historical approach to the issue by examining with special closeness a critical analysis of subliminal perception proferred by one of its early detractors.

There can be little doubt that Charles Eriksen's late 1950s and early 1960s analysis of subliminal perception in particular, and unconscious perception in general, withered investigative interest in the phenomenon. Not only did Eriksen mount a daunting critique of subliminal perception, he offered an alternative interpretation of the available evidence which satisfied most people that unconscious perception had no part in generating the allegedly subliminal effects. Eriksen's (1959, 1960) analyses of unconscious perception still make compelling reading 25 years after they were written, and continue to be cited favorably by contemporary investigators of the phenomena (e.g., Merikle, 1982). In what follows, however, I raise some problematic aspects of Eriksen's critique, while acknowledging that even the ways in which it can be found wanting are nevertheless informative.

In one of his papers on subliminal perception, Ericken (1960) states that

at present there is no convincing evidence that the human organism can discriminate or differentially respond to external stimuli that are at an intensity level too low to elicit discriminated verbal report. In other words, a verbal report is as sensitive an indicator of perception as any other response that has been studied. (p. 298)

And, toward the end of an earlier paper on the same subject, Eriksen (1959) equates "awareness with verbalization, [so that] by definition,...any verbal judgment is one made with awareness" (p. 203). Thus Eriksen's position is that there is no more discriminating response than verbal report, *and* that such discriminative verbal reports are a sufficient criterion for awareness of what is perceived. However, as becomes evident elsewhere in the 1959 paper, verbal discrimination is not a necessary condition for awareness. Just why this is true requires elaboration.

As Dulany and Eriksen (1959) demonstrated, the detection threshold as determined by verbal report is lower than a comparable threshold determined by GSR. This outcome is, however, completely consistent with the fact that GSR will sometimes successfully discriminate the presence/absence of a stimulus that is not successfully discriminated by verbal report. This so-called subception effect (Lazarus & McLeary, 1951) is a psychological fact that Eriksen did not question. What he did dispute focused on how to interpret the subception effect.

Eriksen (1959) himself is quite clear about alternative interpretations of such effects. He states, "In keeping with the definition of awareness in terms of verbalization, this result would certainly suggest the human organism is capable of making discriminations beyond awareness" (p. 196), and that such effects are in fact the clinician's basis for an "inference of unconscious processes or defense mechanisms at work" (p. 202). From Eriksen's point of view, however, the occasional superiority of nonverbal (e.g., affective) discriminations over verbal ones "focuses attention upon the limitations of verbal responses in conveying the individual's perceptual experience" (p. 201).

Eriksen's position seems to be that perceptual experience is *by definition* conscious, and that if verbal report is occasionally insufficient to communicate such experience, then so much the worse for verbal report as an indicator of what the person consciously perceives and discriminates. Moreover, since perceptual experience is inferred from discriminative responses, any such response, verbal or nonverbal, is *by definition* a reflection of a person's conscious experience. Consequently, when verbal response does not successfully discriminate and other response indices do, it is taken as evidence for the inadequacy of language to communicate conscious experience, *not* as evidence for unconscious perception.

If I have adequately (if briefly) characterized Eriksen's position, it seems clear that there is a contradiction at the heart of his argument. He seems to argue that *any* verbal or nonverbal discrimination is, in effect, evidence of conscious perceptual experience. However, such a position means that subliminal perception is a *logical* impossibility, since any evidence for discriminative responsiveness is de facto evidence for conscious (i.e., supraliminal) perception.[1] But if subliminal perception is logically impossible, then its existence is not an empirical issue, despite all of Eriksen's attempts to resolve the issue empirically. In other words, Eriksen's explicit commitment to the empirical resolution of whether subliminal perception exists is at loggerheads with his implicit commitment to the notion that any discriminative response to a stimulus reflects conscious perception.

But that is not all. It is clear that Eriksen forwards the forced-choice, verbal discrimination threshold as a sufficient indicator of awareness because it affords a relatively unambiguous and precise operational definition of an otherwise slippery notion. By committing himself to this methodological definition of awareness, however, he must reject as irrelevant to the entire issue of subliminal perception a plethora of investigations which (even then) indicated that people can verbally discriminate stimuli without any conscious experience of seeing or noticing the discriminated stimuli. Thus Eriksen (1959) states that "an equation of awareness with verbalization, by definition, means that any verbal judgment is one made with awareness irrespective of whether the subject has little or no confidence in the judgment" (p. 203).

There are reasons for questioning Eriksen's position on this matter, however. Consider the distinction between perceiving and noticing introduced earlier in this chapter. This distinction implies that people can in fact perceive and respond discriminatively to information that is not consciously noticed. Furthermore, there is nothing intrinsic to the perceiving-noticing distinction which disallows the possibility of unconscious perception being more faithfully indexed by a discriminative verbal response than by a nonverbal (e.g., affective) response. What this possibility implies, however, is that the epistemological status of a discriminative verbal *response*, indicating the presence or absence of a stimulus, is similar to that of a discriminative GSR response, and that both of these responses are epistemoligially distinct from introspective verbal *reports* regarding the person's consciousness of his or her perceptual experience (Natsoulas, 1967; Lundh, 1979). In other words, whereas a discriminative response (of whatever kind) implies only that a stimulus has been perceived, a verbal (introspective) report implies that the perceptual basis of the discrimination has been noticed. The distinction between discriminative (e.g., verbal) responses and introspective verbal reports preserves the possibility that verbal responses may discriminate better than nonverbal indices. However, this superiority of verbal over nonverbal discrimination can occur without in any way implying that the verbal discrimination threshold suffices as an index of conscious perception. Indeed, discriminative verbal responses may well be achieved without conscious awareness in the very same way and for the very same reasons that perception can occur without noticing.

Empirically this possibility for verbal discrimination without consciously noticing the perceptual basis for it has been dramatically documented by the so-called "blind-sight" phenomena (Weiskrantz, Warrington, Sanders & Marshall, 1974). Briefly, these investigators assessed brain-damaged patients suffering lesions in Area 17 of the visual cortex, resulting in circumscribed scotomas. In one case study, a patient was extensively studied on various discrimination tasks, and was able to discriminate between stimuli at above chance levels. Despite his success, "he was at a loss for words to describe any conscious perception, and repeatedly stressed that he saw nothing at all in the sense of 'seeing,' and that he was merely guessing" (Weiskrantz et al., 1974, p. 721). One implication of this finding is that different parts of the brain may be responsible for detection of stimuli on the one hand, and consciousness of them on the other. Indeed, there is current evidence (e.g., Perenin & Jeannerod, 1975) for a "two visual system" hypothesis, initially proposed by Trevarthen (1968, 1970), which is at least consistent with the notion that lower brain centers are responsible for a preliminary registration of visual information, and that cortical areas may be more important for integrating visual information into awareness. While aspects of this two-visual system hypothesis remain controversial (Campion, Lotto, & Smith, 1983), its relevance for the present problem is obvious.

Although organic damage to the brain may reveal dissociations of perception and awareness most clearly, other literature points to the possibility of a functional dissociation of these mental processes. Hilgard (1977) has explored the importance of such dissociations in hypnosis generally, and others have proposed a similar dissociative account for hysterical (as well as for hypnotically suggested) blindness (Sackeim et al., 1979). What this literature indicates is that verbally discriminated stimuli cannot automatically be assumed to reflect conscious awareness of what is perceived.

In sum, Eriksen's critique of unconscious (or subliminal) perception is not entirely persuasive, (1) because it implies that subliminal perception is logically impossible (and is therefore not an empirical issue), and (2) because it definitionally conflates the critically important distinction between a discriminative verbal response and consciousness of what is perceived (as determined by introspective reports of awareness).

Whereas Eriksen's analysis renders subliminal perception logically impossible, one of its chief defenders turns subliminal perception into a logical necessity. N.F. Dixon (1971) argues that "the most important feature of subliminal perception is *not* that people can respond to stimulation below the awareness threshold, but that they can respond to stimuli of which, *for one reason or another,* they are unaware" (p. 13; italics in original). Thus subliminal perception occurs even when the subject "reports awareness of the stimulus, and of making a response, but professes complete ignorance of any contingency between the two" (p. 13). In other words, subliminal perception is simply a synonym for unconscious responsiveness to external stimulation, however achieved. As I later argue, however, such unconscious responsiveness is a logical necessity. If that is so, then subliminal perception, qua unconscious responsiveness, is also logically necessary.

Clearly, if subliminal perception is to have empirical meaning, neither Eriksen's position nor Dixon's will do. Yet in their own ways, each of these investigators has, at different times, virtually defined the status of subliminal perception for the entire field. In view of the conceptual complexities surrounding the investigation of subliminal perception, future research in the area should keep two important issues in mind: (a) subliminal stimulation must involve some independent assessment of an awareness threshold, (b) below which discriminative responses (verbal or nonverbal) can subsequently be demonstrated.

Granted, this solution leaves open the difficult question of how to define and operationally assess an awareness threshold. Thus Eriksen (1959) argues that "as long as we rely upon the subject himself to report whether or not a verbal judgment was made with awareness, we are in fact using as many different criteria of awareness as we have experimental subjects" (p. 204). As we have seen, Eriksen's solution to this difficulty is simply to define the problem away by identifying the discriminative verbal response as a sufficient condition for awareness. This solution does have the merit of methodological simplicity and precision, but it does so by ignoring the crucial distinction between perceiving and noticing. Perhaps a somewhat facetious illustration will help indicate just what is at stake here.

Consider the differences between optometry and psychology vis-à-vis the problem of vision. Visitors to an optometrist are invariably confronted with an eye chart, and asked to identify alphabetic features that become smaller and smaller with each succeeding line. The myopic among us (and they are legion) very soon find themselves at sea trying to decipher these letters, thereby informing the optometrist about the lens correction required for normal vision. Enter T-scopic psychologist, with a claim that the patient can really see much better than his performance on the eye chart implies. To prove his point, the psychologist introduces said patient to a forced choice discrimination paradigm. That is, the patient is not asked to identify which one of 26 alphabetic features is being presented; rather, he or she is forced to choose on a succession of trials whether a particular feature is an O or a W, a D or a Q, an H or an L, and so on. With letters of the size failed on the optometrist's eye chart (or even smaller), chances are good that the patient will perform very well on such a forced-choice test of vision. Indeed, it is likely that high accuracy can be achieved even though the patient may express little or no decision confidence on many of the trials (Cheesman & Merikle, 1982).

While the psychologist would certainly have demonstrated the ability of myopes to discriminate visual information they were unable to identify on the eye chart, surely it is a Pyrrhic victory over his optometrist colleague. For clearly, the optometrist's criterion of what constitutes "seeing" is far more appropriate to an ecologically complex world than is the psychologist's highly simplified, forced-choice criterion. Indeed, if the psychologist's criterion of what constituted seeing should prevail, we had all best take to the hills, and avoid the highways and byways of the nation, lest squinty-eyed graduates of the forced-choice school of vision drive their automobiles in—and often into—ecological complexity.

The implication of this illustration is that consciousness of what is perceived is frequently necessary for effective adaptation to an ecologically complex world. A rough and ready criterion for such consciousness is that a person be able to *identify* specific features from an indeterminately large set of them. Adopting such a criterion may complicate the researcher's life somewhat, but so be it; the alternative of garroting conceptual subtlety with method-ease, has, in the case of subliminal perception, obscured more than it has revealed. Indeed, the critical methodological decision to identify conscious perception with the ability to discriminate in a forced-choice paradigm (unwittingly) rendered subliminal perception logically impossible, while at the same time interring the crucial distinction between perceiving and noticing. It is time to redress this state of affairs, at least to the extent of permitting subliminal perception the empirical possibility of being genuine.

Memory

There is an interesting distinction between perception and memory that has had compelling implications for models of the mind. To the uninitiated, it seems at least possible that perception is a singular, either-or event; what is "out there" either gets perceived, or it does not. Indeed, one of the reasons subliminal perception may have been so suspect is that it implies a kind of two-stage process of perceiving (preconscious and conscious perception) that does not square with this either-or model. So it is that as late as 1974, Matthew Erdelyi felt it necessary to remind us, in a frequently cited article, that perception is a multistage rather than a single-stage process, and that a sequence of microevents occurs in the process of perceiving even simple features.

Memory, on the other hand, is patently a two-stage process: first there is the occurrence of an event to be remembered, and then there is the memory of the event's occurrence. It is true that when the time between the occurrence and recall of an event is very short, the distinction between memory and perception, especially conscious perception, begins to blur. Nevertheless, under ordinary conditions there are all sorts of things a person can do to aid memory, such as paying close attention to information when it occurs, memorizing or rehearsing material that is extended and complex, and so on. Less clear perhaps, but no less important, are the things people do to forget unpleasant or threatening events that would otherwise haunt or preoccupy the unwilling mnemonist.

Memory then, far more than perception, immediately suggests the extent of a person's contributions to his or her experience of the world. While Freud capitalized on this feature of memory for his theories of personality and psychopathology, recent work in memory has further enriched our understanding about how we retain our past in our present. Consequently, I begin this section with a highly foreshortened review of some of this recent work as it is relevant to the perception-noticing distinction. The reader should be forewarned, however, that the research in memory is very active, and as far as I can tell, there is very little consensus about how best to understand it. What follows, therefore, is by no means a received view, and is doubtless wrong in some of its particulars. It nevertheless seems important to address the issue of memory, even if in a foreshortened, oversimplified way, since it turns out to be so congenial to the view that perceiving and noticing are distinct events in the course of our adaptation to the world.

Although there are different views of just how memory works (see Kihlstrom, this book), many theorists agree that there is a convenient dichotomy to be made between short-term memory on the one hand, and long-term memory on the other (see, however, Lewis, 1979, for a somewhat different view). Furthermore, there seems to be agreement that there is an intimate relationship between short-term memory and consciousness. Some theorists (e.g., Atkinson & Shiffrin, 1968) proposed that information in short-term memory is de facto information in consciousness, and others (e.g., Ericcson & Simon, 1980) seem to imply that information in long-term memory store which is selectively attended ("heeded") is thereby transferred into short-term memory. The specifics of the relationship between short-term memory and consciousness thus still seems to be somewhat a matter of theoretical preference, and in that spirit, I prefer Lundh's (1979) view that information becomes conscious when (1) it is processed to the level of short-term memory and (2) its residence there is selectively attended. Finally, information can enter into short-term memory in two ways: either newly perceived information must be processed to the level of short-term memory, or information from long-term memory must be temporarily transferred into short-term storage before it can become part of one's conscious experience.

A frequently used technique to study the relationship of short-term memory to consciousness involves dichotic listening, wherein a person repeats word for word (shadows) information presented to an attended channel. The fate of information presented to the unattended channel is the major question of interest. It is clear that unattended information is simply lost to recall under conditions in which subjects continue to shadow for some time after the target information is presented on the unattended channel (e.g., Norman, 1969; Glucksberg & Cowen, 1970). Even though long-term memory for material presented on the unattended channel is seriously impaired, short-term memory remains more or less intact, since if shadowing is discontinued within a few seconds after the unattended information is presented, recall for this information is quite good.

This pattern of evidence suggests the following interpretation: Shadowing the attended material requires virtually all of a person's selective attention (Kahneman, 1973). Consequently, when shadowing continues long after the target material is presented on the unattended channel, there is no opportunity to selectively attend this material in order to make it conscious. Moreover, since the target material is not selectively attended, it cannot be rehearsed or in other ways processed into long-term memory storage (Norman, 1976). Since the target material has faded from short-term storage without ever being transferred into long-term storage, it is simply unavailable for later recall. If, however, shadowing is terminated immediately after presentation of target material on the unattended channel, and prior to its fading from short-term memory store, selective attention can be switched to the previously unattended material, thereby making it conscious and available to recall. In sum, consciousness of information depends critically on selective attention to it.

Nevertheless, information need not be conscious in order to be influential. A particularly impressive example of how unattended information can be influential without being selectively attended or consciously recalled was reported by MacKay (1973). In this experiment, subjects wore headphones and were asked to repeat word for word (shadow) short sentences presented to one ear, while ignoring any material presented to the other ear. The shadowed sentences were ambiguous, and could be interpreted in one of two ways. For example, the sentence "They threw stones toward the bank yesterday" can be interpreted quite differently depending on how the word "bank" is understood—either as a river bank, or as a place where money is kept. Every time an ambiguous word appeared on the attended channel, another word, which resolved or "disambiguated" the meaning of the shadowed sentence (e.g., the word "river" or "money") was simultaneously presented on the unattended channel. After shadowing 28 such sentences, subjects were presented with the two disambiguated renditions for each of the original ambiguous sentences, and asked to select the alternative which was recognizably closer to their initial understanding of the sentence.

For ambiguities of the type illustrated above, interpretation of the sentences was significantly shifted in the direction of the disambiguating word presented on the unattended channel.[2] This shift occurred despite the fact that subjects were unable to recall the words presented on the unattended channel. Since the unattended words statistically "tilted" the interpretation of the ambiguous sentences with which they were associated, the assumption is that they must have been processed or analyzed to the level of short-term memory. However, the disambiguating words were not selectively attended, and underwent rapid decay without ever being transferred into long-term memory. Consequently, the unattended information was simply unavailable for subsequent recall.

The rather striking implication of MacKay's (1973) finding and others related to it (e.g., Lackner & Garret, 1972; cf., however, Newstead & Dennis, 1979) is that the transmission of an event's influence through time need not depend upon memory for its initial occurrence; rather, the immediate impact of unattended information may be to bias or skew perceptions, thoughts, and conduct. These effects may themselves be selectively attended and therefore subject to recall, despite the fact that the biasing influence itself can not be remembered. In other words, the human condition spawns more history than memory. A historical event that is unattended and unnoticed can nevertheless be perceived, thereby skewing conscious perception, thought, and action beyond any possibility for recall of the biasing event itself. We will shortly return to this possibility for history without memory.

To summarize, information perceived and processed to the level of short-term memory need not be selectively attended (i.e., noticed) in order to have a demonstrable impact on behavior. Moreover, since unnoticed information is not apt to be processed into long-term memory,[3] it is probably unavailable to later recall attempts. In effect then, whenever an influence has faded from short-term memory without having been selectively attended or transferred into long-term memory, it constitutes a de facto unconscious influence.

As we have seen, experimental inquiry has contributed, either directly or by default, to our understanding of the distinction between perception and noticing. It has pursued these investigations with the tools at its disposal, such as tachistoscopes and tape recorders. Indeed, it is the very nature of the experimental method to administer standard (and frequently frustrating, arduous, or boring) procedures to which the patient subject dutifully responds. By contrast, it is the nature of clinical inquiry to subject patients to close scrutiny of a different kind—one that is less concerned with standardized procedures, and more concerned with the standard sorts of situations that the patient ordinarily generates for himself (Bowers, 1977a). In order to pursue investigations of this kind, the clinician depends heavily on what a patient says and remembers as well as on the accumulation of evidence for things unsaid and forgotten. Indeed, what a person has forgotten can be quite as revealing and influential as what is remembered, or so say clinicians (and novelists) who, far more than experimentalists, have concerned themselves with lapses in memory and consciousness. It is time, therefore, to review briefly two classic views about such mnemonic aberrations, as they have evolved over the last century. One caveat should be entered before doing so, however.

This section has so far been concerned with the so-called perceiving-noticing distinction. In the following discussions of dissociation and repression, the distinction might be better conceived as a memory-noticing distinction. In other words, the locus of influence is going to shift from external, experimentally controlled information, to internal, self-generated information that can be noticed or not, depending on whether it is selectively attended. While there are surely important differences between monitoring external and internal information, here we will not make much of the distinction.

Dissociation

That doyen of the unconscious, Fyodor Dostoyevsky, early in *The Brothers Karamazov,* describes a picture by the Russian painter Kramskoy, called "Contemplation." According to Dostoyevsky (1880/1950):

> There is a forest in winter, and on a roadway through the forest, in absolute solitude, stands a peasant in a torn kaftan and bark shoes. He stands, as it were, lost in thought. Yet he is not thinking; he is "contemplating." If anyone touched him he would start and look at one as though awakening and bewildered. It's true he would come to himself immediately, but if he were asked what he had been thinking about, he would remember nothing. Yet probably he has hidden within himself the impression which had dominated him during the period of contemplation. Those impressions are dear to him and no doubt he hoards them imperceptibly, and even unconsciously. How and why, of course, he does not know either. He may suddenly, after hoarding impressions for many years, abandon everything and go off to Jerusalem on a pilgrimage for his soul's salvation, or perhaps he will suddenly set fire to his native village, and perhaps do both. There are a good many "contemplatives" among the peasantry. (p. 150)

Dostoyevsky is here anticipating by several years Pierre Janet's (1889) seminal work on dissociation whereby "an idea, a partial system of thoughts, emancipated itself, became independent and developed itself on its own account" (Janet, 1905/1965; p. 42). According to Janet, such a dissociated system of ideas is not subject to conscious control or reality testing, nor is it (ordinarily) accessible to recall.

Janet invoked heredity to explain the development of dissociated ideas: people prone to such dissociations were constitutionally weak-willed, and simply did not have enough "mental glue" to keep ideas well connected, especially under stressful conditions. For Joseph Breuer, however, this explanation of preexisting mental weakness simply did not wash. His famous case study, Anna O, was anything but weak minded, but she was nevertheless beset by an extraordinary range of pathological dissociative symptoms (Breuer & Freud, 1893–5/1974). In place of Janet's hereditary account of dissociation, Breuer proposed a distinctly psychological explanation, namely, that dissociative phenomena flourished in persons given to hypnoidal states. According to Breuer, consciousness, memory, and critical appraisal of thoughts and fantasies were impaired for the duration of such altered states of mind. The cause of pathogenic hypnoidal states might be a variety of things, ranging from intense fatigue, affect, very high or low arousal, and so forth.

When the above understanding was applied to Anna O, Breuer pointed out that

> this girl, who was bubbling over with intellectual vitality, led an extremely monotonous existence in her puritanically-minded family. She embellished her life in a manner which probably influenced her decisively in the direction of her illness, by indulging in systematic day-dreaming, which she described as her "private theatre." While everyone thought she was attending, she was living through fairy tales in her imagination; but she was always on the spot when she was spoken to, so that no one was aware of it. She pursued this activity almost continuously while she was engaged on her household duties. (p. 74)

It was this habit for engaging in reverie and daydreaming that set the stage, so to speak, for more profoundly dissociative reactions that occurred as Anna O became increasingly fatigued and frantic with anxiety while she nursed her dying father. In other words, Anna O's increasingly distraught images and fantasies were processed in an altered (hypnoidal) state of mind, and were therefore not subject to recall, conscious control, or reality testing. Instead, these dissociated ideas were irrationally expressed in a panoply of symptoms, in much the same way that a posthypnotic response expresses a previously administered hypnotic suggestion.

In many ways, Joseph Breuer was an early exponent of a "state-specific" view of learning and memory that has increasingly been recognized as an important psychological phenomenon (Overton, 1977). The basic insight here is that the state of mind affects the fate of mental contents, at least insofar as memory of them is concerned. Thus information initially processed in a sad emotional state is much easier to recall in a subsequent sad state than in a subsequent happy state (Bower, 1981), and information processed in a drug state is often more memorable in a similar drug state induced later on than it was during an intervening nondrug state (Swanson & Kinsbourne, 1979).

While it is true that emotional arousal, fatigue, or drugs may generate dissociative reactions of pathological dimensions, there are less extreme, everyday examples of dissociative phenomena that are worth exploring briefly. Consider the experience of reading a book, and suddenly realizing that none of the material has registered for a considerable period of time. When something like this happens, we often say that a person has been lost in thought. Ordinarily, people look upon such interpolated reveries as "off-target" interruptions, and give no thought to recalling them, but instead refocus attention on the material to be read. Clearly, under these circumstances, it is unlikely that the person will ever recall the reveries, since they have not been selectively attended, nor is it likely that they have been processed into long-term memory. Thus reveries or contemplations can be unconscious in the sense that they simply are not selectively attended, and hence remain unnoticed. This state of affairs is very much like the one prevailing in the dichotic listening task mentioned above, except that in the latter case, the lost information is in the form of external information, whereas in the case of reveries, the information at issue is one's own ideas and fantasies.

What happens when a person suddenly realizes that he or she has not been reading, but "contemplating," and decides quickly to shift attention to interior fantasies and reveries? It is clear that considerable recovery of these background fantasies can take place (Freud, 1908/1959; Beck, 1976). However, informal experiments in various classes I have taught suggest that people sometimes have considerable difficulty recovering their interpolated reveries in pretty much the same way that people ordinarily have difficulty recovering their night dreams. It is not at all clear that affect, fatigue, or drugs is operative in these cases of forgetting; rather, it seems to be more a matter of memories being unable to penetrate a "dissociative barrier" (Hilgard, 1977) that is established between the mental organization of an uncritical, unfocused state of mind (in which the fantasies were initially processed) and the mental organization of alert, focused consciousness (which prevails at the time of attempted recall).

It is difficult to determine experimentally whether such unnoticed (dissociated) background fantasies have an impact on the conscious thought and action of the contemplative, but it would be odd if they were entirely impotent in this regard. For example, Freud (1908/1959) told of a patient who was walking down a street and suddenly, inexplicably, broke into tears. Being psychologically minded, the woman quickly reflected back on her state of mind just prior to the crying jag. Although she had not noticed it at the time of occurrence, the woman now recalled having been preoccupied with a highly organized and morose daydream in which she had been first seduced, then impregnated, and finally abandoned by a local pianist who in reality she had never met. Currently, cognitive therapists argue that depression often follows morose and self-derogating fantasies and self-talk of which the patient is largely unaware until instructed to selectively attend the interior flow of fantasy and dialogue (Beck, 1976; Meichenbaum, 1977).

As in the case of unattended information in the dichotic listening paradigm, unattended and unnoticed fantasies or daydreams may well have a psychological impact extending well beyond the person's ability to recall the interior events that initially stimulated it. For example, if the immediate impact of a morose abandonment fantasy is to bias one's self-esteem negatively and to arouse sadness, these effects, themselves subject to selective attention and consciousness, may endure and influence subsequent thought and conduct long after the fantasies stimulating them have become unavailable to recall.

We have here another possibility for history without memory, in which internal fantasies and preoccupations can skew or bias life events. The effects of such biasing may be painfully conscious, while the biasing influence itself remains beyond conscious recall. Attempts to recall such initially unattended mental events may nevertheless proceed, and yield the illusion of memory in the form of confident confabulation. It can only be speculated how often this occurs in some forms of psychotherapy that emphasize the recall of fantasies or memories.

Repression

Thus far there has been no mention of motivational factors in forgetting. Traditionally, motivated forgetting has been referred to as repression, which first became recognized by Sigmund Freud in the book *Studies on Hysteria* (1893–1895/1974) written with his mentor, Joseph Breuer.

In this book Freud raised significant doubts about Breuer's state-specific views of hysteria (so-called hypnoid hysteria) and instead argued for what he termed defense hysteria, in which patients actively resisted recall of memories that were painful. One of his earliest case illustrations of this resistance was in the person of Fraulein Elizabeth von R, who was quite dilatory in complying with Freud's admonitions to let images and ideas just well up in consciousness. The patient's persistent noncompliance with this strategy of recall represented a continuing effort by Elizabeth von R to keep out of consciousness the eroticized affection she felt for her sister's husband. The original rejection of erotic ideas and feelings from consciousness Freud termed repression; resistance referred to the patient's countertherapeutic efforts to maintain the unconscious status of this idea-feeling complex.

What distinguishes repression from ordinary forgetting is the same thing that makes it problematic for many critics—namely, the motivated and selective forgetting of painful or unacceptable ideas—since such forgetting implies a paradoxical awareness of precisely those ideas to be excluded from consciousness. It is as if one has to notice and be conscious of something in order to become unconscious of it.

Interestingly, Freud early in his career recognized this problem and finessed it rather straightforwardly. For example, in his commentary on Elizabeth von R, Freud states that "the patient did not become clearly conscious of her feelings for her brother-in-law, powerful though they were, except on a few occasions, and then only momentarily" (p. 236). He later states that "at least *one* moment of this kind must have occurred. Consciousness, plainly, does not know in advance when an incompatible idea is going to crop up. The incompatible idea . . . must originally have been in communication with the main stream of thought" (p. 238). Thus Freud eliminates the paradoxical features of repression by recognizing that it is a process that takes place through time, and that a prior if brief awareness of the painful material is necessary for its subsequent exclusion from consciousness.

A related issue concerns the frequent assumption that the actual process of repression must itself be unconscious, since conscious effort to forget something would presumably serve as a potent redintegrative cue for the very idea that the person is trying to forget. Consider in this context an editorial footnote to Freud's comment that a patient "wished to forget, and therefore intentionally repressed" (Breuer & Freud, 1893–1895/1974, p. 61). The editor cautions the reader that "the word 'intentionally,' in these instances, merely indicates the existence of a motive and carries no implication of *conscious* intention" (p. 61). Evidently, the editor is here trying to help Freud avoid the apparent paradox of unconscious forgetting that is consciously produced, and he does so by redefining Freud's words in a somewhat idiosyncratic fashion.

However, it is not at all clear that the editor need have bothered. As Erdelyi and Goldberg (1979) have indicated in an illuminating paper, there is nothing paradoxical in intending to forget a painful idea, since the act of forgetting can itself be submitted to the same process of mental evasion as the original idea. "This constitutes nothing other than an intrapsychic version of the 'cover-up of the cover-up,' hardly a novel notion in this post-Watergate era" (p. 366). Moreover, there may be yet other ways in which repression can serve to keep something out of consciousness. It is possible, for instance, that the act of avoiding an idea, though quite conscious at the outset, can with repetition become a habitual and eventually an automatized act that is no longer subject to conscious awareness (LaBerge, 1975).

Finally, there may even be ways in which an idea can be repressed without ever having appeared in consciousness at all, at least as a personally relevant concern. Consider, for example, that a movie can generate an impending sense that "something awful" is going to happen, even if it doesn't telegraph precisely what that "something" is going to be. One could, at that point, walk out of the theater, thereby eliminating any possibility for further knowledge about the specific nature of the threat. Presumably, normal people who go to scary movies do not often leave the film before the horrific coup de grace is delivered, since they know that whatever is eventually depicted on the screen, however ghoulish or grotesque it might be, does not represent a realistic threat to their own personal self-esteem, identity, or existence. In real life, however, this background assurance simply does not exist, so it may indeed be tempting to abort a train of thought in response to early harbingers that "something awful" may soon occur to a person. Once such thought avoidance (repression) has been invoked, the experience of anxiety should be dissipated or eliminated until such time as something occurs to redintegrate the original train of thought (e.g., free association).

The above "early warning" scenario of repression is made possible by the fact that people know about particualr taboos abstractly, without having to experience them in a personally relevant way. Elizabeth von R, for example, surely knew at an abstract level that erotic relationships occurred between adults, and that such relationships might conceivably occur between in-laws, despite social taboos and personal compunctions. At least she could have accepted this possibility as applied to someone besides herself. It was recognizing this abstract possibility as a personal here-and-now issue that was so unacceptable, and which caused her to repress the attraction she felt for her brother-in-law.

Upon reflection, it is difficult to see how repression could take place without some awareness concerning the tabooed status of the repressed idea. For example, a person who had no concept of incest, or who had no idea that it constituted a taboo, would also have no reason to desist either thinking about sexual relations with a consanguineous family member, or acting in accordance with those thoughts—should opportunity and desire coincide. In other words, repression presupposes awareness of the taboo corresponding to the repressed idea.[4] Such a relatively abstract appreciation of tabooed activities is not itself sufficient to trigger repression. However, when a train of thought or fantasy (and associated feelings) begins to portend concrete realization of this taboo in highly personal terms, the stage is set for a full-blown repression—that is, an avoidance of any further thought along such lines.

It should be clear that this conceptualization of repression retains a remnant of the paradox mentioned earlier: a person must be aware of taboos and unacceptable actions at an impersonal, abstract level in order to repress related thoughts and feelings when they threaten to emerge at a very personal level. The full force of the paradox is avoided, however, by a recognition that understanding can go on at different levels simultaneously, such that ideas of unacceptable, tabooed actions—accessible to consciousness at a relatively abstract level—can at the same time be inaccessible to consciousness at the level of concrete, personal significance.

Incidentally, the above comments on repression introduce an issue that will be particularly germane to the final section of this chapter. If repression is in part an avoidant reaction to early portents of a problem as yet undisclosed, then intuition is in part an approach reaction to portents of a solution as yet undiscovered. What both repression and intuition have in common is a presentiment that currently emerging ideas are leading to something important that cannot be fully specified in advance, but which nonetheless generates sufficient emotional valence to determine either avoidant or approach responses (Zajonc, 1980).

THE UNCONSCIOUS AS UNAPPRECIATED OR UNCOMPREHENDED INFLUENCES

Selective attention is the critical process involved in transforming a perceived stimulus into one that is noticed. That is, however, a sense in which the equation of consciousness with noticing is overly restrictive, and does not fully capture what people can be conscious of. For example, simply noticing a stimulus feature or event in no way guarantees appreciation of its influence on thought and action. Such an appreciation requires comprehension (i.e., awareness)[5] of pertinent cause-effect sequences. Moreover, the absence of such comprehension constitutes an extremely important way in which people can remain unconscious of why they behave the way they do.

A particularly graphic illustration of how a stimulus event can be noticed without any appreciation of its influence occurred in my laboratory about 10 years ago when I was conducting studies on the conditioning of picture preferences (Bowers, 1975). A series of postcard reproductions of landscapes and portraits were presented as matched pairs, and subjects were asked on each trial to select whether the landscape or the portrait was preferred. The first 20 trials constituted a baseline condition, during which a subject's natural preference was established. Over the next 90 acquisition trials, I selectively reinforced the subject's initially nonpreferred type of painting. As anticipated, one subject who initially preferred portraits showed an increase in her preference for landscapes as a function of reinforcement. After the conditioning trials were completed, I inquired about her perceptions of the experiment, and the conversation went something like this.

EXPERIMENTER: Did you pick landscapes or portraits more often?

SUBJECT: Landscapes.

EXPERIMENTER: Did you notice whether I said anything during the course of the experiment?

SUBJECT: You said "good" whenever I picked landscapes.

EXPERIMENTER: Do you think your tendency to pick landscapes was influenced by my reinforcement of them?

SUBJECT: Of course not! I picked the landscapes because I liked them better than the portraits. Besides, you only said "good" after I made my choice, so what you said couldn't possibly have influenced my selection of pictures.

Clearly, the subject in the above experiment was able to notice a crucial determinant of her behavior—namely, contingent reinforcement of her painting preferences. Her difficulty was in not appreciating reinforcement *as* determining her preference for landscapes. Presumably, she did not recognize the importance of reinforcement for her selection of paintings because she was not well-informed or sophisticated about the role of reinforcement in shaping behavior. The subject was evidently proceeding on the mistaken assumption that each trial was completely independent of every other trial. Since causes must precede their effects, and since reinforcement always followed her response, she must have reasoned that what I said could not possibly have influenced her selection of landscapes.

Notice that there is nothing irrational or stupid about this line of thinking. Her understanding of the events in question would seem quite reasonable and even compelling to anyone equally uninformed about the nonindependence of the learning trials. However, being unsophisticated or uninformed on this score does not mean that reinforcement has no impact; rather, its influence on thought and/or behavior takes place without the person's comprehension or conscious awareness. In other words, ignorance about the actual impact of a behavioral influence implies that the person's behavior is unknowingly and therefore unconsciously determined by it.

The literature often ignores or confuses the distinction between influences that are unconscious because they are unnoticed, and influences that are unconscious because they are uncomprehended. Recall, for example, that Dixon (1971) invoked the spectre of subliminal perception even under circumstances in which a person was able to notice a response-eliciting stimulus, while nevertheless professing ignorance of its impact on behavior. According to Dixon's view, then, my landscape-preferring subject was being subliminally influenced. By the present analysis, however, subliminal perception should be conceptualized as one particular form of perception sans noticing, rather than as something noticed without comprehension of its effects. In other words, my subject was more a victim of ignorance than of subliminal stimulation.

To summarize, the determinants of thought and behavior are not necessarily as self-evident to consciousness or introspection as they are influential; such determinants can be perceived without being noticed, or noticed without being appreciated as influential. In either case, people's thoughts and actions are determined by factors outside awareness. We are rubbing shoulders here with the "anti-introspectionist" thesis proposed by Nisbett and Wilson in a controversial paper published in 1977. Essentially, these authors argued that people have no direct introspective access to the determinants of their behavior, a notion that seems to many critics both counterintuitive and repugnant. Because Nisbett and Wilson's central proposal is close to mine (and in some measure inspired my thinking about unconscious processes), it is worthwhile to explore rather thoroughly some of the issues that they opened for consideration.

Introspection and Consciousness

Nisbett and Wilson invoked two kinds of empirical evidence in support of their claim that people have no direct or privileged access to the determinants of their behavior.

The first kind of evidence indicated that when people were asked to account for their own behavior, they did not mention certain antecedents that were demonstrably influential, misidentified certain behavioral antecedents as determinative when this was demonstrably not the case, and/or actively rejected the impact of demonstrably influential antecedents when these were proffered by the experimenter as possibly important determinants of the behavior in question.

Perhaps the most graphic and accessible demonstration of these points involved an experiment set up in a shopping mall in which passersby were to judge the quality of five pairs of nylon stockings lined up in a row. After finally selecting the one pair of stockings that seemed superior to the remaining four pairs, subjects were asked why they chose that particular pair of stockings as best. Not surprisingly, the subjects offered a variety of plausible sounding reasons— that is, just the sort of reasons that one would offer in justifying a choice of this sort. People would point to the fact that the stockings they selected were of finer sheer, softer to the touch, lighter and more flattering in color, and so on. In point of fact, however, the stockings were all identical, so that the apparent basis for discriminating the pairs of stockings was more in the eye of the beholder than in the stockings beheld.

What is more, there was a very strong tendency for people to select as superior the pair of stockings that were farthest to the right in the line of five stockings that they were to judge. In other words, the experiment seemed to demonstrate that the participants in the experiment were in fact strongly (but unknowingly) influenced in their judgments by the position that the selected stockings were in relative to the remaining pairs. If, however, the experimenter implied that the subject's selection of the pair of stockings had been influenced by its position, the suggestion was emphatically rejected; after all, the placement a pair of stockings occupies relative to its neighbors is simply not the sort of thing one invokes as a reason for their superior quality.

In sum, the participants in this study offered plausible but erroneous explanations for their choice of a pair of stockings, consistently overlooked the influence of its position on their selection, and rejected out of hand the experimenter's suggestion that the pair of stockings' position may have had something to do with selecting that pair as superior.

The second type of evidence proferred by Nisbett and Wilson in support of their anti-introspectionist thesis is that observers of an act generally identify as its determinants the same antecedents as the actors themselves do (Nisbett & Bellows, 1977). Presumably, private introspections cannot be the basis for the actor's explanation of his or her action if an observer generally arrives at the same account of it. Rather, it seems that observers and actors infer explanations of the latter's behavior from the same publicly available data (e.g., outward behavior, contextual cues, etc.). Specifically, Nisbett and Wilson (1977) argue that both actors and observers explain the actor's behavior in accordance with the cognitive heuristics of representativeness and availability. The representative heuristic relies on the resemblance of an effect to its cause (e.g., attribution of sexual potency to the ingestion of powdered rhinocerous horn). The availability heuristic on the other hand invokes the most immediately available (memorable, salient, vivid) explanation for an effect (e.g., explaining one's irritability as due to a sleepless night). Such representative and availability heuristics are based on a priori causal theories relating action to its determinants. Such theories are generally implicit and unrecognized, are not exposed to critical evaluation, and are therefore often experienced as true, however errant they may prove to be upon independent evaluation.

A corollary of the Nisbett and Wilson (1977) thesis is that when actors happen to provide a correct account of their own actions, it is not because they have privileged introspective access to its determinants. This follows because on those occasions when an actor correctly explains his or her behavior, so too does an observer of it. In other words, both the actor and the observer can be "incidentally correct" (p. 233) in their account of the actor's behavior when there is a coincidental correspondence of the actual determinants of action with representative and/or available explanations of it.

The position outlined by Nisbett and Wilson (1977) and summarized above is controversial because it seems to violate commonsensical ideas about its possibilities for self-knowledge and the conviction that we often and accurately identify the bases for our action (e.g., Smith and Miller, 1978; White, 1980; Ericcson & Simon, 1980). There are indeed some important ways in which Nisbett and Wilson are either mistaken and/or misleading in how they develop their position. We will address these issues in due course. Nevertheless, they are profoundly correct in their major claim that people do not have direct and privileged access to the determinants of their behavior. Moreover, their position is not simply empirically true, but, as we shall see, logically necessary. It therefore provides the strongest possible foundation for the importance of unconscious influences in everyday life.

A Reexamination of the Nisbett-Wilson Position

Let us consider what can be meant by the claim that people do not have privileged introspective access to the determinants of their own behavior, and that introspection is not a "fount of privileged information." This is clearly the central and at the same time most counterintuitive claim made by Nisbett and Wilson (1977). At several places in their paper, the authors refer to introspection as being an "interrogation of memories" regarding why one behaved in a particular fashion. What can such an interrogation reveal? Surely it can recall to mind various events that occurred prior to the behavior to be explained. Sometimes these recalled antecedents may in fact be determinants of the behavior in question, but sometimes not. Surely there is no reason in principle why an interrogation of memory will *necessarily* lead to recall of the determining antecedents of the behavior. Indeed we have already seen that at least some such determinants will forever escape recovery, because they were insufficiently attended and processed in the first place. These determinants are not merely inaccessible to ordinary attempts at recovery, but are unavailable to even extraordinary mnemonic strategies.

The above considerations are thus consistent with the assertion, based on empirical evidence, that people do not necessarily have introspective access to the determinants of their action. Unfortunately, this formulation of Nisbett and Wilson's (1977) position is not really what is at issue. Rather, what they imply and what most people have understood them to mean is that people necessarily have no direct and privileged access to the determinants of their action.[6] This distinction between *not necessarily* having access to the determinants of behavior, and *necessarily not* having such access, is the distinction between an empirical and a logical assertion, and it is what the controversy is really all about.

Even one instance in which a person can legitimately claim introspective access to his or her behavioral determinants means that the more unqualified and radical claim is false. And since most thoughtful people are quite convinced that they do have introspective access to at least some if not all of their behavioral determinants, they assume that the Nisbett and Wilson position must be without merit, or at least extravagantly overstated.

The reason for the controversy and confusion flows from the fact that neither Nisbett and Wilson nor their critics have recognized that the warrant in their radical claim flows from logical and not from empirical considerations. In essence, neither the protagonists nor the antagonists in this dispute have clearly distinguished between the (empirical) possibility of having introspective access to determining antecedents of thought and behavior, and the (logical) impossibility of having introspective access to the causal connection between determining antecedents and their behavioral effects.

Although this may at first glance seem to be a distinction without a difference, closer consideration clarifies that this is most assuredly not the case. Perhaps the best way of documenting the importance of this distinction is to recall that in 1748, David Hume emphasized it in a context that differs only slightly from the present one. He stated:

> When we look about us towards external objects, and consider the operation of causes, we are never able, in a single instance, to discover any power or necessary connexion; any quality, which binds the effect to the cause, and renders the one an infallible consequence of the other. We only find, that the one does actually, in fact, follow the other. The impulse of one billiard-ball is attended with motion in the second. This is the whole that appears to *outward* senses....There is not, in any single, particular instance of cause and effect, anything which can suggest the idea of power or necessary connexion. (Hume, 1748/1936, pp. 328–329)

In essence, Hume's argument is that people can observe antecedents, and they can observe consequences, but they cannot observe the causal connection between them. For *causality is simply not subject to direct observation.*[7] Moreover, the sense of subjective certainty that a particular antecedent caused a particular outcome is not in and of itself evidence of the causal connection between them. Believing something does not make it so, or else every fanatic would be correct in his or her beliefs.

What is true for observation is no less true for introspection. One can introspectively notice and/or recall antecedents of one's behavior, but the causal connection linking the determining antecedents and the behavior to be explained is simply not directly accessible to introspection. Rather, the causal link between antecedents and their consequences is provided by an inference, however implicit and invisible, based in part upon the *comprehension* or *understanding* of the events that are available to observation and/or introspection. And if the understanding is in important ways inadequate or uninformed, then the causal inference will also be found wanting—as was the case in my landscape-preferring subject. It will be recalled that this person was able to identify the reinforcement contingent upon her selection of landscapes, but her naïveté about such matters prevented an informed understanding of its influence on her behavior. And of course, even when a behavioral determinant is (finally) recognized and appreciated for what it is, the causal connection linking the behavior to its determinants has *not* suddenly become directly accessible to observation or introspection, but has instead been comprehended and understood.

It is surely the purpose of psychological research to enhance our comprehension and understanding of causal influences operating on thought and action. Notice, however, that such research would be totally redundant if the causal connections linking thought and behavior to its determinants were directly and automatically self-evident to introspection. So the need for psychological research testifies to the insufficiencies of introspection to deliver a fully informed understanding about the variables controlling thought and action. Indeed, it is the widely recognized insufficiencies of introspection that have led psychologists to place so much faith on the experimental method as a sort of Great White Hope for understanding the whys and wherefores of human behavior. Unsurprisingly, therefore, when a discrepancy occurs between experimentally and introspectively derived accounts of subjects' behavior, it is the research results that almost invariably become the unquestioned arbiter of what actually happened. In other words, experimentally controlled research becomes the "fount of privileged information" for the experimenter that introspection was erroneously assumed to be for the subject. The unquestioned authority of experimental findings to discern the "real" determinants of behavior is highly problematic, however, and needs to be reconsidered.

While a reconsideration of the role of experimentation in understanding human behavior may seem misplaced in a paper concerned with unconscious influences on human thought and action, I hope to show that this is not the case. We certainly cannot do without experimentally controlled studies of human behavior, but there is nothing intrinsic to the method that guarantees its wise and sensitive use. And at its worst, it can bludgeon into submission the gathering doubts and emerging intuitions that would otherwise surface to challenge conventional (but often erroneous) wisdom that is based on experimental findings (Bowers, 1973a, 1977a). In effect, then, the "foibling" of experimental method which follows is propaedeutic to a consideration of intuition in science. And in intuition, we shall find considerable room for the operation of unconscious influences on thought and behavior.

The Insufficiencies of Experimental Research

I have already written at some length about the foibles of experimental methodology as it is often applied in psychology (Bowers, 1973a), and I will not repeat in detail the arguments presented there. The following remarks can be regarded as an extension of my earlier critique. The basic point is that experimentally controlled inquiry simply does not reveal the causal connection linking the independent to the dependent variable. As we have seen, causality is a matter of inference, and inference in turn depends upon how the phenomena in question are understood, no matter what kind of data are available. To be sure, experimental data do have certain advantages, since they can eliminate as erroneous causal inferences that might be consistent with introspective, correlational, naturalistic, or clinical data. By the same token, however, the advantages of experimental data are not absolute, and often permit impoverished or misleading inferences about the phenomenon in question.

To illustrate my point, consider a thought experiment regarding the possible causes of malaria that might have been performed before the disease was well understood. Suppose a perspicacious observer had a hunch that people who slept in rooms with screens on the windows were much less apt to contract malaria. Eschewing correlational for experimental techniques, let us suppose that our intrepid investigator overcomes the various logistical difficulties and manages to randomly assign his subjects to a screened and unscreened condition. After waiting a reasonable amount of time, the investigator simply tabulates the frequency of malaria victims in the two conditions, and finds that, indeed, people in the unscreened condition contract malaria three times more often than their counterparts in the screened condition. Ergo, unscreened windows cause malaria.

At a practical level, this conclusion does have something to recommend it, since the results of the experiment certainly justify the increased use of window screens by the local inhabitants. However, the conclusion that unscreened windows cause malaria does not necessarily suggest anything about the importance of mosquitoes in transmitting the disease. For example, one might be convinced by the experimental results that nighttime miasma is condensed on the screen, before it can reach and infect the potential victim. No doubt a host of other potential explanations of the findings would occur to someone who did not already understand the importance of mosquitoes in the transmission of malarial infections. None of these alternate accounts is apt to lead to other effective antimalarial measures, such as the draining of swamps, the development of insecticides and repellants, and so on. In other words, the simple conclusion that unscreened windows cause malaria is in some ways impoverished and misleading and does not imply or suggest many of the effective preventative measures that a modern understanding of the disease has permitted.

One of the reasons for presenting such a rudimentary example is that the inadequacies of the inference "unscreened windows cause malaria" is so obvious in light of present knowledge and understanding. However, the experimental study of phenomena that are not so well understood can lead the incautious investigator to conclude, erroneously, that the manipulated variable "X" causes the effect "Y."[8]

Keeping this thought experiment in mind, let us consider another imaginary investigation of a sort that more closely resembles some of the work reported by Nisbett and Wilson. Suppose an investigator is interested in romantic love, and decides to manipulate a variable of presumed importance to romantic liaisons, namely, the conditions under which couples meet for the first time. Since anything is possible in a thought experiment, let us assume that the investigator randomly allocated previously "unmet" people of the opposite sex to one of two conditions, a romantic-light and a garish-light condition. In the romantic-light condition, people meet at a restaurant, say, under flattering, low-light conditions, perhaps candlelight. In the control or garish-light condition, people meet for the first time under bright, flickering, and totally unflattering fluorescent lights. Assume for the sake of argument that everything else about the restaurant is the same. Our imaginary investigator then follows up our imaginary subjects about two months after their initial meeting and finds that three times more couples in the romantic- than in the garish-light condition are seriously involved with each other. And suppose further that we can inquire of subjects in the romantic-light condition just why they think they have become romantically involved with their experimental partners. Consider then a hypothetical conversation with George, an interviewee from the romantic-light condition who continues his involvement with Helen, a woman he met in the experiment.

EXPERIMENTER: Tell me, George, do you get along with Helen?
GEORGE: No.
EXPERIMENTER: Is she attractive to you, does she make you feel good?
GEORGE: No and no.
EXPERIMENTER: Is she sexy or supportive; do you and Helen share common interests?
GEORGE: No, no, and no.
EXPERIMENTER: (With growing bewilderment) Is she a good cook, is she thoughtful, does she have a lot of money, or is she expecting a large inheritance?
GEORGE: No, no, no, and no.
EXPERIMENTER: I give up. If you don't get along with Helen, and if she is unattractive, doesn't make you feel good, isn't sexy, is unsupportive, shares no common interests, isn't thoughtful, can't cook, doesn't have any money, and has no immediate prospect of any—just why are you involved with her.
GEORGE: It's because of those damn soft lights.

Such an explanation of his romantic liaison with Helen would permit a conclusion that George was at least a fool, and probably psychologically disturbed as well; this despite the fact that George had identified with consummate accuracy the experimental variable leading to significant group differences in romantic liaisons. In other words, George's tenacity in identifying the soft lights as *the* causal explanation of his affair with Helen condemns him as a man of little wit and less intuition.

The above example clarifies one very important point: If in fact soft lights did lead to more romantic involvements than garish lights, it must have been because they occasioned other, more psychological events to take place, and it is these mediating events that are more proximal and determinative of romance than the soft lighting per se. Still, the soft lighting is not irrelevant to romance; after all, the importance of a romantic atmosphere has been known and exploited by men and women for centuries. So the experimenter has a certain right to maintain that the relationship between soft lights and romance is a causal one, in the same way that the experimenter on malaria had a right to insist that unscreened windows caused malaria. But it is our right to insist in turn that in neither case is the conclusion determined or entailed by the data, but is a judgment or conclusion by the experimenter based on his or her *understanding* of the evidence. And in both cases, I think it is quite arguable that the experimenter's understanding of the connection between antecedent and consequent events is a limited and rather impoverished one.

But if this is true, then we need not conclude that a subject in the soft-light condition would necessarily be in error if he does not identify or accept the soft lights as the causal determinant of his new relationship. Indeed, his understanding of the romantic relationship and its antecedents may invoke a whole different set of variables that he thinks far more influential than the soft lighting, and he may well be correct in claiming that interest in his partner is based on physical attraction, common interests, similar background, and so on. At the very least, the experimental findings do not disprove or invalidate his understanding of why the relationship flourished. And intuitively, the subject's account of his romance seems to be more probing and plausible than the experimenter's insistence on soft lights as *the* determinant of the relationship. Indeed, unless the experimenter is somewhat circumspect about the causal role of the independent variable, he or she runs the risk of looking as foolish and perverse as poor George.[9]

In the context of the above comments, the following important question emerges: When is it more reasonable to accept the experimenter's account of his subject's behavior, and when is it more reasonable to credit the subject's understanding of his behavior as more valid? This is not meant to be a rhetorical question, because there will be occasions when the experimenter's account will be far more plausible, penetrating, and persuasive than the subject's, and other times when the subject's explanation of his or her own behavior will be more telling. The point that should be emphasized, however, is that the experimenter's account will not automatically be more persuasive just because the data on which his or her claims are based are experimentally controlled, whereas the subject's understanding is not. Undue reverence for the results of experimental inquiry is based on the mistaken assumption that proper understanding of a phenomenon only follows the results of controlled inquiry. However, "no inquiry can succeed unless it starts from a true, or at least partly true, conception of the nature of things. Such foreknowledge is indispensable, and all discovery is but a step toward the verification of such foreknowledge" (Polanyi, 1969; p. 130).

A probing experiment is thus not simply one that is methodologically tight, but one that considers variables of critical importance. Good judgment about which variables are critical to an effect under investigation cannot be taught in courses on experimental design, and ultimately it is this intuitive judgment that separates the sagacious mind from a more mundane mentality. Moreover, there is no a priori reason to believe that the experimenter will always be more sagacious than his or her subject in identifying the critically important variables that guide the latter's behavior.

Since the experimenter simply decides, on the basis of prior (mis)understanding, which variables are important to study (Bowers, 1977a), and since the results of the experiment will not, in any case, directly reveal the causal connections between the independent and dependent variables, we can safely conclude that the experimenter does not have a "fount of privileged information" that bubbles up indubitable knowledge, any more than does the subject relying upon introspection. It would be convenient if there were some sort of final and indubitable criterion by which to judge whether the experimenter's or the subject's understanding of the latter's behavior is more valid, but unfortunately, there is none. It is ultimately a matter for the scientific community to decide which understanding of a phenomenon is more plausible (Lakatos, 1970; Polanyi, 1964), and it should be emphasized that in the absence of an indubitable criterion, such plausibility judgments do not differ in principle from plausibility judgments of an individual trying to understand his or her own behavior.

Although Nisbett and Wilson implicitly argue that scientists have something better to offer than merely plausible accounts of their subject's behavior, they are mistaken in this claim. It may nevertheless be true that the experimenter's account of the subject's behavior is better (i.e., more plausible) than that of the subject. But when this occurs, it is not because of the experimenter's access to indubitable information; rather, it is because of the experimenter's access to *pertinent* information that either (a) is not made available to the subject (e.g., the behavior of the control group in a between groups design), or (b) would remain incomprehensible to the subject even if it were made available (e.g., a very young child is unlikely to comprehend the principle of reinforcement which nevertheless helps shape his or her behavior). In other words, it is the differential availability and/or comprehensibility of pertinent information that makes a particular account of the subject's behavior more plausible and persuasive to the scientist than it is to the subject.

In sum, since data are never indubitable (Bowers, 1977a,b) and never entail particular conclusions about them (Kaplan, 1964), plausibility in light of the available evidence is all that can be claimed in support of one's understanding of the phenomena in question.

Reflections on Consciousness and Comprehension

What has emerged in this section is the very strong link that exists between consciousness and comprehension: influences on thought and behavior that are not comprehended are, de facto, unconscious influences. Moreover, we have seen that comprehension does not derive directly from observation or introspection of causal influences operating on behavior; nor are such causal influences directly revealed by experimental research on human behavior (conventional wisdom to the contrary notwithstanding). Rather, comprehending the influences at work on one's thought and behavior involves some sort of theory or conceptualization that "fills the gap," so to speak, between behavior and its determining conditions. This theorizing about thought and behavior can be implicit and informal, as it is for most people who are trying to figure out why they have behaved in a particular way; or it can derive from explicit and formal inquiry. In either case, however, the attempt to understand any particular thought or behavior presupposes the occurrence of the thought and behavior to be understood. Stated more generally, thinking and behavior are logically prior to any particular theory of thought and action.

What is more, both thought and action on the one hand, and any explanation of them on the other, *necessarily* have unconscious determinants. This is so because of the intimate relationship between consciousness and comprehension. As indicated earlier, there is no direct or unmediated access, either by observation or introspection, to the causal connections linking thought and behavior to their determining antecedents. Until such time as these relationships are conceptualized, therefore, we have little or no comprehension of why we have thought or acted in a particular manner. And as long as the thought and behavior in question remain uncomprehended, they are, in effect, unconsciously determined.

Most people, however, abhor such a conceptual or explanatory vacuum, as far as their own behavior is concerned. As Freud argued:

> There seems to be a necessity for bringing psychical phenomena of which one becomes conscious into causal connection with other conscious material. In cases in which the true causation evades conscious perception one does not hesitate to attempt to make another connection, which one believes, although it is false. (Breuer & Freud, 1893–95/1974, p. 125)

However, when the thought and behavior in question are incorrectly or inadequately conceptualized, it means that their actual determinants remain uncomprehended and unconscious. Only a correct account of behavior can make the unconscious determinants of thought and action conscious. Unfortunately, as we have seen, there is no indubitable criterion for knowing when a theory or conceptualization is correct (cf., Popper, 1979; Lakatos, 1970; Weimer, 1979). All we can have is a theory that is more and more plausible, given the available evidence. This state of affairs implies that any particular explanation of a course of thought or action, however plausible and compelling it may be, is nonetheless incomplete and subject to doubt, leaving at least some uncomprehended and therefore unconscious influences operating on the thought or action being investigated. This ultimate insufficiency of theory to the phenomena being explained is of course as true when it is thinking or behavior in general (rather than a particular thought or action) that is under investigation.

Finally, since any attempt to theorize about thought and action is itself a thinking or doing, such theorizing suffers from the same inability to comprehend itself that it suffers vis-à-vis the thought and behavior it is trying to conceptualize and understand. In other words, theories of thinking and thought, even theories that propose unconscious determinants of thought and action, have uncomprehended (i.e., unconscious) influences guiding and determining their evolution. In fact, it should now be clear that any theory at all, as an embodiment of human thinking and conceptualization, is necessarily subject to unconscious determinants, and that this is no less true when the theory is about unconscious determinants of human thought and action. It is in this sense that any theory of unconsciousness is logically presupposed by unconscious influences which help to determine and shape the theory in question.

INTUITION

The emphasis up to this point in the chapter has been to show that a good deal of human thought and conduct is subject to influences outside of conscious awareness. Nisbett and Wilson (1977) emphasize the down side of this insight by repeatedly demonstrating how people err in accounting for their own behavior. However, the fact that people are frequently mistaken in identifying truly influential factors operating on their thought and behavior means that human behavior and thought is sensitive and responsive to information that is not noticed or comprehended. Whereas Nisbett and Wilson emphasize the *inability* of people to identify and appreciate truly controlling factors that unconsciously influence their thought and action, I would like to stress the *ability* of persons to be influenced and informed by considerations that are not explicitly represented in conscious awareness (Bowers, 1981). Intuition is precisely this possibility for being tacitly informed (Polanyi, 1964). Indeed, we can define intuition as sensitivity and responsiveness to information that is not consciously represented, but which nevertheless guides inquiry toward productive and sometimes profound insights. Thus while Nisbett and Wilson have emphasized the extent to which people's explanations of their own thought and action are typically *mis*informed by influences operating outside of awareness, we emphasize here how these selfsame thoughts and actions can be tacitly and productively *informed* by unconscious considerations. A good place to begin this exploration involves the distinction between causes and reasons.

Causes and Reasons

The distinction at issue has been recognized by philosophers for some time (e.g., Peters, 1958; Louch, 1966), but has only recently wended its way into the psychological literature (Buss, 1978; Harvey & Tucker, 1979; Kruglanski, 1979; Locke & Pennington, 1982). However, my use of this distinction will differ somewhat from most previous treatments of it. The basic point to be made here is that the reason-cause distinction recognizes that the relationship between a phenomenon and its determinants differs from the relationship that exists between a phenomenon and its explanation: the former relationship is a causal one; the latter is characterized by "good reasons."

It is true that science (for the most part) presupposes a deterministic universe in which the phenomena to be explained have particular causes. However, as we have seen, science can not directly reveal these causal connections. Rather, it can only submit evidence in support of a particular explanation or conceptualization of the phenomenon under investigation. This evidence becomes the *reason* for accepting or crediting the explanation as probative or valid. The mounting evidence does not entail the explanation, but simply renders it more and more plausible. Nevertheless, even an apparently irresistible explanation can eventually turn out to be limited, inconclusive, or simply incorrect.

It is precisely this possibility for error that distinguishes the explanation of a phenomenon from its determinants. The *actual* causes of a phenomenon cannot be mistaken (any more than they can be directly and immediately discerned); only the current scientific explanation (and the reasons for espousing it) can be in error. For example, the actual causes of ocean tides, whatever they may be, can never be mistaken, whereas it is conceivable that the lunar theory of tides is more limited or inconclusive than is presently appreciated.

The clear distinction between a phenomenon's determinants on the one hand and our current explanation of them on the other, has some important implications. In the first place, the distinction implies that the determinants of the phenomenon under consideration are separate and distinct from the determinants of our thoughts and theories about it. For example, ocean tides as a natural (geophysical) phenomenon may be importantly determined by the moon, but our lunar explanation of the tides as a psychological (brain-mind) event clearly is not. If the lunar *theory* of tides were as determined by phases of the moon as the tides themselves apparently are, then the theory could no more be mistaken than the occurrence of the tides it presumably explains. But a theory must stand in some possibility of being wrong (falsifiable), or its status as a scientific claim is thrown into doubt (Lakatos, 1970).

Secondly, the fact that an explanation is not determined by the exact same variables as the phenomenon it explains does not mean that explanations have no determinants. However, the determinants of the explanation are totally irrelevant to the explanation's validity. In other words, a theory's ability to understand and explain a phenomenon depends very little if at all on identifying the determinants of the theory itself; access to the (genetic, neurophysiological, historical, intellectual) determinants of a theory is simply irrelevant to an appraisal of the theory's validity. A theory is judged in terms of how well it explicates and predicts, not in terms of its "pedigree." A closely related point is that the determinants of insight into a phenomenon have no evidential value regarding the phenomenon under investigation. For example, Kekule's famous dream of snakes swallowing their tails (see below) is not in any sense evidence for the hexagonal shape of the benzene ring, however important the dream may have been as a determinant of Kekule's insight into the closed structure of benzene. A denial of the point in hand is tantamount to belief in revealed knowledge, whereby dreams, omens, and other "signs" are taken as direct evidence for the truth of an assertion.

Finally, since the determinants of a scientific explanation are distinct from the determinants of the phenomenon being explained, conscious awareness (i.e., comprehension) of the latter does not entail or imply conscious awareness of the former. More emphatically, awareness (i.e., comprehension) of a phenomenon's determinants is completely consistent with nonawareness of the explanation's determinants. In fact, it is probably rare for a scientist to appreciate the origins of his insights, and Kekule's snake dream is so intriguing in part because it is such an unusual example of a scientist having access to a probable determinant of his ideas. In general, however, scientific understanding is guided at least in part by tacit factors that are not articulated or explicit, and which can remain out of awareness even when the results of such investigations have been explicated and accepted (Polanyi, 1964).

In sum, the determinants of a phenomenon's explanation are distinct from those of the phenomenon explained. This distinction means, among other things, that the conduct of inquiry is informed not only by explicit evidence regarding a phenomenon and its determinants, but also by various implicit, tacit, and unconscious influences that guide our thinking and understanding of the phenomenon. These "silent" guides to scientific inquiry are the basis of intuition.

Intuition: Two Examples

Let us turn now to a couple of examples of a truly important discovery in science that illustrates such intuitive processes. Although I am going to emphasize two particular examples, any number of illustrations from the history of science could be invoked to make the same point (e.g., Platt & Baker, 1969). And while the examples are anecdotal, this alone is not a good reason to ignore them. Dealing with phenomena as elusive as intuition means that we cannot afford to overlook any reasonable source of insight, even at the risk of being misinformed. In any event, I shall later present some preliminary evidence for intuition from recent research in my own laboratory.

Consider, then, the famous discovery of the benzene ring by Auguste Kekule. According to Kekule, he was dozing by the fire when in his mind's eye he saw snakelike structures cavorting before his eyes. And then suddenly: "But look! What was that? One of the snakes had seized hold of its own tail, and the form whirled mockingly before my eyes. As if by a flash of lightning I awoke" (in Hein, 1966; p. 10). What had suddenly occurred to Kekule was that benzene did not have an open structure as had been supposed previously, but rather a closed, hexagonal structure. The Kekule dream is in one respect unusual, in that most sudden insights leave no residue of their origins. The literature on creativity is replete with anecdotes of how people experienced the occurrence of important insights as if they were some sort of visitation or intervention by an outside agency—God, Mephistopheles, muse, or whatever (Koestler, 1964). This bolt-out-of-the-blue experience is probably misleading, however. There are good reasons to suppose that the sudden insight so fills consciousness with its importance that there is little room for, or interest in, recalling the mental events occurring just prior to the sudden flash of inspiration (Durkin, 1937; Ericcson & Simon, 1980). Nevertheless, the example is instructive in showing how dreamlike reveries or contemplations that are ordinarily not noticed or recalled can have a profound and sometimes productive impact on our conscious thought and experience.

What yet wants explaining is Kekule's dream. It seems to me that there are at least four ways of trying to account for this extraordinarily prescient vision. The first explanatory model we can refer to as the deus ex machina model, whereby God simply generates the dream in Kekule's sleeping brain, leaving it for the dreamer to recognize its significance for a current scientific preoccupation—namely, the structure of benzene. There is a long religious tradition in which this kind of deus ex machina intervention is at least implicit. If it is true, there is nothing that a mere psychologist can hope to fathom, and we can simply resign ourselves to ignorance.

A second model of explanation is more secular—namely, the lottery or roulette model. By this account, Kekule's dream is a random event uninfluenced by anything in Kekule's previous life, yet profoundly altering the subsequent course of his own personal life, and that of the history of science into the bargain. In other words, Kekule's dream was a bit like a winning number in an intellectual lottery—a strictly random event that nevertheless changes the course of scientific history.

A third account we can call the teleological or omen model. Using this model, the dream is not a reflection of Kekule's past history, but is instead both caused by and an omen of future events, namely, Kekule's imminent discovery of the shape of the benzene molecule. In sum, like the biblical Joseph's insight into the dream of seven fat and seven lean cattle, Kekule's dream was a portent of things to come.

It will perhaps come as no surprise that I do not favor any of the above models as a satisfactory account of Kekule's dream. Rather, I prefer what we can call, for want of a better term, the intuitive model. By this account, Kekule's dream was a symbolic condensation or representation of information that he already knew implicitly, but had not yet consciously understood. By this model, Kekule's dream was informed by his thorough immersion in the currently available knowledge of chemistry, and by his continual preoccupation with the problem to be solved. This total immersion of the scientist in his field seems to be an important condition of genuine creativity in it. But as necessary as such immersion may be for discovery, it is at the same time a potentially limiting factor on the possibility for a creative breakthrough.

At first blush, it may seem paradoxical that the same condition of thorough immersion in a scientific subject matter can be both a necessary and a limiting condition on the possibility for inspired insight. But a moment's thought reveals that it is really not so puzzling or paradoxical. The alert and focused mind, informed by explicit evidence and knowledge in an area of inquiry, is also a mind saddled by conscious expectations of what is likely or probable. Such expectations are, of course, not always correct, and can often be seriously misleading (Nisbett & Ross, 1980). Indeed, a genuinely important discovery or insight is considered creative in part because it is highly unusual and novel, which is to say, unexpected or improbable (Getzels & Jackson, 1962).

In light of the above considerations, it is perhaps not surprising that time after time one can read of original ideas emerging out of states of reverie, or at the very least, when the investigator was not consciously pursuing the solution to a problem (Platt & Baker, 1969). It is at such a time that relatively unlikely associations of available ideas, information, and images are apt to connect, unhindered by conscious goals, expectations, or strategies of problem solving (Spence & Holland, 1962; Koestler, 1964; Rugg, 1963; Arieti, 1976).

An especially compelling example of the facilitative effect of low arousal on creative thought (Simonton, 1980) was reported by the Nobel Laureate, Otto Loewi (1960). His most famous experiment involved demonstrating the chemical transmission of nerve impulses on effector organs. The experiment occurred to him in the middle of the night, whereupon he awoke and jotted down the gist of it on a slip of paper. Although he could not decipher his writing the next morning, he awoke at 3:00 A.M. the following night with the same experiment fully formed in his mind. On this occasion, he went directly to the laboratory and performed the experiment successfully.

In retrospect, it was clear to Loewi that the experiment had been steeping in his mind for a long time. Seventeen years earlier, the hypothesis of chemical transmission of neural impulses had occurred to him, but without the accompanying notion of how to validate his hunch. Two years before he finally performed his nocturnal experiment, he had conducted a very similar investigation for another purpose. It was the nighttime juxtaposition of a 17-year-old hypothesis with a 2-year-old experimental procedure that led to his Nobel-Prize-winning work.

Loewi's reflection about this experiment is instructive: "If carefully considered in the daytime, I would undoubtedly have rejected the kind of experiment I performed [as improbable]....It was good fortune that at the moment of the hunch I did not think but acted immediately" (p. 18).

In sum, I argue that Kekule's dream of snakes with tails in their mouths and Loewi's nocturnal insight represented an improbable joining or juxtaposition of available information that was permitted symbolic expression in an undirected dream state, a juxtaposition that is less likely to have occurred in an alert and focused mind dominated by conscious expectations, rather than by unfettered but informed fantasy (Bowers & Bowers, 1979).

It is these private, idiosyncratic, and often unconscious sources of ideas and inspiration that psychology typically overlooks (or even eschews) in its reconstruction of the scientific enterprise. Instead, "science" is frequently identified with the anointed methods of inquiry that lead to (allegedly) warranted claims about the phenomenon under investigation (Andreski, 1972). There is something reassuring about this identification, since it makes the rules of inquiry entirely rational, explicit, and comprehensible to anyone trained in their use. The sources of inspiration—being almost entirely inexplicit, nonrational, and incomprehensible—are also vaguely threatening to the public image of science as an orderly if not routine enterprise. But the cost of denying the human side of science has been formidable, particularly in psychology. For example, as Neisser (1982) has recently noted, research in memory has for years been bogged down in essentially methodological issues. This trend is the lasting legacy of Ebbinghaus's decision to employ nonsense syllables for his memory research—the better to eliminate contributions of an individual's personal history and private experience to mnemonics. The result, according to Neisser, is that research on memory has almost nothing to do with the fascinating questions that initially stimulated research about how memory operates in everyday life.

If memory has been treated so circumspectly by psychology, it is not at all surprising that intuition has been virtually ignored (but see Westcott, 1968; Bastick, 1982; Polanyi, 1964; Turvey, 1974). Indeed, intuition is currently in the "bad books" of many cognitive psychologists, who argue that it is responsible for massive and chronic errors in judgment (e.g., Kahneman & Tversky, 1973; Ross, 1977; Tversky & Kahneman, 1974). If, as implied by these authors, intuition has been misappropriated from the context of discovery and is instead being utilized as the court of final appeal in the context of justification, then there is indeed a problem. The question is, how can we sort out a legitimate role for intuition in scientific inquiry from more problematic ones?

The Scientific Study of Intuition

Meno's paradox, according to Plato, consists of the following dilemma:

> A man cannot inquire either about what he knows, or about that which he does *not* know; for if he already knows, there is no need for inquiry, and if he does not know, he does not know the very subject about which he is to inquire ....We cannot learn (come to *know*) anything unless we already know (have learned) it....[On the other hand, how] can one exhibit a knowledge of things for which one's prior learning experience has given no prepration? (Weimer, 1973, p. 16)

Plato's resolution of this paradox is his theory of anamnesis, which argues that there is no new learning at all, but only recollection of what is already known of true forms as they reappear in particulars.

Plato's statement of the paradox is more prescient than his resolution of it. The question to which he is seeking an answer is: "Where do new ideas come from?"—the answer to which generations of Ph.D. candidates would love to know. The process of conceiving a dissertation topic certainly doesn't *feel* like an act of recall, but more like an effort to precipitate something previously unthought and entirely novel.

It seems to me that intuition resolves the paradox better than Plato's theory of anamnesis. What is required of intuition is that in the context of a particular problem, it puts into association two or more previously unconnected ideas that the person has already had, a process that Koestler (1964) has termed bisociation. But why do just these particular ideas come together in a sudden flash of insight or discovery? One possible answer to that question is this: The particular ideas are "bisociated" because they are embedded in and reflect an emerging coherence that is tacitly perceived *prior* to becoming fully conscious (i.e., noticed). Recently, a graduate student, Claude Balthazard, and I began to investigate whether people can in fact perceive coherence before explicitly noticing the basis for it. While the program of research is just beginning, one preliminary finding is particularly accessible and illuminating.

Subjects in a pilot investigation were provided with a series of 60 paired word triads. One of the triads in each pair was culled from Mednick and Mednick's (1962) Remote Associates Test (RAT) (or from similarly derived lists of associates); the other triad was generated by placing together three words from *different* RAT items (or comparably nonassociated words). The subjects of course did not know in advance which triad was compiled of associates, and which was compiled of non-associated words. The task was to achieve the solution to the solvable triad if at all possible. Subjects had only eight seconds to do so, however, and if they were unable to solve the genuine RAT item in this time frame, they were to select (by sheer guessing if necessary) which of the two triads was solvable. By proceeding in this fashion we could examine all of the unsolved triads that were nevertheless selected as solvable. (Readers may at this point wish to try their luck with the pair of word triads that appear at the end of the chapter (Figure 6.1), making sure to permit themselves only an eight second's look, solving the genuine RAT item if possible, but failing that, guessing which of the two triads can be solved.)

The data are compelling. Across the 60 paired triads and eliminating from consideration all those items that were successfully solved, the solvable triad was correctly identified on the average of 58% of the time, which is quite significantly above chance. Some subjects were more intuitive than others, in that successful selection of the solvable triads ranged from a mean of about 51% for the least intuitive subjects to about 62% for the most intuitive. Other phases of the research project support the notion that people display stable individual differences in their ability to perceive coherence tacitly (Polanyi, 1964). (Incidentally, the solvable triad in the example at the end of the chapter is B, and the answer to it is "silver." Fifteen percent of the subjects in our study solved this problem, and 73% of the subjects who did not solve it nevertheless selected it as the solvable triad).

The implication of these findings is that people can have a presentiment of coherence before they can explicitly identify the basis for it. Moreover, even prior to its being explicitly noticed and identified, perceived coherence seems to guide thought and action tacitly. We have evidently struck a familiar chord here, namely, the perceiving-noticing distinction. Previously, however, the emphasis was on the perception of coherent information of a relatively concrete kind, such as tachistoscopically presented letters or words. The short exposure durations of these features made them difficult to perceive consciously (i.e., notice), while nevertheless informing a discriminative response in a forced-choice paradigm. As we have seen, however, coherence can also be difficult to notice because it is relatively abstract—which is to say, separate and distinct from the convergence of word-clues that reflect and reveal it. And evidently, such a relatively abstract coherence can also inform thought and behavior before being consciously perceived. It is of course this process of being tacitly informed by perceived (but as yet unnoticed) coherence that I have termed intuition.

It is clear that this view of intuition is an extension of the perceiving-noticing distinction which emerged from controlled laboratory contexts. Once the perceiving-noticing distinction is recognized in that domain, however, its relevance for the broader context of discovery should come as no surprise. For example, simply perceiving coherence is not sufficient for scientific discovery; consciously recognizing the coherence is a critical step in this process. Therefore, when perceived coherence crosses an awareness or identification threshold and becomes noticed, we have the beginning of and basis for comprehension. Perceiving, then noticing, and finally comprehending *patterns* of coherent evidence characterizes discovery and discourse in science.

As previously noted, the present analysis of intuition provides a much different perspective on the phenomenon than recent and rather disparaging accounts of it. The current literature concerning judgment under uncertainty (e.g., Tversky & Kahneman, 1974) stresses the inaccurate decisions made by subjects whose judgments are intuitively rather than normatively based. The conclusion to be drawn from the available evidence depends on whether a cup is regarded as half empty or half full. Surely, intuitive judgments can often be in error; for example, people are incorrect 42% of the time in identifying the solvable triad in our word task. And there may be times when relying on intuitive judgments while ignoring decisive (e.g., base rate) information leads to less accurate judgment than necessary. However, there are times when pertinent information is simply unavailable or insufficient to the solution of a problem, and under these conditions, intuitive judgments may be our best hope for making progress.

CONCLUSION

The social sciences can be considered a "consciousness-raising" enterprise that attempts to identify in a disciplined, explicit way the various kinds of implicit influences on human perception, thought, and action (Bowers, 1981). However, becoming sophisticated about (previously implicit) influences on one's behavior can minimize and may even entirely disarm the "power" of such influences to control thought and action—or at least provide the basis for an informed choice regarding whether such potential influences should become influences in fact (Neisser, 1976; Sheibe, 1978). For example, in my painting-preference study mentioned earlier (Bowers, 1975), many subjects who were informed and sophisticated about operant conditioning regarded my contingent reinforcement of their stated preferences as a clear and untoward attempt to manipulate their preferences. Consequently, they refused to alter their pattern of responding.

It is precisely because such explicit knowledge can undermine otherwise subtle (implicit, tacit, unconscious) influences on behavior that social psychologists in particular try to obtain naïve subjects for their experiments, rather than advanced students in psychology or otherwise well-informed people knowledgeable about the hypotheses and issues under investigation. Moreover, such studies often employ deception, misdirection, and other camouflage techniques in order to preserve the subject's naïveté. In effect, such investigators intuitively recognize and exploit the possibility for the implicit control of human behavior; but at the same time, their use of naïve subjects and deceptive techniques constitutes de facto recognition that such implicit unrecognized control is by no means inevitable and can, in fact, be undermined by the use of sophisticated subjects or by employing manipulations that are too salient and figural to remain unrecognized for what they are (Bowers, 1981).

While such sophistication can protect a person against undue influence, it can be a two-edged sword. Being sophisticated and worldly-wise, so to speak, can indeed somewhat limit the impact of subtle influences on thought and action. However, we have seen that the effect of explicit knowledge and the conscious expectations it establishes may also work to limit the likelihood of being genuinely informed by tacit features of one's experience. It appears that awareness or consciousness of subtle influence attempts can protect us against their effect on thought and behavior; but at the same time, such sophistication or consciousness can establish expectations that diminish the likelihood of being tacitly and implicitly informed.

It seems to me that this Janus-faced character of consciousness is an important theme throughout humanity's attempt to understand itself. It is surely one of the basic motifs behind the biblical depiction of the Fall: As one becomes more conscious and sophisticated about oneself and the world, there is the danger of becoming ever less innocent and open to the creative sources of one's being. Finding a balance between sophistication and inspiration can be a subtle and difficult process that seems most often swayed by the need to remain unfooled. This is not the poet's choice, however, and the minority view is well expressed in Robert Frost's poignant comment about the perfect moment of "unbafflement":

> "Once to have known it, nothing else will do.
> Our days all pass awaiting its return."

What we can now perhaps add to poetry is this: Our days of labor and expectant waiting are occasionally interrupted by our reveries, our contemplations, and our dreams, and it is perhaps the surfacing of this unconscious, night side of thinking that permits some of our best ideas to see the light of day.

NOTES

1. Conceivably, Eriksen would claim that this logical point is problematic, on the grounds that if GSR had discriminated stimuli at lower exposure levels than did verbal report, then the existence of subliminal perception would indeed have been demonstrated empirically. This line of defense is not entirely persuasive, however. In the first place, such a pattern of evidence could be explained away in exactly the same fashion that the subception effect was. That is, the superiority of GSR over verbal discrimination could be seen as evidence for the inadequacy of language to express conscious perception—not as evidence for unconscious perception. More fundamentally, however, appealing to the superiority of GSR over verbal discrimination as the empirical basis for subliminal perception simply misses the point: subliminal perception is not a matter of whether one response system discriminates better than another one, but whether the stimulus discrimination threshold is below the threshold for noticing the discriminated stimulus. Eriksen simply does not address this question seriously, yet it is the center of gravity of the entire issue.

2. It should be noted that this disambiguation of attended by unattended information only worked with surface structure ambiguities of the kind illustrated in the text above. Deep structure ambiguities (e.g., "They thought the shooting of the hunters was dreadful") were *not* successfully disambiguated by appropriate information on the unattended channel. In other words, conscious processing of unattended information seems required before it can help resolve such deep structure ambiguities.

3. There is a subtlety here that needs to be mentioned. Even though unattended (i.e., unnoticed) information is not apt to be recalled, there is some evidence (Marcel, 1980) that it can later be recognized. This means that the material in question must have made some contact with long-term memory store, even if not fully processed into it.

4. Evidently, unconscious influences due to repression presuppose consciousness. It is for this reason that full-blown repression probably is restricted to humans. Repression is simply one of the costs of the human condition.

5. Perhaps we should refer to perceived but unnoticed events as having "type 1" unconscious influence, and noticed but uncomprehended events as having a "type 2" unconscious influence. However, such a convention is expositionally awkward, and besides, context usually clarifies which of these two kinds of unconscious influences is being considered.

6. Readers familiar with the Nisbett and Wilson paper will quite possibly object to this strong formulation of their position, and they can quite rightly point to the fact that nowhere do the authors explicitly state that people necessarily have no access to the determinants of their behavior. In fact, they seem sometimes to soften their position by implying that actors might occasionally have an advantage over observers in understanding the former's behavior. However, this concession does not in any way imply that the actor has privileged introspective access to the determinants of his or her behavior; rather it demonstrates privileged access only to one's own history of behavior. In principle this behavior is publicly accessible, though practically it is quite possible that only the actor knows about it. Finally, in an APA debate (Nisbett & Bowers, note 1) Nisbett himself recognized that in the original paper with Wilson he was making a logical point, not an empirical one. Therefore, the logical formulation of his argument, that people necessarily have no introspective access to the determinants of their behavior, is one that should be made explicit.

7.   It is perhaps important to acknowledge that Hume's claim, though generally regarded as having passed the test of time, remains for some as counterintuitive today as it was when it was first formulated. Indeed, Harre and Madden (1975) have recently challenged Hume's insight: "We do not perceive an avalanche and then subsequent destruction but the avalanche destroying the village and vegetation of the countryside, just as we do not perceive waves and then subsequent disappearance of shoreline but the waves eating away the shoreline" (p. 53). In addition, these authors appeal to the experiments of Michotte (1963) to indicate that people do in fact perceive causality. While it is true that Hume may have been bemused by the latter's work, Michotte himself recognizes that Hume "would have been led to revise his views [only] on the psychological origin of the popular idea of causality. He would probably have appealed in his explanation to the 'causal impression' rather than to habit and expectation. This causal impression, however, would have been for him...nothing but an illusion of the senses....Moreover it is probable that his philosophical position would not have been affected in the least" (p. 256). That is, Hume's analysis would continue to deny that the psychological "impression" of causality bears any necessary correspondence to the occurrence of causality in the world. After all, a child's vivid impression that swaying trees cause the wind to blow is simply false by an adult's understanding, and an adult's impression that letting go of something causes it to fall is, at the very least, a partial and in some ways, misleading account of why unsupported objects fall. Some sort of conceptual understanding of events is essential to the perception of "waves eating away the shoreline," even though in cases such as this, the conceptual contributions to "perceived causality" can be overlearned, automatic, and largely invisible to introspection.

8.   The reader is surely familiar with the following comment, paraphrased from countless sources: "It is impossible for correlational data to yield a causal account of the phenomena under investigation; experimental investigations are necessary to identify causal influences."

9.   It might be objected that the above example is spurious, since it derives persuasive force from the fact that there is a considerable time lag between the independent and the dependent variables. This objection is problematic for two reasons. First of all, many studies in psychology involve considerable delay between intervention and assessment (e.g., psychotherapy outcome studies), so our fictional experiment is by no means singular in its assessment of remote effects. Secondly, and more importantly, a protracted temporal interval between independent and dependent variables simply helps to highlight how subjects can sometimes provide better accounts of their own behavior than the experimenter, but a delay is not essential for such subject superiority. In particular, a demand characteristic interpretation of the experimental results (Orne, 1969) is often more telling than the causal account preferred by the experimenter. The latter assumes some sort of direct "causal" link between the independent and dependent variables. By contrast, the demand characteristic account of an experimental outcome implies that other factors besides the independent variable are having a pronounced impact on the subject's behavior. These other factors can be contemporaneous with the introduction of the independent variable, and can therefore influence the course of an experiment even when the outcomes assessed are temporally proximal to the experimental manipulation. The subject need not notice (i.e., become aware of) such demand characteristics in order to perceive and therefore be influenced by them (e.g., Bowers, 1973b). However, when

A	B
Mouth	Coin
Sixteen	Quick
Lines	Spoon

Figure 6.1.   A paired word triad.

the demand characteristics are noticed, they can be introspectively reported, and in that case, what the subject says by way of accounting for his or her behavior may well be more probative than what the experimenter can say of it by virtue of the experimental results.

REFERENCE NOTE

Nisbett, R. & Bowers, K.S. Debate: Introspective awareness to higher order cognitive processes: Do we know more than we know? Chaired by John H. Harvey at the 87th Annual Convention of the American Psychological Association, New York City, September 2, 1979.

REFERENCES

Andreski, S. *Social sciences as sorcery.* London: Deutsch, 1972.

Arieti, S. *Creativity: The magic synthesis.* New York: Basic Books, 1976.

Atkinson, R.C., & Shiffrin, R.M. Human memory: A proposed system and its control processes. In K.W. Spence & J.T. Spence (Eds.), *The psychology of learning and motivation: Advances in research and theory* (Vol. 2). New York: Academic Press, 1968.

Bastick, T. *Intuition: How we think and act.* New York: Wiley, 1982.

Beck, A.T. *Cognitive therapy and the emotional disorders.* New York: International Universities Press, 1976.

Bower, G. Mood and memory. *American Psychologist, 1981, 35,* 129–148.

Bowers, K.S. Situationism in psychology: An analysis and a critique. *Psychological Review,* 1973, *80,* 307–336.a

Bowers, K.S. Hypnosis, attribution, and demand characteristics. *International Journal of Clinical and Experimental Hypnosis,* 1973, *21,* 226–238.b

Bowers, K.S. The psychology of subtle control: An attributional analysis of behavioral persistence. *Canadian Journal of Behavioral Science,* 1975, *7,* 78–95.

Bowers, K.S. There's more to Iago than meets the eye: A clinical account of personal consistency. In D. Magnusson & N.S. Endler (Eds.), *Personality at the crossroads: Current issues in interactional psychology.* Hillsdale, N.J.: Erlbaum, 1977.a

Bowers, K.S. Science and the limits of logic: A response to the Mahoney-DeMonbreun paper. *Cognitive therapy and research,* 1977, *1,* 239–246.b

Bowers, K.S. Knowing more than we can say leads to saying more than we can know: On being implicitly informed. In D. Magnusson (Ed.), *Toward a psychology of situations: An interactional perspective.* Hillsdale, N.J.: Erlbaum, 1981.

Bowers, P.G., & Bowers, K.S. Hypnosis and creativity: A theoretical and empirical rapprochement. In E. Fromm & R.E. Shor (Eds.), *Hypnosis: Developments in research and new perspectives* (2nd ed.). New York: Aldine, 1979.

Breuer, J., & Freud, S. *Studies on hysteria.* Harmondsworth, England: Pelican, 1974. (Originally published 1893–1895.)

Buss, A.R. Causes and reasons in attribution theory: A conceptual critique. *Journal of Personality and Social Psychology,* 1978, *36,* 1311–1321.

Campion, J., Lotto, R., & Smith, Y.M. Is blindsight an effect of scattered light, spared cortex, and near-threshold vision? *Brain and Behavior Science,* 1983, *6,* 423–448.

Cheesman, J., & Merikle, P. An investigation of perception without awareness using a variant of the Stroop colour word task. Paper read at Canadian Psychological Association Convention, Montreal, Canada, June 1982.

Corteen, R., & Wood, B. Autonomic responses to shock-associated words in an unattended channel. *Journal of Experimental Psychology,* 1972, *94,* 308–313.

Dixon, N.F. *Subliminal perception: The nature of a controversy.* New York: McGraw-Hill, 1971.

Dixon, N.F. *Preconscious processing.* New York: Wiley, 1981.

Dostoyevsky, F. *The brothers Karamozov.* New York: Vintage, 1950. (Originally published 1880.)

Dulany, D.E., Jr., & Eriksen, C.W. Accuracy of brightness discrimination as measured by concurrent verbal responses and GSRs. *Journal of Abnormal and Social Psychology,* 1959, *59,* 418–423.

Durkin, H.E. Trial-and error, gradual analysis, and sudden reorganization: An experimental study of problem solving. *Archives of Psychology,* 1937, *210,* 1–85.

Erdelyi, M.H. A new look at the new look: Perceptual defense and vigilance. *Psychological Review,* 1974, *81,* 1–25.

Erdelyi, M.H., & Goldberg, B. Let's not sweep repression under the rug: Toward a cognitive psychology of repression. In J.F. Kihlstrom & F.J. Evans (Eds.), *Functional disorders of memory.* Hillsdale, N.J.: Erlbaum, 1979.

Ericcson, K.A., & Simon, H.A. Verbal reports as data. *Psychological Review,* 1980, *87,* 215–251.

Eriksen, C.W. Unconscious processes. In M.R. Jones (Ed.), *Nebraska symposium on motivation, 1958.* Lincoln: University of Nebraska Press, 1959.

Eriksen, C.W. Discrimination and learning without awareness: A methodological survey and evaluation. *Psychological Review,* 1960, *67,* 279–300.

Freud, S. Hysterical phantasies and their relation to bisexuality. In S. Freud, *Collected papers* (Vol. 2). New York: Basic Books, 1959. (Originally published 1908.)

Getzels, J.W., & Jackson, P.W. *Creativity and intelligence: Explorations with gifted students.* New York: Wiley, 1962.

Glucksberg, S., & Cowen, G.N. Memory for nonattended auditory material. *Cognitive Psychology,* 1970, *1,* 149–156.

Harre, R., & Madden, E.H. *Causal powers.* Totowa, N.J.: Rowman and Littlefield, 1975.

Harvey, J.H., & Tucker, J.A. On problems with the cause-reason distinction in attribution theory. *Journal of Personality and Social Psychology,* 1979, *37,* 1441–1446.

Hein, G.E. Kekule and the architecture of molecules. In R.F. Gould (Ed.), *Advances in chemistry series: Kekule centennial.* Washington, D.C.: American Chemical Society, 1966.

Hilgard, E.R. *Divided consciousness: Multiple controls in human thought and action.* New York: Wiley, 1977.

Hume, D. An enquiry concerning human understanding. In B. Rand (Ed.), *Modern classical philosophers.* Boston: Houghton Mifflin, 1936. (Originally published 1748.)

Janet, P. *L'Automatisme psychologique.* Paris: Alcan, 1889.

Janet, P. *The major symptoms of hysteria.* New York: Hafner, 1965. (Originally published 1907.)

Kahneman, D. *Attention and effort.* New York: Prentice-Hall, 1973.

Kahneman, D., & Tversky, A. On the psychology of prediction. *Psychological Review,* 1973, *80,* 237–251.

Kaplan, A. *The conduct of inquiry: Methodology for behavioral science.* San Francisco: Chandler, 1964.

Koestler, A. *The act of creation.* New York: Macmillan, 1964.

Kruglanski, A.W. Causal explanation, teleological explanation: On radical particularism in attribution theory. *Journal of Personality and Social Psychology,* 1979, *37,* 1447–1457.

LaBerge, D. Acquisition of automatic processing in perceptual and associative learning. In P. Rabbitt & S. Dornic (Eds.), *Attention and performance* (Vol. 5). New York: Academic Press, 1975.

Lackner, J.R. & Garrett, M.F. Resolving ambiguity: Effects of biasing context in the unattended ear. *Cognition,* 1972, *1,* 359–372.

Lakatos, I. Falsification and the methodology of scientific research programmes. In I. Lakatos and A. Musgrave (Eds.), *Criticism and the growth of knowledge.* Cambridge: Cambridge University Press, 1970.

Lazarus, R.S., & McCleary, R.A. Autonomic discrimination without awareness: A study of subception. *Psychological Review,* 1951, *58,* 113–122.

Lewis, D.J., Psychobiology of active and inactive memory. *Psychological Bulletin,* 1979, *86,* 1054–1083.

Lewis, J.L. Semantic processing of unattended messages using dichotic listening. *Journal of Experimental Psychology,* 1970, *85,* 225–228.

Locke, D., & Pennington, D. Reasons and other causes: Their role in attribution processes. *Journal of Personality and Social Psychology,* 1982, *42,* 212–223.

Loewi, O. An autobiographic sketch. *Perspectives in Biology and Medicine,* 1960, *4,* 3–25.

Louch, A.R. *Explanation and human action.* Oxford: Basil Blackwell, 1966.

Lundh, L-G. Introspection, consciousness, and human information processing. *Scandinavian Journal of Psychology,* 1979, *20,* 223–238.

MacKay, D. Aspects of the theory of comprehension, memory and attention. *Quarterly Journal of Experimental Psychology,* 1973, *25,* 22–40.

Mahoney, M.J. Psychotherapy and the structure of personal revolutions. In M.J. Mahoney (Ed.), *Psychotherapy process: Current issues and future directions.* New York: Plenum, 1980.

Marcel, A. Conscious and preconscious recognition of polysemous words: Locating the selective effects of prior verbal context. In R.S. Nickerson (Ed.), *Attention and performance* (Vol. 8). Hillsdale, N.J.: Erlbaum, 1980.

Mednick, S.A., & Mednick, M.T. *Examiner's manual: Remote associates test.* Boston: Houghton-Mifflin, 1962.

Meichenbaum, D. *Cognitive-behavior modification.* New York: Plenum, 1977.

Merikle, P.M. Unconscious perception revisited. *Perception and psychophysics,* 1982, *31,* 298–301.

Michotte, A. *The perception of causality.* New York: Basic Books, 1963.

Natsoulas, T. What are perceptual reports about? *Psychological Bulletin,* 1967, *67,* 249–272.

Neisser, U. *Cognition and reality.* San Francisco: Freeman, 1976.

Neisser, U. *Memory observed: Remembering in natural contexts.* San Francisco: Freeman, 1982.

Newstead, S.E., & Dennis, I. Lexical and grammatical processing of unshadowed messages: A re-examination of the MacKay effect. *Quarterly Journal of Experimental Psychology,* 1979, *31,* 477–488.

Nisbett, R.E., & Bellows, N. Verbal reports about causal influences on social judgments: Private access versus public theories. *Journal of Personality and Social Psychology,* 1977, *35,* 613–624.

Nisbett, R., & Ross, L. *Human inference: Strategies and shortcomings of social judgment.* Englewood Cliffs, N.J.: Prentice-Hall, 1980.

Nisbett, R.E., & Wilson, T.D. Telling more than we can know: Verbal reports on mental processes. *Psychological Review,* 1977, *84,* 231–259

Norman, D.A. Memory while shadowing. *Quarterly Journal of Experimental Psychology,* 1969, *21,* 85–93.

Norman, D.A. *Memory and attention: An introduction to information processing.* New York: Wiley, 1976.

Orne, M.T. Demand characteristics and the concept of quasi-controls. In R. Rosenthal & R.L. Rosnow (Eds.), *Artifact in behavioral research.* New York: Academic Press, 1969.

Overton, D.A. Major theories of state dependent learning. In B. Ho, D. Chute, & D. Richards (Eds.), *Drug discrimination and state dependent learning.* New York: Academic Press, 1977.

Perenin, M.T., & Jeanrrod, M. Residual vision in cortically blind hemifields. *Neuropsychologia,* 1975, *13,* 1–7.

Peters, R.S. *The concept of motivation.* London: Routledge & Kegan Paul, 1958.

Platt, W., & Baker, R.A. The relation of the scientific "hunch" to research. *Journal of Chemistry Education,* 1969, *8,* 1969–2002.

Poetzl, O. The relationship between experimentally induced dream images and indirect vision. *Psychological Issues* (Monograph No. 7), 1960, *2,* 41–120. (Originally published 1917.)

Polanyi, M. *Personal knowledge: Toward a postcritical philosophy.* New York: Harper, 1964.

Polanyi, M. Knowing and being. In M. Grene (Ed.), *Knowing and being: Essays by Michael Polanyi.* Chicago: University of Chicago Press, 1969.

Popper, K. *Objective knowledge: An evolutionary approach.* Oxford: Clarendon Press, 1979.

Posner, M.I., & Snyder, C.R.R. Attention and cognitive control. In R.L. Solso (Ed.), *Information processing and cognition.* Hillsdale, N.J.: Erlbaum, 1975.

Ross, L. The intuitive psychologist and his shortcomings: Distortions in the attribution process. In L. Berkowitz (Ed.), *Advances in Experimental Social Psychology,* Vol. 10. New York: Academic Press, 1977.

Rugg, H. *Imagination.* New York: Harper & Row, 1963.

Sackeim, H.A., Nordlie, J.W., & Gur, R.C. A model of hysterical and hypnotic blindness: Cognition, motivation, and awareness. *Journal of Abnormal Psychology,* 1979, *88,* 474–489.

Scheibe, K. The psychologist's advantage and its nullification: Limits of human predictability. *American Psychologist,* 1978, *33,* 869–881.

Shevrin, H., & Fritzler, D.E. Visual evoked response correlates of unconscious mental processes. *Science,* 1968, *161,* 295–298.

Simonton, D.K. Intuition and analysis: A predictive and explanatory model. *Genetic Psychology Monographs,* 1980, *102,* 3–60.

Smith, E.R., & Miller, F.D. Limits on perception of cognitive processes: A reply to Nisbett and Wilson. *Psychological Review,* 1978, *85,* 355–362.

Spence, D.P. Conscious and preconscious influences on recall: Another example of the restricting effects of awareness. *Journal of Abnormal and Social Psychology,* 1964, *68,* 92–99.

Spence, D.P., & Holland, B. The restricting effects of awareness: A paradox and an explanation. *Journal of Abnormal and Social Psychology,* 1962, *64,* 163–174.

Swanson, J.M., & Kinsbourne, M. State-dependent learning and retrieval: Methodological cautions and theoretical considerations. In J.F. Kihlstrom & F.J. Evans (Eds.), *Functional disorders of memory.* Hillsdale, N.J.: Erlbaum, 1979.

Trevarthen, C.B. Two mechanisms of vision in primates. *Psychological Forschung,* 1968, *31,* 299–337.

Trevarthen, C. Experimental evidence for a brain-stem contribution to visual perception in man. *Brain Behavior and Evolution,* 1970, *3,* 338–352.

Triesman, A., & Geffen, S. Selective attention: Perception or response. *Quarterly Journal of Experimental Psychology,* 1967, *19,* 1–17.

Turvey, M.T. Constructive theory, perceptual systems, and tacit knowledge. In W.B. Weimer & D.S. Palermo (Eds.), *Cognition and symbolic processes.* Hillsdale, N.J.: Erlbaum, 1974.

Tversky, A., & Kahneman, D. Judgments under uncertainty: Heuristics and biases. *Science,* 1974, *185,* 1124–1131.

Weimer, W. Psycholinguistics and Plato's paradoxes of the Meno. *American Psychologist,* 1973, *28,* 15–233.

Weimer, W.B. *Notes on the methodology of scientific research.* Hillsdale, N.J.: Erlbaum, 1979.

Weiskrantz, L., Warrington, E.K., Sanders, M.D., & Marshall, J. Visual capacity in the hemianopic field following a restricted occipital ablation. *Brain,* 1974, *97,* 709–728.

Wescott, M.R. *Toward a contemporary psychology of intuition: A historical, theoretical and empirical inquiry.* New York: Holt, Rinehart & Winston, 1968.

White, P. Limitations on verbal reports of internal events: A refutation of Nisbett and Wilson and of Bem. *Psychological Review,* 1980, *87,* 105–112.

Wolitsky, D.L., & Wachtel, P.L. Personality and perception. In B.B. Wolman (Ed.), *Handbook of general psychology.* Englewood Cliffs, N.J.: Prentice-Hall, 1973.

Zajonc, R.B. Feeling and thinking: Preferences need no inferences. *American Psychologist,* 1980, *35,* 151–175.

CHAPTER 7

The Nature of
Unconscious Processes:
A Cognitive-Behavioral
Perspective

DONALD MEICHENBAUM AND J. BARNARD GILMORE

In 1890, William James wrote: "The 'unconscious' is the sovereign means of believing whatever one likes in psychology and of turning what might become a science into a tumbling ground for whimsies" (p. 163). Though James cannot be characterized as a behaviorist, his sentiments about the concept of unconscious processes have been shared by generations of behavioristic psychologists. No other concept so clearly divides the traditional behavioral from the psychodynamic camp. Psychodynamic theory and practice are grounded in respect for, and attention to, the elusive unconscious in all its dynamic complexity. But traditional behavioral therapists and theorists eschew the very suggestion of unconscious processes, and they challenge the implication that in these constructs there might reside any heuristic values for theory, for assessment, or for therapy.

In recent years there have been attempts to bridge the gaps that separate the behavioral and psychodynamic approaches (cf. Goldfried, 1982; Marmor & Woods, 1980; Wachtel, 1977). We are convinced that this effort is fruitful, and even mandatory. We believe that where the gap is widest, between the divergent attitudes concerning the existence or importance of an "unconscious," there are bridges to be built that can be of great benefit to both sides, permitting new forms of professional trade and commerce between them. This chapter represents our attempt to begin the construction of just such a bridge.

The authors are grateful to Patricia Bowers and Dennis Turk for their constructive editorial comments.

273

COGNITIVE EVENTS

It is with the introduction of "cognition" into the behavioral camp that consideration of "unconscious" events became inevitable (Mahoney, 1980). A decade ago it seemed that all psychology was "going cognitive" (Dember, 1974). In the clinic the cognitive cross-fertilizations were expressed as cognitive-behavior modification (Mahoney, 1974; Meichenbaum, 1977) and cognitive therapy (Beck, Rush, Shaw & Emery, 1979). The "cognition" which was introduced implied and embraced three aspects: cognitive events, cognitive processes, and cognitive structures. Each of these aspects has its links to unconscious processes as those processes are understood in psychodynamic circles. Our discussion focuses on each aspect in turn.

Cognitive events are conscious, identifiable thoughts and images. They occur in the individual's stream of consciousness or they can be readily retrieved upon request. Mandler (1979) has noted that such conscious events exist under four conditions. First, conscious thoughts and images occur during the construction and integration of new thought and action structures. Typically, thoughts and actions are conscious before they become well integrated and automatic. For example, learning to drive a car is initially a conscious process. But with skill, the driver acts automatically and "unconsciously." "Go slowly, be careful, check before pulling out, down shift" and so forth, often characterize the thoughts of the novice driver. With proficiency, these verbalizations drop out of the repertoire and the behavioral act of driving the car becomes automatic. Cognitive-behavioral theory recognizes these *automatic* schemas as significant for theory, assessment, and therapy. And so, in such automatic events (behaviors, thoughts, and accompanying feelings), we recognize one form of "unconsciousness."

A second condition during which cognitive events are active occurs when the individual has to exercise choices and judgments, as is the case in uncertain or novel situations. Whenever individuals have to weigh possible outcomes and consequences (covert trial-and-error judgments), conscious processes may come into play with a corresponding illumination of the underlying and typically "hidden" automatic schemas.

A third condition for the emergence of cognitive events is during periods of "trouble shooting." When one's mental or cognitive plans are interrupted, when a habitual way of acting fails, or when a cognitive plan or sequence is not brought to conclusion, consciousness is brought into play in a problem-solving capacity.

Mandler's fourth condition for the emergence of cognitive events is recall. (Recall of memories is often accompanied by attributions, expectations, and associated emotions about the future as well.) For example, if you were asked to sit back in your chair, close your eyes, and recall in detail a scene in which you became upset, and to report on the thoughts, images, and feelings you had before, during, and after that stressful incident, then the content of your verbal response would exemplify what is here being called cognitive events.

Parenthetically, it is worth noting that being asked to recall one's thoughts or cognitive events, as in the imagery recall assessment, does *not* imply that the individual actually had such thoughts at the time of the stressful incident. Upon reflection, one may produce some postperformance rationalization ("I must have had those thoughts if I behaved in that manner"), or one's recall may be biased or influenced by one's present mood or the demand characteristics of the recall situation. A variety of cognitve and social processes that the individual is not directly aware of may influence the (re)construction of one's cognitive events (Nisbett & Ross, 1980). It is exactly these potential biasing processes that constitute the cognitive processes that are of such great concern to cognitive-behavior therapists, and these will be examined in the next section.

Each of the four conditions described by Mandler, whereby cognitive events can become objects of conscious scrutiny and report, illuminates a corresponding condition in which cognitions are latent and/or unobserved. Beck (1976) has called these unobserved cognitions "automatic thoughts." He describes them as being discrete, specific, unquestioned, idiosyncratic ideas that occur (outside of awareness) autonomously. Meichenbaum (1977) has referred to the same events, calling them part of the "internal dialogue."[1] This dialogue incorporates, among other things, attributions, expectancies, evaluations of the self or task, task-irrelevant thoughts, and so forth. Automatic events are not limited to cognitions, according to the cognitive-behavioral perspective. Images, symbolic "words" and gestures, and accompanying affect are frequently present as well. The role of affect in cognitive-behavioral theory is especially central (Meichenbaum & Gilmore, 1982) and it is especially "automatic" in its function. We will comment further on the role of affect throughout this chapter.

Cognitive events constitute one of three referents for the "cognition" implied by the cognitive-behavioral perspective. Cognitive processes and cognitive structures constitute the other two, and they will be discussed below. Clearly, however, there can be no effective cognitive-behavioral assessment, therapy, or research unless methods exist for uncovering the unseen cognitive events introduced above. A full discussion of the methods for observing those cognitive events that may not normally be visible is given in Meichenbaum, Burland, Gruson, and Cameron (1983), in Meichenbaum and Butler (1980) and in Meichenbaum, Henshaw, and Himel (1982).

COGNITIVE PROCESSES

Cognitive processes refer to those processes that shape mental representations, transforming them and constructing schemes of experience and action. Reciprocally, cognitive processes will themselves be influenced by cognitive structures such as those which guide the focus of attention and information upon which these processes will act. These processes—which include search and storage mechanisms, inferential processes, and retrieval processes—often operate at an automatic or unconscious level. Under most circumstances we do not attend to the ways in which we process information and under many circumstances we cannot. In the same way that we engage in a variety of physiological processes (breathing, stomach contractions, and so forth) without awareness, a similar analogy can be drawn to how we process information. This does *not* mean that one's awareness could not be focused on one's breathing, or for that matter on one's style of thinking; but under normal circumstances we usually do *not* focus attention on these automatic processes. One usually does *not* attend to the processes involved in the appraisals we may make of situations or that are active during the recall of events or during the drawing of conclusions. As Langer (1978) and Thorngate (1976) have observed, in most well-rehearsed social situations our behavior is "mindless." In these situations cognitive processes operate automatically unless they are interrupted for some reason. In the same way that driving a car becomes automatic and occurs with little forethought (unless interrupted) the manner in which an individual processes information typically occurs in a similar automatic fashion. An example of this comes from the study of metacognitions. Metacognitions are important in cognitive-behavior theory. They represent an interface between that which is normally out of conscious awareness and that which is accessible to assessment, therapy, and research.

Metacognition

Imagine that you, the reader, are at a party, talking animatedly, when suddenly you block on someone's name—"What's her name?" At this point, imagine someone interrupts you saying:

> I have a sort of unusual request. I noticed that you blocked on a person's name and I wonder if you would share with me for a moment what you are doing as you try to retrieve this name?

With some forebearance you indulge this "data snoop" and you report:

> Well, if you insist. I guess I will start off by imagining the last time I saw this person, where it was, what we were doing, and so forth.

In other words what is being reported is an effort to retrieve this name by means of association (i.e., metaphorically massaging the engram in which the name is stored).

> Now if that doesn't work then I will go through the alphabet—A, B, C, and so on, and see if the systematic use of a mnemonic helps me to retrieve the name. Then maybe I will solicit help from my friend Jan. I will say, "You know the woman I never liked, the one who wears the tacky dresses, what's her name."

This latter technique reflects the ability to strategically use someone else's "head" in the retrieval process. One doesn't merely ask "Oh, what's her name?" but instead knows exactly how to produce the relevant associations to foster retrieval, namely, "the one I never liked who wears tacky dresses."

If this also fails I'd probably say that such things happen to me, and if I just keep talking the name might occur to me later.

In short, you are conveying a sense of efficacy about your own cognitive processes.

Finally, I would decide to do nothing. I never liked her in the first place and it is certainly not all that important to recall her name. I can tell if the effort at searching my memory will pay off or not, and if it won't I am not going to exert further effort.

This answer to the query "What are you doing to retrieve the unremembered name?" illustrates what is meant by metacognition. Each of us has a good deal of knowledge about our own cognitive processes, and each of us has the ability to guide and control important cognitive strategies. That knowledge and those abilities are what we mean by "metacognition." Under most conditions, individuals engage in metacognitive activity in an automatic nonreflective manner (see Meichenbaum et al., 1983). We retrieve names, overcome memory blocks, seek and process information automatically. These "unconscious" activities are well-rehearsed and practiced. It is, however, possible to learn to see and change the manner in which many of our cognitive processes operate, using metacognitive skills such as those just illustrated (Meichenbaum & Asarnow, 1979).

Whereas most of the work on metacognitiion has been in the area of memory (Flavell & Wellman, 1977; Kreutzer, Leonard, & Flavell, 1975), investigators have also studied metacognition in relation to attentional processes (Miller & Bigi, 1979), to reading comprehension (Meyers & Paris, 1978; Ryan, 1980), to self-control (Mischel, Mischel & Hood, 1978), and to self-monitoring and communication (Markman, 1977). In each of these studies, the individual's knowledge and manner of information processing (his or her cognitive strategies) affected performance. From the perspective of the present chapter, the important point is that metacognitive activities and metacognitive knowledge often function in an automatic unconscious manner.

In summary, metacognitive skills, such as those that direct and control thinking, appear to be overlearned during the middle and later years of childhood (Flavell, 1979). Like the automated performance of a well-practiced pianist, they often occur without conscious awareness or direction. Even before the recent explosion of interest in cognition, the existence of automated metacognitive schemes was recognized, as for instance by Miller, Galanter, and Pribram (1960) in their concept of the *plan*. But metacognition alone does not determine the course of thinking, for there is an inseparable affective component to the control of thought as well. Miller et al. (1960) recognized this fact too when they noted that under certain conditions, mood states (e.g., elation, anxiety, depression, etc.) change the manner in which information is processed. Cognitive-behavioral theory likewise recognizes this position. Cognitive processes respond to affective processes, and vice versa.

Affect and Cognitive Functioning

Cognitive-behavioral theory does not assign primacy either to affect or to cognition. Instead it adopts a transactional perspective that sees both cognition and affect as interdeterministic and interdependent (cf. Bandura, 1978; Lazarus, 1982). There is growing research evidence for the role affect plays in modulating cognitions and metacognitions. For example, research by Bower (1981) and Teasdale (1983) indicates that when subjects are in a depressed mood produced by hypnotic induction, a mood induction procedure, or a psychiatric illness, their cognitive processes are altered. When depressed, speed of information processing is slowed. There is differential recall of negative events. Similarly, there is some evidence that positive moods can influence the recall and influence of positive, as compared to negative, events (Isen, Shalker, Clark, & Karp, 1978; Masters & Santrock, 1976; Mischel, Ebbesen, & Zeiss, 1976). Moreover, such biasing processes occur automatically or unintentionally, without the subject's awareness.

Depressed thoughts and feelings have an impact on the client's behavior in turn, often leading to inactivity that can then contribute to biochemical changes that may further exacerbate the cognitive and affective components of depression (Akiskal & McKinney, 1975). In addition, the depressed individual has a depressed impact on others, thus contributing to the very social avoidance and rejection that the depressive often complains about (Coyne, 1976). More significantly, the depressed individual is often unaware of how (1) the current mood colors and influences the manner in which information and events are being appraised, processed, stored, and retrieved; (2) behavior (inactivity) is exacerbating the depressive process; and (3) unusual social behavior inadvertently is contributing to the very processes that maintain depression. In short, a complex depressive pattern may occur at an automatic, "unconscious" level.

Cognitive-behavioral therapy attempts to make the client aware of this unnoticed automatic pattern (Beck et al., 1979). Cognitive-behavioral therapy proposes that if one wishes to change the depressed individual's behavior (or for that matter the behavior of any individual) there is a need to develop an awareness of unconscious maladaptive thoughts and feelings and their effects on behavior. In other words, one cannot change a behavior without having it first deautomatized or interrupted. The maladaptive behavioral, cognitive, and affective processes that are habitual (i.e., not premeditated) must first be returned to a deautomatized condition. This is the sense in which we would speak of making the unconscious conscious. This "forced consciousness" increases the likelihood for successful interruption of the chain of events that would otherwise operate in an automatic and self-defeating manner. In many instances, such increased awareness will be a necessary but not sufficient condition for behavioral change.

Other Cognitive Processes

Recent work in cognitive and social psychology has described a number of specific cognitive processes that work unnoticed, and so unconsciously. Among these would be the availability heuristic and the representativeness heuristic formulated by Tversky and Kahnemann (1977). The "confirmation bias" described by Taylor and Crocker (1981) and by Snyder and Swann (1976, 1978) is another such unnoticed cognitive process that may influence dysfunctional behaviors. Confirmation bias can be exacerbated by the self-fulfilling processes described by Frank (1974). In each case, a cognitive process that is unnoticed by the client can lead to unrealistic thinking and behavior. The cognitive-behavioral therapist assists the client to identify and examine the impact of these dysfunctional processes. Moreover, the therapist teaches a scientific form of hypothesis testing that can make maladaptive inferential processes known to the client and susceptible to conscious correction. The relationship of processes of this type to nonconscious thinking and behaving is significant and so deserves some further elaboration.

Kahnemann and Tversky (1973) introduced the concepts of the availability and the representativeness heuristics in the context of discussions of judgment under uncertainty conditions. The availability heuristic is characterized by the use of the most available (salient, ready at hand) information or thought as if it were the most relevant and predictive. Availability refers to the ease with which relevant instances come to mind as a basis for judging frequencies of occurrence, that is, the likelihood of a given event or outcome. The ease with which information is brought to mind may be influenced by such factors as recency, saliency, or stereotypic preconceptions, even though these factors may be irrelevant, and may bias both predictions and decision making (Nisbett & Ross, 1980). The representativeness heuristic evaluates information according to the degree to which it matches and represents the nature of the information in conscious awareness at the time. The representativeness heuristic is employed when one is deciding how likely it is that a given event or person is a member of a certain category (i.e., matches the essential features of some schema). As Turk and Salovey (1983) indicate, the automatic use of the representativeness heuristic often causes us to underutilize important base-rate information, and to maintain preconceptions despite contradictory information. (Also see the related work on illusory correlation by Chapman & Chapman, 1969).

The availability heuristic leads to error insofar as the most salient thought may easily be irrelevant, inappropriate, and misleading. The representativeness heuristic leads to error insofar as outcomes depend on more than the degree to which they would be well-representative of the current state of things. The tendencies to expect the simplest and most frequent outcomes in life can influence cognition despite their consciously known fallibility. For example, depressed individuals may be predisposed to attend selectively, in an automatic fashion, to those features of events that are representative of their shortcomings, while ignoring those features that are disconfirmatory. This amplifies the depressed person's view of himself or herself as worthless (Turk & Salovey, 1983). Cognitive-behavioral therapy makes a particular effort to discover the situations in which these automatic egocentric biasing tendencies are generally operating, so that steps may be taken in these situations to stop the dysfunctional cycle.

Research on confirmatory bias has uncovered additional cognitive processes that are frequently automatic in function and significant in modifying behavior, affect, and cognition. Snyder and Swann (1976, 1978) provided subjects with set inducing hypotheses about the personalities of certain target individuals. Subjects were then asked to test these hypotheses by interviewing the target individuals. It was found that subjects regularly looked for and found evidence that was consistent with their initial hypotheses, rather than for evidence which could show these hypotheses to be incorrect. This biased search strategy of the subjects had more profound effects as well, for it also influenced the behaviors of the target individuals in a manner leading them to produce behaviors that seemed to confirm the original mental set of the subjects. Subjects were unaware that their manner of interviewing was producing a biased sample of behavior from the targets. Here too an automatic cognitive process was affecting perception and thinking without conscious awareness.

Frank (1974) used the term "pseudoconfirmation" to refer to a process by which an untested assumption leads to behavior that very probably will evoke respondent behavior confirming this initial assumption. The initial assumption acts as a self-fulfilling prophecy. An example would be someone who imagines others to be very competitive and who, consequently, behaves competitively toward them. This in turn elicits competitive counterresponses that "confirm" the competitiveness of the world (Kelley & Stahelski, 1970). Snyder (1981) has summarized the social psychological research in support of such confirmatory processes in his fine chapter entitled "Seek and ye shall find." Such untested assumptions lead many depressed patients to confirm their own hypothesized undesirableness by defensive social behaviors that contribute to social rejection. This rejection is "available," then interpreted as being "representative," inevitable, and proof of the initial assumption of low personal worth. Thus the client's behavior may create responses in others that confirm maladaptive beliefs. In this way a self-defeating cycle may be created and perpetuated. This entire cognitive process is invariably "unconscious."

COGNITIVE STRUCTURES

The concept of cognition implies events, processes, and structures. We have discussed the first two of this triad and now we propose to consider the place of cognitive structures in cognitive-behavioral theory. Although the term "cognitive structures" had been used earlier by the philosopher Immanuel Kant (see Korner, 1955) and the developmentalist James Baldwin (1894), the term first became popular in psychology through the efforts of Tolman (1932), Bartlett (1932) and Lewin (1935). Since then, cognitive structures have frequently been hypothesized and made the basis for theory. Notable examples include such concepts as Abelson's (1976) "scripts"; Bandura's (1978) "self-systems"; Kelly's (1955) "personal constructs"; Miller, Galanter, and Pribram's (1960) "plans"; Morris's (1975) "structures of meaning"; Minsky's (1975) "frames"; Parkes's (1971) and Frank's (1974) "assumptive worlds"; Piaget's "schemata", (Piaget, 1926/1955; Flavell, 1963) and Sarbin's "roles" (Sarbin & Coe, 1972).

Kovacs and Beck (1978) have captured the meaning of "cognitive structures" very well. They state:

> Cognitive structures are relatively enduring characteristics of a person's cognitive organization. They are organized representations of prior experience; different aspects of experience are organized through different schemata.... A schema allows a person to screen, code, and assess the full range of internal or external stimuli and to decide on a subsequent course of action.... Silent assumptions or premises, bits of information and conclusions provide the content of a cognitive schema. A schema is a relatively enduring structure that functions like a template; it actively screens, codes, categorizes, and evaluates information. By definition, it also represents some relevant prior experience. (pp. 526, 528–529)

The schemata or controlling assumptions that Kovacs and Beck describe are rarely explicitly formulated. They may be thought of as being implicit or as operating at an unconscious level. These schemata may operate as peremptory ideas, that is, those that Klein (1970) described as precluding all doubt, question, or delay, admitting no refusal and being truly imperative. In other words, cognitive structures operate as "perceptual readiness hypotheses" that influence the way situations and events are appraised. As Lazarus (1982) recently noted, such implicit appraisal processes do *not* imply anything about deliberate reflection, rationality, and awareness. Appraisal processes do *not* necessarily imply awareness of the underlying cognitive structures on which they rest. The concept of schemata has been embraced by cognitive social psychologists, who view it as a mental organization of experience which influences the way information is processed and the way behavior is organized (Hastie, 1981; Silver, Wortman, & Klos, 1982; Taylor & Crocker, 1981).

Along these same lines Neisser (1976) described the role of a schema as follows:

> A schema is that portion of the entire perceptual cycle which is internal to the perceiver, modifiable by experience, and somehow specific to what is being perceived. The schema accepts information as it becomes available at sensory surfaces and is changed by that information: it directs movements and exploratory activities that make more information available, by which it is further modified.... The functions of schemata may be clarified by some analogies. In one sense, when it

is viewed as an information-accepting system, a schema is like a *format* in a computer-programming language. Formats specify that information must be of a certain sort if it is to be interpreted coherently.... A schema is not merely like a format; it also functions as a *plan* of the sort described by Miller, Galanter, and Pribram in their seminal book. Perceptual schemata are plans for finding out about objects and events, for obtaining more information to fill in the format.... The analogy between schemata and formats and plans is not complete. Real formats and plans incorporate a sharp distinction between form and content, but this is not true of schemata. The information that fills in the format at one moment in the cyclic process becomes a part of the format in the next, determining how further information is accepted. The schema is not only the plan but also the executor of the plan. It is a pattern of action as well as a pattern *for* action. (p. 54, original emphasis)

Hastie (1981) has proposed that schemata are highly interdependent and that they are embedded in a hierarchical organization. The various levels of the schema hierarchy embody information about prototypic features of events as well as procedural information or instrumental scripts (i.e., mental organizations of behavioral sequences that follow from a plan for accomplishing a goal). The role of schemata has been studied most extensively in the areas of reading comprehension (e.g., Bransford & Franks, 1971; Bransford & Johnson, 1972) and social judgments (Cantor & Mischel, 1977; Taylor & Crocker, 1981).

George Kelly (1970) anticipated the current interest in cognitive structure with his personal construct theory. Kelly's personal construct theory describes the ongoing cycle of framing personal interpretations of the world and then reassessing them in light of ensuing events. For Kelly, a personal construct is a way in which to view the world or to impute meaning to one's experience. However, the cognitive work of building, evaluating, and rebuilding these constructs is rarely done at a conscious level; instead these constructs and the work of remodeling them remain tacit and unarticulated (Neimeyer, 1980). To underscore this tacit process, consider the distinction offered by Kelly between the construal process he postulates and more typical forms of cognition. He states:

It would be quite understandable, linguistic traditions being what they are, if you were to visualize construing as a verbalized or conscious act. But that need not be so. Constructs can be *preverbally* symbolized and a person can have a hard time representing constructs to himself except as raw experience. There is not necessarily anything either cognitive or affective about this kind of construing. (1969, pp. 197–198, original emphasis)

For Kelly, constructs are not solely cognitions. In order to underscore this point Kelly observes:

A person is not necessarily articulate about the constructions he places upon his world. Some of his constructions are not symbolized by words.... Even the elements which are construed may have no verbal handles by which they can be manipulated and the person finds himself responding to them with speechless impulse. Thus, in studying the psychology of man-the-philosopher, we must take into account his subverbal patterns of representation and construction. (Kelly, 1955, p. 16)

Kelly's conceptualization of a complicated unverbalized meaning is reminiscent of Polanyi's (1958) notion of tacit knowledge. Polanyi indicated that people know a great deal more than they can articulate, and as Bowers (1981) noted, people behave "in accordance with information that is not consciously represented, but which is nevertheless registered and trusted as an important clue to reality" (p. 184). Like Polanyi, Kelly did *not* draw a dichotomous distinction between conscious and unconscious processes, but instead spoke of different levels of cognitive awareness. With this brief historical background to the concept of cognitive structures, we can now turn our attention to the question of the functions of cognitive structures.

Functions of Cognitive Structures

The concept of cognitive structures has been introduced to account for the limits of one's information processing. At any given time we are able to attend to and process only a small portion of internal and external input. One's attention serves a "gating function," delimiting the range of potential inputs. The construct of cognitive structures is used by cognitive-behavioral theories to explain the processes that guide and control one's attention.

Cognitive structures should be thought of as theoretical constructs offered to explain the perception, interpretation, transformation, organization, and recall of information. The need for such a concept was evident in the 1930s when the concept of a schema was introduced. As first proposed by Bartlett (1932) and Woodworth (1938), the concept of a schema was offered to explain the construction of perception and the distortion of memory. The schema was viewed as a cognitive template imposed on the world, leading to selective perception and permitting one to fill in the gaps of information that are missing. As Taylor and Crocker (1981) note, schemas enable the perceiver to identify stimuli quickly, chunk an appropriate unit, fill in information missing from the stimulus configuration, and select a strategy for obtaining further information, solving a problem or reaching a goal. Thus schemata serve both encoding and representational functions as well as interpretative and inferential functions.

Recently, Markus (1977) demonstrated that the concept of a schema can be extended to information about oneself. Markus views self-schemata as cognitive generalizations about the self, derived from past experiences that organize and guide the processing of self-related information contained in the individual's social experience. These schemata function as selective mechanisms that determine which information is attended to, how it is structured, what importance is attached to it, and what happens to it subsequently. The accessibility of schemata is an important factor in determining the sources of environmental stimulation that will receive attention, how attended information will be interpreted and encoded, and whether it will be remembered.

Self-schemata are viewed as self-serving, biasing the encoding process (that is, how information is perceived, classified, stored, and selectively retrieved). Markus found that information which is congruent with one's self-concept is processed more easily and confidently than incongruent information. Moreover, an individual is resistant to counterschematic information and in the context of psychotherapy this may be a major source of client resistance (see Meichenbaum and Gilmore, 1982).

Turk and Speers (1983) have commented on the nature of cognitive structures. They argue that each schema embodies two components, an ideational component and an affective component. The ideational component consists of information and definitions (i.e., defining characteristics and prototypic exemplars). The affective component consists of affective valences related to the stimulus domain. Thus not only is information coded and stored, but so is affect. One can trigger a particular schema by eliciting a set of emotions. The schema thus activated in turn determines which emotions, thoughts, and behaviors are accessed.

The concept of cognitive structures or schemata is similar to Kuhn's (1970) notion of scientific *paradigms* which control and screen information that challenges a particular perspective, expectancy, or understanding. Like paradigms, one's cognitive structures may operate at an automatic or unconscious level. Both the scientist and the client are often unaware of the manner in which their schemata guide and influence their perceptions of the world and their behavior.

Examples of such implicit unconscious processes are not limited to the domains of psychology and psychotherapy. Harman (1981) has described anthropological examples of people from one tribe having a different "reality" or consensual belief system (set of schemata) by means of which they perceive the world quite differently than do members of another tribe. Each tribe's belief system is validated by experience. Belief systems shape perceptions and they in turn contribute to the validation process. The tribe's constellation of implicit beliefs, with accompanying expectations, serves as a framework for perceiving and evaluating inputs. Moreover, the members of each tribe have a confirmatory bias to seek and find data that are supportive of their initial beliefs.

It is important to appreciate, however, that although such confirmatory biases exist, schemata are not intractible, and they can be altered by means of disconfirmatory evidence. A major feature of cognitive-behavioral intervention is to make clients aware of their tendency to adopt a confirmatory stance and to encourage them to view their thoughts as hypotheses worthy of testing, instead of viewing them as unalterable truths. The therapist uses a variety of clinical ploys to cajole and challenge the client to perform personal experiments, in the therapy session as well as *in vivo,* in order to collect data that are disconfirmatory.

Cognitive structures or schemas about oneself may change *without* formal psychotherapy. Various consciousness-raising movements such as "Black pride," or "Women's lib," and so forth, can be seen as attempts to help individuals appreciate the tacit nature of their already existing schemata and to encourage the development of different schemata, feelings, and behaviors.

There are many ways to alter an individual's schemata. One procedure for change is to focus directly on the cognitive structure by means of direct challenges that present contrary information. However, given the tendency for schemata to be self-serving and to resist counterschematic input, such direct assaults may *not* prove the most therapeutically effective means of intervention. We each have a tendency to ignore information that is *contradictory* to our self-image. An alternative treatment approach is to engage the client in a collaborative venture in which he or she comes to appreciate the potential biasing impact of certain schemata and works to collect data that may disconfirm a maladaptive schema.

Since schemata have both an ideational and affective component, the client can learn to monitor the conditions that trigger a particular schema (that is, the client can perform a situational and affective analysis). For instance, consider the example in which you are asked to sit back and recall a time when you became stressed, and to note the feelings and thoughts you had before, during, and after that incident. We then ask the question: "In what other situations do you have similar thoughts and feelings?" By conducting a situational analysis of such feelings and thoughts, we can explore what is common across these various stressful situations. Are there particular themes or current concerns that emerge across such stressful situations? For some of us the common theme may involve the challenge to our sense of control, whereas for others the major dominant concern may involve a need for social approval, and for still others a violation of our sense of justice may be central to our stress, and so forth. In fact, a stressful situation may elicit a variety of competing concerns and complex feelings with their accompanying automatic scripts, expectations, behavioral routines, and interpersonal consequences.

Imagine a client who found himself, all too often, overreacting to daily hassles. As Wachtel (1982) has noted, one should try to understand the regularities in such an individual's behaviors, feelings, and thoughts. One way to do this is to try to answer the question: What would this person have to want or think in order to behave that way so frequently? In attempting to answer this question in a collaborative manner with the client, the therapist and client attempt to formulate a working hypothesis as to the cognitive structures, current concerns, hidden agendas, or what Malan (1979) and Strupp and Binder (1982) call the "psychodynamic focus" that the client brings to bear across situations. In addition, the therapist and client consider the possibility that such cognitive structures may exert their influence without the client's awareness or understanding. It is possible that the client is not conscious of the goals, or at least of parts of the goals that influence and guide behavior. In this sense, the cognitive structures may exert their influence in an unconscious manner.

One objective of cognitive-behavioral therapy is to increase the client's self-awareness in such a way that he or she can appreciate how specific cognitive structures are influencing the way events are being perceived, memories recalled, and expectancies and behaviors produced. By means of a "collaborative empiricism" (Beck et al., 1979) clients are encouraged to become their own "personal scientist" (Mahoney, 1974), personally conducting experiments that may yield data which disconfirm dysfunctional assumptions about the world, or which, to use the term suggested by Alexander and French (1946), provide "corrective emotional experiences." Some clients may need to be taught specific cognitive and behavioral skills to perform such corrective experiments and to be open to such emotional experiences. With repeated attempts (or multiple trials) and guidance from the therapist, the client can begin to collect data or *evidence* that demonstrates the extent to which his or her cognitive structures may need to change. Meichenbaum (1977) and Meichenbaum and Gilmore (1982) have described this process as an evidential theory of behavior change.

Influencing Cognitive Structures

Several examples can be offered illustrating how an individual's (or group's) meaning system, current concerns, and schemata affect behavior. The first example comes from a sociological study of a Chicago street gang (Keiser, 1969). Based on his observations and his interviews with gang members, Keiser hypothesized that one major schema or meaning system could account for a great deal of the gang's behavior. The gang members divided situations into two categories of rather colorfully labeled events: (1) high-risk activities (for example, "humbugging," "gang-banging," "wolf-packing," and "hustling"), and (2) low-risk activities ("gigs," "games," "sets" and "pulling jive"). It was in the former set of risk activities that one earned peer acceptance (earned one's "rep," displayed "heart," or showed one was no "punk"). Thus acceptance by one's peers in the gang represented a primary current concern that influenced how situations were perceived (in terms of risk levels, with the associated potential for raising or lowering group esteem); it influenced which emotions were experienced (in terms of their timing and significance), and it influenced which behaviors were engaged in (approach or avoidance). The need for status in the gang, and for the social approval of peers, produced a readiness set or appraisal system which operated automatically in influencing the thoughts, feelings, and behaviors of the gang members.

For Keiser, the need for peer approval and the appraisal of riskiness of situations reveal the existence of a superordinate cognitive structure. We call structures of this kind *core organizing principles* ("cops").[2] "Cops" are theoretical constructs in the Cronbach and Meehl (1955) sense of the term. "Cops" explain and predict present and future behavior. One cannot prove the existence of "cops," but one can infer their presence from a number of convergent sources of data in the same way that one confirms other scientific concepts such as "gravity" and "perception" (Garner, Hake, & Eriksen, 1953). "Cops" are cognitive structures that are a useful fiction. Each is a theoretical construct and a working hypothesis to explain behavior. One tenet of the cognitive-behavioral model is that "cops" can (and generally do) operate, and influence behavior, without any conscious awareness of them by the individual. "Cops" represent a "tacit knowledge" that guides and influences thoughts, feelings, and behavior.

We can illustrate the role of "cops" with a clinical case in which a client found himself becoming overly upset at a variety of daily hassles to the point where help was needed. A situational analysis of these various stressful situations revealed a common emotional theme. These feelings of irritation, frustration, and anger were all elicited in situations in which the client felt that an injustice had been perpetuated on him or on others (e.g., being shortchanged, or seeing the weak being taken advantage of, etc.). When a developmental analysis was conducted or when he could recall having had similar feelings and thoughts in the past, he was able to report instances in childhood in which he had observed his immigrant father having had to "eat crow" (i.e., not standing up for his rights when an injustice was suffered). The client used these experiences and their accompanying feelings to construct a personal credo or an implicit set of rules of living (a "core organizing principle") whereby he would *never* allow anyone to take advantage of him or the members of his family. This credo guided his progress through law school, and it became a "readiness set" or "cognitive template" for appraising life's various situations. Thus for example, his response to finding himself shortchanged by a waiter was extreme. This was due not only to the specifics of the immediate situation, but also to the "meaning" this event held for this man, given his "cops." The stress this client felt was set up by a life theme that had become latent in a dominating cognitive structure. The client's natural tendency to adopt a confirmatory bias prevented him from exploring the possibility that what he perceived as being deliberately shortchanged might instead have been due to some other source of error. His somewhat "paranoid" social style elicited an immediate defensive hostility in others, further confirming the client's sense of being deliberately victimized. Thus a vicious cycle was completed, only to be recycled again and again. This overlearned pattern operated in an automatic unconscious manner.

This client's main presenting problem developed from his preoccupation with a need for "justice" (as he defined that) and was exacerbated by his rigidity in not being open to disconfirmatory data and to other competing hypotheses (cognitive structures). He evaluated each social interaction in terms of his peremptory ideas about equity; usually seen from the standpoint of himself as victim. Wachtel (1982) describes the process leading to such a state as the "cumulative skewing of experiences through the course of development. These experiences lead to patterns which, whatever their origins in the person's history, are maintained in the present by their present consequences" (p. 597). We may add that this skewing and interactive process invariably occurs without the individual's direct conscious awareness or intention, and with a tangential conscious participation that is itself conditioned upon earlier "cops."

We begin to see then how much the emphasis on cognition and feelings influence cognitive-behavioral theory and associated clinical practice. In particular, the present focus on cognitive structures has parallels with the unconscious "complexes" employed by the more psychodynamic traditions. Yet major differences remain between the cognitive-behavioral and psychodynamic traditions, differences that hinge on differential implicit roles played by wish and motivation and by the role of behavioral interventions in changing cognitive structures. These matters can be illustrated with a case described by Silvan Tomkins (1979). This case affords another example of how cognitive structures, in particular the concept of "cops," play a role in the cognitive-behavioral understanding of human psychology.

Tomkins describes the case of a man who was driving along a beautiful solitary country road on a sunny day when he became intensely and inappropriately enraged upon the brief appearance of a distant truck. Tomkins explains this incident in terms of what he calls a "preemptive metaphor." As an only child this man had gone mute for six months (apparently in rage) upon the birth of his brother. Tomkins views the pastoral driving scene as an analogue for the warm, solitary relationship enjoyed with the mother. The truck symbolized the unexpected appearance of the younger brother who spoiled everything. For Tomkins then, this episode reflected an unconscious metaphor for the "nuclear scene," with attendant motivational and wishful drives being expressed. For the cognitive-behavioral theorist, this episode represents the result of the action of certain cognitive events, cognitive processes, and cognitive-affective structures which may occur at an automatic (unconscious) level, as well as a result of their interpersonal consequences.

The cognitive-behavioral therapist would first attempt to determine the nature of the driver's cognitive events (conscious thoughts and feelings) and accompanying feelings that occurred before, during, and after the appearance of the truck. How did the client's mood affect what he attended to, selectively recalled, and which attributions he employed to explain his behavior? The client would be encouraged to explore whether the stimulus for the rage was not perhaps different than the consciously recognized truck. Perhaps the triggering stimulus was really an unremembered news item on the car radio, or an unremembered thought from the day before. It is clear that the real causes of behavior need not be the attributed causes (Nisbett & Ross, 1980; Bowers, this book).

The assessment would continue by determining if the client has similar thoughts and feelings in other situations in which he becomes enraged? Do any themes emerge, do any cognitive structures help to explain this pattern of reactions? What is the developmental history of such structures? If such core organizing principles of cognitive structures emerge, then it seems plausible that they have had important developmental precursors.

Although one may question Tomkins's equation of objective stimulus events (e.g., pastoral scene with this man's relationship with his mother, and the appearance of the truck with sibling rivalry), the rejection of a specific metaphor does not preclude the potentially important role of "cops" or cognitive structures in guiding and influencing ongoing behavior without one's awareness. The development of each cognitive structure may have been influenced, if not started, by early childhood events such as the birth of a sibling. Would the fact that in Tomkins's example the driver's baby brother loved trucks and grew up to become a truck driver make Tomkins's metaphor more plausible? Would the fact that the mother loved to paint pastoral scenes improve the plausibility of the preemptive metaphor? Tomkins does *not* provide such information about the brother or about the mother. Instead, these questions raise the issue concerning which conditions we might consider to influence associative meanings affecting someone's behavior—meanings which the individual may *not* fully recognize. Simply put, behavior (e.g., becoming enraged) may be influenced by unconscious processes or implicit meaning systems, as well as being influenced by a number of conscious and directly observable environmental events.

Core organizing principles or cognitive structures serve many of the same purposes for cognitive-behavior therapists as those served for Freud by the concept of unconscious processes. Each metaphor tries to make sense out of patients' verbalizations and behaviors that on the surface seem bewildering. By examining the patient's dreams, fantasies, slips of the tongue, early memories, and associations Freud inferred the presence of unconscious conflicts. For Freud, such unconscious conflicts represent ideas and desires that have been repressed. The "unconscious" and "repression" are closely linked in Freudian theory. Freud stated: "The repressed is a prototype of the unconscious." This interdependence between the unconscious and repression has always presented a major dilemma to researchers. The unconscious is never easily accessible to consciousness, so how can we ever hope to know its contents or its influence? Rather than view unconscious processes as the repository of unverbalized needs that have grown out of arrested psychosexual development and that have been subjected to repression, one can instead view unconscious processes in terms of information-processing mechanisms (i.e., cognitive processes and structures) that may be subject to independent cross-validations. When viewed this way, the investigation of unconscious processes is clearly neither foolhardy nor the domain of whimsies. As Mahoney (1980) noted, it then represents a challenging and inescapable task.

Summary

From the cognitive-behavioral perspective, cognitive structures are systems which provide meaning to experience. These theoretical constructs are postulated to be responsible for the nature of an individual's observable thoughts, feelings, and behaviors. In turn, such feelings, thoughts, and consequences from one's own earlier behavior can elicit further cognitive schemata. Thus a cognitive-behavioral model of "the psyche" is an interactive one, with cognitions, affects, and their supporting schemata all being mutually interdetermined and mutually restrictive.

An individual's cognitive structures serve as a kind of "executive processor" holding the "blueprints" for thinking, feeling, and behaving. The set of cognitive structures is the "meaning system" that functions to put behavior into motion, and then to guide the choice and direction of particular sequences of thoughts, feelings, and behaviors. Cognitive structure also determines the continuation, interruption, or change of direction of ongoing thought, affect, and behavior. The meaning that individuals impute to situations and to events functions to influence their expectations and appraisals, setting into motion cognitive events or internal dialogues with their accompanying feelings and behavior. In this way, the core organizing principles ("cops") of an individual are theoretical constructs that we feel are particularly useful in explaining and predicting behavior.

The cognitive impact on behavioral therapy and behavioral theory has been great. We have now traced this impact in regard to the concepts of cognitive events (the significance of thoughts and affects), cognitive processes (the significance of covert reasoning, heuristics, and covert emotional biasing) and cognitive structures (the significance of schemata and core organizing principles). Each of these three aspects of cognition implies an unconscious domain that is important to recognize and understand. We can see in these unconscious domains many points of similarity with the concept of unconscious function offered by psychodynamic theories. It is important to understand that in cognitive behavioral assessment, therapy, and research, what is not conscious is seen as being highly significant. This is a reversal of the original behavioral point of view, and deserves emphasis.

Naturally, however, there remain important differences between the cognitive-behavioral view of the unconscious and the psychodynamic view. The cognitive-behavioral approach questions the theoretical axiom that postulates a dynamic unconscious maintained by the energies of repression. In general, the psychodynamic model that takes unconsciousness to be the charcoal forged by the kiln of pain and conflict, ready to glow with heat again if properly rekindled, is questioned by a cognitive-behavioral perspective. Cognitive-behavioral theory attributes the significant places of pain and conflict to the conscious impediments these put up against attempts to change oneself in the ways intended in therapy (cf. Meichenbaum & Gilmore, 1982). Pain and conflict are often, and most importantly, sources of resistance which are not necessarily denied or hidden.

Moreover, a cognitive-behavioral approach focuses upon a developmental-transactional analysis of behavior (along the lines of social learning theory), one that considers unconscious processes (as described herein) to be only one of several influences on behavior. As much weight is placed on environmental consequences in determining behavior as on developmental factors in influencing cognitive structures. The emphasis placed by psychodynamic theorists on arrested stages of psychosexual development in causing "unconscious conflicts" is questioned by cognitive-behavioral theorists. While developmental factors are seen as important precursors for the shaping of cognitive structures, these factors are viewed as both more individually and culturally determined and contemporaneously influenced than is often proposed by psychodynamic models. In a cognitive-behavioral model, there is no commitment to an "energy model" of psychodynamic conflicts or to a particular mental or motivational model of the mind (i.e., id, ego, superego processes). Instead, there is an attempt to develop a taxonomy of cognitive events, processes, and structures and to develop a testable theoretical model of how these processes interact with each other as well as with feelings, behaviors, and environmental consequences.

Clearly, however, both the psychodynamic and the cognitive-behavioral schools share in common a most significant derivative from their concepts of the unconscious, that is, they share a commitment to what we might call "raising consciousness." For the cognitive-behavioral therapist, however, "raising consciousness" is *not* considered sufficient to foster behavioral change. The cognitive-behavioral therapist employs the full armamentarium of behavior therapy to help the client "work through" or perform behavioral assignments in order to collect the data that will lead to changes. This change is reflected in altered cognitive and affective events, processes, and structures as well as in the client's behavioral repertoire and the consequences resulting from it. Such techniques as self-monitoring, behavioral and imagery rehearsal, graded *in vivo* assignments, cognitive restructuring, and the like are used to help the client alter the meaning and impact of maladaptive unconscious processes. Although both psychodynamic and cognitive-behavioral approaches pay homage to the concept of unconscious processes, each employ different therapeutic tactics to change these processes. Cognitive-behavioral treatment approaches are more likely to be briefer, more directive, and more behavioral than are psychodynamic treatment approaches. But even these differences are obscured if one recalls that Freud's initial interventions were also of a brief variety and often quite directive (Strupp & Binder, 1982). As the passions that separate therapeutic approaches subside and the logical analysis of techniques and concepts are undertaken, a constructive exchange between approaches can begin. In order to nurture such an exchange, we conclude our discussion with an attempt to better understand the concept of the "unconscious" in psychology.

TOWARD A CONCEPTUALIZATION OF THE UNCONSCIOUS

Part of the difficulty in explicitly defining the concept of the unconscious is not only with the slippery nature of unconscious processes, but also with the clouded nature of scientific concepts. Neisser (1979) has considered these problems with regard to the concept of intelligence. Since his analysis has relevance for issues surrounding the concept of the unconscious, we will consider it in some detail. Neisser argues that the concept of intelligence, like many scientific and everyday concepts, is fuzzy-edged, having many associated features and operations. No single characteristic defines a given concept. Instead, concepts are defined by the degree to which examples of the concept show *prototypicality,* and by the degree to which a *family of resemblance* exists among various examples of the concept.

The notion of prototypicality comes from the work of Rosch and her colleagues (Rosch, 1975, 1978; Rosch & Mervis, 1975; Rosch, Mervis, Gray,

Johnson, & Boyes-Braem, 1976). They have argued that a concept is best defined by the fit between any example and the prototype exemplar. Neisser discusses the nature of prototypicality by trying to define an everyday concept such as "chairness." One can give many examples of different types of chairs—dining room chairs, car seats, stools, bean bag chairs, and so forth. Each of these examples differs in some important feature, yet they each fall within the category of "chairness." To use Rosch's term, they have more category "in-ness" than "out-ness." However, such judgments depend upon the prototype that we hold of "chair." For Neisser, the prototypic chair has a horizontal surface, is man-made out of relatively permanent material, is portable, and was built to be sat upon. Insofar as any example matches this prototype, it fits the category of "chairness." Neisser argues that a similar prototypic analysis can be performed for the definition of scientific concepts such as intelligence. One must identify theoretically relevant dimensions in formulating a prototype. Then one can judge how well each example fits the prototype. A similar prototype analysis can be applied to the concept of the unconscious. However, before attempting to perform such an analysis, let us first briefly consider Neisser's second definitional strategy, namely, the Wittgensteinian approach, defining concepts by means of formulating a family of resemblance.

Wittgenstein (1953) illustrated the concept of a family of resemblance with his discussion of the concept of "gameness." Consider, for example, such varied games as board games, card games, ball games, Olympic games, and so forth. What is common to each of these that defines "gameness?" Is it amusement, skill, competition? Wittgenstein noted that there is nothing common to *all* games, but embedded in the definition of the concept "gameness" is a *network of overlapping similarities,* a "family of resemblance." No one game has all of the attributes; and each game has somewhat different attributes. Some games require skills, others do not Some are competitive and others are not. But sufficient overlap exists so that one can come up with a definition of "gameness." There is no single feature that all games have in common, but rather one attempts to search for the boundary conditions that separate games from nongames.

The same difficulties that apply to defining the concepts of "chairness" and "gameness" apply to the concepts of "unconscious" and "conscious." There is no sharp boundary between conscious and unconscious processes, just as there is no sharp distinction between games and nongames. The concept of the unconscious, like the concept of "gameness," can be defined by means of identifying similarities that occur across examples. The implicit definitions of the unconscious, shared it seems by most clinicians whatever may be their appraisals concerning the utility of those definitions, are not easy to map. We admire, and would like to recall here, Bowers's (this book) simple assertion about what constitutes an unconscious determinant of behavior. He writes: "Determinants of thought and action which are not noticed or appreciated as such constitute unconscious influences." We would add to this beginning definition of the unconscious, unnoticed and unappreciated determinants of affect, about which psychology has more varied hypotheses than is the case for the causes of thought or action.

What then might be the nature of the family of resemblances that points to "unconsciousness"? Consider the range and variety of the most prominent examples that have been offered in this book to illustrate the concept of unconscious events, processes and structures: dreaming, sleep talking and sleep walking, habitual automatic behavior and thinking styles, subliminal perception and hidden preattentive processes, metacognitive activity, various forms of psychopathology such as dissociative states, altered states due to drugs or hypnotic induction, blind sight, defense mechanisms such as repression, action slips, tacit knowledge, intuition, pseudoconfirmatory behavior, and core organizing principles. Bowers's definition, with affect added, nicely subsumes each of these. But we are left with the next level of analysis at which it becomes useful to attempt to change a definition by exclusion ("not noticed and not appreciated") into a definition implying the presence of conditions that produce unconsciousness or prevent consciousness. *Why* do we fail to notice and fail to appreciate the determinants of action, thought, and affect?

There can be a number of reasons why these determinants go unnoticed and unappreciated. They may be inherently invisible because they require mental capacities that are not yet, or will never normally be, available for use. They may be functionally invisible, requiring an attention and set that does not currently exist even if each of these could be produced from a change in motivation or situation. In this latter case, there may never have been the attention or set that would render conscious what is still unconscious. Bowers has discussed how anticipatory avoidances may result in this state. On the other hand, a person may once have been conscious of what is now unattended and unappreciated. The change to a new unconsciousness may be the result of "repression," of "automaticity," or of normal learning experiences which happen to have "misled" or temporarily blinded the person. The challenge is to better specify these various reasons, these various situations, resulting in unconsciously controlled action, emotion, and thought.

The effort to meet this challenge and the effort to formulate families of resemblance and prototypes of unconscious processes, reflect a commitment to a basic presupposition, namely, that those aspects of mental activity that are in or subject to awareness comprise but a small portion of the total activity of the human mind. The precise formulations of the family of resemblance, and the prototypes we seek, must await future work. But that work must be done, because some concept beyond conscious mental experience is needed to explain behavior. The present cognitive-behavioral analysis of unconscious processes is designed to raise, once again, the proposition that one's thoughts, feelings, and actions are informed and influenced by factors that are not consciously represented. Insofar as we have been successful in explicating the nature of unconscious processes, a rapprochement between the behavioral and psychodynamic views of behavior and behavior change are possible. An integrative cognitive-behavioral approach which examines the relationships between thoughts, feelings, behaviors and their consequences holds the promise for a much enriched understanding of the "unconscious."

NOTES

1. Beck (1976) comments that "for a good part of their waking life, people monitor their thoughts, wishes, feelings, and actions. Sometimes there is an internal debate as the individual weighs alternatives and courses of action and makes decisions. Plato referred to this phenomenon as 'internal dialogue.'" As Beck's quote illustrates the present cognitive-behavioral perspective has had many historical forerunners.
2. We are indebted to our colleague Dick Steffy for coining the acronym "cops"—core organizing principles.

REFERENCES

Abelson, R.P. Script processing in attitude formation and decision making. In J. Carroll & J. Payne (Eds.), *Cognition and social behavior.* Hillsdale, N.J.: Erlbaum, 1976.

Akiskal, H., & McKinney, W. Overview of recent research in depression. *Archives of General Psychiatry,* 1975, *32,* 285–305.

Alexander, F., & French, T. *Psychoanalytic therapy: Principles and applications.* New York: Ronald Press, 1946.

Baldwin, J. *Mental development in the child and the race.* New York: Macmillan, 1894.

Bandura, A. The self-system in reciprocal determinism. *American Psychologist,* 1978, *33,* 344–358.

Bartlett, F. *Remembering.* Cambridge: Cambridge University Press, 1932.

Beck, A., Rush, A., Shaw, B., & Emery, G. *Cognitive therapy of depression.* New York: Guilford Press, 1979.

Bower, G. Mood and memory. *American Psychologist,* 1981, *36,* 129–148.

Bowers, K. Knowing more than we can say leads to saying more than we can know: On being implicitly informed. In D. Magnusson (Ed.), *Toward a psychology of situations.* Hillsdale, N.J.: Erlbaum, 1981.

Bransford, J., & Franks, J. The abstraction of linguistic ideas. *Cognitive Psychology,* 1971, *2,* 331–350.

Bransford, J., & Johnson, M. Contextual prerequisites for understanding: Some investigations of comprehension and recall. *Journal of Verbal Learning and Verbal Behavior,* 1972, *11,* 717–726.

Cantor, N., & Mischel, W. Traits as prototypes: Effects on recognition memory. *Journal of Personality and Social Psychology,* 1977, *35,* 38–48.

Coyne, J. Toward an interactional description of depression. *Psychiatry,* 1976, *39,* 14–27.

Chapman, L., & Chapman, J. Illusory correlation as an obstacle to the use of valid psychodiagnostic signs. *Journal of Abnormal Psychology,* 1969, *74,* 271–287.

Cronbach, L., & Meehl, P. Construct validity of psychological tests. *Psychological Bulletin,* 1955, *52,* 281–302.

Dember, W. Motivation and the cognitive revolution. *American Psychologist,* 1974, *29,* 161–168.

Flavell, J. *The developmental psychology of Jean Piaget.* Princeton, N.J.: Van Nostrand, 1963.

Flavell, J. Metacognition and cognitive monitoring: A new area of cognitive-developmental inquiry. *American Psychologist,* 1979, *34,* 906–911.

Flavell, J., & Wellman, H. Metamemory. In R. Kail & J. Hagen (Ed.), *Perspectives on the development of memory and cognition.* Hillsdale, N.J.: Erlbaum, 1977.

Frank, J. *Persuasion and healing* (2nd ed.). New York: Schocken, 1974.

Freud, S. Repression. *Standard Edition* (Vol. 14). London: Hogarth Press, 1958. (Originally published 1915.)

Garner, W., Hake, H., & Eriksen, C. Operationism and the concept of perception. *Psychological Review,* 1953, *63,* 149–159.

Goldfried, M. On the history of therapeutic integration. *Behavior Therapy,* 1982, *13,* 572–593.

Harman, W. Human consciousness research: Problems and promises of an emerging science. Paper presented at the American Psychological Association. August, 1981.

Hastie, R. Schematic principles in human memory. In E. Higgins, C. Herman, & M. Zanna (Eds.), *Social cognition: The Ontario Symposium.* Hillsdale, N.J.: 1981.

Isen, A., Shalker, T., Clark, M., & Karp, L. Affect, accessibility of material in memory, and behavior: A cognitive loop? *Journal of Personality and Social Psychology,* 1978, *36,* 1–12.

James, W. *The principles of psychology* (VOl. 1). New York: Holt, 1890.

Kahnemann, D., & Tversky, A. On the psychology of prediction. *Psychological Review,* 1973, *80,* 237–251.

Keiser, L. *The vice lords: Warriors of the streets.* New York: Holt, Rinehart & Winston, 1969.

Kelley, H., & Stahelski, A. Errors in perception of intentions in a mixed-motive game. *Journal of Experimental Social Psychology,* 1970, *6,* 370–400.

Kelly, G. *The psychology of personal constructs.* New York: Norton, 1955.

Kelly, G. Personal construct theory and the psychotherapeutic interview. In B. Maher (Ed.), *Clinical psychology and personality: The selected papers of George Kelly.* New York: Wiley, 1969.

Kelly, G. A brief introduction to personal construct theory. In D. Bannister (Ed.), *Perspectives in personal construct theory.* New York: Academic Press, 1970.

Klein, F. *Peremptory ideas in perception, motive and thought.* New York: Knopf, 1970.

Korner, S. *Kant.* Harmondworth, England: Penguin Books, 1955.

Kovacs, M., & Beck, A. Maladaptive cognitive structures and depression. *American Journal of Psychiatry,* 1978, *135,* 525–533.

Kreutzer, M., Leonard, C., & Flavell, J. An interview study of children's knowledge about memory. *Monographs of the Society for Research in Child Development,* 1975, *40,* 159.

Kuhn, T. *The structure of scientific revolutions.* Chicago: University of Chicago Press, 1970.

LaBerge, D., & Samuels, S. Towards a theory of automatic information processing in reading. *Cognitive Psychology,* 1974, *6,* 293–323.

Langer, E. Rethinking the role of thought in social interaction. In J. Harvey, W. Ickes, & R. Kidd (Eds.), *New directions in attribution research* (Vol. 2). Hillsdale, N.J.: Erlbaum, 1978.

Lazarus, R. Thoughts on the relations between emotion and cognition. *American Psychologist,* 1982, *37,* 1019–1024.

Lazarus, R. The stress and coping paradigm. In C. Eisdorfer (Ed.), *Models for clinical psychopathology.* New York: Spectrum, 1981.

Lazarus, R., & Launier, R. Stress-related transactions between persons and environment. In L. Pervin & M. Lewis (Eds.), *Perspectives in interactional psychology.* New York: Plenum Press, 1978.

Lewin, K. *A dynamic theory of personality.* New York: McGraw-Hill, 1935.

Mahoney, M. *Cognition and behavior modification.* Cambridge, Mass.: Ballinger, 1974.

Mahoney, M. Psychotherapy and the structure of personal revolutions. In M. Mahoney (Ed.), *Psychotherapy process.* New York: Plenum, 1980.

Malan, D. *Individual psychotherapy and the science of psychodynamics.* London: Butterworth, 1979.

Mandler, G. Thought processes, consciousness and stress. In V. Hamilton & D. Warburton (Eds.), *Human stress and cognition: An information processing approach.* London: Wiley, 1979.

Mandler, G. Stress and thought processes. In L. Goldberger & S. Breznitz (Eds.), *Handbook of stress.* New York: Macmillan, 1982.

Markman, G. Realizing that you don't understand: A preliminary investigation. *Child Development,* 1977, *48,* 986–992.

Markus, H. Self-schemata and processing information about the self. *Journal of Personality and Social Psychology,* 1977, *35,* 63–78.

Marmor, J., & Woods, S. (Eds.) *The interface between psychodynamic and behavioral therapies.* New York: Plenum, 1980.

Mason, J. A reevaluation of the concept "non-specificity" in stress theory. *Journal of Psychiatric Research,* 1971, *8,* 323–333.

Masters, J., & Santrock, J. Studies in self-regulation of behavior: Effects of contingent cognitive and affective events. *Developmental Psychology,* 1976, *12,* 334–348.

Meichenbaum, D. *Cognitive behavior modification: An integrative approach.* New York: Plenum, 1977.

Meichenbaum, D., & Asarnow, J. Cognitive-behavioral modification and metacognitive development: Implications for the classroom. In P. Kendall & S Hollon (Eds.), *Cognitive-behavioral interventions: Theory, research and procedures.* New York: Academic Press, 1979.

Meichenbaum, D., Burland, S., Gruson, L., & Cameron, R. Metacognitive assessment. In S. Yussen (Ed.), *Growth of reflection.* New York: Academic Press, 1983.

Meichenbaum, D., & Butler, L. Cognitive ethology: Assessing the streams of cognition and emotion. In K. Blankstein, P. Pliner, & J. Polivy (Eds.), *Assessment and modification of emotional behavior.* New York: Plenum, 1980.

Meichenbaum, D., Butler, L., & Joseph L. Toward a conceptual model of social competence. In J. Wine & M. Smye (Eds.), *The identification and enhancement of social competence*. New York: Guilford Press, 1982.

Meichenbaum, D., & Gilmore, B. Resistance: From a cognitive-behavioral perspective. In P. Wachtel (Ed.), *Resistance in psychodynamic and behavioral therapies*. New York: Plenum, 1982.

Meichenbaum, D., Henshaw, D., & Himel, N. Coping with stress as a problem-solving process. In W. Krohne & L. Laux (Eds.), *Achievement, stress and anxiety*. Washington, D.C., Hemisphere Press, 1982.

Meyers, M., & Paris, S. Children's metacognitive knowledge about reading. *Journal of Educational Psychology*, 1978, *70*, 680–690.

Miller, G., Galanter, E., & Pribram, K. *Plans and structure of behavior*. New York: Holt, 1960.

Miller, P., & Bigi, L. The development of children's understanding of attention. *Merrill-Palmer Quarterly*, 1979, *25*, 235–250.

Minsky, M. A framework for representing knowledge. In P. Winston (Ed.), *The psychology of computer vision*. New York: McGraw-Hill, 1975.

Mischel, W., Ebbesen, E., & Zeiss, A. Determinants of selective memory about the self. *Journal of Consulting and Clinical Psychology*, 1976, *44*, 92–103.

Mischel, W., Mischel, H., & Hood, S. *The development of delay gratification*. Unpublished manuscript, Stanford University, 1978.

Morris, P. *Loss and change*. Garden City, N.Y.: Anchor Press/Doubleday, 1975.

Neimeyer, R. The structure and meaningfulness of tacit construing. In H. Bonarius, R. Holland, & S. Rosenberg (Eds.), *Personal construct psychology: Recent advances in theory and practice*. London: Macmillan, 1980.

Neisser, U. *Cognition and reality: Principles and implications of cognitive psychology*. San Francisco: Freeman, 1976.

Neisser, U. The concept of inteligence. *Intelligence*, 1979, *3*, 217–227.

Nisbett, R., & Ross, L. *Human inference: Strategies and shortcomings of social judgment*. Englewood Cliffs, N.J.: Prentice-Hall, 1980.

Parkes, C. Psychosocial transitions: A field for study. *Social Science and Medicine*, 1971, *5*, 101–115.

Piaget, J. *The language and thought of a child*. New York: New American Library, 1955. (Originally published 1926.)

Polyanyi, M. *Personal knowledge: Towards a post-critical philosophy*. Chicago: University of Chicago Press, 1958.

Rosch, E. Universals and specifics in human categorization. In R. Brislin, S. Bochner, & W. Lonner (Eds.), *Cross-cultural perspectives on learning*. New York: Halsted, 1975.

Rosch, E. Human categorization. In N. Warren (Ed.), *Studies in cross-cultural psychology*. London: Academic Press, 1978.

Rosch, E., & Mervis, C. Family resemblances: Studies in the internal structure of categories. *Cognitive Psychology*, 1975, *7*, 573–605.

Rosch, E., Mervis, C., Gray, W., Johnson, D., & Boyes-Braem, P. Basic objects in natural categories. *Cognitive Psychology*, 1976, *8*, 382–439.

Ryan, E. Identifying and remediating factors in reading comprehension: Toward an instructional approach for poor comprehenders. In T. Waller & G. MacKinnon

(Eds.), *Advances in reading research* (Vol. 2). New York: Academic Press, 1980.

Sarbin, T., & Coe, W. *Hypnosis: A social psychological analysis of influence communication.* New York: Holt, Rinehart & Winston, 1972.

Shevrin, H., & Dickman, S. The psychological unconscious: A necessary assumption for all psychological theory? *American Psychologist,* 1980, *35,* 421–434.

Silver, R., Wortman, C., & Klos, D. Cognitions, affect and behavior following uncontrollable outcomes: A response to current human helplessness research. *Journal of Personality,* 1982, *50,* 480–513.

Snyder, M. Seek, and ye shall find: Testing hypotheses about other people. In E. Higgins, C. Herman, & M. Zanna (Eds.), *Social cognition: The Ontario symposium.* Hillsdale, N.J.: Erlbaum, 1981.

Snyder, M., & Swann, W. When actions reflect attitudes: The politics of impression management. *Journal of Personality and Social Psychology,* 1976, *34,* 1034–1042.

Snyder, M., & Swann, W. Hypothesis-testing processes in social interaction. *Journal of Personality and Social Psychology,* 1978, *36,* 1202–1212.

Strupp, H., & Binder, J. *Time limited dynamic psychotherapy (TLDP): A treatment manual.* Unpublished manuscript, Vanderbilt University, 1982.

Taylor, S., & Crocker, J. Schematic bases of social information processing. In E. Higgins, C. Herman, & M. Zanna (Eds.), *Social cognition: The Ontario symposium.* Hillsdale, N.J.: Erlbaum, 1981.

Teasdale, J. Negative thinking in depression: Cause, effect, or reciprocal relationship? In L. Joyce-Moniz, F. Lowe, & P. Higson (Eds.), *Theoretical issues in cognitive-behavioral therapy.* New York: Plenum, 1983.

Thorngate, W. Must we always think before we act? *Personality and Social Psychology Bulletin,* 1976, *2,* 31–35.

Tolman, E. *Purposive behavior in animals and men.* New York: Century, 1932.

Tomkins, S. Script theory: Differential magnification of affects. *Nebraska symposium on motivation.* Lincoln: University of Nebraska Press, 1979.

Turk, D., & Salovey, P. *Cognitive structures, cognitive processes, and cognitive-behavior modification: I. Client issues.* Unpublished manuscript, Yale University, 1983.

Turk, D., & Speers, M. Cognitive schemata and cognitive processes in cognitive behavior modification: Going beyond the information given. In P. Kendall (Ed.), *Advances in cognitive-behavioral research and therapy* (Vol. 2). New York: Academic Press, 1983.

Tversky, A., & Kahneman, D. Causal schemata in judgments under uncertainty. In M. Fishbein (Ed.), *Progress in social psychology.* Hillsdale, N.J.: Erlbaum, 1977.

Wachtel, P. *Psychoanalysis and behavior therapy: Toward an integration.* New York: Basic Books, 1977.

Wachtel, P. What can dynamic therapies contribute to behavior therapy? *Behavior Therapy,* 1982, *13,* 594–609.

Wittgenstein, L. *Philosophical investigations.* New York: Macmillan, 1953.

Woodworth, R. *Experimental psychology.* New York: Holt, 1938.

Author Index

Aarons, L., 176
Abelson, R. P., 281
Abse, D. W., 177
Adelson, J., 124
Ahern, M., 122, 127
Akiskal, H., 278
Alberts, W. W., 223
Alexander, F., 77, 78, 286
Anderson, J. R., 156, 162, 165, 166, 170
Andreski, S., 200
Antrobus, J. S., 174, 176
Aoki, B., 122
Arieti, S., 260
Aristotle, 221
Arkin, A. M., 174, 176
Asarnow, J., 277
Aschaffenburg, G., 38
Atkinson, R. C., 161, 236

Baddeley, A. D., 177
Baldwin, J., 281
Balint, M., 83
Ballard, P. B., 166
Balthazard, C., 262
Bandura, A., 151, 278, 281
Barber, T. X., 153, 154, 182, 183
Bartlett, F. C., 165, 189, 281, 283
Bastick, T., 261
Beck, A., 241, 274, 275, 278, 281, 286, 294
Bellows, N., 247
Bendefelt, F., 173
Benedikt, M., 18
Bergman, A., 89, 94
Bernheim, H., 41, 157
Berrington, W. P., 132
Bertenthal, B. I., 111, 133, 141
Biggs, J., 92, 93, 106, 135
Bigi, L., 277
Binder, J., 285, 291

Binet, A., 10, 12, 19, 29, 44, 157
Bjork, R. A., 177
Black, A. H., 157
Bliss, E. L., 119, 132, 134
Blos, P., 130
Bogen, J., 83
Bonaparte, M., 11, 58
Bower, G. H., 92, 118, 123, 161, 177, 180, 278
Bowers, K. S., ix, x, xi, xii, 5, 6, 174, 179, 180,
    182, 184, 186, 187, 239, 250, 254, 256, 260,
    263–266, 283, 288, 292, 293
Bowers, P. G., 174, 260
Boyes-Braem, P., 282
Brady, J. P., 172
Braff, D., 160
Brandsma, J. M., 173
Bransford, J., 282
Brennemann, H. A., 186, 187
Brenner, C., 120
Breuer, J., 10–12, 53, 54, 240, 242, 243, 255
Broadbent, D. E., 163, 164
Broughton, J., 94, 124, 135
Brown, A. L., 134, 137
Brown, J. A., 166
Bruner, J. S., 90, 118, 164, 170
Brunswick, E., 1
Buddin, B. J., 95, 123
Bullock, D., 106
Burland, S., 275
Buschke, H., 166
Buss, A. R., 256
Butler, L., 275
Byrne, P. N., 122

Caharack, G., 118, 188
Cameron, J. L., 119
Cameron, R., 275
Campbell, D. T., 152
Campion, J., 234

Campos, J. J., 106
Cantor, N., 151, 168, 282
Carlston, D. L., 167
Case, R., 84, 90, 92, 111
Cavé, M., 17
Cermack, L. S., 165
Chandler, M. J., 94, 131
Chapman, J., 279
Chapman, L., 279
Charcot, J. M., 19, 20, 26, 27, 37, 49, 53, 157, 171
Chaves, J. F., 153
Cheesman, J., 235
Cherry, E. C., 163, 164
Chertok, L., 42
Chevreul, M. E., 28
Chomsky, N., 156, 168
Clark, M., 278
Cleckley, H., 132, 135
Codet, H., 20
Coe, W. C., 174, 184, 281
Cohen, D. B., 175
Cole, L. E., 17
Collis, K., 92, 97, 106, 135
Cooper, L. M., 177
Corballis, M. C., 160
Corrigan, R., 94
Corteen, R., 230
Cortese, C., 188
Cott, A., 159
Cowen, G. N., 237
Coyne, J., 278
Craik, F. I., 165, 166
Crawford, H. J., 184
Crocker, J., 279, 281, 283
Cronbach, L., 286
Cross, D. G., 180
Crowder, R. G., 162
Crutchfield, L., 186

Dallas, M., 188
Damaser, E. C., 179, 180
Daniels, G., 81
Darwin, E., 31
Davison, G. C., 170
Decarie, T. G., 141
Deloache, J. S., 134, 137
Dember, W., 274
Dement, W. C., 119
de M'Uzan, M., 80
Dennis, I., 238
de Paulo, B. M., 118
Descartes, R., 18

Deutsch, D., 160, 164, 191, 192
Deutsch, F., 77
Deutsch, G., 160
Deutsch, J. A., 160, 164, 191, 192
Dewey, J., 89, 90, 150
Diamond, R., 160
Dickman, D., 156
Dixon, N. F., 164, 231, 234, 246
Dodge, K. A., 119
Dodson, J. D., 108
Doolittle, H., 44
Dostoyevsky, F., 239
Dulany, D. E., 232
Durkin, H. E., 259

Ebbesen, E., 278
Eccles, J. C., 160
Eich, J. C., 177, 178, 180
Eichorn, D. H., 111
Eissler, K., 77
Ellenberger, H. F., 6, 9, 16–18, 26, 28, 29, 34, 157
Ellman, G. J., 174
Emery, G., 274
Emmons, W. H., 176
English, A. C., 155
English, H. B., 155
Erdelyi, M. H., 164, 166, 170, 229, 230, 236, 243
Ericsson, K. A., 153, 237, 248, 259
Eriksen, C. W., 152, 164, 231–235, 265, 286
Evans, F. J., 176, 177, 179–181

Fechner, G. T., 18
Feffer, M., 82, 90, 91, 112, 113, 132
Fein, G. G., 107
Feinstein, B., 223
Feldman, D. H., 100
Ferenczi, S., 43
Fine, R., 17, 77
Fischer, K. W., xii, 5–7, 90, 92, 93–95, 98, 100–102, 106–108, 111, 112, 114, 122, 125, 126, 128, 129, 133, 135, 137, 138, 141
Fiske, D. W., 152
Flavell, J. H., 93, 106, 134, 135, 137, 277, 281
Fliess, W., 20, 58
Flournoy, T., 67, 69–71
Forel, A., 28
Foulds, G. A., 172
Foulkes, D., 133
Frame, C. L., 119
Frank, J., 279, 280, 281
Frankel, F., 84

Franks, J., 282
Freeman, T., 119
French, T., 286
Freud, A., 61, 89, 109, 120, 131, 134, 137
Freud, S., xii, 1, 4–9, 11–13, 21–25, 53, 54, 58,
    61, 62, 88–91, 111, 113, 116, 119–121, 126,
    128, 130, 132, 138–140, 150, 156–158, 160,
    163, 170, 179, 215, 216, 223, 225, 227, 228,
    236, 240–243, 255, 289, 291
Friedländer, A. A., 15, 38
Fritzler, D. E., 230
Fromm, E., 119

Galanter, E., 277, 281, 282
Galin, D., 160
Garner, W. R., 152, 286
Garrett, M. F., 238
Gazzaniga, M. S., 160
Geffen, S., 230
Genero, N., 152
Getzels, J. W., 260
Gill, M. M., 110
Gilmore, B., xii, xiii, 6–8, 284, 286, 290
Glenberg, A. M., 177
Glucksberg, S., 237
Godden, D. R., 177
Goldberg, B., 164, 170, 243
Goldfried, M., xiiii, 273
Goodenough, D. R., 175
Graham, C. H., 213
Gray, A. L., 182
Gray, W., 291
Greaves, G. B., 172
Greene, D., 180
Greenspan, S. I., 48
Grosz, H. J., 172
Gruson, L., 275
Guillain, G., 20
Guntrip, H., 109
Gur, R. C., 230
Gurney, E., 10
Gwynn, M. I., 184

Haan, N., 109, 131, 138
Hake, H. W., 152, 286
Hand, H. H., 94, 95, 101, 102, 107, 122, 125
Harackiewicz, J. M., 180
Hardt, J. V., 159
Harman, W., 284
Harre, R., 266
Harter, S. H., 92, 94, 123, 124, 133, 135, 136
Hartmann, H., 9
Harvey, J. H., 256

Hastie, R., 158, 167, 281, 282
Hayden, B., 118
Hebb, D. O., 42
Heiberg, A., 84
Hein, G. E., 258
Helmholz, 141
Henshaw, D., 275
Herbart, J. F., 9, 18
Herink, R., 42
Hewitt, E. C., 42, 184, 185
Hilgard, E. R., 6, 9, 10, 32, 41, 42, 89, 119, 132,
    150, 154, 157–159, 164, 171, 172, 182–189,
    191, 231, 241
Hilgard, J. R., 184
Himel, N., 275
Hintzman, D. L., 167
Hirst, W., 118, 188, 192
Hochberg, J., 150, 168
Hogarty, P. S., 111
Holland, B., 260
Holt, R. R., 90, 92, 109–112
Hood, S., 277
Hoppe, K., 83
Hoskovec, J., 177
Hull, C. L., 22, 181
Hume, D., 249, 266

Isen, A., 278

Jackson, P. W., 106, 260
Jacobson, E., 176
Jacoby, L. L., 166, 188
James, W., 21, 117, 119, 149–151, 155–157,
    162, 186, 192, 273
Jameson, D. H., 172
Janet, J., 29, 43
Janet, P., xii, 4, 6, 7, 9, 10, 13–15, 19, 26, 27,
    31–40, 43, 49, 51, 52, 57, 77, 118, 157–159,
    171, 189, 216, 217, 239
Jaynes, J., 150, 182
Jeannerod, M., 234
Jennings, S., 125, 141
Jessor, R., 1, 2
Johnson, L. C., 174
Johnson, M. K., 182, 184, 282, 292
Johnson, R. F., 150
Jones, B., 182
Jones, E., 10, 11, 13, 14
Jones, J., 172
Jung, C. G., 13, 37

Kahnemann, D., 186, 190, 192, 237, 261, 263,
    279

Kales, A., 176
Kamiya, J., 152, 154, 159
Kant, E., 9, 281
Kaplan, A., 254
Karp, L., 298
Karush, A., 81
Kaufman, L., 156, 168
Keim, C. S., 182
Keiser, L., 286
Kekule, A., 257–260
Kelly, G., 280–283
Kenny, S. L., 124
Keppel, G., 166
Kernberg, O., 83, 89, 92, 94, 95, 97, 118, 120, 124, 127, 136, 141
Kihlstrom, J. F., 6, 42, 168, 180–184, 236
Kinsbourne, M., 240
Kitchener, K. S., 124
Klein, D. B., 9, 155, 164
Klein, F., 281
Klein, G. S., x
Kleinbard, 166
Kletti, R., 173
Klos, D., 281
Knox, V. J., 183–186
Koch, D. A., 94
Koestler, A., 258, 260, 262
Kolers, P. A., 188
Kohut, H., 83, 127, 141
Koulack, D., 175
Kovacs, M., 281
Kreutzer, M., 277
Kruglanski, A. W., 256
Kuhn, T., 284
Kutas, M., 154

LaBerge, D., 243
Lackner, J. R., 238
Ladame, P. U., 15, 38
Laforgue, R., 20
Lakatos, I., 254, 255, 257
Lamborn, S., 126
Langer, E., 276
Laurence, J-R., xii, 4, 7, 42, 43, 158, 184, 185
Lazarus, R., 232, 278, 281
LeDoux, J. E., 160
Leibnitz, G. W., 9
Leonard, C., 277
Lepper, M., 180
Lester, D., 171
Lester, E. P., 89
Leventhal, H., 154
Lewin, K., 281

Libet, B., 223
Liddell, D. W., 172
Liebeault, A., 157
Link, N. F., 122
Lloyd, B. B., 151
Locke, D., 256
Lockhart, R. S., 165, 166
Loewi, O., 260
Loftus, E. F., 90, 166, 167
Loftus, G. R., 90, 166, 167
Lorand, S., 77
Lotto, R., 234
Louch, A. R., 256
Ludwig, A. M., 151, 173
Lundh, L-G., 172, 229, 230, 232, 237

McCall, R. B., 111
McCauly, M., 122
McCleary, R. A., 232
McConkey, K. M., 42, 43, 180, 183
McDonald, R. D., 182, 184
McDougall, J., 81, 82
McGhie, A., 119
McGuire, W., 13
MacKay, D., 237, 238
McKinney, W., 278
MacLean, P., 83
Madden, E. H., 266
Mahler, M. S., 89, 92, 94, 95, 98, 141
Mahlerstein, A. J., 122, 127
Mahoney, M., 274, 286, 289
Maine de Biran, F. P., 19, 30
Malan, D., 285
Malcolm, J., 43, 154
Malfara, A., 182
Mandler, G., 118, 150, 154, 168, 170, 274
Marcel, A., 265
Markman, G., 277
Markus, H., 283
Marmor, J., 273
Marquis, D. G., 171
Marshall, J., 233
Martin, M. F., 172
Marty, P., 80
Marx, K., 151
Masters, J., 278
Medin, D. L., 151
Mednick, M. T., 262
Mednick, S. A., 262
Meehl, P., 286
Meichenbaum, D., x, xii, xiii, 6–8, 241, 274, 275, 277, 284, 286, 290
Melton, A. W., 165

Merikle, P., 231, 235
Mervis, C., 291
Mesmer, A., 157
Meyers, M., 277
Michotte, A., 266
Miller, F. D., 248
Miller, G., 272, 281, 282
Miller, P., 277
Minsky, M., 281
Mischel, H., 119, 277
Mischel, W., xii, 119, 272, 278, 282
Modell, A. H., 119
Moray, N., 163
Morgan, A. H., 182–184
Morris, P., 281
Moscovitch, M., 182
Mulholland, T. B., 159
Myers, F. W. H., 10

Nace, E. P., 180
Nasby, N., 118
Natsoulas, T., 150
Neale, J. M., 171
Neimeyer, R., 282
Neisser, U., 42, 90, 118, 158, 162, 165, 182,
    188, 190, 192, 230, 261, 263, 281, 291, 292
Nelson, E., 188
Nemiah, J. C., xii, 5, 7, 9, 80, 81, 83, 171
Newell, A., 161
Newstead, S. E., 238
Nisbett, R. E., 152, 153, 156, 168, 170, 180,
    228, 246–249, 251, 255, 256, 260, 265, 279
    288
Nogrady, H., 42, 43, 184, 185
Nordlie, J. W., 230
Norman, D. A., 161, 191, 192, 237
Noyes, R., 173

Obstoj, I., 183
O'Connell, D. N., 182
Orne, M. T., 119, 132, 152–154, 159, 179, 180,
    182, 183, 266
Osgood, C. E., 87, 120
Overton, D. A., 177, 178, 240

Paget, K. F., 94
Paris, S., 277
Parkes, C., 281
Pattie, F. A., 135
Pavlovski, A. P., 159
Pearlstone, Z., 163
Penfield, W., 166
Pennington, D., 256

Perenin, M. T., 234
Perry, C. W., xii, 4, 7, 42, 43, 158, 183–185
Peterfreund, E., x
Peters, J. E., 187
Peters, R. S., 256
Piaget, J., xii, xiii, 7, 89, 90, 93, 94, 111, 112,
    141, 151, 281
Pichon, E., 11
Pillemer, D. B., 134, 182
Pine, F., 89, 94
Pipp, S. L., xii, 5–7, 90, 92, 93, 106, 125, 133,
    141
Plato, 221, 261, 294
Platt, W., 258
Plotkin, W. B., 159
Poetzl, O., 230
Polanyi, M., 4, 5, 253, 254, 256, 258, 261, 283
Popper, K., 160, 255
Posner, M. I., 230
Postman, L., 164, 165, 170
Powers, W. T., 151
Prechtal, H. F., 108
Pribram, K., 277, 281, 282
Prince, M., 9, 10, 60, 66, 158, 171, 188
Putnam, F. W., 119, 132
Pylyshyn, Z., 156

Raab, D., 218
Rapoport, D., 92, 111
Raye, C. L., 174, 182
Raymond, F., 51
Reaves, C. C., 118, 188
Reder, L. M., 166
Reid, G., 173, 174
Ribot, T., 19
Richet, P., 19, 23, 30
Roazan, P., 44
Roberts, R. J., 114, 122
Robinson, D. N., xii, 5, 218, 221
Rock, I., 156, 168
Rogers, C., x
Rosch, E., 151, 291, 292
Rosenbaum, M., 119, 132
Ross, L., 228, 260, 261, 279, 288
Roth, M., 173
Rozen, P., 156
Rubin, K. H., 107
Rugg, H., 260
Rush, A., 274
Russell, S. L., 95, 101, 122
Ryan, E., 277

Sackeim, H. A., 230, 234

Salovey, P., 279, 280
Sameroff, A., 106
Sanders, M. D., 233
Santrock, J. P., 278
Sarbin, T. R., 174, 184, 281
Sartre, J., x
Schacter, D. L., 181
Schafer, R., 118
Scheibe, K. E., 182, 263
Scherer, S. E., 122
Schimek, J. S., 90, 92, 111, 112
Schneider, W., 118, 163
Schreber, D., 67
Sedman, G., 173
Segalowitz, S. J., 160
Selman, R. L., 94
Shalker, T., 278
Shapiro, D., x
Shaw, B., 274
Sheehan, P. W., 179, 180, 183
Shevach, B. J., 159
Shevrin, H., 156, 230
Shiffrin, R. M., 118, 161, 163, 236
Sidis, B., 10
Sifneos, P., 80, 81
Shipko, S., 83
Shor, R. E., 182
Siegler, R. S., 92
Silver, R., 281
Silverman, I., xi
Silvern, L., 122, 127
Simon, C. W., 153, 161, 176
Simon, H. A., 237, 248
Simonton, D. K., 230, 260
Skinner, B. F., 150, 225
Smith, E. E., 151, 177
Smith, E. R., 241, 248
Smith, S. M., 151
Snyder, C. R., 230
Snyder, M., 279, 280
Sobesky, W. E., 122
Spanos, N. P., 42, 154, 182, 184, 185
Speers, M., 284
Spelke, E. S., 118, 188, 192
Spence, D. P., 230, 260
Sperling, G., 218, 219
Sperry, R. W., 150, 160
Springer, S. P., 160
Stahelski, A., 280
Stam, H. J., 184
Steffy, R., 294
Sternberg, S., 223
Stevenson, J. A., 186

Stoyva, J., 152
Strupp, H., 285, 291
Suci, G. J., 97
Sullivan, H. S., xii, 92, 94, 97, 118, 120, 123, 124, 136
Sutcliffe, J. P., 172, 182
Swann, W., 279, 280
Swanson, J. M., 240
Szasz, T. S., 174

Taine, H., 18
Tannebaum, P. H., 97
Taylor, S., 279, 283
Taylor, W. S., 172
Teasdale, J., 278
Tellegen, A., 154
Templer, D. I., 171
Thigpen, C. H., 132, 135
Thomson, D. M., 166
Thorn, W. A., 181
Thorngate, W., 276
Tolman, E., 281
Tomkins, S., 288, 289
Trevarthen, C. B., 234
Triesman, A. M., 163, 230
Tucker, J., 94, 95, 101
Tucker, J. A., 256
Tulving, E., 163, 165–167, 181
Turk, D., 279, 280, 284
Turvey, M. T., 261
Tversky, A., 261, 263, 279

Underwood, B. J., 166

Vaillant, G. E., 109, 131, 134, 138
Vandenberg, B., 107
Van Parys, M., 94, 95, 101, 125
Vygotsky, L., 126

Wachtel, P. L., x–xiv, 90, 118, 120, 231, 273, 285, 287
Walsh, B., 183
Warrington, E. K., 233
Waterman, J. M., 122
Watson, J. B., 150
Watson, M. W., 94, 95, 98, 101, 112, 125, 129
Waugh, N. C., 161
Weimer, W. B., 255, 261
Weiskrantz, L., 222, 233
Welford, A. T., 118
Wellman, H., 134, 137, 277
Werner, H., 89, 114
Wescott, M. R., 261

White, P., 248
White, R. W., 159
White, S. H., 134
Whyte, L. L., 155
Wickelgren, W. A., 165
Wilbur, C. B., 173
Williams, H. L., 176
Wilson, T. D., 113, 152, 156, 168, 170, 228,
    246–249, 251, 256
Winograd, T., 167
Wittgenstein, L., 212, 292
Wolff, P. H., 88, 90, 92, 108, 111,
    132

Wolitsky, D. L., xi
Wood, B., 230
Woods, S., 273
Woodworth, R., 283
Wortman, C., 281
Wright, E. W., 223
Wundt, W., 7, 149

Yerkes, R. M., 108

Zajonc, R. B., 120, 230, 244
Zeiss, A., 278
Zimmerman, J. A., 172

Subject Index

Abstraction, 94, 123
ACT model, *see specific memory processes*
Affect, 39, 53, 60, 61, 91, 102, 108, 110, 112,
    114, 118, 119, 120, 131, 132, 133, 136,
    139, 233, 240, 244, 275, 277, 278, 284
Aggression, 21, 26, 63, 65, 66, 170
Alexithymia, 80, 81, 83, 84
Anxiety, 55, 61–66, 225
   signal, 61, 66, 120, 240, 243
Appraisal processes, 279–281
Attention, 219, 283
   divided, 192, 197. *See also* Dissociation
   selective, 32, 33, 150, 162, 164, 167, 168,
      170, 191, 229, 237, 241, 242, 244, 275,
      276, 280, 293
   see also Inattention; Information processing
Attributional processes, 180, 275
Automaticity, 118, 168, 243, 274, 277, 293
   automatisms, psychological, 28, 29, 31, 158,
      189
   automatic writing, 60, 157, 221

Behaviorism, 1, 150, 153, 159, 229
Blind sight, 222–225, 233

Case studies:
   Alice V., 54–57, 58, 59, 61, 65
   Anna O., 240
   Boy S., 109, 111, 112, 114, 117
   Cora P., 62, 65, 67
   Elizabeth von R., 242, 243
   Girl K., 116
   Grace C., 71–76
   John G., 78–81
   Jonah, 173
   Leonine, 27
   Marie, 17, 34, 49–51, 57, 77
   P.N., 172
   of phobia (Morton Prince), 60–61

   Miss Vé, 67–71, 75
   Woman C, 109–119, 127, 136
Catharsis, 13, 53, 57
Censor, 21–24
Cognitive events, 274, 275, 280
   automatic thoughts, 221, 274, 275
   images, 55, 56, 59, 61, 274
   internal dialogue, 241, 275, 290, 294
Cognitive processes, 275–280, 289, 290
   cognitive heuristics, *see* Mental heuristics
   metacognition, 276–278
Cognitive structures, 275, 280–284, 290
   core organizing principles, 8, 286, 288, 289,
      290
   schemata, xiii, 7, 158, 189, 192, 281–285,
      289
Cognitive-behavioral therapy, 241, 273, 274,
      278, 280, 284, 285, 288, 291
Coherence, 228, 262, 263
Collaborative empiricism, 286
Commissurotomy, cerebral, 84, 160, 215, 221,
      222
Conflict, psychological, 54, 57–59, 65, 80, 82,
      83
Conscious(ness), 25–27, 149, 151, 160, 163,
      164, 168, 229, 236, 237, 244, 246, 254,
      291
   altered state of, 30, 150–155, 157
   as comprehension, 228, 245, 249, 250, 254,
      255, 258, 263
   as control, 1–3, 114, 134, 150, 154, 180, 189,
      190
   divided, 188–193
   experience, 3, 4, 21, 22, 132, 150, 151, 193,
      214, 230, 233, 237
   field of, ix, 31, 32, 217
   levels of, 19, 31
   as monitoring, 26, 134, 137, 150, 154, 180,
      189, 239, 294

Conscious(ness) (*Continued*)
   perception, ix, 1, 3, 4, 169, 182, 192, 219,
      229, 232–235, 263, 265
   of self, 31, 221, 223
   shrinkage of or restriction in, 13, 27, 33, 39
   stream of, 158, 159, 186, 193, 274
   unity of, 160
Corrective emotional experience, 286
Creativity, 31, 35, 258, 259, 264

Décalage horizontal, 93
Defense mechanisms, 59–62, 65, 76, 109, 131,
      138, 157, 217, 232
   avoidance, 61
   displacement, 61, 66, 110–112
   projection, 61, 66, 75
   reaction formation, 4, 63, 64, 65
   regression, 75, 122
   suppression, 69, 170
   see also Repression
Demand characteristics, 37, 39, 43, 180, 182,
      184, 185, 266, 267, 275
Depersonalization, *see* Memory, disturbances or
      anomolies
Depression, 55, 62, 63, 65, 66, 217, 220, 241,
      278, 280
Dissociation, 6, 10, 13, 30, 32, 36, 40, 41, 51,
      53, 57, 70, 84, 89, 132, 135, 141, 157,
      158, 159, 171, 174, 178, 181–188,
      194–197, 231, 234, 239–242
   active dissociation, 90, 115, 119–121, 131,
      132, 139
   désagrégation, 10, 19, 27, 30–34, 39–42, 158
   double consciousness, 25, 30, 33, 160, 187
   idée fixe, 12, 25, 30, 34, 35, 216
   passive dissociation, 115–119, 139
   see also Hypnosis; Multiple personality;
      Somnambulism; Unconscious processes
Dream, 35, 111, 113, 119, 120, 133, 134, 135,
      157, 175, 220, 223, 257–260
   formation, 15, 21, 22
   interpretation, 14, 36, 38, 39
   latent content of, 22
   manifest content of, 22
   nightmare, 56, 67
Dynamic Psychiatry, First, 157, 158, 170, 178

Ego, 19, 24, 16, 52, 54, 62, 109, 158
Emotion, *see* Affect

Family of resemblance, 281–293
Fantasy, 58, 59, 66, 76, 78, 79, 80, 240, 241,
      242, 244, 260
Free association, 14, 24, 37, 76, 133, 136, 243

Hypnoidal state, 54, 240
Hypnosis, xii, 6, 10, 14, 16, 18–20, 27, 28, 30,
      33, 35, 41, 43, 50, 51, 60, 119, 120, 132,
      133, 151, 153–155, 157, 178–187, 234
   age regression, 51, 182, 185
   forensic use of, 167
   hidden observer, 119, 136, 183, 184, 185,
      187
   hypnotic analgesia, 42, 184, 187
   posthypnotic amnesia, 32, 134, 179, 180,
      194, 195
   posthypnotic response, 179, 180
   posthypnotic suggestion, 28, 32, 41, 179–180
   simulation of, 181–185
   trance logic, 182, 183, 185
Hypnotizability, 42, 84, 134, 135, 155, 177,
      179, 183, 185, 187
Hysteria, 11, 12, 18, 20, 26, 27, 28, 32, 33, 37,
      49, 51, 53, 58, 70, 82, 84, 151, 157, 171
      174, 187, 216
   blindness, functional, *see* Perceptual
      anomalies
   conversion, 29, 77, 160
   defense hysteria, 54, 242
   fugue, 157, 171, 172, 174, 187
   hypnoid hysteria, 54, 240, 242
   la belle indifference, 171

Id, 26, 62
Inattention, 224, 225, 237, 238, 241, 265
Information processing, xi, 6, 161, 197, 216,
      217, 219, 225
   attention, *see* Attention
   feature detection, 162, 168
   memory, *see* Memory
   pattern recognition, 162, 168
   sensory registers, 161
Introspection, 19, 30, 150, 153, 156, 168, 213,
      224, 228, 230, 233, 234, 246–250, 254,
      265, 266, 267
Intuition, 5, 26, 228, 244, 250, 256–263

Knowledge:
   compilation, 170
   declarative, 158, 167–169, 194, 195
   procedural, 158, 167–170, 194, 195
   self-knowledge, 25, 168, 248
   tacit, 5, 256, 258, 262, 263, 264, 283, 287

Memory:
   as a cognitive process, 27–30, 90, 231,
      236–239, 248, 261
   activation of associative networks, 162,
      165, 166, 169, 181, 193, 194

ACT model of, 162, 170, 181, 193, 194
attention, *see* Attention
availability-accessibility distinction, 156, 160, 163, 166, 167, 175, 181, 193–194
encoding specificity, 177, 178
episodic memory, 167, 173, 181, 194, 195
iconic memory, 162
long-term memory, 236, 237, 265
multistore model of, 161–163, 175
primary memory, 162–165, 175
recall, cued, 162, 166, 167
recall, free, 166, 167, 195, 275
recognition memory, 166, 194
rehearsal, elaborative, 162
rehearsal, maintenance, 162
secondary memory, 162–165, 175
semantic memory, 167, 173, 181, 195
sensory memory, 161, 162, 165
short-term memory, 162, 221, 230, 236, 237
unistore model of, 163–170
disturbances or anomalies:
amnesia, 132, 172, 173, 174, 221. *See also* Dissociation; Hypnosis; Hysteria; Repression
childhood amnesia, 134, 181
confabulation, 35, 39, 167, 242
cryptomnesia, 174
déjà vu, 174, 187
depersonalization, 173, 187
derealization, 173
hypermnesia, 166
jamais vu, 174
state dependent memory, *see* State dependent learning and retention
traumatic memories, 18, 33–39, 50, 51, 53, 57–59
Meno's paradox, 261
Mental heuristics, 279, 280
availability, 247, 248, 279
confirmatory bias, xii, 279, 280, 284, 287
representativeness, 247, 248, 279
Methodology, xiii, 6, 7, 27, 238, 239, 260
experimental, 250–254, 266
Motivation, 39, 52, 61, 108, 117, 119, 179, 180, 230, 242, 290
Multiple personality, 6, 10, 32, 33, 119, 132–136, 157, 171, 172, 174, 187

Neodissociation theory, xii, 6, 10, 32, 41, 42, 188–197
Noticing, comprehension distinction, 228, 244–256, 265, 293

Object relations theory, 83, 94, 141
Oedipus complex, 38, 58, 59, 75, 109, 112, 118, 127–131, 140

Perception, 90, 112, 194, 231, 236, 283
perceptual defense, xi, 164
perceptual synthesis, 27, 28, 29, 169
span of apprehension, 218
subliminal, xi, 164, 197, 223, 231–236, 246, 265
techniques for studying
backward masking, 162, 218, 221, 222
cued retrieval, 218, 221
delayed auditory feedback, 182
dichotic listening, 182, 237, 241
forced-choice discrimination, 223, 233, 235, 263
see also Conscious perception
Perception, noticing distinction, 6, 7, 18, 164, 169, 170, 223, 224, 228, 229–244, 259, 262, 263, 265, 266, 279, 293
Perceptual anomalies, 182, 183
anesthesia, 12, 33, 50, 51, 171
functional blindness, 34, 50, 51, 172, 234
hallucinations, 70, 72, 171, 182, 183, 223
Personal construct theory, 282
Personal identity, 172, 221, 222
Personality, 30, 31
Pleasure principle, 18, 109
Preconscious, *see* Unconscious
Preemptive metaphor, 288
Primary process, 88–90, 109, 110–115, 121, 128, 139, 157, 160, 196
condensation, 110–112, 127–131, 139, 140
displacement, *see* Defense mechanisms
wish fulfillment, 21, 58, 110–112, 288
Prototypicality, 291, 292
Psychoanalysis, x, 7, 8, 13–17, 28, 34–42, 54, 88–91, 108, 111, 115, 119, 156–159, 170, 196, 215–217, 220, 225, 227
structural model, 20, 23, 26, 62
topographic model, 18, 20, 21, 26, 61
Psychoneurosis, 10, 13, 28, 35, 36, 82
phobia, 60, 66, 84
traumatic origins of, 49–51, 53, 56, 57, 58, 77, 88, 132, 133, 171
unconscious conflicts in, 24, 58, 61, 288, 289, 290
see also Hysteria; Sex
Psychophysics, 212, 213, 221
Psychophysiological correlates, 154, 212, 215, 220, 226
AER (Average evoked response), 217–219
EEG, 154, 159, 177, 218–220, 224

Psychophysiological correlates (*Continued*)
EMG, 220
EOG, 220
endorphins, 217
GSR, 232, 233, 265
Psychosis, 71–74
Psychosomatic disorders, 29, 76–81, 83
conflict model, 80–81
deficit model, 81–82
Psychotherapy, 34–36, 42–44, 127, 220, 225

Reality testing, 75, 239
Reason-cause distinction, 256–258
Reinforcement, 229, 245, 246, 264
Remote Associates Test, 262
Repression, x, 5, 6, 13, 18, 21, 23, 24, 36–42,
54, 58, 59, 61, 62, 74, 77, 80–82, 89,
91, 120, 121, 131, 132–138, 139, 140,
159, 170, 175, 196, 213–215, 217, 219,
225, 231, 239, 242–244, 265, 289, 290,
293
Resistance, 23, 24, 58, 292
Reverie, 70, 239, 240, 241, 259, 260, 264

Salpêtrière, 20, 26, 27, 34, 49, 53
Schizophrenia, 91, 119, 132, 133, 136, 151
Self-identity, 221
Self-perception, 29, 30, 32, 33, 35, 193, 194
Sex, 8, 21, 26
sexual abuse, 132
sexual activity, 2, 54, 56, 61, 68, 243, 244
sexual conflict, 68, 70, 242, 244
sexual etiology of neurosis, 12, 15, 18, 37,
38, 54–57, 58, 59, 62, 65, 71, 170
Skills theory:
abstractions, 94, 102, 104–106, 123, 124,
134, 135, 140
affective splitting, 92, 93, 95, 97, 100, 102,
115, 116, 118, 120–122, 125–127, 129,
139, 140
compounding, 100, 101
environmental support, 106, 107, 113, 117,
121, 126, 127, 139
gap hypothesis, 91, 112, 113, 121, 128, 138
fractionation, xii, 89, 92, 93, 101, 108, 114,
116, 119, 139
integration, 89, 93, 100, 101, 102, 116, 139
levels, 95, 96, 108, 115, 117, 139
optimal level, 93, 100, 106–108, 115, 116,
139
overextended skill, 113
representations, 94–97, 102, 104, 105, 115,
116, 123, 124, 134, 137
sensorimotor actions, 94, 124, 125

sensorimotor development, 124, 125, 141
shift of focus, 101, 117, 133
skill acquisition and generalization, 92, 93
tiers, 93, 94, 96, 102, 108, 126, 139
Sleep, 22, 154, 174–179, 224
learning, 175–177
REM sleep, 154, 175, 176, 177, 178, 220
suggestion, 177–178, 224
talking, 175–177
vigiambulism, 221, 224
walking, 175–177
Slips of the tongue, 40, 41
Somnambulism, 6, 27, 28, 30, 32, 33, 35, 50,
157, 171, 176, 213
"Split brain," Commissurotomy, cerebral
State dependent learning and retention, 92,
175, 177, 178, 240, 242
Stress, 33, 40, 54, 76, 82, 83, 171, 240,
275, 285
Subception, 232
Suggestibility, 31, 33, 157
Suggestion, 28, 39, 177, 178, 180
Superego, 23, 25, 26, 62, 67–69, 109
Symptom formation, 10, 12, 20, 51–54, 57, 58,
60, 61, 66, 81, 82, 84

Task complexity, 112, 113, 117, 122
Task interference, 159, 185, 186, 194
Thought and thinking, 54, 90, 168, 255, 256,
275
automatic, 274, 275, 287
delusional, 122
divided, 192, 193
primary process, *see* Primary process
secondary process, 7, 109, 111, 112, 115,
157
unconscious, xii, 2, 8, 51, 90, 91, 108, 112,
114, 115, 124, 155, 158, 264, 278, 280.
See also Primary process.
Threshold:
awareness, 223, 234, 263
detection, 232
discrimination, 232, 265
noticing, 230, 265
perceptual, 224, 230
Transference, 38, 71, 74
Two-visual system hypothesis, 234

Unconscious, ontological problem, of 212
Unconscious, taxonomy of, 224–225
Unconscious processes, ix, xii, 5, 17, 19, 20,
22, 26, 40, 42, 77, 82, 84, 88, 90, 91,
100, 155, 157, 163, 213, 214, 216, 232,
273–275, 280, 284, 289, 290, 291, 292

co-conscious(ness), 119, 120, 132–136, 140, 157, 158, 183, 188, 190
conflicts, *see* Psychoneurosis
defense, xi, 57, 59, 66
dipsychism, 25, 157, 192
inference, unconscious, 19, 141, 156
polypsychism, 158
preconscious, 21–26, 156, 163, 164, 170

subconscious, 11, 25, 31, 32, 35, 36, 44, 52, 157, 158, 170, 193, 194, 196, 197
thought, *see* Thought and thinking
Unconscious structure, 91, 108, 109, 112, 115, 117, 121–138, 141, 156
Unconscious system (Ucs), 21, 22, 24, 25, 26, 40, 62, 156, 160

Yerkes-Dodson Law, 108

Psychology and Psychiatry in Courts and Corrections: Controversy and Change
  by Ellsworth A. Fersch, Jr.
Restricted Environmental Stimulation: Research and Clinical Applications
  by Peter Suedfeld
Personal Construct Psychology: Psychotherapy and Personality
  edited by Alvin W. Landfield and Larry M. Leitner
Mothers, Grandmothers, and Daughters: Personality and Child Care in
Three-Generation Families
  by Bertram J. Cohler and Henry U. Grunebaum
Further Explorations in Personality
  edited by A. I. Rabin, Joel Aronoff, Andrew M. Barclay, and Robert A. Zucker
Hypnosis and Relaxation: Modern Verification of an Old Equation
  by William E. Edmonston, Jr.
Handbook of Clinical Behavior Therapy
  edited by Samuel M. Turner, Karen S. Calhoun, and Henry E. Adams
Handbook of Clinical Neuropsychology
  edited by Susan B. Filskov and Thomas J. Boll
The Course of Alcoholism: Four Years After Treatment
  by J. Michael Polich, David J. Armor, and Harriet B. Braiker
Handbook of Innovative Psychotherapies
  edited by Raymond J. Corsini
The Role of the Father in Child Development (Second Edition)
  edited by Michael E. Lamb
Behavioral Medicine: Clinical Applications
  by Susan S. Pinkerton, Howard Hughes, and W. W. Wenrich
Handbook for the Practice of Pediatric Psychology
  edited by June M. Tuma
Change Through Interaction: Social Psychological Processes of Counseling and
Psychotherapy
  by Stanley R. Strong and Charles D. Claiborn
Drugs and Behavior (Second Edition)
  by Fred Leavitt
Handbook of Research Methods in Clinical Psychology
  edited by Philip C. Kendall and James N. Butcher
A Social Psychology of Developing Adults
  by Thomas O. Blank
Women in the Middle Years: Current Knowledge and Directions for Research and Policy
  edited by Janet Zollinger Giele
Loneliness: A Sourcebook of Current Theory, Research and Therapy
  edited by Letitia Anne Peplau and Daniel Perlman
Hyperactivity: Current Issues, Research, and Theory (Second Edition)
  by Dorothea M. Ross and Sheila A. Ross
Review of Human Development
  *edited by Tiffany M. Field, Aletha Huston, Herbert C. Quay, Lillian Troll,
  and Gordon E. Finley*
Agoraphobia: Multiple Perspectives on Theory and Treatment
  edited by Dianne L. Chambless and Alan J. Goldstein
The Rorschach: A Comprehensive System, Volume III: Assessment of Children and Adolescents
  by John E. Exner, Jr. and Irving B. Weiner
Handbook of Play Therapy
  edited by Charles E. Schaefer and Kevin J. O'Connor
Adolescent Sexuality in a Changing American Society: Social and Psychological Perspectives
for the Human Service Professions (Second Edition)
  by Catherine S. Chilman
Failures in Behavior Therapy
  edited by Edna B. Foa and Paul M.G. Emmelkamp
The Psychological Assessment of Children (Second Edition)
  by James O. Palmer